Apple Intelligence
For Masterminds

How to Create Intelligent Applications
for iPhones, iPads and Macs

J.D Gauchat
www.jdgauchat.com

The source code for this book is available at **www.formasterminds.com**

Copyright Registration Number: 1238235

ISBN: 978-1-7779782-8-0

1st Edition 2026 John D Gauchat

Table of Contents

Chapter 1
App Development
1.1 - Requirements **1**
1.2 - Setup **1**
1.3 - Xcode **2**
Playground 3
Projects 6

Chapter 2
Apple Intelligence
2.1 - Overview **9**
2.2 - Introduction to Artificial Intelligence **9**
The Human Brain 10
Artificial Neural Networks 12
Models 15
Model Architectures 16
Apple Models 17

Chapter 3
Xcode
3.1 - Code Completion **19**
3.2 - Coding Assistant **21**
External Models 29
Local Models 32

Chapter 4
Integrated Tools
4.1 - Tools **37**
4.2 - Image Playground **37**
Image Playground Interface 37
Image Creator 42
4.3 - Genmojis **46**
Storing Genmojis 50
Advanced Implementation 53
4.4 - Writing Tools **61**
Advanced Implementation 64

Chapter 5
Foundation Models
5.1 - Foundation Models Framework **71**
Session 71
Instructions 78
Streaming 80

Sampling ... 82
Guided Generation ... 85
Dynamic Schemas ... 94
Tool Calling ... 100
Availability ... 109
Errors ... 113
Storing Sessions ... 122
Adapters ... 129

Chapter 6

Text Models

6.1 - Natural Language ... 143
Language Recognizer ... 143
Tokenizer ... 148
Tagger ... 150
Embeddings ... 157
6.2 - Translation Framework ... 164
Translation Interface ... 164
Translation Tasks ... 167
Batch Translation ... 179

Chapter 7

Vision Framework

7.1 - Overview ... 187
7.2 - Image Analysis ... 187
Image Classification ... 187
Attention Based Saliency ... 196
Image Aesthetics ... 201
Barcode Detection ... 203
7.3 - Text Analysis ... 208
Text Recognition ... 208
Document Recognition ... 212
7.4 - Human Body Analysis ... 223
Face Detection ... 224
Body Detection ... 232
Hand Detection ... 239
7.5 - Core Image ... 245
Barcodes ... 250
Person Segmentation ... 251

Chapter 8

Audio Models

8.1 - Sound Processing ... 257
8.2 - Speech Analyzer ... 257
File Transcription ... 260
Live Transcription ... 265
Translating Speech ... 273
8.3 - Voice Synthesizer ... 276
Voice Configuration ... 278
Voice Selection ... 279

Premium Voices 282
Controlling the Synthesizer 285
8.4 - Sound Analysis 288
Audio File Analysis 290
Live Audio Analysis 295

Chapter 9

Siri

9.1 - App Intents Framework 301
App Intents 301
App Shortcuts 306
Dialog 310
Parameters 311
Errors 324
App Entity 326
Snippet View 335
Siri Tips 347

Chapter 10

Additional Models

10.1 - Custom Models 351
Create ML 351
Core ML 360
Pre-trained Models 367
10.2 - External Models 369
OpenAI 370
API Key 370
API 372
Cloudflare 378
Workers 378
Wrangler 381
OpenAI Library 385
Implementation 388
AI Gateway 395

Chapter 11

Neural Networks

11.1 - How Neural Networks Work 399
Network Architecture 399
Training Cycle 400
Forward Propagation 401
Error Functions 407
Back Propagation 411
Optimization 423
Training 427
11.2 - MLX Framework 429
Network Data 431
Forward Propagation 438
Loss Functions 443
Back Propagation 444

Optimization 444
Network Architecture 445
Training 446

About this Book

This book covers essential concepts and advanced techniques you need to develop professional applications with Apple Intelligence. Depending on your current level of knowledge and experience, some topics may feel challenging at first. If a section seems difficult or does not apply to your immediate goals, feel free to move ahead. You can always return to those topics later when they appear in practical examples or become relevant to your own projects.

Every topic introduced in this book is explained through fully functional examples that you can try on your own. We recommend opening Xcode and experimenting with the code as you learn, but you can also download the projects from our website to work through the material at your own pace (**www.formasterminds.com**).

The examples in this book were created for instructional purposes and may not always follow established best practices. There are many programming patterns and techniques you can apply, and the right approach depends on the needs of your application and your development goals. We recommend you to explore the options presented in this book, but also experiment and develop your own.

IMPORTANT

In this book, we assume the reader has a basic understanding of the Swift programming language and the Apple frameworks used to create user interfaces, including SwiftUI and UIKit. All the examples in this book are fully functional, so this background is not strictly required to follow along, but we recommend becoming more familiar with these topics to fully leverage the potential of Apple Intelligence. For more information on Swift and SwiftUI, read our books *Swift Programming Language for Masterminds* and *SwiftUI Framework for Masterminds*. Apple's official documentation is available at **developer.apple.com**. References to frameworks and APIs can be found at **developer.apple.com/documentation**.

Chapter 1

App Development

1.1 - Requirements

Developing applications that integrate Apple Intelligence comes with a few requirements, but most modern hardware already satisfies these conditions and the necessary tools and accounts are available for free. Here is what we need to get started.

Mac Computer
Apple Intelligence requires the system to be equipped with an Apple silicon chip (M1, M2, M3, or M4) and running the latest version of macOS (currently macOS Tahoe 26).

Xcode
Xcode is the software provided by Apple for development. To develop applications with Apple Intelligence, we need version 26 or later.

Mobile Device
Applications developed with Apple Intelligence can be tested on the Mac, but it is recommended to try them out on a real iPhone or iPad if we want to deploy to those devices. Apple Intelligence requires the device to be equipped with an A17 Pro or newer processor and running the latest version of iOS or iPadOS (currently iOS 26 and iPadOS 26).

1.2 - Setup

Apple Intelligence is currently in beta, which means it may be disabled on some devices, but we can easily enable it from the system settings. All we need to do is click the Apple icon in the menu at the top of the screen, select System Settings, open the Apple Intelligence & Siri panel (Figure 1-1, number 1), and activate Apple Intelligence and Siri (Figure 1-1, number 2 and number 3).

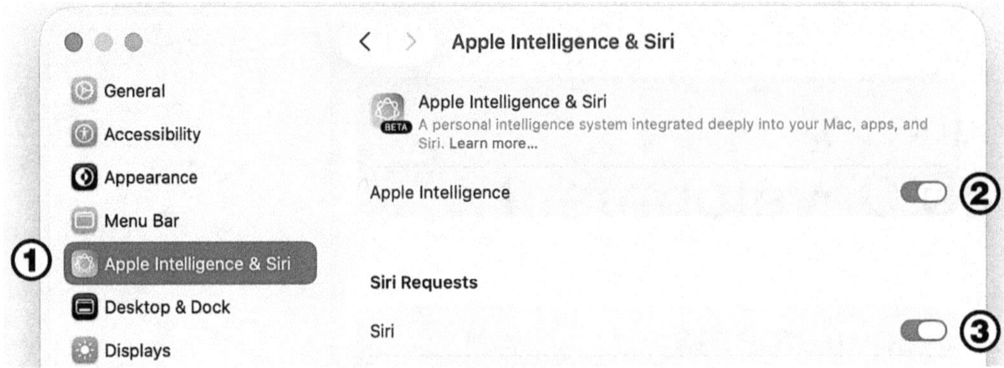

Figure 1-1: *Apple Intelligence options*

If we use Apple Intelligence features on a mobile device, the system may need to download additional resources before they become available. In such cases, a warning message appears indicating that the resources are being downloaded, as shown below.

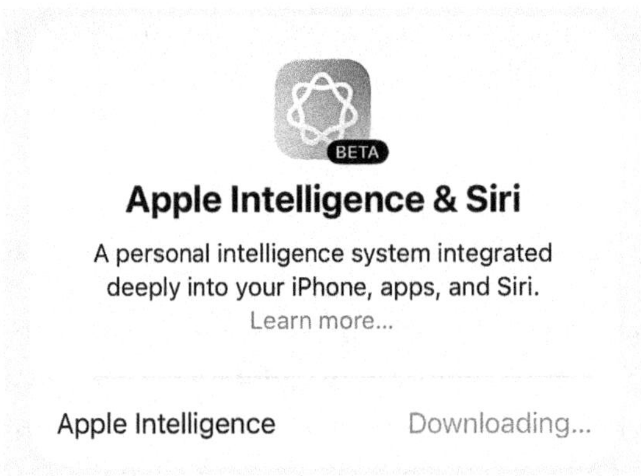

Figure 1-2: *Apple Intelligence downloading resources*

1.3 - Xcode

Once we have our Mac running macOS Tahoe 26 and Apple Intelligence enabled, the next step is to install Xcode 26. To install Xcode, open the App Store from the Applications folder in Finder, and then search for the term "Xcode" (Figure 1-3, number 1). The window will display the Xcode icon along with a Get button to install it (Figure 1-3, number 2).

Figure 1-3: *Xcode in the App Store*

> **IMPORTANT**
>
> Xcode can also be downloaded from Apple's developer website (**developer.apple.com/download/**). The website not only includes the latest version of Xcode but also beta versions that we can test before they are released to the market.

After downloading Xcode, we can run the application from the Applications folder in Finder. The following is Xcode's welcome screen.

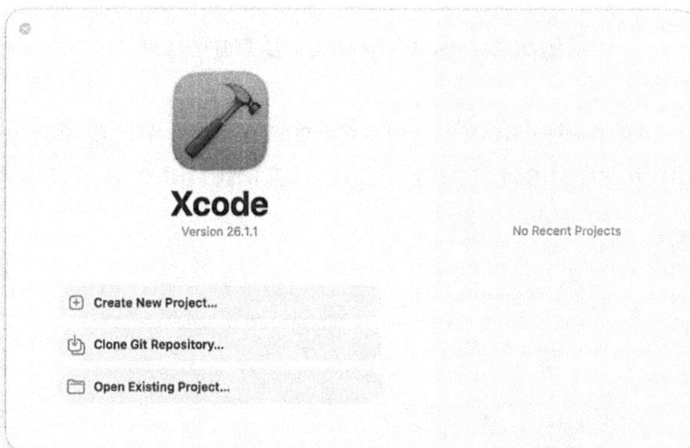

Figure 1-4: *Xcode's welcome screen*

The welcome screen provides a list of recent projects on the right and buttons on the left to create a new project (Create New Project), clone a project stored in a repository (Clone Git Repository), or open a project on our computer (Open Existing Project).

Playground

When working with Apple Intelligence, we will constantly need to perform tests, and the best way to do this is by using Playground. Playground is a tool provided by Xcode that allows us to test our code before incorporating it into our applications. Playground files are created using the Playground option in the File menu at the top of the screen.

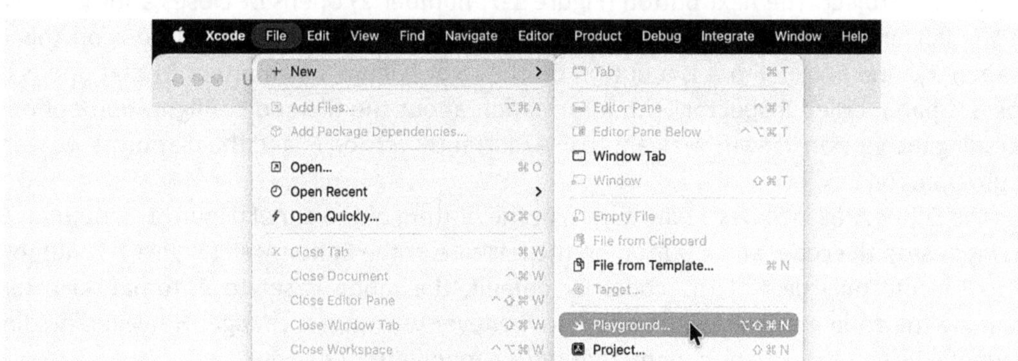

Figure 1-5: *Playground option*

After clicking this option, a window opens with a list of icons for selecting the template we want to use. To test our Apple Intelligence code, all we need is a Blank template, as shown below.

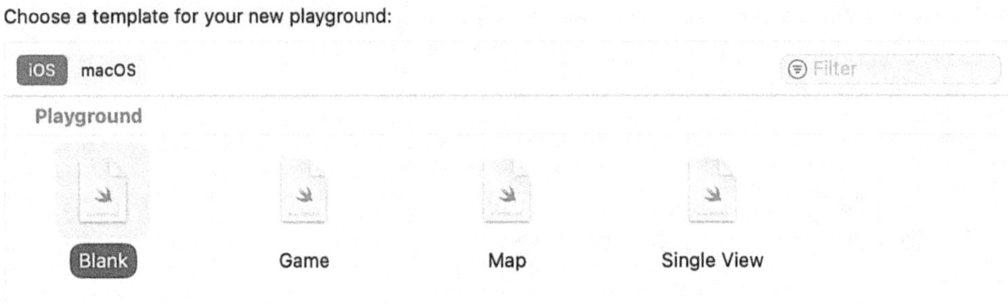

Figure 1-6: *Playground templates*

After selecting the template, Xcode asks for the name of the Playground file and where we want to store it, and then shows the Playground interface on the screen.

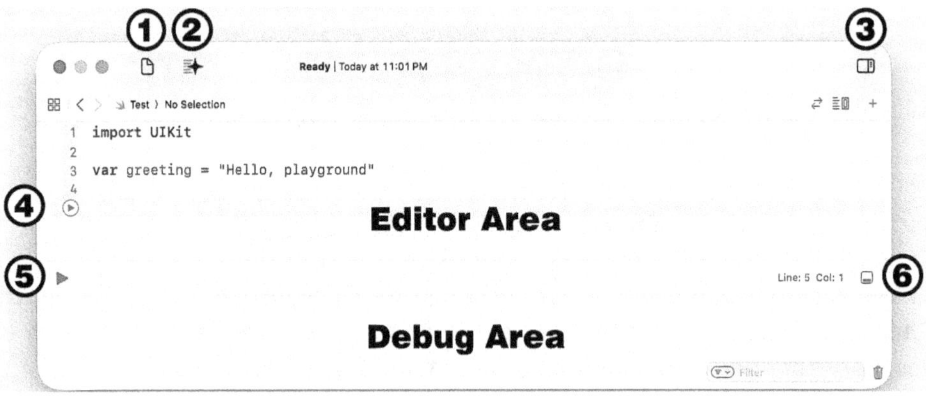

Figure 1-7: *Playground's interface*

Playground presents a simple interface with a toolbar at the top and two main areas: the **Editor** area, where we write our code, and the **Debug** area at the bottom, where we can read the errors produced by the code and print our own messages (Figure 1-7, number 6). The toolbar includes three buttons. The button on the left (Figure 1-7, number 1) opens or closes a panel on the left called **Navigator**, which shows the list of files included in the current Playground project. The next button (Figure 1-7, number 2) opens or closes another panel on the left with a **Coding Assistant** that can help us generate our code (more on this in Chapter 2). And finally, there is a button on the right (Figure 1-7, number 3) that opens or closes a panel called **Inspector** with information about the file and configuration options, including the version of Swift we want to use (currently version 6) and the platforms we want to program for.

The Editor Area includes a Play button at the bottom of the panel (Figure 1-7, number 5) to run or stop the code, and a button on the left side of the Editor Area (Figure 1-7, number 4) to execute only part of the code. By default, the mode is set to Automatically Run, meaning the code executes automatically whenever we make a change. However, holding down the Play button opens a menu that lets us modify this behavior.

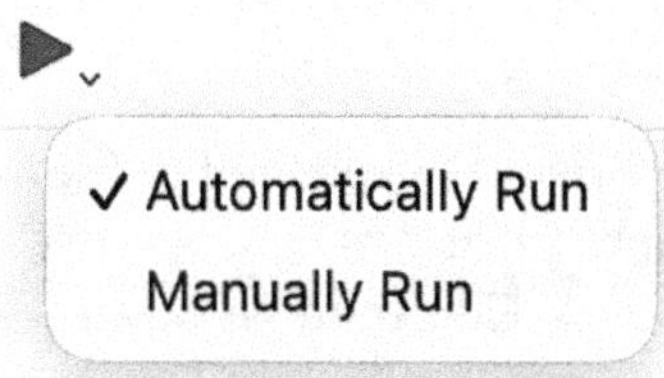

Figure 1-8: *Playground's running mode*

When the code is executed, Xcode opens a canvas on the right side of the Editor area to show the results.

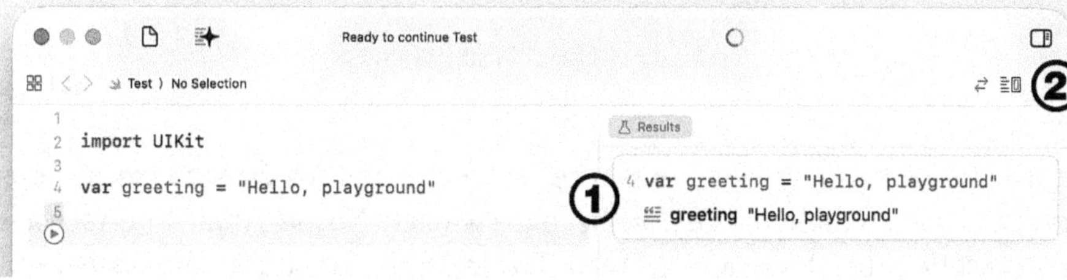

Figure 1-9: *Results*

The canvas displays the results of the execution of the code one line at a time, so we can check the values of variables and see how they change over time (Figure 1-9, number 1). If we don't need this feature, we can press the Editor Options button at the top of the Editor area (Figure 1-9, number 2) and select the option Show Editor Only.

If there is additional information available, such as an image or a map, the canvas includes a Quick Look icon on the right of each description to show it. For example, we can add a line to our code to load an image and then click on this icon to display the image on the canvas (Figure 1-10, number 1).

Figure 1-10: *Quick Look icon*

Do It Yourself

Install Xcode 26 on your Mac, as explained in Figure 1-3, or download it from **developer.apple.com**. Once installed, open Xcode, go to the menu at the top of the screen, click File, then New, and select the Playground option to create a new Playground file (see Figure 1-5). Xcode will ask you to select a template, as shown in Figure 1-6. Select the Blank option and press Next. Enter a name and save the file. You should see an interface similar to Figure 1-7. Click the Play button to run the code. You should see something similar to Figure 1-9.

Projects

Playground is useful when we need to test some code, but if we want to create applications that users can install on their devices, we have to switch to Xcode's main interface and create a project. An Xcode project includes all the information and resources necessary to build an application. The welcome window, shown in Figure 1-4, presents a button called Create New Project to start a new project (the option is also available from the File menu). When we click this button, a window appears allowing us to select the type of project we want to create.

Figure 1-11: *Project templates*

This window includes templates to create applications for every Apple device and operating system, including iOS for iPhones and iPads, macOS for Mac computers, watchOS for the Apple Watch, tvOS for Apple TV, and visionOS for Apple Vision Pro. With the introduction of SwiftUI, we can now create apps for all devices using the same framework, and therefore there is an additional option called *Multiplatform*. A Multiplatform project is set up to create an application for iPhones, iPads, and Mac computers using SwiftUI (we can add more platforms later). All we need to do is open the Multiplatform section and select the App template, as shown in Figure 1-11. Once this option is selected, we must configure the project, as shown below.

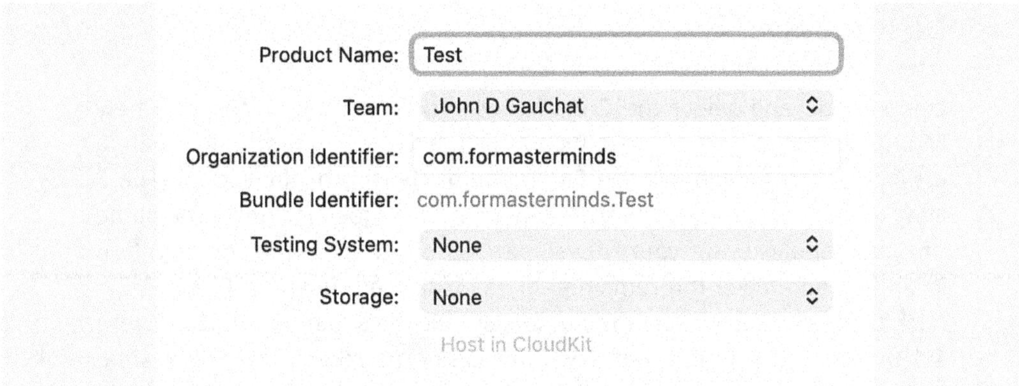

***Figure 1-12:** Project configuration window*

The information required to create applications with Apple Intelligence is the same as for any other project. We need the Product Name, which becomes the name of our application, the Team account so the project is assigned to our development team (this could be our personal developer account or our company's account), the Organization Identifier to identify the app (it is recommended to specify it using an inverted domain, as we have done in our example), and finally the testing and storage systems we want to use in our app if necessary.

Once the project is created, Xcode generates some files according to the selected template and presents the main interface on the screen.

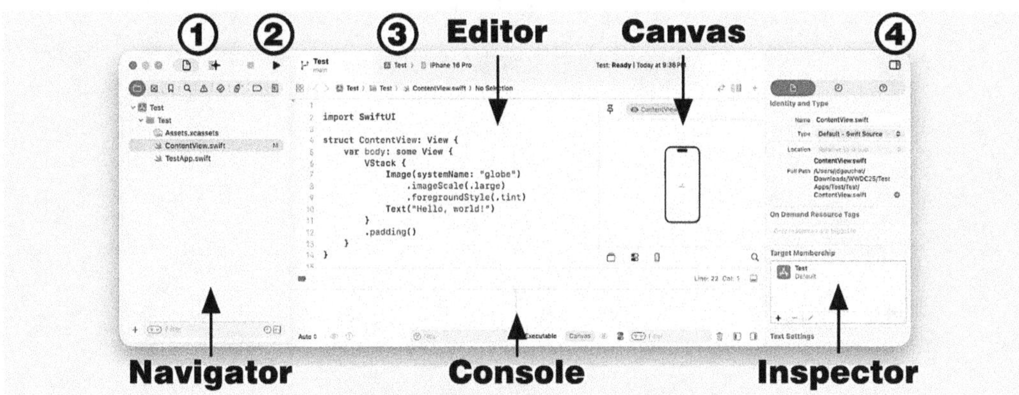

***Figure 1-13:** Xcode's interface*

Xcode's main interface is similar to the Playground interface introduced earlier. At the top, we have a toolbar with buttons to open and close additional panels (Figure 1-13, number 1 and number 4); a button to run the application (Figure 1-13, number 2); and a tool to select the simulator or device where we want to run it (Figure 1-13, number 3). As with the Playground interface, the panel on the left can show the **Navigator** with the list of files or the **Coding Assistant** to help us write our code (Figure 1-13, number 1). In the middle is the **Editor** for editing file contents, and next to it is the **Canvas** to show the result of executing our code. On the right is the **Inspector** panel, which offers configuration options and additional tools to edit files, and at the bottom we have the **Console** for debugging and displaying messages.

Do It Yourself

Open Xcode and select the Create New Project option to create a new Multiplatform project, as described in Figure 1-11. The option to create a project is also available in the File menu at the top of the screen (**File > New > Project**). Enter the information for your project, including the name of your application, your developer account, and the organization identifier, and leave the remaining fields blank, as shown in Figure 1-12. Click the Next button. You should now see Xcode's main interface (Figure 1-13). Select the ContentView.swift file to see the code in the Editor area. To learn more about Xcode and how to create applications with SwiftUI, read our book *SwiftUI Framework for Masterminds*.

Chapter 2

Apple Intelligence

2.1 - Overview

Artificial intelligence systems have been part of our lives for years, quietly working behind the scenes to perform simple tasks like recommending which movie to watch, which song to listen to, or which product to buy. Recent advances in research, however, have allowed these systems to evolve, making them more influential than ever before. Today, tools like ChatGPT (**www.chatgpt.com**), Suno (**www.suno.com**), or Gemini (**gemini.google.com/app**) are used by hundreds of millions of people around the world to work more efficiently, generate new ideas, and find inspiration.

Artificial intelligence tools have become so popular that every company now wants to build its own chatbot or image generator. Apple is no exception, but rather than focusing on standalone tools, the company chose to expand on the technologies it had already developed and integrate artificial intelligence directly into its platforms. This effort culminated in 2024 with the launch of *Apple Intelligence*.

Despite what its name suggests, Apple Intelligence is not a single product but a collection of systems that enhance the functionality of Apple's devices to create a seamless experience for users. With Apple Intelligence, users can generate images on the fly while texting a friend, design custom emojis as they type, refine emails before sending them, correct text directly in their favorite editors, apply filters to photos and videos as soon as they are taken, and perform complex tasks with ease.

Initially, Apple Intelligence was accessible only within Apple's own systems and applications. Some features were available to third-party apps, but only as fixed functionalities that developers could not customize or control. Since 2025, however, Apple opened access to these tools, enabling us to work with them directly and finally unlock the full potential of artificial intelligence within our own apps.

2.2 - Introduction to Artificial Intelligence

The purpose of artificial intelligence is to build machines capable of thinking and reasoning like a human being, so every attempt to build these systems begins with an understanding of how the human brain works.

IMPORTANT

This section provides an introduction to artificial intelligence models. While this information is not required to use Apple Intelligence, it is recommended for those who want a better understanding of what's happening under the hood. We will explore artificial intelligence models in greater detail in Chapter 11.

The Human Brain

The fundamental unit of the human brain is the neuron. A neuron is a specialized cell that can receive and transmit signals from and to other neurons. It has terminals on one side to collect signals from surrounding neurons and terminals on the opposite side to send signals outward.

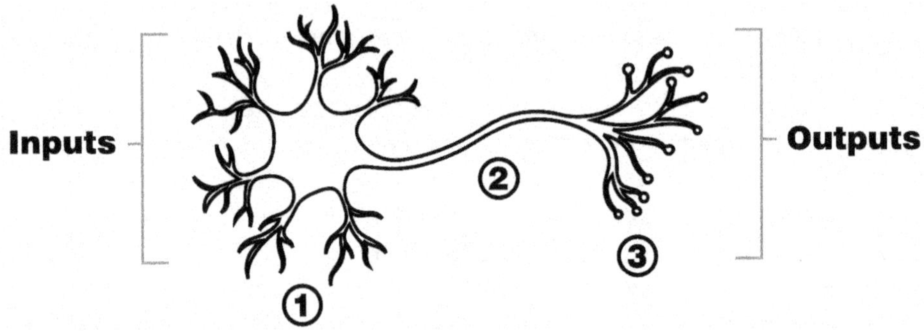

Figure 2-1: *Neuron*

As shown in Figure 2-1, a typical neuron is composed of *dendrites* (number 1), which are terminals connected to the neuron's body; a thin extension that stretches out from the body called the *axon* (number 2); and terminals at the end of the axon called *axon terminals* (number 3). Signals from other neurons are received by the dendrites and sent to the body as electrical signals. If these signals are strong enough, they trigger a series of chemical reactions that cause the inside of the neuron to become temporarily more positive, creating an electrical impulse that is then sent down the axon and passed to other neurons through the axon terminals, as shown below.

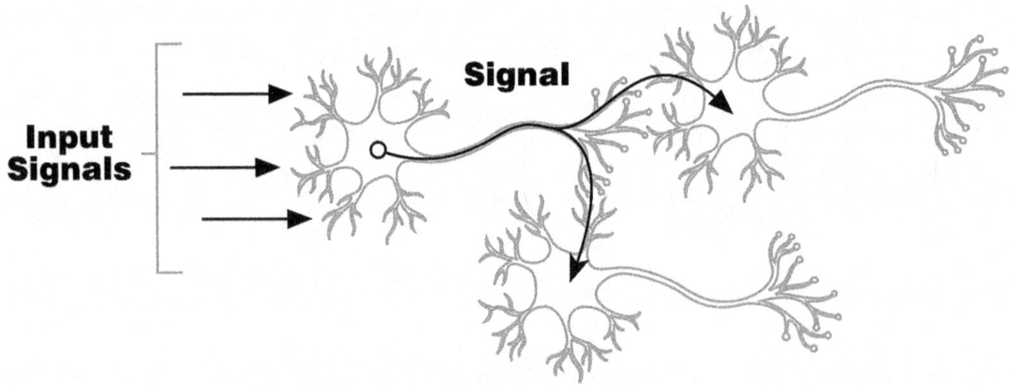

Figure 2-2: *Neural Network*

Neurons can receive signals from thousands of other neurons, but they only fire when the combined electrical charge reaches a certain level. In other words, a neuron transmits a signal to nearby neurons only if the signals it receives are strong and frequent enough to raise its internal charge above its firing threshold (typically around –60 millivolts). As a result, some neurons will send a signal while others remain inactive, creating a pattern of interconnected neurons that set a path for the signal to follow, as shown below.

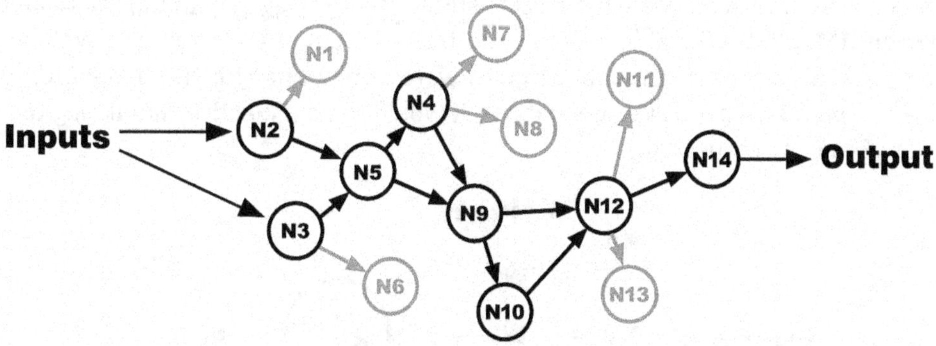

Figure 2-3: *Neural Pattern*

In this example, the two neurons on the left (N2 and N3) receive input signals strong enough to activate them. They in turn send signals to three other neurons (N1, N5, and N6), but only one of them becomes active (N5) because it is the only one that reaches the activation threshold. The process continues through the network: if the incoming signals are strong enough, the downstream neurons will also activate, forming a pattern of interconnected neurons that ultimately leads to the activation of the final neuron on the right (N14).

This process occurs over and over throughout the brain, forming an immense network of patterns of interconnected neurons that represent every piece of information we use to survive. When an input is received by the brain, it activates a specific neural pattern, which produces an output that may, in turn, trigger another neural pattern, continuing the chain until a memory is recalled or an action is carried out. For example, the smell of food might activate a pattern in a worm's brain, which then triggers a movement-related pattern, eventually activating the neural pattern that coordinates the muscles needed for the worm to crawl toward the food.

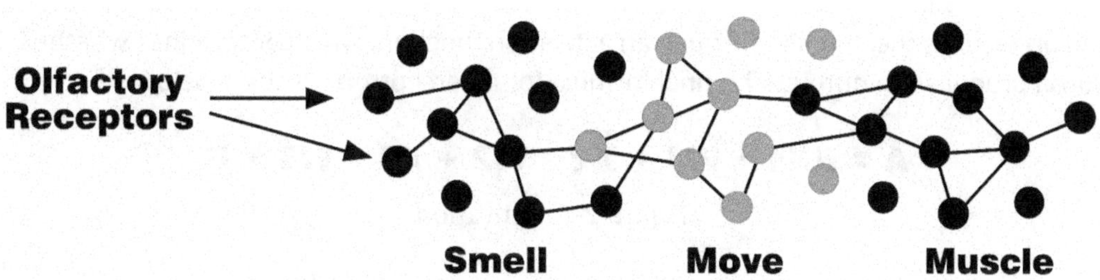

Figure 2-4: *Interconnected Neural Patterns*

This is what makes the brain so powerful. By building these patterns of interconnected neurons, the brain can generate different responses to different inputs and guide our behavior in ways that help us understand and navigate the world. Everything we know, including our memories, what we love and hate, and how we see the world and ourselves, is stored as networks of interconnected neurons. They make us who we are and have therefore been the main subject of artificial intelligence research since the very beginning.

Artificial Neural Networks

The earliest attempts to replicate biological neural networks began with the invention of the perceptron. The perceptron was a simple electronic model of a neuron, complete with its own inputs and outputs. If the input signals were strong enough, the perceptron would activate and produce an output signal; if not, it would remain inactive, simulating the basic behavior of a biological neuron.

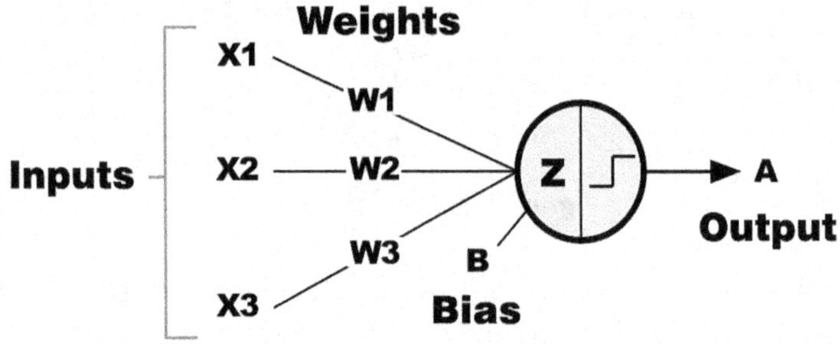

Figure 2-5: *Perceptron*

Figure 2-5 shows the configuration of a single perceptron. It includes input values (**X1**, **X2**, and **X3**), the weights that determine how much each input contributes to the activation of the neuron (**W1**, **W2**, and **W3**), and a constant known as the bias (**B**), which acts as an additional parameter to help the neuron reach its activation threshold and prevent it from becoming permanently inactive. To determine the output of the perceptron, we first multiply the input values by their corresponding weights, and the results of these multiplications are then added together along with the bias. This result is known as the *weighted sum*, and it is expressed by the following formula.

$$Z = X1 * W1 + X2 * W2 + X3 * W3 + B$$

Figure 2-6: Weighted sum

This result is then passed through an activation function, which determines whether the neuron produces an output. The final formula for a perceptron is shown below.

$$A = f(X1 * W1 + X2 * W2 + X3 * W3 + B)$$

Figure 2-7: Activation

This formula may seem complicated because of the number of values involved, but it is actually quite simple. All we do is to perform basic mathematical operations. As an example, we can reproduce our perceptron using real values.

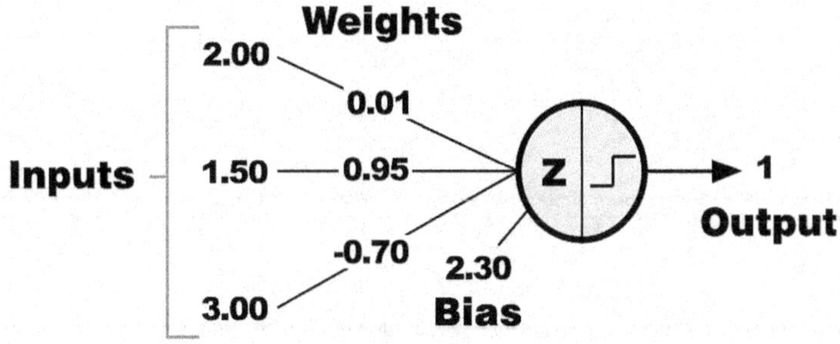

Figure 2-8: Perceptron Values

To get this perceptron's activation value, all we need to do is replace the values in the previous formula and calculate the result.

A = 2.00 * 0.01 + 1.50 * 0.95 + 3.00 * -0.70 + 2.30
A = f(1.645)
A = 1

Figure 2-9: Calculating the perceptron's activation value

In Figure 2-9, we multiply each input by its corresponding weight, add them all together along with the bias, and then apply the activation function to the result. In this example, we use the same activation function as in the original perceptrons. This is a step function that returns 0 if the result is negative and 1 if it is equal to or greater than zero, indicating whether the perceptron is inactive (0) or active (1). In our case, the weighted sum is 1.645, which is greater than 0, so the activation function returns 1, meaning the perceptron is active.

IMPORTANT

While using 0 and 1 to decide whether a perceptron is active or not proved effective at first, it had some limitations. Modern perceptrons use activation functions that produce values across a range, making networks more flexible and powerful. We will study these functions and their benefits in detail in Chapter 11.

Naturally, a single perceptron cannot accomplish much on its own. The first artificial networks were built with hundreds of perceptrons working in parallel to process simple images. The results were promising, but after years of research it became clear that those systems were not enough to solve complex problems. As computers advanced, researchers experimented with new architectures and gradually developed the structure we recognize in most artificial neural networks today. In this structure, perceptrons are organized into layers, with each perceptron in one layer connected to every perceptron in the next, as shown below.

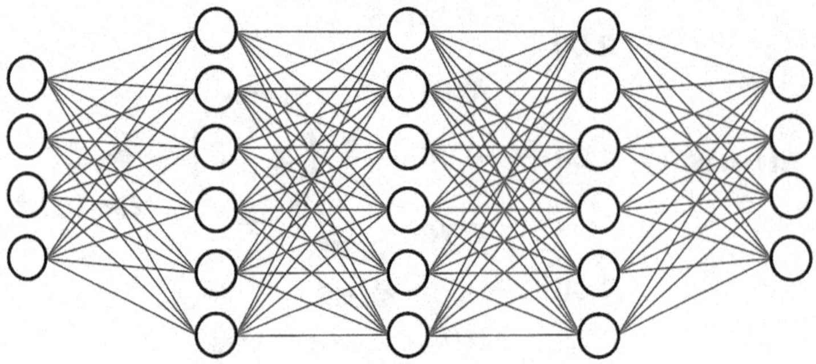

Figure 2-10: *Multilayer Perceptron*

In this architecture, perceptrons are referred to as nodes or neurons. Each neuron in one layer has a set of weights that determine how it influences the activation values of the neurons in the next layer. These activation values are calculated in the same way as before, one neuron at a time, as illustrated below.

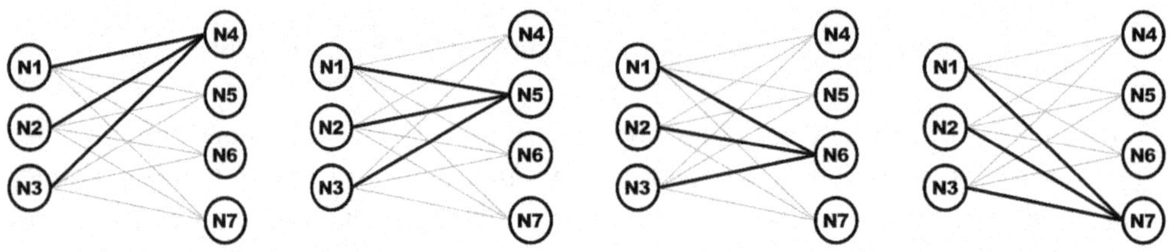

Figure 2-11: *Calculating the activation value of each neuron in a layer*

Figure 2-11 shows the first and second layers of a hypothetical neural network and how the activation values of the neurons in the second layer are calculated. In the diagram on the left, we calculate the activation value of the first neuron in the second layer (**N4**) by multiplying the activation values of the neurons in the first layer by the weights connected to that neuron. The same process is then repeated for each neuron in the second layer (**N5**, **N6**, and **N7**), always using only the weights associated with those specific neurons.

This process repeats throughout the network. We begin by assigning the input values as the activation values of the neurons in the first layer, then use those values to calculate the activation values of the neurons in the next layer, and continue this process layer by layer until we reach the last one, as shown below.

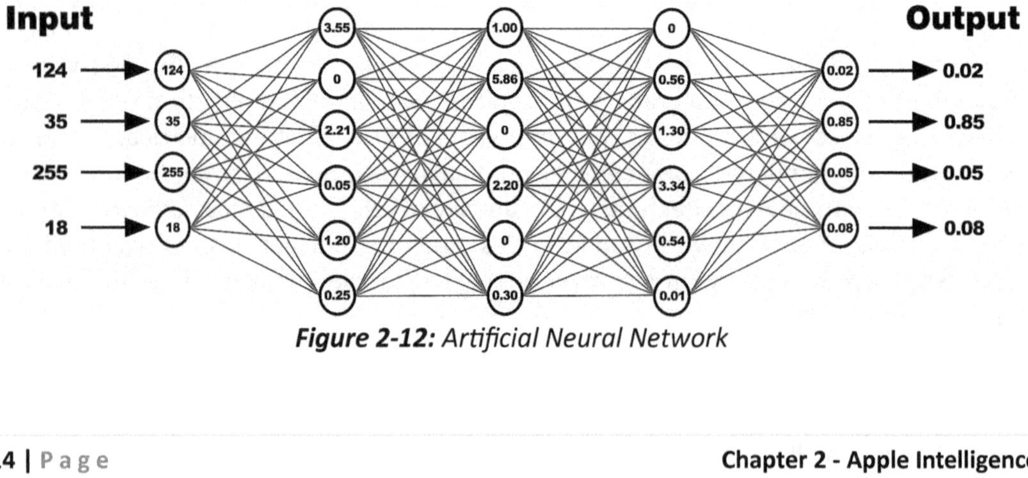

Figure 2-12: *Artificial Neural Network*

As illustrated in Figure 2-12, the activation values of the neurons in the last layer represent the final output of the network. Although they are calculated just like the activation values for any other neuron, these values are important because they represent the solution to our problem. For example, if we design a network to determine whether an image contains a cat or a dog, the neurons in the output layer will have values that indicate the content of the image, as shown below.

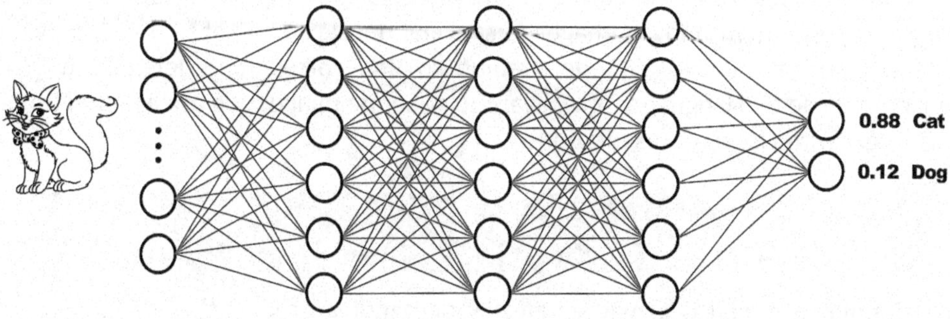

Figure 2-13: *Artificial Neural Network designed to identify images of cats and dogs*

In this example, the network has an input layer with enough neurons to take every pixel of an image and an output layer with two neurons: one that represents cats and the other that represents dogs. When we feed the image on the left into the network, the cat neuron outputs 0.88 and the dog neuron outputs 0.12. This indicates that the network has predicted an 88% probability that the image contains a cat, which is indeed the correct result.

This is exactly how neural networks work, and why they have become so useful. By processing input values through layers of neurons connected by weights and biases, neural networks form patterns that allow them to find associations between inputs and outputs. And this capability goes far beyond identifying objects in an image. Following the same procedure, neural networks can translate languages, generate original text, respond to user input, create new images and videos, and perform many tasks at a level comparable to human performance.

Models

Neural networks do not come preconfigured to identify cats and dogs, translate languages, or generate text. They must be trained. Training is the most complex and demanding aspect of working with neural networks, but at its core, it simply means adjusting the weights and biases of every neuron so that the output values match the target values. For example, if we design a network to detect cats and dogs in images, we must adjust the weights and biases so that when we input the image of a cat, the neuron representing cats produces the higher activation value, and when we input the image of a dog, the neuron representing dogs produces the higher value.

Every data sample we input into the network will be different, so we need to process many samples, adjust the weights and biases for each one of them, and repeat the same procedure until the network produces the correct output for every case. Once the network performs well on the training data, we evaluate it using new inputs, such as images of cats and dogs the network hasn't seen before, and if the results are satisfactory, we consider the network successfully trained.

The outcome of this entire process is what we call a *model*. A model is the trained version of the network. It has the same architecture as the original network (the same number of layers and neurons) but with weights and biases that has been adjusted to perform well in real-world applications. Models are what we interact with whenever we use an artificial intelligence system. Each time we rely on these systems, we are accessing a model, that is a network that has already been trained to recognize and process the type of data we are working with. If we want to identify cats and dogs in our pictures, we use a model trained with thousands of images of cats and dogs. If we want to translate text from English to Spanish, we use a model trained to find correlations between words and sentences in those two languages. If we want to generate images, we use a model trained to associate text with visual representations.

IMPORTANT

Training a model is a mathematically demanding process that relies on concepts such as matrices and derivatives. In this chapter, we focus on the fundamental ideas behind this process. We will learn how training works and how to train our own models in Chapter 11.

Model Architectures

The model we used as reference in previous sections is a classification model. A classification model identifies the category or class that the input data belongs to (e.g., distinguishing between cats and dogs). The original perceptrons were designed to perform exactly this type of task. Researchers would create a layer of hundreds of perceptrons to classify images into categories. For decades, this was the limit of what neural networks could achieve, but in the early 2000s, new techniques, more powerful hardware, and access to larger datasets transformed the field, allowing networks to tackle far more complex problems.

The first major improvement came around 2002, when a research team from the University of Toronto discovered more effective ways to implement and train an architecture called the **Restricted Boltzmann Machine** (RBM). This network consists of two layers of neurons: one for processing input data and another for capturing hidden features that represent patterns in the data. By uncovering these patterns, RBMs could generate new content, identify correlations, classify natural language, and more. Building on these results, around 2006 the same research team developed a more advanced architecture called the **Deep Belief Network** (DBN), which combined multiple Restricted Boltzmann Machines in sequence, creating a layered system capable of learning increasingly complex features from data. The success of Deep Belief Networks demonstrated for the first time that multilayer architectures (later called **Deep Learning** networks), could be trained effectively. This was confirmed by the same team in 2012 when they developed **AlexNet**, a deep convolutional network with dozens of layers that could recognize thousands of objects in images with performance comparable to that of humans.

AlexNet ignited a revolution, drawing unprecedented attention to Deep Learning networks and accelerating research across the entire field. This breakthrough not only led to more accurate classification models but also enabled the creation of new architectures capable of generating content, such as **Generative Adversarial Networks**, which produced remarkably realistic images, and improved **Recurrent Neural Networks**, which could capture semantic relationships between words and generate coherent text for the first time.

The evolution of Recurrent Neural Networks is arguably the most significant of these recent improvements, as it led to the development of a game-changing architecture called **Transformers**. Recurrent Neural Networks process information sequentially and therefore had difficulty handling long texts. The attention mechanism introduced by the Transformer architecture solved this problem by allowing the model to consider the entire text at once, making it possible for a network to understand context and generate more meaningful results. This new architecture made it possible to capture contextual meaning across entire documents, allowing models to process large amounts of text, including long documents and even entire books. As a result, researchers were able to scale these systems dramatically, giving rise to what are now known as **Large Language Models** (LLMs). Built with billions or even trillions of parameters, these models can learn complex language patterns from massive text collections, enabling them to answer questions, generate content, and engage in conversations that increasingly resemble human communication.

All these innovations have brought us to the present, where we now have models capable of sustaining natural conversations and generating original content, multimodal systems that combine different architectures to deliver fully integrated multimedia experiences, and agents that can coordinate multiple models to perform complex tasks in sequence, all accessible from the comfort of our homes and personal devices.

Apple Models

Models vary in size and capability. In general, the larger the model, the more powerful and versatile it becomes. Today, some models are so large they can only run in massive data centers, while others are compact enough to operate efficiently on a mobile device. Despite these differences, all models can excel at their intended tasks. From the start, Apple recognized this potential and chose to bring artificial intelligence to the masses by developing highly efficient models that run locally on their devices and operating systems. Many of these models are now seamlessly integrated into Apple's ecosystem, providing users with a smooth, consistent experience across devices and applications.

Because Apple's focus is on making artificial intelligence accessible to everyone, they not only provide models we can integrate into our apps but also offer simple tools designed to assist users with everyday tasks. These include **Writing Tools** for editing and composing text, **Genmoji** for creating personalized emojis, and **Image Playground** for generating custom images.

Figure 2-14: *Integrated tools*

As we will see later, these tools can be integrated into our apps with little to no effort, but they only scratch the surface of what Apple's models are capable of. To fully leverage the potential of Apple Intelligence, we need to work with the dedicated frameworks Apple provides for this purpose. These frameworks are organized into six distinct domains: the **Foundation Models** framework for accessing an on-device large language model; the **Vision** framework for processing images and videos; the **Natural Language** framework for analyzing text; the **Translation** framework for translating human language; the **Speech** framework for speech recognition; and the **Sound Analysis** framework for classifying audio.

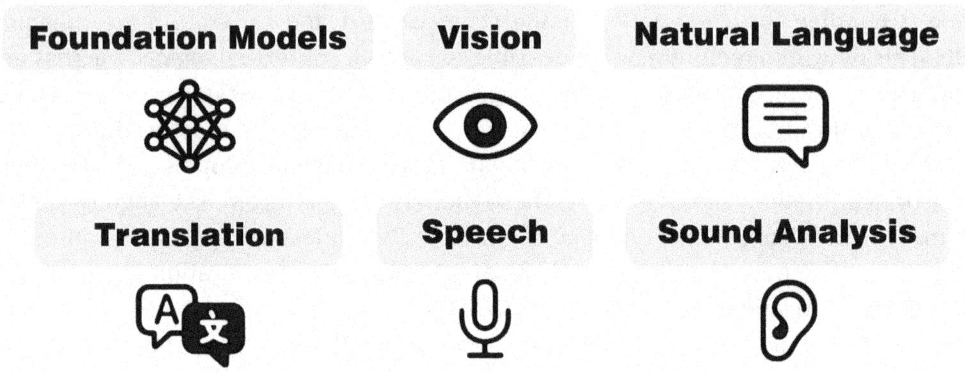

Figure 2-15: *Apple Intelligence frameworks*

No matter how comprehensive Apple's models may be, they will not always offer the exact features our apps require. For this reason, Apple also provides everything developers need to train and deploy custom models, including access to third-party models and tools for experimenting and building our own. These tools include **Create ML** for training models with custom data, **Core ML** for managing both custom models and those developed by the community, and the **MLX** framework for experimenting and learning how models work.

Figure 2-16: *Machine Learning frameworks*

All the frameworks introduced in this section form the foundation of Apple Intelligence and are the central focus of the remainder of this book. In the following chapters, we will explore these frameworks, examine the models they use to perform their tasks, and learn how to implement them to build intelligent and powerful applications that run seamlessly across all Apple platforms.

Chapter 3

Xcode

3.1 - Code Completion

In addition to the models we can integrate into our applications, Apple has also embedded intelligent models directly into Xcode to assist developers in building those applications. One of the first tools we encounter is code completion, which is enabled by default. This feature suggests code as we type and allows us to easily insert it by pressing the Tab key. For example, if we create a function called **`loadImage()`**, Xcode will recognize that we are likely trying to build a function that loads an image from the web and will propose the appropriate code to implement it.

```
    func loadImage() async -> UIImage {
        let url = URL(string: "https://example.com/image.jpg")!
    }
```

Figure 3-1: *Code completion*

In this example, Xcode suggests making the function asynchronous, returning a **`UIImage`** object (or an **`Image`** view, depending on the context), and creating a new **`URL`** structure as soon as we begin typing the code. In this case, Xcode suggested only one line of code, but it can suggest more depending on what we are working on. For example, if we press the Tab key to accept the suggestion shown in Figure 3-1, Xcode will automatically complete the rest of the code for the function, including a line to read the contents of the image and another to return it, as shown below.

```
    func loadImage() async -> UIImage {
        let url = URL(string: "https://example.com/image.jpg")!
        let data = try! Data(contentsOf: url)
        return UIImage(data: data)!
    }
```

Figure 3-2: *Completion of multiple lines of code*

As long as the suggested code is what we want, we can keep pressing the Tab key and let Xcode write the program for us. But Xcode can do more than generate single lines of code. If the function performs a simple task, Xcode can generate the entire code for us in a single step. For example, if we start writing the name of a function called **`formatDate()`**,

Xcode will understand that we are creating a function to format a date and will not only define the function's attributes and return types but also suggest all the code for the function, as shown below.

```
func formatDate(_ date: Date) -> String {
    let formatter = DateFormatter()
    formatter.dateFormat = "yyyy-MM-dd HH:mm:ss"
    return formatter.string(from: date)
}
```

Figure 3-3: *Completion of a function*

Behind Xcode's code completion tool is a large language model that can suggest not only code but also text. For example, if we start typing the value for a **`String`** property, Xcode will suggest what to write next.

```
import SwiftUI

var text = "This is my first SwiftUI project"
```

Figure 3-4: *Text completion*

Every time we type, Xcode will show a suggestion. If we like it, we can press the Tab key to insert it into our code; if we don't, we can press Escape to ignore it or simply keep writing our own code. However, if the tool becomes annoying or doesn't provide the help we need, we can disable it in Settings. To do this, we must select Settings from the Xcode menu at the top of the screen, go to the Editing tab, click on Completion, find the Display Code Prediction setting, and open the drop-down menu, as shown below.

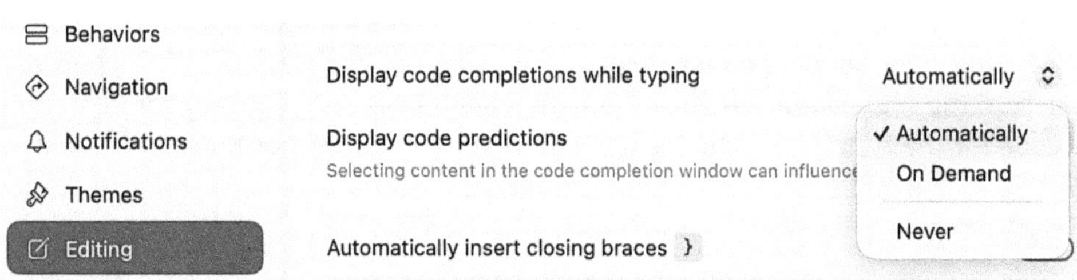

Figure 3-5: *Display Code Prediction option*

There are three options available: Automatically, On Demand, and Never. Automatically lets Xcode decide when to show suggestions, On Demand shows suggestions only when we press the combination of keys Control + Option + Space, and the Never option completely disables the feature.

Do It Yourself

Open your Playground file or create a new one. Define a function with a name that clearly indicates its purpose, such as `loadImage()` or `generateLabel()`. As soon as you start typing, you should see suggestions from Xcode. Press the Tab key to accept a suggestion and observe how Xcode can predict the code you intend to write.

IMPORTANT

Code completion is available only in Xcode 26 running on macOS 26, and Apple Intelligence must be enabled, as explained in Chapter 1, Figure 1-1. The model suggests code based on the surrounding code and its context. If you try the previous examples on your own computer, the results may vary.

3.2 - Coding Assistant

Xcode predictions are based on the code we have typed so far, so they usually don't follow best practices and have a limited scope. For example, in the code suggested in Figure 3-2, some instructions were implicitly unwrapped, which can lead to crashes if the image we are trying to download is not found. For this reason, Xcode's completion feature should be used only to help us type faster, but to generate new code or write large pieces of code we should resort to the Coding Assistant. This tool is available from a panel on the left that opens when we press the Coding Assistant button on the toolbar (Chapter 1, Figure 1-7, number 2).

At the moment, the Coding Assistant does not work with models provided by Apple but instead uses external models from third-party companies, like ChatGPT and Claude. To set up these models, we can click the Set Up Intelligence button on the panel, or go to the Xcode menu at the top of the screen, select Settings, and then click Intelligence.

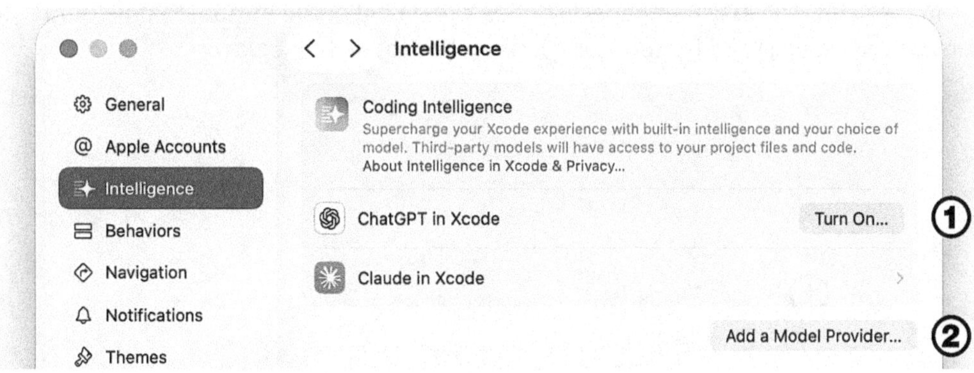

Figure 3-6: *Coding Assistant Setup*

As of this writing, there are two options available: we can enable the models that Apple has built into Xcode, such as ChatGPT or Claude (Figure 3-6, number 1), or manually connect Xcode to other models (Figure 3-6, number 2). From the two built-in options, ChatGPT is the most convenient because it can be used with a free account. To get started, we simply press the Turn On button, accept the terms, and Xcode will be ready to work with this model.

The free version of ChatGPT allows only a limited number of requests per day. After performing a few requests, we may receive a warning indicating how long we must wait before accessing the model again. While the daily request limit for free accounts is sufficient for many developers, we can sign in with a paid ChatGPT account to extend these limits by clicking the ChatGPT option again and pressing the Sign In button (Figure 3-7, number 1).

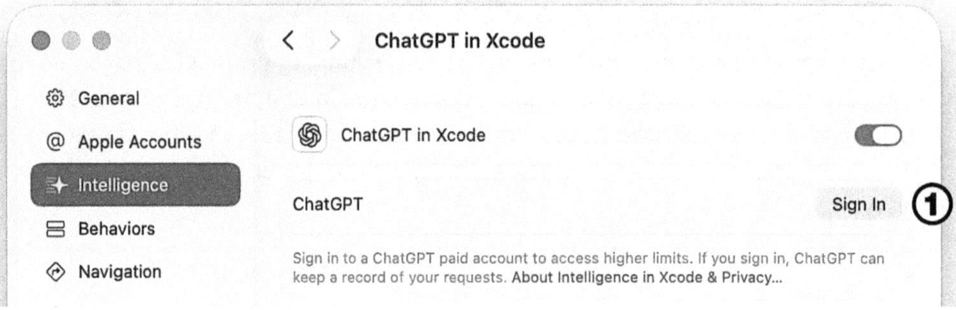

Figure 3-7: *Signing in to a paid ChatGPT account*

> **IMPORTANT**
>
> There is no explicit information about how many requests we can make to ChatGPT before reaching a limit. If you find yourself hitting these limitations with a free account, you can subscribe to ChatGPT Plus to extend them (**www.chatgpt.com**) or open an account with Claude (**www.claude.ai**) to use that model instead. At the time of this writing, ChatGPT and Claude subscriptions costs $20 USD per month.

Once our free or paid account is enabled, we can start using the Coding Assistant to get the help we need. The assistant panel includes a text field at the bottom to type our request (Figure 3-8, number 1) and buttons for configuration, as shown below.

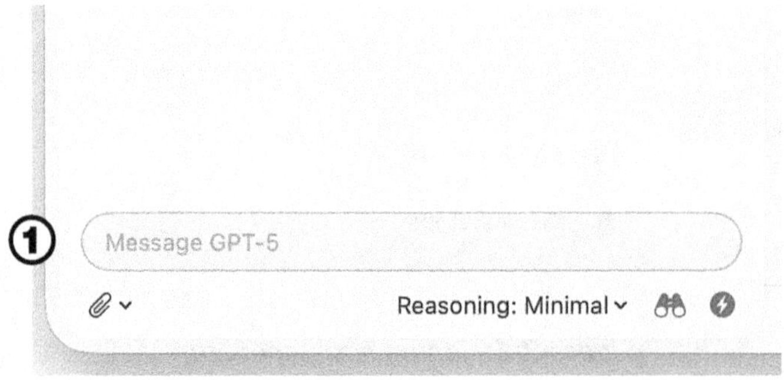

Figure 3-8: *Coding Assistant panel*

The assistant works like any other chatbot. We can ask questions or give direct instructions of what we want. For example, we can ask the assistant to add code to the **`ContentView`** view created by the Multiplatform App template, as shown below.

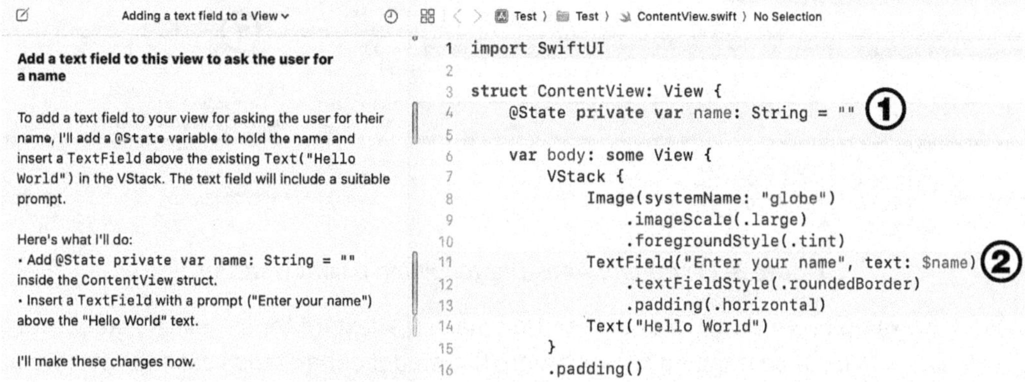

***Figure 3-9:** Coding Assistant request*

The example in Figure 3-9 asks the assistant to "Add a text field to this view to ask the user for a name." The assistant understands that we are referring to the **`ContentView`** view currently open in the editor and that it needs to add a **`@State`** property to store the value entered by the user (number 1), as well as a **`TextField`** view to allow the user to enter his or her name (number 2). Note that in this example it not only added the **`TextField`** view but also set the placeholder text to "Enter your name" and configured the view to have rounded borders and horizontal padding.

After a request is completed, we will see a report at the bottom of the assistant that includes two buttons: one on the left to display a summary of all the changes made (Figure 3-10, number 1), and another on the right to revert the changes (Figure 3-10, number 2). This allows us to review what has been changed throughout the project and go back to the previous state if we don't like it.

***Figure 3-10:** Revert button*

Every time we enter a new request, it becomes part of an ongoing conversation, allowing the model to use it as a reference for future requests. This means that we can ask the assistant to make additional changes to what it has already done, and it will understand what we are referring to. For example, we can ask it to replace the **`TextField`** view it generated earlier with a **`TextEditor`** view.

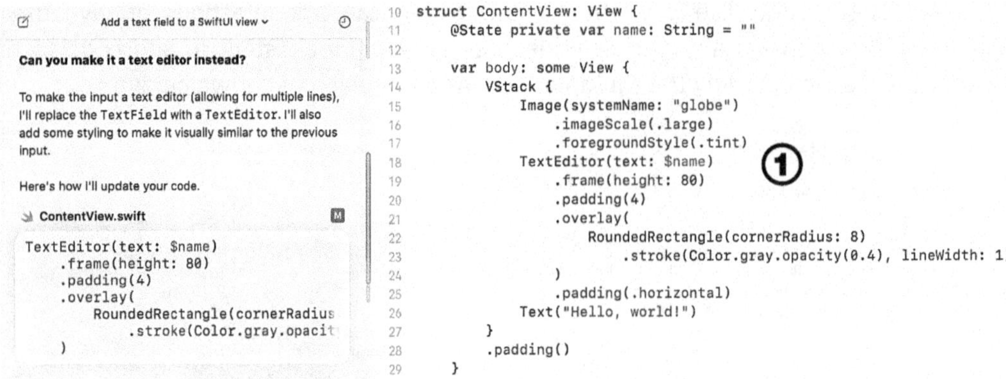

Figure 3-11: *Coding Assistant following a conversation*

In this example, we simply asked, "Can you make it a text editor instead?", and because this request is part of an ongoing conversation, the model understands exactly what we are referring to and not only replaces the **`TextField`** view with a **`TextEditor`** view but also adds all the necessary modifiers to ensure the text editor looks like the previous view, keeping the design of the user interface the same.

When we perform a request, the model takes into consideration all the requests in the current conversation and also every file and code in our project. If we want the model to interpret our request in the context of a symbol, like a class, a structure, or a file, we can use the **@** character. When we type the character, the assistant shows a list of all the symbols we can choose from.

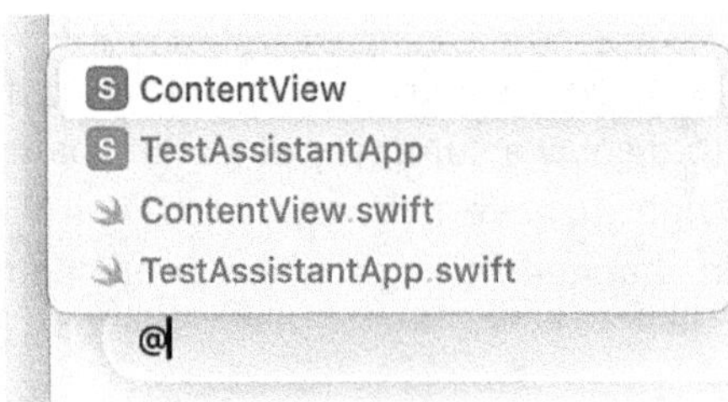

Figure 3-12: *Choosing symbols for reference*

After a symbol is selected, the assistant turns it into an entry for our request, so we can then type what we want to do with it. For example, in Figure 3-12, we are working with a new project called TestAssistant, which includes the **`ContentView`** view, the initial **`App`** structure created by the template, and the two files that store this code. If we select the **`TestAssistantApp`** structure or the TestAssistantApp.swift file and ask the system to create a new function, it will add the function to that structure, regardless of what is currently selected in the editor.

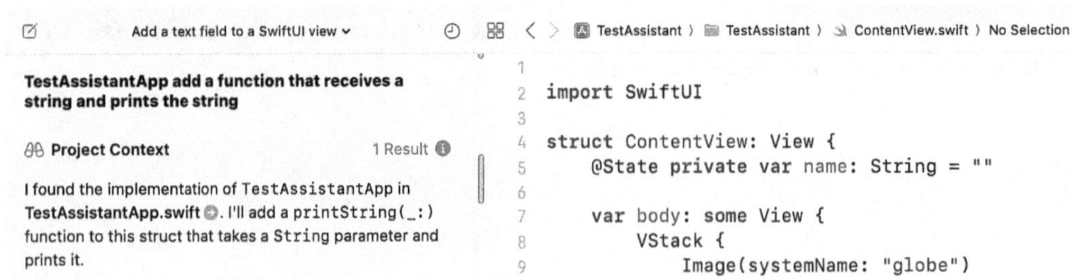

Figure 3-13: *Coding Assistant working on a specific file*

In this example, we ask the model to create a new function that takes a **String** value as a parameter and prints it to the console, but because we specify the symbol **TestAssistantApp**, the model finds the **TestAssistantApp** structure and adds the new function to that file, even though the ContentView.swift file is currently open in the editor.

Another way to ask the assistant to work on a specific symbol or section of our code is by using the Coding Tool. We can open this tool from the editor by selecting a symbol and clicking the button that appears on the left side of the editor (Figure 3-14, number 1), or by holding the Control key, clicking on a symbol, and then selecting the Show Coding Tools option from the menu (Figure 3-14, number 2).

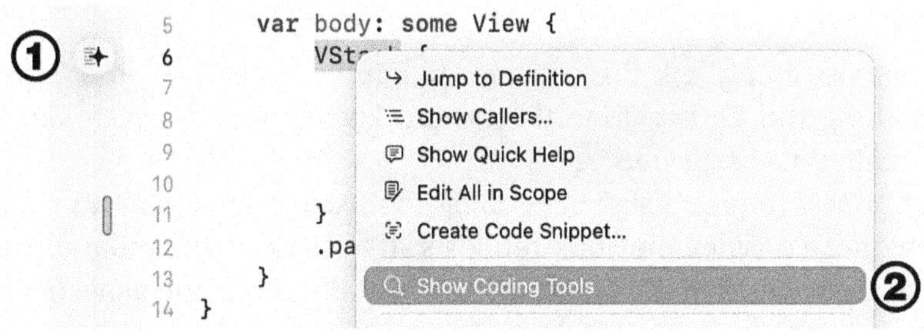

Figure 3-14: *Coding Tools option*

Once we select the option, Xcode displays a small window next to the code with a text field for typing our request, along with buttons for performing predetermined tasks. There is an Explain button to generate a description of what the symbol does and a Document button to insert this description into the code for documentation purposes. At the bottom, there are two additional options: one to generate a Playground for testing a structure or class (available only when a structure or class is selected) and another to generate a preview if the selected symbol is a view.

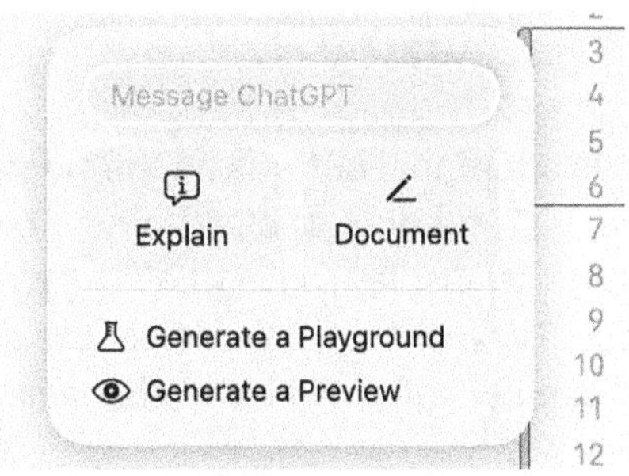

Figure 3-15: *Coding Tools window*

If we enter a request in this window, the assistant will generate content based on the symbol or code we used to open the tool. For example, we can select the **VStack** in the **ContentView** view we have been working on and ask the assistant to embed it in a **ZStack**.

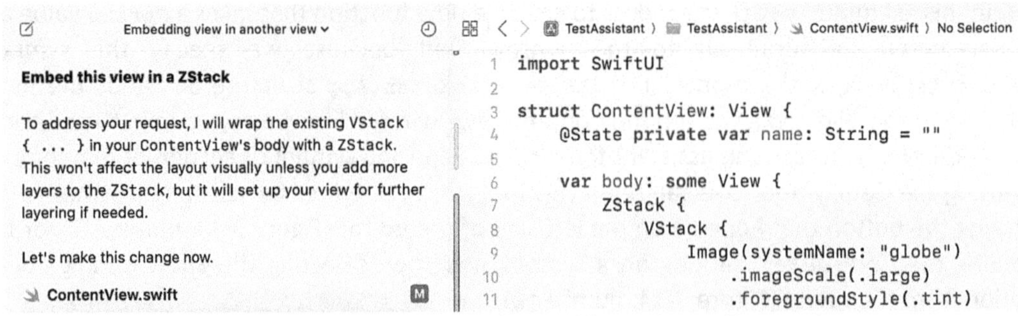

Figure 3-16: *Request performed from the coding tool*

In this example, we simply ask the assistant to "Embed this view in a ZStack," but because we do it using the Coding Tool, the system knows exactly which view we are referring to and modifies it as expected.

When we enter a new request using the Coding Tool, Xcode starts a new conversation, so the model does not consider previous requests. If we want to continue a previous conversation, we can select it from the dropdown menu at the top of the panel (Figure 3-17, number 2).

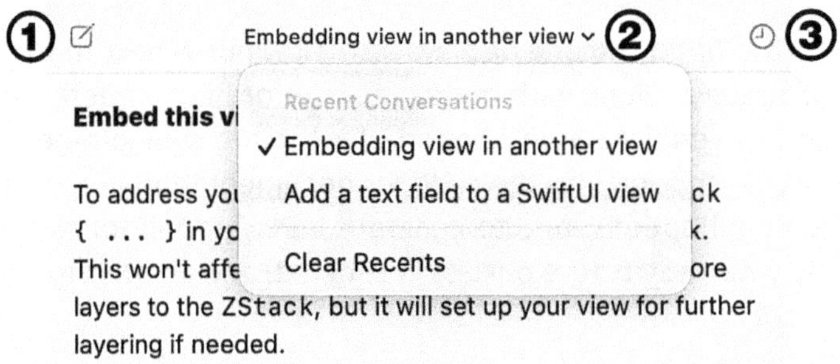

Figure 3-17: *List of conversations*

The panel also includes two additional buttons on the sides to manage the conversation. The button on the left (Figure 3-17, number 1) starts a new conversation, while the button on the right (Figure 3-17, number 3) displays a list of all the changes the assistant has made during the current conversation. For example, if we select the conversation we started at the beginning of our project, we can see a list of all the changes made to the code so far and revert to a previous state if needed.

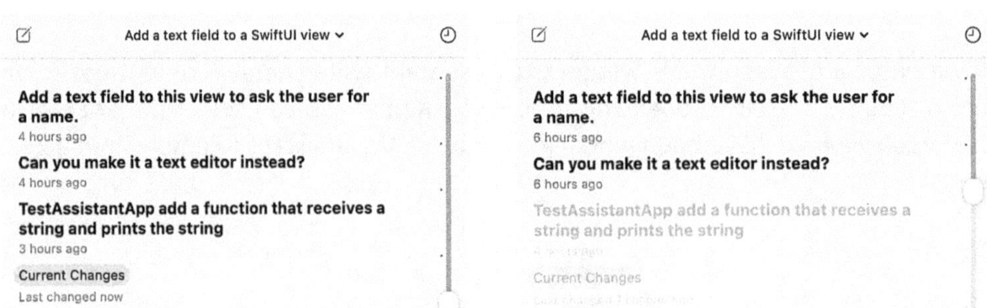

Figure 3-18: *Modification history*

The assistant includes a slider on the right that allows us to revert to any previous state. As we move it up, the corresponding requests are grayed out, and their changes are removed from the code in the editor. If we like what we see, the panel also includes a Restore button at the bottom to make the changes permanent.

Other than asking the assistant to generate code for us, we can also ask questions. For example, if we don't understand how the code works or what a class or a function is doing, we can just ask. For example, we can ask the assistant why the State property in the view is set to private.

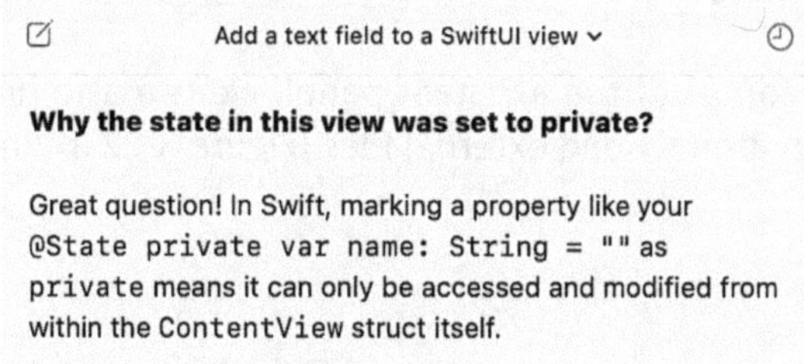

Figure 3-19: *Assistant responding questions*

Unless we specify otherwise, either by referencing a symbol with the @ character or by using the Coding Tool, the assistant will always produce a response based on the contents of our project and previous requests, but we can change this behavior from the buttons at the bottom of the panel (Figure 3-20, number 1).

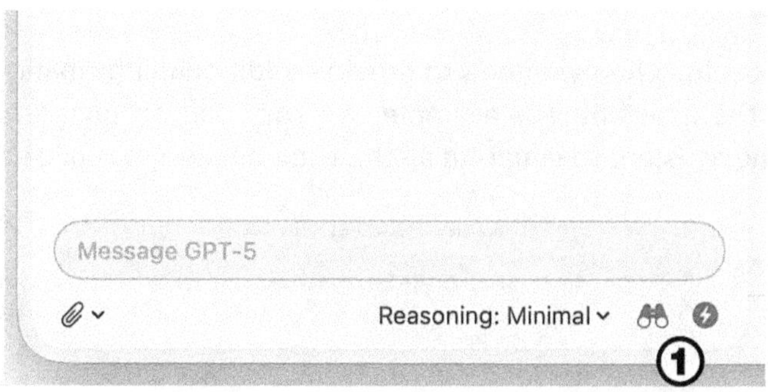

Figure 3-20: *Coding Assistant configuration*

The first button determines whether the model should consider the content of the project when responding to a request (enabled by default). If this option is disabled, the assistant will provide more generic answers. The second button controls whether the assistant automatically applies the changes. If we disable this feature, the assistant will not apply the changes directly but will generate a proposal that includes the recommended code. Clicking on these proposals opens a popup window where we can review the changes and manually apply them to our code, as shown below.

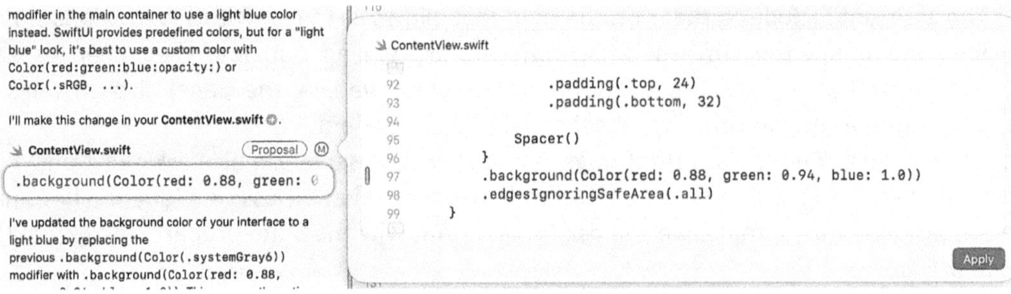

Figure 3-21: *Manually applying changes*

At the bottom-left corner of the assistant panel, we can also find another button that opens a menu with an option to load external files (Figure 3-22, number 1).

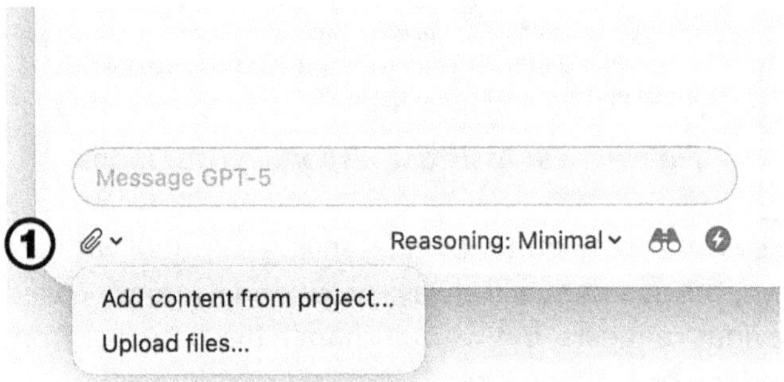

Figure 3-22: *Attachments button*

This option is useful when we need to provide additional information, such as code or images, to guide the assistant. For example, we can load an image of a user interface mockup and ask the assistant to generate all the code needed to replicate that interface.

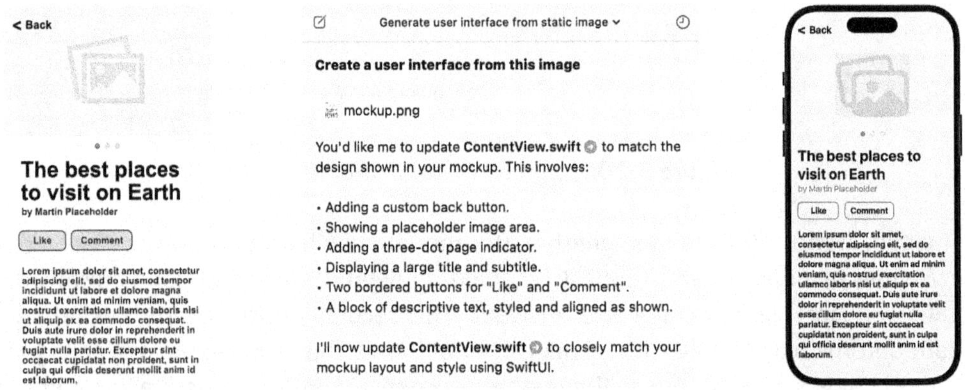

Figure 3-23: *Interface generated by the assistant from a mockup*

Figure 3-23 shows the mockup used for this example on the left and the interface produced by the assistant on the right. The assistant modified the ContentView.swift file, adding all the views necessary to create the interface without requiring us to type any code.

Do It Yourself

Create a new Multiplatform project. Download the **mockup.png** file from our website or use your own. Click the button at the bottom left corner of the assistant panel (Figure 3-22, number 1), select Upload Files, and load the image file. Once the image is loaded, enter the request "Create a user interface from this image." After a few seconds, the assistant should add the code to your **ContentView** view, and you should see the interface displayed on the canvas.

The Coding Assistant can also help us fix errors in our code. When we encounter an error, Xcode displays a label beside it with an X button on the left. Clicking this button opens a popup window with information about the error and a button to ask the assistant for a solution.

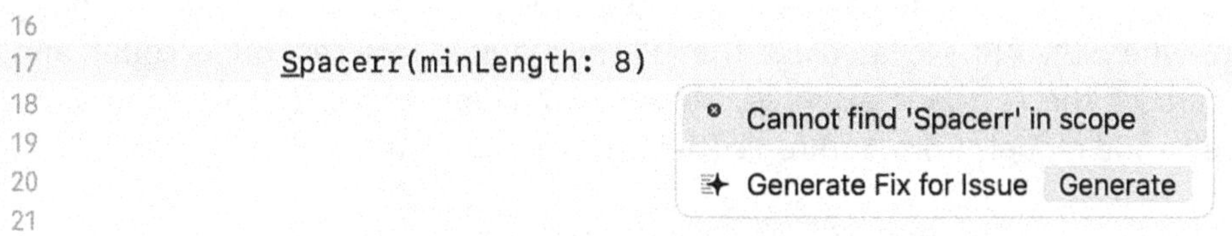

Figure 3-24: *Error message*

In this example, we made a typo when writing the name of the **Spacer** view. If we click Generate, the assistant detects the typo and fixes the error for us.

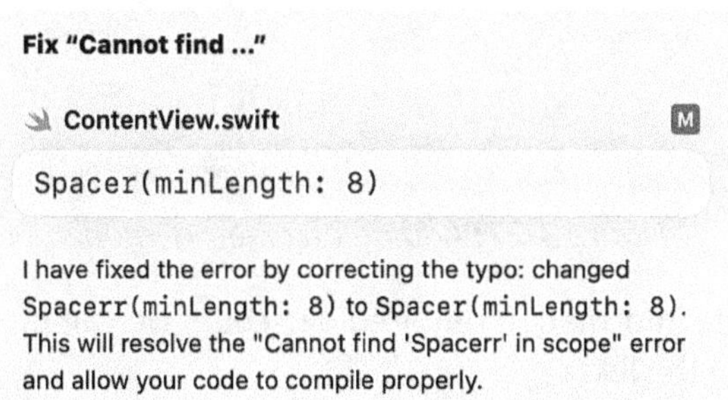

Figure 3-25: *Error fixed by the Coding Assistant*

External Models

As mentioned before, Xcode comes with built-in support for ChatGPT and Claude, but we can also work with any other external model we want. In the Settings panel, there is a button called Add a Model Provider (see Figure 3-6, number 2) that allows us to connect Xcode to additional models. Clicking this button opens a window with two tabs: one for entering the information needed to connect to an external model hosted on the internet (Internet Hosted) and another for connecting to a model running locally on our computer (Locally Hosted).

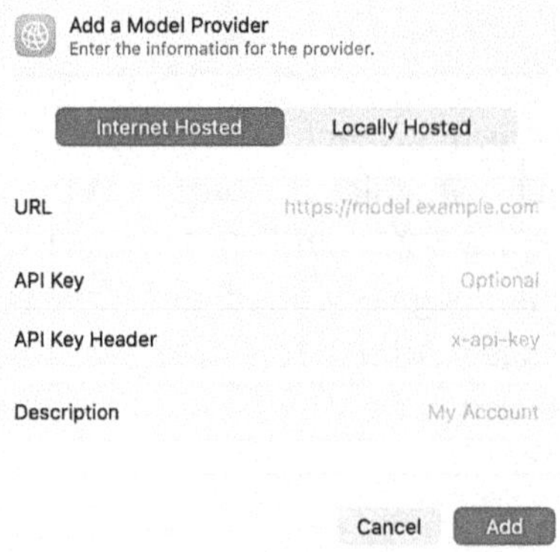

Figure 3-26: *Adding a model*

External models are offered by various companies, such as OpenAI, Anthropic, and Mistral. These companies host their models on their own servers and provide access through APIs. Although these are complex programming interfaces that we would normally need to learn to use, Xcode handles the entire process for us. All we need to do is provide the URL where the API is located and the API key required to access our account, and Xcode takes care of the rest. For example, Figure 3-27 below shows the configuration values needed to add models from Anthropic (the providers of Claude).

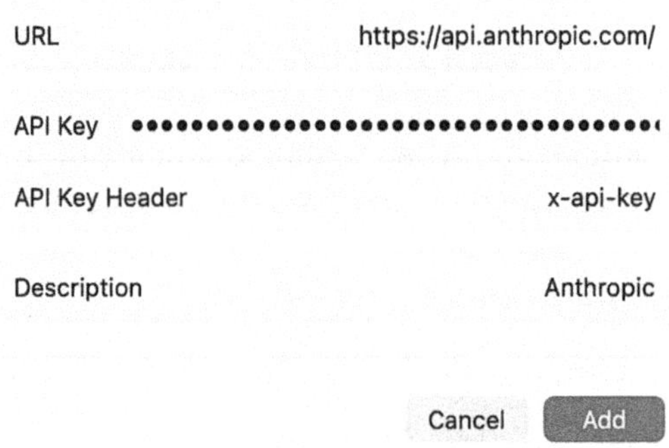

Figure 3-27: *Adding an external model*

After entering all the information required by Xcode, we can press the Add button, and the provider is added to the list.

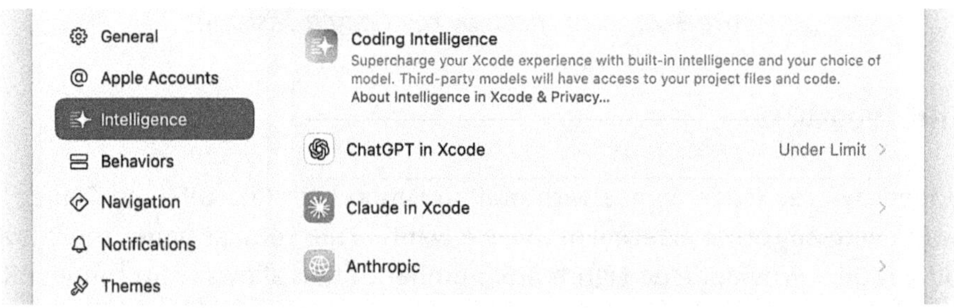

Figure 3-28: *Anthropic provider added to the list*

Companies usually offer multiple versions of their models, each with different characteristics. By default, all of these models are added to Xcode, but we can click the provider's name to view the full list and enable or disable only the ones we need.

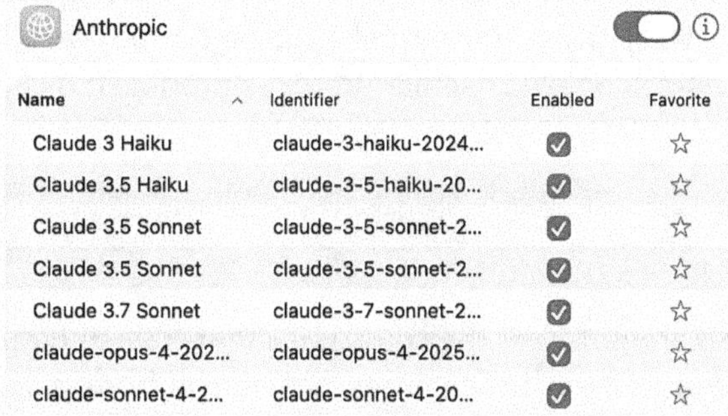

Figure 3-29: *List of models offered by the provider*

After the models have been added to Xcode, we need to select them from the Coding Assistant panel. The option appears next to the button used to create a new conversation (Figure 3-30, number 1).

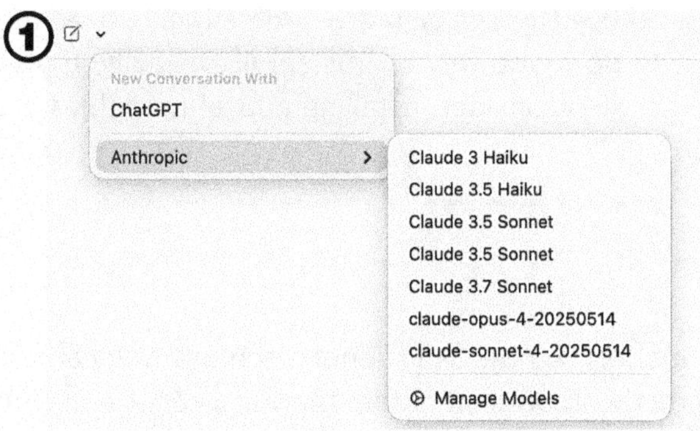

Figure 3-30: *Selecting the model*

Once the model is selected, a message appears on the panel indicating which model is in use, and we can start performing requests, just as we did before with ChatGPT.

Do It Yourself

If you want to test the Anthropic models used in this example, go to **https://console.anthropic.com**, create an account, find the API Keys option in the menu, and click the Create Key button to generate a key. (Currently, the system requires an initial deposit of at least $5 USD to obtain an API key and access the model.) After getting the key, open the Xcode menu at the top of the screen, click Settings, select Intelligence, and click Add a Model Provider (Figure 3-6, number 2). You will see the form shown in Figure 3-26. Enter the URL **https://api.anthropic.com/**, the API key you created on Anthropic's website, and the text **x-api-key** for the API key header. Click the Add button. You should see the new provider on the list, as shown in Figure 3-28. (If you don't see the provider or the models, restart Xcode.) Close Settings, open the Coding Assistant panel, click the button to select a model (Figure 3-30, number 1), and choose one from the list. (Of all the models provided by Anthropic, Sonnet 4.5 is currently recommended for working with Swift.) Once the model is selected, perform a request as before. You should see results similar to those produced by ChatGPT.

IMPORTANT

External models are not free; the companies that train and maintain these models charge based on usage. Fees can range from a few cents per request to several dollars, depending on the model and the number of words processed in both the request and the response. It is a good idea to try different models to find the one that best fits your needs and budget. In addition to ChatGPT, two of the most popular options at the moment are Claude Sonnet by Anthropic (**https://www.anthropic.com/**) and Codestral by Mistral (**https://mistral.ai/**). When using an API, you only pay for what you use. While this can be more flexible than a fixed monthly fee, costs may still add up if you rely on the service heavily. If you are on a budget, you might also consider installing a local model, as explained in the next section.

Local Models

In addition to external models, Xcode also supports the use of local models. These models are installed and run directly on our computer, offering a cost-free solution with the added reassurance that no code is being sent to external servers beyond our control.

To install and run a local model, we need a model manager. Currently, the most popular options are Ollama (**https://ollama.com/**) and LM Studio (**https://lmstudio.ai/**). Both offer user-friendly interfaces that simplify the process and allow us to use any model we want, but Ollama is currently recommended for developers due to its flexibility and performance. To use Ollama, we first need to download the application from their website at **https://www.ollama.com/download/**.

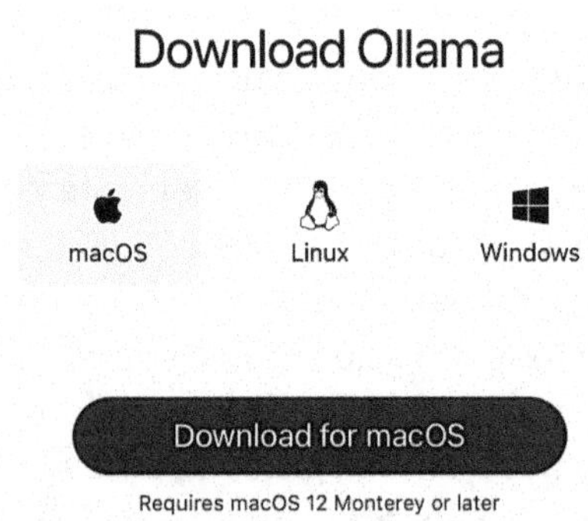

Figure 3-31: *Ollama's download page*

When the application is running, an icon appears in the menu bar at the top of the screen, indicating that it is active in the background. Clicking the icon opens a menu with an option to launch the interface.

Figure 3-32: *Ollama's menu*

Ollama's interface is similar to other chatbots like ChatGPT. It includes a button in the top-left corner to open a side panel that lists all the conversations we had with the models (Figure 3-33, number 1), a main panel where we can view the current conversation and enter a new request (Figure 3-33, number 2), and a button in the bottom-right corner of this panel to select the model (Figure 3-33, number 3).

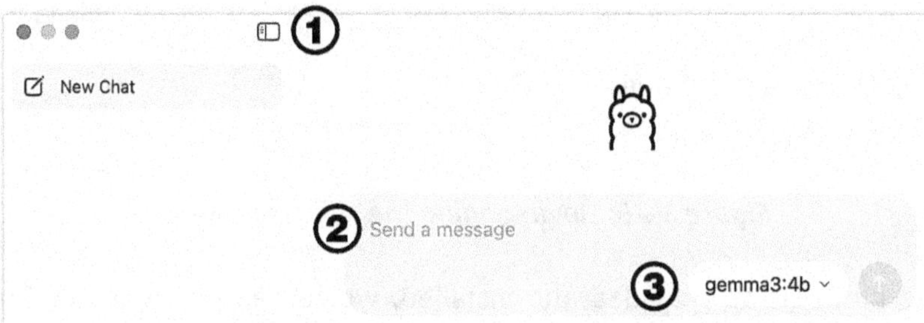

Figure 3-33: *Ollama's interface*

The button for selecting the model opens a list of all models installed on the system, along with a few suggested options to choose from, and an input field at the top to search for more (Figure 3-34, number 1).

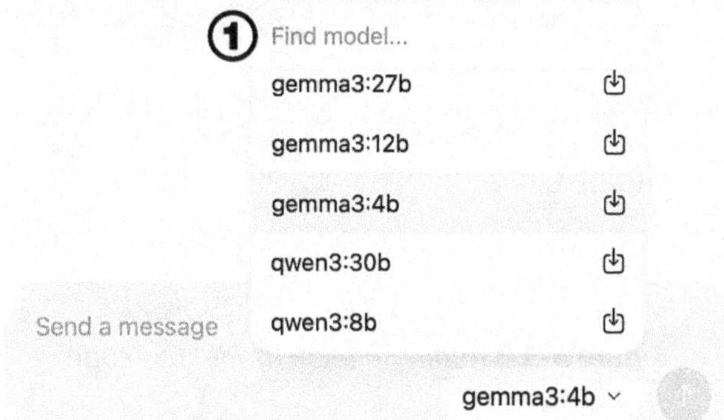

Figure 3-34: *Model options*

There are many models available for coding. Some of the most popular at the moment are Qwen, Codestral, and Llama, but new ones are released every month. As an example, we will install Qwen 2.5 Coder with 7 billion parameters. This model is recommended for working with Swift, and the 7 billion parameter version is compact enough to run on most Mac computers. Ollama's interface doesn't show this model in the list, so we have to search for it using the search bar by entering the full name, as shown below.

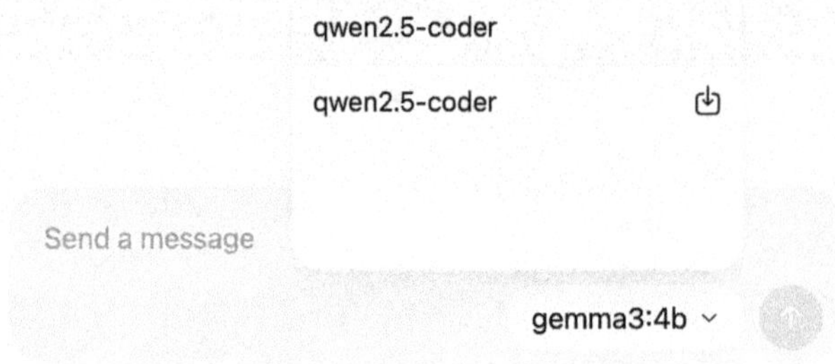

Figure 3-35: *Searching for a model*

When we find the model we want, we click on it to select it. If the model is already installed on our computer, Ollama will use it to process our requests; otherwise, the model will be downloaded and installed automatically as soon as we type our first request.

Figure 3-36: *Downloading the selected model*

Once the model is downloaded and installed, we can add it to Xcode. The option is available in Settings, but this time we need to open the Locally Hosted tab (Figure 3-37, number 1).

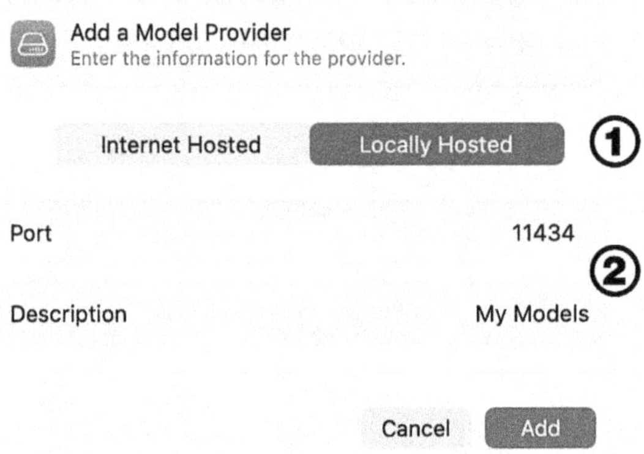

Figure 3-37: *Adding a local model to Xcode*

Ollama operates as a local server on our computer, similar to a web server. To communicate with this server, we need to send requests to a specific port number. In the case of Ollama, the port is **11434**. To connect Xcode with Ollama, we must enter this number, provide a name for the account, and click the Add button, as shown in Figure 3-37, number 2. The account is added below the ChatGPT account, as before, and we can click on it to select the models we want to enable.

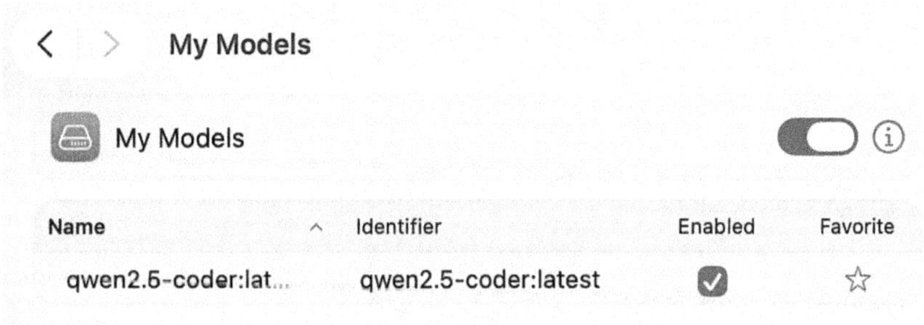

Figure 3-38: *List of local models*

Once the models are enabled, we can select them from the list in the Coding Assistant (Figure 3-30) and begin typing our request. The responses should be very similar to those previously received from ChatGPT and Anthropic, but now the model runs locally on our computer, so there are no usage fees to worry about.

Do It Yourself

Visit **https://www.ollama.com/download/** and click the Download For macOS button to download the app (Figure 3-31). Double-click the Ollama.dmg file to install the application, then run it. You should see the icon in the menu bar at the top of the screen (Figure 3-32). Click the icon and select Open Ollama. Click the button to select the model (Figure 3-33, number 3), and search for the name "qwen2.5-coder" (Figure 3-35). Click the model to select it, and enter a request (e.g., "Hello"). Ollama should begin downloading the model (Figure 3-36). After the model is downloaded and installed, open Xcode, go to the Xcode menu at the top of the screen, click Settings, select the Intelligence option, click Add a Model Provider (Figure 3-6, number 2), and open the Locally Hosted tab (Figure 3-37, number 1). Enter the port number **11434** and a name for the account, then press the Add button. You should be able to select the Qwen 2.5 Coder model from the Coding Assistant. Remember to make sure that the model is enabled and restart Xcode if it doesn't appear on the list.

IMPORTANT

Local models come in different sizes to accommodate various computer configurations. For example, models with fewer than 4 billion parameters (weights and biases) can typically run well on Mac computers with 8 gigabytes of memory, though the exact requirements depend on the model's architecture and configuration. Larger models produce better results but require significantly more memory and processing power. Always check the documentation for the specific model you plan to install to ensure it will work on your system and deliver the results you expect. For a full list, visit **https://ollama.com/search?q=coding**.

Chapter 4
Integrated Tools

4.1 - Tools

Apple Intelligence introduces a new generation of integrated tools that allow users to express themselves more effectively. With these tools, users can refine and correct text, generate images, and create customized emojis through intuitive interfaces that are available system-wide, including our own apps.

4.2 - Image Playground

Among these tools, Image Playground is one of the easiest to implement, as it offers a straightforward API that integrates seamlessly with SwiftUI applications. Using this API, we can present the Image Playground interface directly within our app and allow users to create any image they want.

Figure 4-1: *Image Playground interface*

Image Playground Interface

The Image Playground interface provides everything users need to enter a prompt, create images, and refine the results. To present this interface, the **Image Playground** framework offers the following modifier.

imagePlaygroundSheet(isPresented: Bool, **concepts:** [ImagePlaygroundConcept], **sourceImage:** Image?, **onCompletion:** Closure, **onCancellation:** Closure)

This modifier presents a sheet with the Image Playground interface and returns the image created by the user. The **isPresented** argument is a Binding property of type **Bool** that opens or closes the interface, the **concepts** argument is an array of **ImagePlaygroundConcept** structures that provide the information needed to generate the image, the **sourceImage** argument is an optional **Image** view that the system can use as a reference, the **onCompletion** argument is a closure called with the image generated by the user, and the **onCancellation** argument is a closure called when the user cancels the process.

The Image Playground interface provides all the tools the user needs to generate an image, so all we have to do to offer this functionality in our app is to implement the **imagePlaygroundSheet()** modifier and process the image in the **onCompletion** closure, as shown below.

Listing 4-1: Processing an image generated by Image Playground

```
import SwiftUI
import ImagePlayground

struct ContentView: View {
   @State private var openPlayground: Bool = false
   @State private var image = UIImage(named: "nopicture")!

   var body: some View {
      VStack {
         Image(uiImage: image)
            .resizable()
            .frame(width: 300, height: 300)
         Button("Create Image") {
            openPlayground = true
         }
         .padding()
         .buttonStyle(.borderedProminent)
         .disabled(openPlayground)
         Spacer()
      }
      .imagePlaygroundSheet(isPresented: $openPlayground, onCompletion: {
         url in
         if let newImage = UIImage(contentsOfFile: url.path) {
            self.image = newImage
         }
      })
   }
}
```

In this example, we first import the **Image Playground** framework to gain access to its tools, and then define two State properties: one called **openPlayground** to determine whether the sheet is presented or not, and another called **image** to store the image generated by the user. Here, the **image** property is initialized with a placeholder image.

In the body, we include an **Image** view to show the image to the user, a button to open the sheet, and implement the **imagePlaygroundSheet()** modifier to present the interface. Note that we also apply the **disabled()** modifier to the button so that it cannot be pressed while the sheet is open.

When the button is pressed, the **imagePlaygroundSheet()** modifier presents the Image Playground interface, where the user can type instructions to generate an image. Once the image is created, it is stored in a temporary file, and the URL to that file is passed to the closure specified in the **onCompletion** argument. Inside this closure, we use the URL to create a new **UIImage** object from the generated file and assign it to the **image** property so it can be displayed on the screen. The result is shown below.

Figure 4-2: *Generating images with Image Playground*

Do It Yourself

Create a new Multiplatform project. Download the **nopicture.png** image from our website and add it to the Assets Catalog. Update the ContentView.swift file with the code in Listing 4-1. Run the application on a device compatible with Apple Intelligence. Press the Create Image button. After a few seconds, the Image Playground interface should appear. Type your prompt (e.g., "Cute dog with a hat") and press the button to start the process. After the image is generated, you should see something similar to Figure 4-2, center. Press the OK button in the top-right corner to approve the image. The generated image should appear in the interface, as shown in Figure 4-2, right.

IMPORTANT

Apple Intelligence tools do not work in the simulator; they require a device with supported hardware. The examples in this chapter are designed to run on iPhone or iPad models with an A17 Pro processor or newer. Also, note that when testing on a physical device, the interface may take a few seconds to become responsive. This is a temporary issue that occurs only when you run the application from Xcode.

In this example, we let the user specify the instructions to generate the image within the Image Playground interface, but the `imagePlaygroundSheet()` modifier also includes the **concepts** argument, which we can use to provide these instructions directly from our app. The instructions are defined by the `ImagePlaygroundConcept` structure, which includes several type methods to create predefined instances. The following are the most frequently used.

text(String)

This method creates a structure with a short description of what the generated image should depict.

extracted(from: String, **title:** String?)

This method creates a structure that extracts the main concepts from a longer piece of text to determine what the generated image should depict. The **from** argument is the text the system should analyze, and the **title** argument is an optional string representing the title of that text.

To define the instructions, we can use any information inserted by the user or provide our own. In the following example, we include a `TextField` view to let the user provide the instructions from our app.

Listing 4-2: Specifying the instructions from the application

```
import SwiftUI
import ImagePlayground

struct ContentView: View {
   @State private var openPlayground: Bool = false
   @State private var image = UIImage(named: "nopicture")!
   @State private var instructions: String = ""

   var body: some View {
      VStack {
         Image(uiImage: image)
            .resizable()
            .frame(width: 300, height: 300)
         TextField("Describe the image", text: $instructions)
            .textFieldStyle(.roundedBorder)
            .padding()
         Button("Create Image") {
            openPlayground = true
         }
         .padding()
         .buttonStyle(.borderedProminent)
         .disabled(openPlayground || instructions.isEmpty)
         Spacer()
      }
      .imagePlaygroundSheet(isPresented: $openPlayground, concepts:
         [.text(instructions)], onCompletion: { url in
         if let newImage = UIImage(contentsOfFile: url.path) {
            self.image = newImage
```

```
                self.instructions = ""
            }
        })
    }
}
```

The implementation of the **imagePlaygroundSheet()** modifier is the same as before, but now it includes the **concepts** argument to provide the instructions. In this case, we expect a short text from the user, so we use the **text()** method to generate the instruction. Now the Image Playground interface will start generating the image with these instructions as soon as it opens.

Do It Yourself

Update the **ContentView** view with the code in Listing 4-2. Run the application again on your device. Type your instructions in the text field and press Create Image. After a few seconds, the Image Playground interface should appear and automatically start generating the image based on your instructions.

Image Playground can generate different types of images, including animations, illustrations, and sketches, and it can also generate images based on the appearance of a person found in your Photos app. The framework includes the following modifiers to configure this behavior.

imagePlaygroundGenerationStyle(ImagePlaygroundStyle)

This modifier defines the style of the image. The argument is a structure with the type properties **animation**, **illustration**, **sketch** and **all**.

imagePlaygroundPersonalizationPolicy(ImagePlaygroundPersonalizationPolicy)

This modifier specifies whether the interface should allow the user to base the image on a person. The argument is an enumeration with the values **automatic**, **enabled** and **disabled**.

To configure the interface, we can declare these modifiers right after the **imagePlaygroundSheet()** modifier, as shown below.

Listing 4-3: Configuring the Image Playground interface

```
.imagePlaygroundSheet(isPresented: $openPlayground, concepts:
   [.text(instructions)], onCompletion: { url in
   if let newImage = UIImage(contentsOfFile: url.path) {
      self.image = newImage
      self.instructions = ""
   }
```

```
})
.imagePlaygroundGenerationStyle(.sketch)
.imagePlaygroundPersonalizationPolicy(.disabled)
```

In this example, we set the style to **sketch** and disable personalization, so the image is generated as a sketch and the button to select a person from the Photos app is no longer available.

> **Do It Yourself**
>
> Add the **imagePlaygroundGenerationStyle()** and **imagePlayground-PersonalizationPolicy()** modifiers below the **imagePlayground-Sheet()** modifier, as shown in Listing 4-3. Run the application again on your device. The image should be generated as a sketch, and the button to select a person should no longer appear.

Image Creator

Although Image Playground presents an interface that users are familiar with, our app may have different requirements. In such cases, we can use the **ImageCreator** class. This class is included in the **Image Playground** framework to allow us to generate images programmatically. The following is the method defined by the class for this purpose.

images(for: [ImagePlaygroundConcept], **style:** ImagePlaygroundStyle, **limit:** Int)

This method asks the model to generate images based on the instructions provided by the arguments. The **for** argument is an array of **ImagePlaygroundConcept** structures that contain the information needed to generate the image. The **style** argument is an **ImagePlaygroundStyle** structure that defines the style of the image. This structure includes the following type properties: **animation**, **illustration**, **sketch**, and **all**. And the **limit** argument specifies the maximum number of images to generate.

The **images()** method returns an asynchronous sequence of **CreatedImage** structures containing the images generated by the model. The **CreatedImage** structure includes the following property to access the image.

cgImage

This property returns a **CGImage** object with the image generated by the model.

As mentioned, the values are returned asynchronously, so we must define a **for await in** loop that waits for the model to finish processing each image. The following example shows how to generate a single image and display it to the user using this approach.

Listing 4-4: Generating images programmatically

```
import SwiftUI
import ImagePlayground

struct ContentView: View {
   @State private var image = UIImage(named: "nopicture")!
   @State private var creating: Bool = false
   @State private var instructions: String = ""

   var body: some View {
      VStack {
         Image(uiImage: image)
            .resizable()
            .frame(width: 300, height: 300)
         TextField("Describe the image", text: $instructions)
            .textFieldStyle(.roundedBorder)
            .padding()
         Button("Create Image") {
            creating = true
            Task {
               await createImages()
            }
         }
         .padding()
         .buttonStyle(.borderedProminent)
         .disabled(creating || instructions.isEmpty)
         Spacer()
      }
   }
   func createImages() async {
      do {
         let creator = try await ImageCreator()
         let images = creator.images(for: [.text(instructions)], style:
            .illustration, limit: 1)

         for try await img in images {
            image = UIImage(cgImage: img.cgImage)
         }
         creating = false
         instructions = ""
      } catch {
         print("Error: \(error)")
      }
   }
}
```

This example implements the same interface as before, but this time we use a separate property called **creating** to disable the button while the model generates the image. The button now executes an asynchronous function called **createImages()** to handle the entire process. Inside this function, we create an instance of the **ImageCreator** class and then call the **images()** method with the user's instructions, the **illustration** style, and a limit of 1 to receive only one image in response. Note that the initialization of the **ImageCreator** class is asynchronous, so we also must wait for this process to be over before continuing.

Once the image is received, we create a **UIImage** object and assign it to the **image** property to show it to the user. The result is the same as before, except this time the image is generated in the background without opening the interface.

Do It Yourself

Update the `ContentView` view with the code in Listing 4-4. Run the application on your device. You should see the same interface as before. Type your instructions in the text field and press the Create Image button to generate an image. After a few seconds, the image will be generated in the background and displayed on the screen.

When we use the Image Playground interface, the system automatically checks whether Image Playground is available and displays a message if it isn't, but when the images are generated directly from the model, we must check availability ourselves. The framework provides the following Environment property for this purpose.

`supportsImagePlayground`

This property returns a Boolean value indicating whether Image Playground is available on the system.

This is an Environment property, so all we need to do is create our own property using the `@Environment` property wrapper and then check its value. As an example, we are going to build an app that takes advantage of the model's ability to generate multiple images at once, but disable the button when Image Playground is not available.

Listing 4-5: Generating multiple images programmatically

```
import SwiftUI
import ImagePlayground

struct ContentView: View {
   @Environment(\.supportsImagePlayground) private var support

   @State private var images: [UIImage] = [UIImage(named: "nopicture")!]
   @State private var creating: Bool = false
   @State private var instructions: String = ""

   var body: some View {
      VStack {
         ScrollView(.horizontal) {
            LazyHStack(spacing: 0) {
               ForEach(images.indices, id: \.self) { index in
                  Image(uiImage: images[index])
                     .resizable()
                     .frame(width: 300, height: 300)
                     .containerRelativeFrame(.horizontal)
               }
            }
         }
         .scrollTargetBehavior(.paging)
         .frame(height: 320)
```

```
        TextField("Describe the image", text: $instructions)
            .textFieldStyle(.roundedBorder)
            .padding()
        Button("Create Image") {
            creating = true
            Task {
                let tempImages = await createImages()

                if !tempImages.isEmpty {
                    self.images = tempImages
                }
                creating = false
                instructions = ""
            }
        }
        .disabled(creating || instructions.isEmpty || !support)
        .padding()
        .buttonStyle(.borderedProminent)
        Spacer()
    }
  }
  func createImages() async -> [UIImage] {
    var tempImages: [UIImage] = []
    do {
        let creator = try await ImageCreator()
        let images = creator.images(for: [.text(instructions)], style:
            .illustration, limit: 4)
        for try await image in images {
            tempImages.append(UIImage(cgImage: image.cgImage))
        }
    } catch {
        print("Error: \(error)")
    }
    return tempImages
  }
}
```

In this example, we create a property called **support** to retrieve the value of the **supportsImagePlayground** property and use it to disable the button. The button is now disabled while the model is generating images (**creating**), when the user hasn't entered any instructions (**instructions.isEmpty**), or when Image Playground isn't supported (**!support**).

The rest of the process is similar to what we did before, except this time we generate four images instead of one. In the **createImages()** method, we create a temporary array to store the images returned by the model, return this array, and assign it to the **images** property so they can be displayed to the user. To present the images, we use a horizontal **ScrollView** that arranges the views side by side. The result is shown below.

Figure 4-3: *Generating multiple images*

Do It Yourself

Update the **`ContentView`** view with the code in Listing 4-5. Run the application on your device. Enter the instructions and press the Create Image button. After a few seconds, the first image should appear on the screen, and you should be able to scroll through all of them, as shown in Figure 4-3.

IMPORTANT

Apple Intelligence tools may be disabled not only due to lack of hardware support but also because the required models are still being downloaded. When using these tools for the first time on a mobile device, the system may need to download the models, and the interface will not become available until the process is complete. In our examples, when **`ImageCreator`** returns an error, we simply print a message to the console. However, you should always inform users of the situation and re-enable the button so they can try again once the models have finished downloading.

4.3 - Genmojis

Genmoji is a tool similar to Image Playground, but it uses a model trained to create small images that can be used as emojis. With this tool, users can describe what they want and generate personalized emojis that reflect their current ideas or emotions.

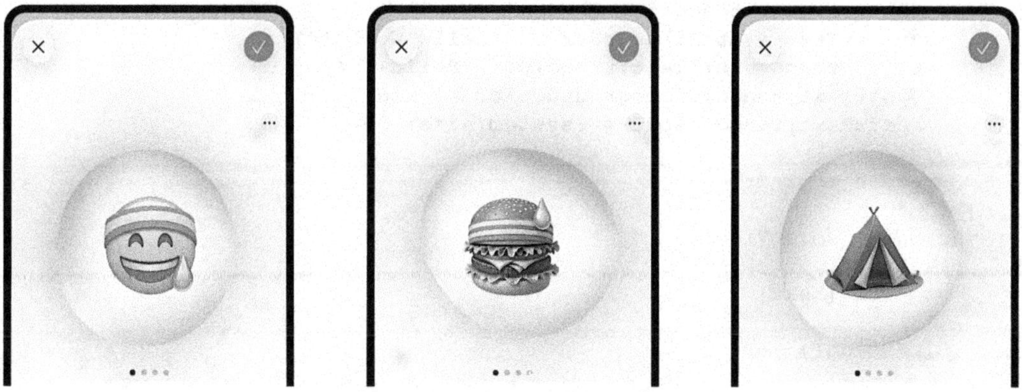

***Figure 4-4:** Genmoji interface*

Genmojis can be embedded in text like any other emoji, and most views can display them without issues. However, to handle these values, we need to use a data type capable of managing attributed content. For this purpose, the **Foundation** framework provides the **`AttributedString`** structure. This structure can store not only Genmojis but also strings with various attributes, such as bold or italic fonts, different sizes, colors, and more. The following is the structure's initializer.

`AttributedString``(String, `**`attributes:`**` AttributeContainer)`

This initializer creates an attributed string with the string specified by the first argument. The **attributes** argument is an optional value used to define initial attributes.

The **`AttributedString`** structure conforms to the **`AttributedStringProtocol`** protocol, which among others, defines the following method to search for strings within a text.

`range(of:`` String)`

This method returns a **`Range`** value that represents the position of the string specified in the **of** argument within the attributed string, or **`nil`** if the string is not found.

Once we obtain the range of the text we want to modify, we can apply SwiftUI attributes to it. For this purpose, the **Foundation** framework provides the **`SwiftUIAttributes`** structure, which includes properties that help us define these attributes. The most frequently used are **`backgroundColor`** and **`foregroundColor`** to set the color of the text, **`font`** to specify the characteristics of the font, and **`adaptiveImageGlyph`** to handle Genmojis. The following example demonstrates how to apply these attributes to a text.

Listing 4-6: Assigning attributes to a text

```
import SwiftUI

struct ContentView: View {
```

```
   var text: AttributedString {
      var attText = AttributedString("Hello World!")
      if let range = attText.range(of: "Hello") {
         attText[range].foregroundColor = .red
         attText[range].font = .system(size: 30)
      }
      return attText
   }
   var body: some View {
      VStack {
         Text(text)
      }
      .padding()
   }
}
```

In this example, we define a computed property called **`text`** that returns an attributed string and display it using a **`Text`** view. The computed property first creates an attributed text with the string "Hello World!", then finds the range of the word "Hello" within the string, and finally applies a foreground color and a new font size to the characters in that range. The result is shown below.

Figure 4-5: *Attributed text*

Do It Yourself

Create a new Multiplatform project. Update the **`ContentView`** view with the code in Listing 4-6. Run the application on the simulator or the canvas. You should see the attributes applied to the text, as shown in Figure 4-5.

Although we can assign these attributes programmatically, Apple's systems also include built-in tools that users can use for this purpose. When we store the text in an **`AttributedString`** property, the system automatically provides these tools for editing, including a button to generate Genmojis. The following example shows how to define a **`TextEditor`** view that supports this functionality.

Listing 4-7: Defining a `TextEditor` view that supports attributed text

```
import SwiftUI

struct ContentView: View {
   @State private var text: AttributedString = ""
```

```
    var body: some View {
        VStack {
            TextEditor(text: $text)
                .padding()
                .scrollContentBackground(.hidden)
                .background(Color.gray.opacity(0.2))
                .clipShape(RoundedRectangle(cornerRadius: 12))
        }.padding()
    }
}
```

Because the **text** property stores an **AttributedString** value, we can now format the text and insert Genmojis. The formatting options are available from the contextual menu that appears when we tap the view, while the Genmoji option becomes available when we tap the emoji button on the keyboard. This opens a panel that displays all standard emojis, along with a text field at the top to describe the Genmoji and a button to generate it (Figure 4-6, number 1). After pressing this button, an interface similar to the one provided by Image Playground appears. Once the Genmoji is generated, we can add it to our text by pressing the OK button (Figure 4-6, center).

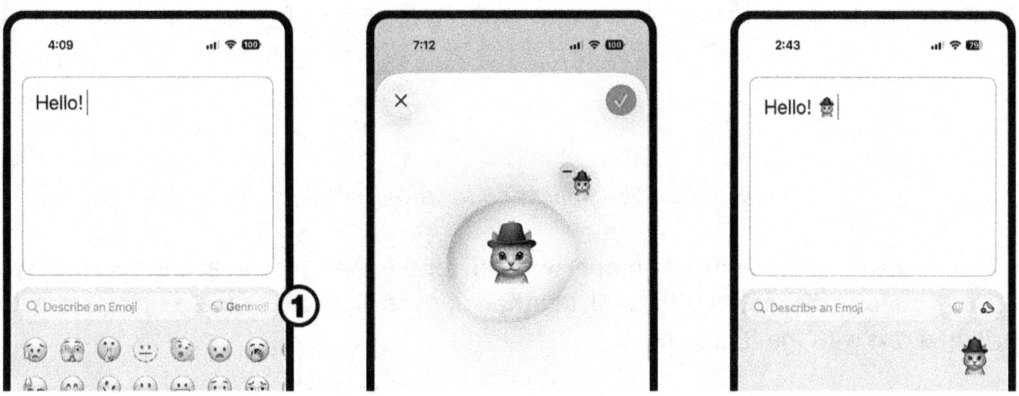

Figure 4-6: *Using Genmojis*

Do It Yourself

Update the **ContentView** view from the previous example with the code in Listing 4-7. Run the application on your device. Tap the **TextEditor** view, then tap the emoji button on the keyboard, enter the instructions for the Genmoji (e.g., "Cute cat with a hat"), and tap the Genmoji button (Figure 4-6, number 1). After the Genmoji is generated, press the OK button to approve it. You should see the Genmoji inserted into your text (Figure 4-6, right). To learn more about attributed strings and text formatting, read our book *SwiftUI Framework for Masterminds*.

Storing Genmojis

Genmojis are inserted in the text like any other characters, but they are not simple characters, they are personalized images with specific formats and requirements. This means that we can't store or share them as plain text; we must first process their values. Fortunately, Core Data now supports the **AttributedString** type, so if all we need is to store them in a database, the process is straightforward.

To demonstrate how to work with these values, we are going to create a small application that allows users to store notes. We need one view for listing all the notes stored in the database, another for entering the notes' titles and texts, and a third for displaying the content of each note, as shown below.

Figure 4-7: *Application to store Genmojis*

The following is the SwiftData model we need for this example. It has a property of type **String** to store the note's title and another of type **AttributedString** to store the attributed text with the Genmojis.

Listing 4-8: Storing attributed strings

```
import SwiftUI
import SwiftData

@Model
class Note: Identifiable {
   var id: UUID = UUID()
   var title: String
   var text: AttributedString

   init(title: String, text: AttributedString) {
      self.title = title
      self.text = text
   }
}
```

The next step is to set up the model container in the **App** structure's environment so all views have access to it.

Listing 4-9: Setting up the model container

```
import SwiftUI
import SwiftData

@main
struct TestGenmojiApp: App {
   var body: some Scene {
      WindowGroup {
         ContentView()
            .modelContainer(for: [Note.self])
      }
   }
}
```

Now we can work on our interface. The **ContentView** view must list all the notes already stored in the database and provide a button to add more.

Listing 4-10: Listing notes

```
import SwiftUI
import SwiftData

struct ContentView: View {
   @Query var listNotes: [Note]

   var body: some View {
      NavigationStack {
         if listNotes.isEmpty {
            Text("No notes available. Add one!")
               .font(Font.system(size: 16))
               .foregroundStyle(Color(.secondaryLabel))
               .padding(20)
         }
         List(listNotes) { note in
            NavigationLink(destination: NoteView(note: note)) {
               Text(note.title)
            }
         }
         .toolbar {
            ToolbarItem(placement: .topBarTrailing) {
               NavigationLink(destination: AddNote()) {
                  Image(systemName: "plus")
               }
            }
         }
      }
   }
}
```

This view displays the list of notes by title and includes a toolbar button to open a view for creating a new note. The following is the code for this view.

Listing 4-11: Adding notes

```
import SwiftUI
import SwiftData

struct AddNote: View {
    @Environment(\.modelContext) var dbContext
    @Environment(\.dismiss) var dismiss
    @State private var inputTitle: String = ""
    @State private var inputText: AttributedString = ""

    var body: some View {
        VStack {
            TextField("Insert Title", text: $inputTitle)
                .textFieldStyle(.roundedBorder)
                .padding()
            TextEditor(text: $inputText)
                .padding()
                .scrollContentBackground(.hidden)
                .background(Color.gray.opacity(0.2))
                .clipShape(RoundedRectangle(cornerRadius: 12))
            HStack {
                Spacer()
                Button("Save") {
                    let newNote = Note(title: inputTitle, text: inputText)
                    dbContext.insert(newNote)
                    try? dbContext.save()
                    dismiss()
                }.buttonStyle(.borderedProminent)
                    .disabled(inputTitle.isEmpty || inputText.description.
                        isEmpty)
            }.padding()
        }.padding()
    }
}
```

In this view, we have two State properties: one to store a simple **String** value for the title and another of type **AttributedString** for the text, so the user can insert Genmojis. The views are configured as before, but now there's a Save button at the bottom of the interface that creates a **Note** instance with the values provided by the user and inserts it into the database.

When the user selects a note from the list, we open a view to show it on the screen. The following is the code for this view.

Listing 4-12: Displaying notes

```
import SwiftUI
import SwiftData

struct NoteView: View {
    let note: Note

    var body: some View {
        VStack(alignment: .leading, spacing: 8) {
```

```
                Text(note.title)
                    .font(.title)
                    .padding(.bottom, 8)
                ScrollView {
                    Text(note.text)
                        .font(Font.system(size: 16))
                        .multilineTextAlignment(.leading)
                        .textSelection(.enabled)
                }
                .frame(maxWidth: .infinity, alignment: .leading)
                Spacer()
            }.padding(20)
        }
    }
```

Since **`Text`** views can handle both **`String`** and **`AttributedString`** values, the code for this view is simple. We receive the **`Note`** selected by the user and then use two **`Text`** views to show the values of the **`title`** and **`text`** properties on the screen.

Do It Yourself

Starting from the previous project, create a new file called NotesModel.swift for the code in Listing 4-8. Update the **`App`** structure with the code in Listing 4-9 and the **`ContentView`** view with the code in Listing 4-10. Create a new file called AddNote.swift for the code in Listing 4-11, and another called NoteView.swift for the code in Listing 4-12. Run the application on your device. Press the + button to add a note. Provide a title and insert a Genmoji in the text. Press Save. You should see the note in the list (Figure 4-7, left). Select the note. You should see the content of the note, including the Genmojis (Figure 4-7, right). To learn more about SwiftData, read our book *SwiftUI Framework for Masterminds*.

Advanced Implementation

Apple Intelligence is still being integrated into every Apple technology and framework. This means that these tools are not available everywhere. For example, in the previous application, we used a **`TextField`** view to let the user enter the note's title, but the value was stored as plain text. This is because the **`TextField`** view does not yet support **`AttributedString`** values. If we want users to be able to insert Genmojis in a text field, we need to implement the **`UITextField`** class from the **UIKit** framework and provide the value for this view as an **`NSAttributedString`** object instead of an **`AttributedString`** structure.

The **`UITextField`** class creates a text field similar to the **`TextField`** view in SwiftUI, but unlike **`TextField`**, it can also work with attributed strings. All we need to do is to specify the following property to tell the system that we are working with Genmojis.

supportsAdaptiveImageGlyph

This property sets or returns a Boolean value that determines whether the view supports personalized images (Genmojis) as input.

To transform **AttributedString** structures into **NSAttributedString** objects, the **NSAttributedString** class includes the following initializer.

NSAttributedString(AttributedString)

This initializer creates an **NSAttributedString** object from the value specified by the attribute.

To convert an **NSAttributedString** object back into an **AttributedString** structure, the **AttributedString** structure provides a similar initializer.

AttributedString(NSAttributedString)

This initializer creates an **AttributedString** structure from the value specified by the attribute.

It may sound complicated, but implementing a **UITextField** view in a SwiftUI application is actually quite simple. All we need to do is create a representable view. A representable view is a structure that implements the functionality required to create the UIKit view and connect it to the SwiftUI interface. This functionality is defined by the **UIViewRepresentable** protocol, which includes three methods that we must implement to represent a **UITextField** view: the **makeUIView()** method to create and return the view; the **updateUIView()** method to update the **UITextField** view with values coming from the SwiftUI interface; and the **makeCoordinator()** method to update the SwiftUI interface with the values inserted by the user and respond to additional delegate methods if necessary. In the following example, we implement a basic representable view to provide the **UITextField** view for our application.

Listing 4-13: Creating a Representable view for a UITextField view

```
import SwiftUI

struct CustomField: UIViewRepresentable {
   @Binding var input: AttributedString

   func makeUIView(context: Context) -> UITextField {
      let view = UITextField()
      view.borderStyle = .roundedRect
      view.attributedText = NSAttributedString(input)
      view.supportsAdaptiveImageGlyph = true
      view.delegate = context.coordinator
      return view
   }
```

```
    func updateUIView(_ uiView: UITextField, context: Context) { }
    func makeCoordinator() -> CoordinatorTextField {
        return CoordinatorTextField(input: $input)
    }
}
class CoordinatorTextField: NSObject, UITextFieldDelegate {
    @Binding var inputCoordinator: AttributedString

    init(input: Binding<AttributedString>) {
        self._inputCoordinator = input
    }
    func textFieldDidChangeSelection(_ textField: UITextField) {
        if let text = textField.attributedText {
            inputCoordinator = AttributedString(text)
        }
    }
}
```

The Representable view requires a Binding property to pass values between the view and the SwiftUI interface. In this example, we define a property called **input** of type **AttributedString** to manage this value. In the **makeUIView()** method, we create the **UITextField** view, set its font size to 20, apply a rounded border, initialize it with the value of the **input** property, and enable Genmoji support by setting the **supportsAdaptive-ImageGlyph** property to **true**. Note that because the **UITextField** view works with **NSAttributedString** values, we must convert the value coming from the SwiftUI view into an **NSAttributedString** object before assigning it to the view.

In the coordinator, we implement the **textFieldDidChangeSelection()** method. This delegate method is called by the **UITextField** view every time the user types or deletes a character, so we can use it to send the value entered by the user back to the SwiftUI interface. Now we can use a **CustomField** view instead of a **TextField** view in our SwiftUI interface to allow users to insert attributed text. The following is our implementation for this example.

Listing 4-14: Using a representable view to allow the user to type Genmojis

```
import SwiftUI

struct ContentView: View {
    @State private var inputTitle = AttributedString("")

    var body: some View {
        VStack {
            Text("Insert Title")
                .font(.title)
            CustomField(input: $inputTitle)
                .frame(height: 40)
            Spacer()
        }
        .padding()
    }
}
```

This view defines a property called `inputTitle` to store the value entered by the user, and includes a `CustomField` view to provide the text field where the user can type. When the user enters a value in the `UITextField` view, the delegate method assigns it to the Binding property, and this value is then passed to the `inputTitle` property, so we can later store it in a database or display it to the user, as we did before.

The `CustomField` view behaves like any other SwiftUI view, so we can define its size and combine it with other views. In this case, we give it a size appropriate for this type of view and place it at the top of the screen, as shown below.

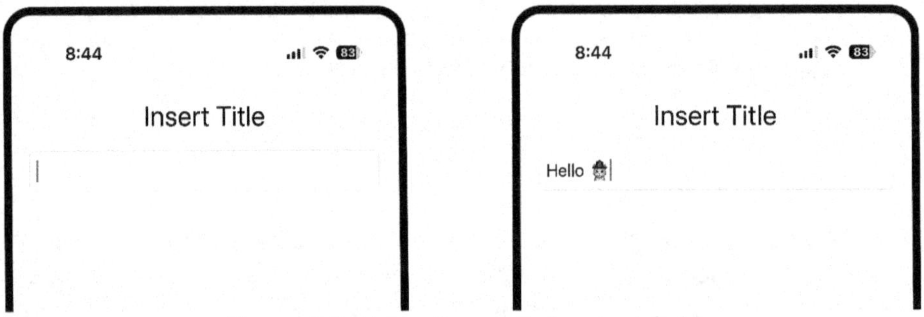

Figure 4-8: *Using Genmojis in a text field*

Do It Yourself

Create a new Multiplatform project. Create a new file called CustomField.swift for the code in Listing 4-13. Update the `ContentView` view with the code in Listing 4-14. Run the application on your device. You should be able to insert Genmojis into the text field. To learn more about representable views and UIKit, read our books *Advanced SwiftUI for Masterminds* and *UIKit for Masterminds*.

The `NSAttributedString` class is not only required when working with legacy views from UIKit but also when we need to perform additional operations on Genmojis beyond simply storing them in a database. For example, if we want to share attributed text containing Genmojis or save it to a file, we need to convert it to data. The `NSAttributedString` class provides the following method for this purpose.

```
data(from: NSRange, documentAttributes: Dictionary)
```

This method returns a `Data` structure containing the attributed string encoded in the format specified by the arguments. The **from** argument defines the range of characters to encode, and the **documentAttributes** argument is a dictionary whose keys and values specify the data format. For attributed strings that include Genmojis, we must specify the `documentType` key and a `DocumentType` structure as the value. To define the format for Genmojis, the structure includes the properties `html` and `rtfd`.

To convert the data back into an `NSAttributedString` object, the class includes the following initializer.

NSAttributedString(data: Data, **options:** Dictionary, **documentAttributes:** Pointer?)

This initializer creates an **NSAttributedString** object with the format specified by the arguments. The **data** argument is the content to convert, the **options** argument defines how the data should be interpreted (for example, as RTFD or HTML), and the **documentAttributes** argument is an optional pointer that can be used to retrieve metadata about the document, such as its type, encoding, or layout information.

In theory, we should be able to provide a **TextEditor** view with an **AttributedString** value for the user to type and format the text, and then convert that **AttributedString** into an **NSAttributedString** value before turning it into data. However, the conversion between these types is currently unreliable, so in practice, we need to work directly with **NSAttributedString** values, which means we must again replace the SwiftUI views with UIKit views.

In the following example, we use UIKit views and **NSAttributedString** values to create a simple application where users can enter text and press a button to save it to a file, so the next time the application is launched, they can continue typing where they left off.

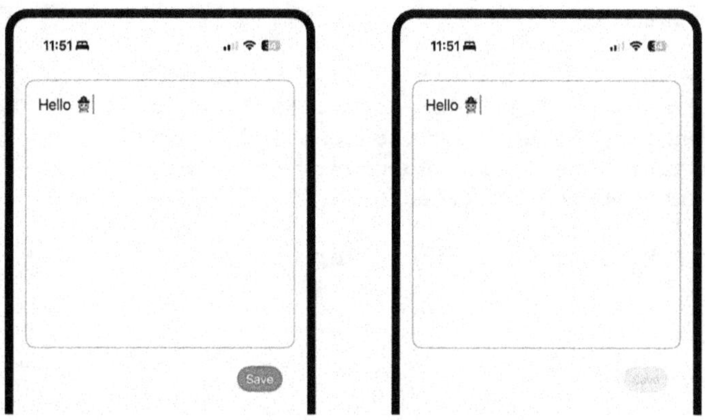

Figure 4-9: *Application to store Genmojis in files*

First, we need to define a class to process the data. The class must include two methods: one to convert the **NSAttributedString** object into data and save it to a file, and another to read the file and convert the data back into an **NSAttributedString** object. The following is our implementation of this class.

Listing 4-15: Loading and saving an NSAttributedString value

```
import SwiftUI

class ApplicationData {
   let manager: FileManager
   let directories: [URL]?

   static let shared: ApplicationData = ApplicationData()
   private init() {
      manager = FileManager.default
      directories = manager.urls(for: .documentDirectory, in:
         .userDomainMask)
   }
```

```
    func openFile() -> NSAttributedString {
        var text = NSAttributedString(string: "")

        guard let docURL = directories?.first else { return text }
        let fileURL = docURL.appendingPathComponent("myFile.rtfd")
        do {
            if manager.fileExists(atPath: fileURL.path) {
                // Read file and convert data into NSAttributedString
                if let content = manager.contents(atPath: fileURL.path) {
                    let ns = try NSAttributedString(data: content,
                        documentAttributes: nil)
                    text = ns
                }
            }
        } catch {
            print("Error loading file: \(error)")
        }
        return text
    }
    func saveFile(text: NSAttributedString) {
        guard let docURL = directories?.first else { return }
        let fileURL = docURL.appendingPathComponent("myFile.rtfd",
isDirectory: true)
        do {
            // Convert NSAttributedString into data and save it
            let data = try text.data(from: NSRange(location: 0, length: text.
                length), documentAttributes: [.documentType:
                NSAttributedString.DocumentType.rtfd])
            try data.write(to: fileURL)
        } catch {
            print("Error saving file: \(error)")
        }
    }
}
```

Most of this class is just standard code for reading and saving a file. In the **openFile()** method, we get the URL of our app's Documents folder, then append the name of our file (myFile.rtfd) to that URL, check whether the file exists using the **fileExists()** method of the **FileManager** class, read its contents with the **contents()** method, and then create an **NSAttributedString** object with the data and return it. On the other hand, the **saveFile()** method follows the opposite process. Again, we get the URL of our app's Documents folder and append the name of our file (myFile.rtfd), but this time we convert the **NSAttributedString** object containing the text inserted by the user into a **Data** structure using the **data()** method and write it to the file. Note that in this example, the data is saved in the RTFD format, which is recommended when working with Genmojis because it can store rich text along with attachments, such as images or animations, in a single package.

Now that we have the methods to store and retrieve the text, we need to define a representable view that allows us to use a UIKit text view in our SwiftUI interface. In this case, we must implement the **UITextView** class, which is the equivalent of the **TextEditor** view in SwiftUI. The following is the representable view for this example.

Listing 4-16: Representable view to provide the `UITextView` view

```
import SwiftUI

struct CustomEditor: UIViewRepresentable {
   @Binding var input: NSAttributedString

   func makeUIView(context: Context) -> UITextView {
      let view = UITextView()
      view.isEditable = true
      view.allowsEditingTextAttributes = true
      view.supportsAdaptiveImageGlyph = true
      view.delegate = context.coordinator

      let defaultFont = UIFont.systemFont(ofSize: 20)
      view.typingAttributes[.font] = defaultFont
      view.attributedText = input
      return view
   }
   func updateUIView(_ uiView: UITextView, context: Context) {
      uiView.attributedText = input
   }
   func makeCoordinator() -> CoordinatorTextView {
      return CoordinatorTextView(input: $input)
   }
}
class CoordinatorTextView: NSObject, UITextViewDelegate {
   @Binding var inputCoordinator: NSAttributedString

   init(input: Binding<NSAttributedString>) {
      self._inputCoordinator = input
   }
   func textViewDidChange(_ textView: UITextView) {
      inputCoordinator = textView.attributedText
   }
}
```

This representable view is similar to the one implemented before, except this time we are representing a **`UITextView`** view instead of a **`UITextField`** view and working directly with **`NSAttributedString`** values, so the Binding property must be declared using this data type. In addition, the delegate methods for the **`UITextView`** view are defined by the **`UITextViewDelegate`** protocol, so the method we need to implement to send the text entered by the user back to the SwiftUI view is **`textViewDidChange()`**.

The representable view with the **`UITextView`** view is now ready, so we can use it in our SwiftUI interface to allow the user to enter text. The following is our implementation of this interface.

Listing 4-17: Letting the user save and load attributed text

```
import SwiftUI

struct ContentView: View {
   @State private var appData = ApplicationData.shared
```

```
   @State private var inputText = NSAttributedString(string: "")
   @State private var isDisabled: Bool = false

   var body: some View {
      VStack {
         CustomEditor(input: $inputText)
            .padding()
            .overlay(
               RoundedRectangle(cornerRadius: 12)
                  .stroke(Color.secondary, lineWidth: 1)
            )
         HStack {
            Spacer()
            Button("Save") {
               appData.saveFile(text: inputText)
               isDisabled = true
            }
            .buttonStyle(.borderedProminent)
            .disabled(inputText.length == 0 || isDisabled)
            .padding()
         }
      }
      .padding()
      .onChange(of: inputText, initial: true) { old, value in
         isDisabled = false
      }
      .onAppear {
         inputText = appData.openFile()
      }
   }
}
```

This view doesn't introduce anything we haven't seen before. It includes a State property called **inputText** to store the text entered by the user, the new **CustomEditor** view to let the user edit the text, and a button that calls the **saveFile()** method in the **ApplicationData** object to store the text in a file. When the app launches, we call the **openFile()** method to read the last text saved by the user and assign it to the **inputText** property, allowing the user to continue from where he or she left off.

Do It Yourself

Create a new Multiplatform project. Create a file called ApplicationData.swift for the code in Listing 4-15, and a file called CustomEditor.swift for the code in Listing 4-16. Update the **ContentView** view with the code in Listing 4-17. Run the application on your device. Type some text with Genmojis, then stop the application from Xcode and run it again. This will force the app to load the text from the file. You should see the text and the Genmojis you typed earlier displayed on the screen again. To learn more about how to store and load files, read our book *Advanced SwiftUI for Masterminds*.

IMPORTANT

Genmojis are a new technology and therefore they are not supported everywhere. Fortunately, there are several techniques we can use to work around these limitations. For example, we can convert Genmojis into images and insert them between the text, replace them with textual descriptions of what they represent, or convert the attributed string into data to share it with other applications or devices, as shown in the last example. The best approach depends on the requirements of your application and may change as Apple continues to expand and integrate Apple Intelligence tools across frameworks and systems. For more information on the options currently available to work with Genmojis, visit our website and follow the links for this chapter.

4.4 - Writing Tools

Apple provides access to a large language model through an interface called Writing Tools, which allows users to correct and improve their writing. This interface is available anywhere the user can edit text, including our own apps. If our interface contains a view where the user can type text, such as a **TextField** or a **TextEditor**, the system automatically enables this feature. All the user has to do is tap the view and select the Writing Tools option (Figure 4-10, number 1).

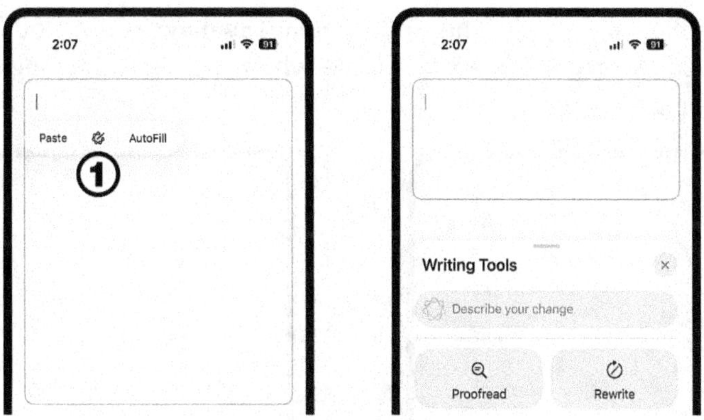

Figure 4-10: *Writing Tools*

Although it's not a bad idea to have this tool available in our app, the **View** protocol includes the following modifier to disable it.

writingToolsBehavior(WritingToolsBehavior)

This modifier defines how Writing Tools behave within a view. The argument is a structure with the following properties: **automatic**, **complete**, **disabled**, and **limited**.

Users expect system tools like Writing Tools to be available everywhere they need them, but there may be situations where it's best to disable them. For example, if we have an interface with input views to enter a title and a note, as we did in previous examples, we may want to disable the tools when the user is typing the title and leave them available only when they are typing the note, as shown below.

Listing 4-18: Disabling Writing Tools

```
import SwiftUI

struct ContentView: View {
   @State private var inputTitle: String = ""
   @State private var inputText: String = ""

   var body: some View {
      VStack {
         TextField("Insert Title", text: $inputTitle)
            .textFieldStyle(.roundedBorder)
            .padding()
            .writingToolsBehavior(.disabled)
         TextEditor(text: $inputText)
            .padding()
            .scrollContentBackground(.hidden)
            .background(Color.gray.opacity(0.2))
            .clipShape(RoundedRectangle(cornerRadius: 12))
      }.padding()
   }
}
```

In this example, we apply the **writingToolsBehavior()** modifier only to the **TextField** view, so Writing Tools are available when the user is typing the note but not when they are typing the title.

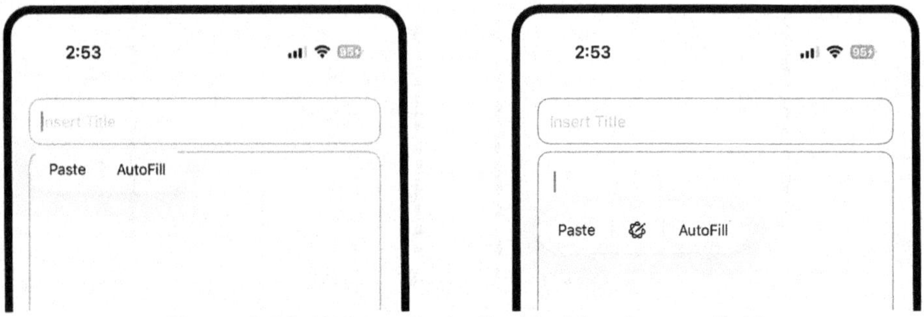

Figure 4-11: *Writing Tools disabled for the text field*

Most users know how to open the editing menu because they've been using it for years to copy, paste, and format their text. However, if our application focuses heavily on text, we may want to provide a clear and accessible option to open Writing Tools. At the moment, SwiftUI does not include a built-in way to open this interface, but we can rely on UIKit tools to do it.

The **UIKit** framework defines all the classes required for our app to run, including the **UIApplication** class to control the application, and the **UIResponder** class to handle events coming from the system or the user. When the user presses the Writing Tools button on the interface (Figure 4-10, number 1), the **UIApplication** object sends a message to the **UIResponder** object, which then calls a method to open the interface. If we want to do this ourselves, we must trigger the process programmatically. The following is the method we need to call from the **UIResponder** object for this purpose.

showWritingTools(Object)

This method opens the Writing Tools interface. The argument is a reference to the object that triggered the event.

To send the message to the responder, the **UIApplication** class includes the following method.

sendAction(Selector, **to:** Object, **from:** Object, **for:** UIEvent)

This method sends a message asking the responder to perform a specific action. The first argument identifies the action to perform, the **to** argument specifies the object that should receive the message, the **from** argument specifies the object that sends the message, and the **for** argument is an object that provides information about the event that caused the **UIApplication** object to send the message.

To open the Writing Tools interface using this method, we only need to specify the **showWritingTools()** method as the action and can ignore the remaining arguments, as shown in the following example.

Listing 4-19: Creating a button to open the Writing Tools interface

```
import SwiftUI

struct ContentView: View {
   @State private var inputText: String = ""
   @FocusState private var isFocused: Bool

   var body: some View {
      NavigationStack {
         VStack {
            TextEditor(text: $inputText)
               .focused($isFocused)
               .padding()
               .scrollContentBackground(.hidden)
               .background(Color.gray.opacity(0.2))
               .clipShape(RoundedRectangle(cornerRadius: 12))
         }.padding()
         .toolbar {
            ToolbarItem(placement: .topBarTrailing) {
               Button(action: {
                  isFocused = true
                  Task {
                     let app = UIApplication.shared
                     app.sendAction(#selector(UIResponder.
                      showWritingTools(_:)), to: nil, from: nil, for: nil)
                  }
```

```
                    }, label: {
                        Image(systemName: "apple.writing.tools")
                    })
                }
            }
        }
    }
}
```

The **UIResponder** object performs the action on the first responder, which is the element in the interface that currently has focus and is therefore responding to user events. This means that we must ensure that the **TextEditor** view is focused before performing the action. In this example, we accomplish this by defining a **FocusState** property and assigning it to the view with the **focused()** modifier. When the user presses the button, we set this property to **true**, effectively moving the focus to the view, and then send the message to the responder to open the interface. The result is shown below.

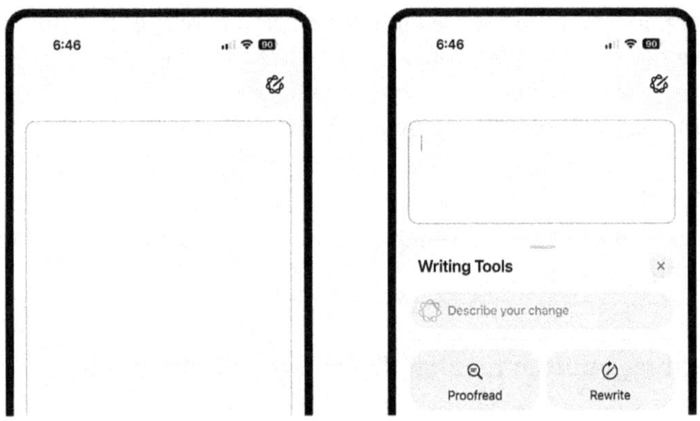

***Figure 4-12:** Custom button to open Writing Tools*

Do It Yourself

Create a new Multiplatform project. Update the **ContentView** view with the code in Listing 4-19. Run the application on your device. You should see a button on the toolbar to open the Writing Tools interface. Press the button. You should see the interface appear at the bottom of the screen, as shown in Figure 4-12.

Advanced Implementation

As with Genmojis, Writing Tools are still being gradually integrated into Apple's technologies and frameworks, so their most advanced features are not yet available everywhere. For example, one of the capabilities currently supported by this tool is the ability to perform specific actions when the user begins or finishes editing text. However, this functionality is only accessible through the delegate object of a **UITextView**, which means we must implement this view and its delegate to add this feature to our app. The delegate of a

UITextView is defined by the **UITextViewDelegate** protocol, which includes the following methods for working with Writing Tools.

textViewWritingToolsWillBegin(UITextView)

This method is called by the system to notify that the user is about to start interacting with Writing Tools.

textViewWritingToolsDidEnd(UITextView)

This method is called by the system to notify that the user has finished interacting with Writing Tools.

textView(UITextView, **writingToolsIgnoredRangesInEnclosingRange:** NSRange)

This method is called by the system to determine whether Writing Tools should ignore any range of characters within the text.

The implementation of these methods is straightforward. We simply need to define a coordinator that conforms to the **UITextViewDelegate** protocol and implement the methods to perform the desired actions (see Listing 4-16). For example, we can create a coordinator that processes the text entered by the user before and after it has been corrected by Writing Tools.

Listing 4-20: Processing the text before and after is modified by Writing Tools

```
import SwiftUI

struct CustomEditor: UIViewRepresentable {
   @Binding var input: String

   func makeUIView(context: Context) -> UITextView {
      let view = UITextView()
      view.font = .systemFont(ofSize: 20)
      view.text = input
      view.delegate = context.coordinator
      return view
   }
   func updateUIView(_ uiView: UITextView, context: Context) {
      uiView.text = input
   }
   func makeCoordinator() -> CoordinatorTextView {
      return CoordinatorTextView(input: $input)
   }
}
class CoordinatorTextView: NSObject, UITextViewDelegate {
   @Binding var inputCoordinator: String

   init(input: Binding<String>) {
      self._inputCoordinator = input
   }
   func textViewDidChange(_ textView: UITextView) {
      inputCoordinator = textView.text
   }
```

```
    func textViewWritingToolsWillBegin(_ textView: UITextView) {
        print("Old Text: \(textView.text ?? "Empty")")
    }
    func textViewWritingToolsDidEnd(_ textView: UITextView) {
        print("New Text: \(textView.text ?? "Empty")")
    }
}
```

In this example, we've implemented a simple **UITextView** to process plain text, but the rest of the code for the representable view remains the same as before. For the interface, we only need an instance of this view, as shown below.

Listing 4-21: Interface to test delegate methods

```
import SwiftUI

struct ContentView: View {
    @State private var inputText: String = ""

    var body: some View {
        VStack {
            CustomEditor(input: $inputText)
                .padding()
                .overlay(
                    RoundedRectangle(cornerRadius: 12)
                        .stroke(Color.secondary, lineWidth: 1)
                )
        }.padding()
    }
}
```

The **CustomEditor** view provides access to the **UITextView**, so when the user types in this view, the delegate methods in the coordinator are called. In this example, we simply print messages to the console when the user begins and finishes editing, so we will see output in the console when editing starts and again after the correction generated by the model is accepted.

Do It Yourself

Create a new file called CustomEditor.swift with the code in Listing 4-20. Update the **ContentView** view with the code in Listing 4-21. Run the application on your device and type some text. Tap on the editor to open the contextual menu and select the option to open Writing Tools. Press the Proofread button. You should see a message printed to the console with the current text. Accept the changes. You should then see another message printed to the console with the updated text.

Another method provided by the **UITextViewDelegate** protocol is **textView(UITextView, writingToolsIgnoredRangesInEnclosingRange:)**. This method allows us to specify which parts of the text should be ignored by Writing Tools. For example, if our application expects users to enter text that includes sections enclosed in square brackets, and those sections should not be modified, we can locate these sections and return an array of **NSRange** values representing their positions, so Writing Tools knows exactly which characters to ignore.

Listing 4-22: Selecting the text to be edited by Writing Tools

```
class CoordinatorTextView: NSObject, UITextViewDelegate {
    @Binding var inputCoordinator: String

    init(input: Binding<String>) {
        self._inputCoordinator = input
    }
    func textViewDidChange(_ textView: UITextView) {
        inputCoordinator = textView.text
    }
    func textView(_ textView: UITextView,
        writingToolsIgnoredRangesInEnclosingRange enclosingRange: NSRange)
            -> [NSValue] {
        var result: [NSValue] = []
        let nsText = textView.text as NSString
        let text = nsText.substring(with: enclosingRange)

        let regex = /\[([^\]]*)\]/
        let matches = text.matches(of: regex)
        for match in matches {
            let innerRange = NSRange(match.range, in: text)
            result.append(NSValue(range: innerRange))
        }
        return result
    }
}
```

The delegate method receives an **NSRange** value representing the length of the entire text being edited by Writing Tools. In this example, we first isolate that portion of the string, and then use a regular expression and the **matches()** method to extract every section of text enclosed in square brackets. The delegate method must return an array of **NSValue** objects, so we convert the ranges found by the **matches()** method into **NSRange** values, wrap them in **NSValue** objects, add these objects to the array, and return it. Now Writing Tools knows which parts of the text to ignore, so it only edits the rest, as shown below.

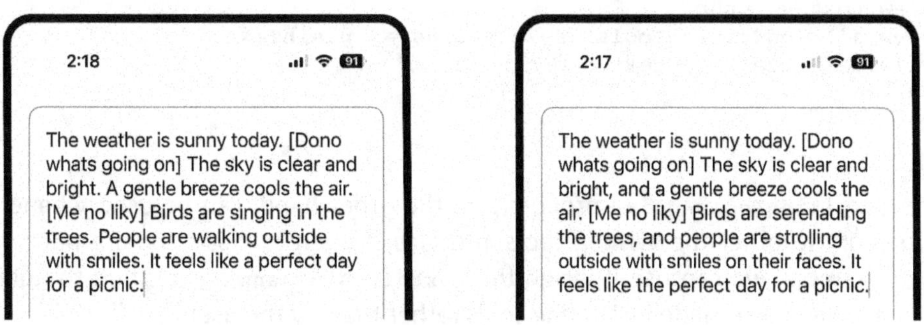

Figure 4-13: *Writing Tools editing only parts of the text*

Do It Yourself

Update the **CoordinatorTextView** class with the code in Listing 4-22. Run the application and type some text that includes sections enclosed in square brackets, as shown in Figure 4-13. Tap on the editor and select the option to open Writing Tools. Press the button to rewrite the text. You will see the model processing each section individually, excluding the text between square brackets. To learn more about regular expressions and the **matches()** method, read our book *Swift Programming Language for Masterminds*.

When working with UIKit views, we also have access to properties that allow us to configure the interface and check its state. The following are the ones currently available.

writingToolsResultOptions

This property determines the type of content that Writing Tools should work with. It is a **UIWritingToolsResultOptions** structure that includes the type properties **plainText**, **richText**, **list**, and **table**.

isWritingToolsActive

This property returns a Boolean value indicating whether Writing Tools are currently active.

By default, Writing Tools support plain and rich text but not tables. If we want the model to process only plain text or to include tables, we must set the **writingToolsResultOptions** property of the **UITextView** to the desired values. For example, since our current application works exclusively with plain text (**String** values), we can configure our **UITextView** to ensure that we only receive responses in that format.

Listing 4-23: Configuring the Writing Tools results

```
func makeUIView(context: Context) -> UITextView {
    let view = UITextView()
    view.font = .systemFont(ofSize: 20)
    view.text = input
    view.allowedWritingToolsResultOptions = .plainText
    view.delegate = context.coordinator
    return view
}
```

The **isWritingToolsActive** property, on the other hand, can be used whenever we need to verify whether the Writing Tools interface is open or closed before performing a task. For example, we can use it inside the **textViewDidChange()** method to determine whether a change was made by Writing Tools rather than by the user.

Listing 4-24: Detecting if Writing Tools is open

```
func textViewDidChange(_ textView: UITextView) {
   if textView.isWritingToolsActive {
      print("Changes performed by Writing Tools")
   }
   inputCoordinator = textView.text
}
```

IMPORTANT

The **UIKit** framework also offers tools to control Writing Tools when working with custom text editors and can be configured to operate with web views. The topic is beyond the scope of this book. For more information, visit our website and follow the links for this chapter.

Chapter 5

Foundation Models

5.1 - Foundation Models Framework

The **Foundation Models** framework provides access to a large language model that runs on device. This is the same model that powers many of the features included in Apple Intelligence, which means we can use it to perform a wide range of tasks, from generating content, to classifying items, summarizing text, answering questions, and more. Since the model operates entirely on the device (without requiring an Internet connection), it has been adapted and optimized to fit within the hardware limitations of mobile devices. As a result, it cannot perform all the tasks handled by models running in large data centers. For example, we can ask it to answer questions or compose long pieces of text, but it may not be accurate when responding to real-world questions or performing tasks that require advanced reasoning. Regardless, the model remains capable of performing many everyday tasks and can also be connected to external tools to expand its knowledge base and functionality.

Session

Large language models can perform generic tasks such as answering questions, following instructions, or processing text. To work with a model, we provide a prompt describing what we want it to do and then wait for the response. To be able to follow these conversations, the model operates within a session. The framework provides the following class to create and manage these sessions.

`LanguageModelSession(model:` `SystemLanguageModel)`

This initializer creates a session to interact with the model. The **model** argument is an object that determines the type of model to use.

If not specified, the system uses a generic model suitable for most tasks. The framework provides the following class to specify which model to use.

`SystemLanguageModel(useCase:` `UseCase)`

This initializer creates a **`SystemLanguageModel`** instance that specifies which model to use. The **useCase** parameter identifies the intended purpose of the model. Currently, two options are available: **`general`**, to specify the default model, and **`contentTagging`**, for a model specialized in tagging content.

The **SystemLanguageModel** class also includes the following type property to provide access to the model by default.

default

This type property returns a reference to the base version of the Foundation model.

After starting a session, we must send prompts to the model for processing. The **LanguageModelSession** class provides the following method to send a prompt and receive the response.

respond(to: Prompt, **generating:** Type, **includeSchemaInPrompt:** Bool, **options:** GenerationOptions**)**

This method sends a prompt to the model and returns its response. The **to** argument specifies the prompt, the **generating** argument defines the data type that represents the schema the model should follow, the **includeSchemaInPrompt** argument determines whether the schema should be included in the request (**true** by default), and the **options** argument is a structure that configures how the model generates its response.

The **respond()** method returns a **Response** structure, which includes the following properties to provide the information.

content

This property returns the model's response. The response is a **String** value unless a different type is explicitly specified.

transcriptEntries

This property returns an array with all the entries (prompts and responses) that the model has processed so far.

A session can handle only one prompt at a time. If we send a second prompt while another is still being processed, the system will return an error. To ensure the model is ready to process our request, the **LanguageModelSession** class includes the following property.

isResponding

This property returns a Boolean value that indicates whether the model is currently processing a prompt (**true**) or is available to handle a new one (**false**).

By default, a session automatically uses the model by default, so if all we need is a quick response, we can simply initialize a **LanguageModelSession** object and send the request with the **respond()** method. In the following example, we ask the model to write a paragraph and then display the response on the screen.

Listing 5-1: Prompting the model

```
import SwiftUI
import FoundationModels

struct ContentView: View {
   @State private var response = ""

   var body: some View {
      VStack {
         Button("Send") {
            let prompt = "Write a paragraph describing a unicorn"
            let session = LanguageModelSession()
            if !session.isResponding {
               Task {
                  do {
                     let answer = try await session.respond(to: prompt)
                     response = answer.content
                  } catch {
                     response = "Error accessing the model: \(error)"
                  }
               }
            }
         }
         .buttonStyle(.borderedProminent)

         Text(response)
            .font(Font.system(size: 18))
            .padding()
         Spacer()
      }
      .padding()
   }
}
```

In this example, we first import the **Foundation Models** framework to access these tools and then define a button to perform the request. The button creates a standard session using the **`LanguageModelSession()`** initializer, checks whether the model is already processing a request by reading the **`isResponding`** property, and if the model is available, sends our prompt using the **`respond()`** method. The **`respond()`** method is asynchronous and can throw errors, so we perform the request inside a **`Task`**, wait for the response, and then assign the value of **`content`** to a property to display it on the screen.

The model will do its best to generate a response that closely matches our prompt. In this case, we asked for a description of a unicorn, and that's exactly what we get, as shown below.

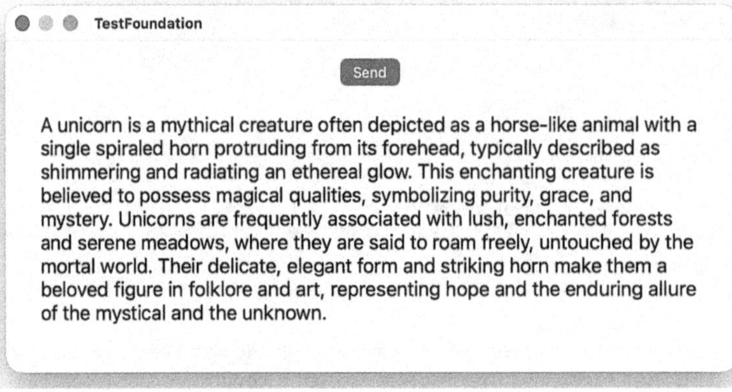

Figure 5-1: *The model's response*

Do It Yourself

Create a new Multiplatform project. Update the **`ContentView`** view with the code in Listing 5-1. In Xcode's toolbar, select My Mac from the Scheme menu to run the application on your Mac. Press the Send button. After a few seconds, you should see a description of a unicorn, as shown in Figure 5-1.

In the previous example, each time we press the button, a new session is created, causing the model to lose context and making it unable to follow the conversation. If we send another prompt, the model won't be able to reference the previous prompts and responses. To maintain continuity, we must persist the session by storing it in an object that is not destroyed after every prompt. In the following example, we separate the code that manages the session from the view, so we get full control over the session. First, we need to define a class for our data, as shown below.

Listing 5-2: Persisting the session

```
import SwiftUI
import FoundationModels
import Observation

@Observable class ApplicationData {
   var response: AttributedString = ""
   var prompt: String = ""

   @ObservationIgnored var session = LanguageModelSession()

   static let shared: ApplicationData = ApplicationData()
   private init() { }

   func sendPrompt() async {
      do {
         let answer = try await session.respond(to: prompt)
```

```
            // Add response to chat box
            var newResponse = AttributedString("\(answer.content)\n\n")
            newResponse.font = .system(size: 16, weight: .regular)
            response.append(newResponse)
         } catch {
            response.append(AttributedString("Error accessing the model:
\(error)\n\n"))
         }
         prompt = ""
      }
   }
```

In this class, we just define the properties needed to manage the values for the view, along with a method called **sendPrompt()** to send the prompt to the model and process the response. The **response** property is defined as an **AttributedString** so we can use different attributes to distinguish the user's prompt from the model's reply. The rest of the process is the same as before: we create the session using the **LanguageModelSession()** initializer, and when the **sendPrompt()** method is called from the view, we send the prompt to the model using the **respond()** method.

In the view, we need a text field to let the user type the prompt and a scrollable **Text** view to display the conversation. The following is our implementation of this view.

Listing 5-3: Using Foundation Models to create a chat box

```
import SwiftUI
import FoundationModels

struct ContentView: View {
   @State private var appData = ApplicationData.shared
   @State private var position = ScrollPosition(idType: String.self)

   var body: some View {
      VStack {
         ScrollView {
            Text(appData.response)
               .padding()
               .textSelection(.enabled)
               .id("textID")
         }
         .frame(minWidth: 350, maxWidth: .infinity, minHeight: 300,
            alignment: .leading)
         .background(Color.gray.opacity(0.2))
         .clipShape(RoundedRectangle(cornerRadius: 12))
         .scrollPosition($position)

         HStack {
            TextField("Insert Prompt", text: $appData.prompt)
               .textFieldStyle(.roundedBorder)
               .disabled(appData.session.isResponding)
            Button("Send") {
               Task {
                  if !appData.prompt.isEmpty {
                     // Insert prompt in chat box
                     var newPrompt = AttributedString("\(appData.
                        prompt)\n\n")
```

```
                    newPrompt.font = .system(size: 16, weight: .bold)
                    appData.response.append(newPrompt)

                    // Send prompt to model
                    await appData.sendPrompt()
                 }
              }
           }
           .buttonStyle(.borderedProminent)
           .disabled(appData.session.isResponding)
        }
     }
     .padding()
     .onChange(of: appData.response) {
        position.scrollTo(edge: .bottom)
     }
   }
 }
```

This is just a standard SwiftUI view. The only thing related to the Foundation Model is that we use the **isResponding** property to disable the text field and the Send button while the model is processing a request. When the user presses Send, we store the prompt in the **response** property to display it on the screen, and then call the **sendPrompt()** method to send it to the model. Once a response is received, we also store it in the **response** property and clear the text field so the user can type again. Note that the **ScrollView** view is set to scroll to the bottom every time a new message is added to the **response** property, so the user can follow the conversation. The result is shown below.

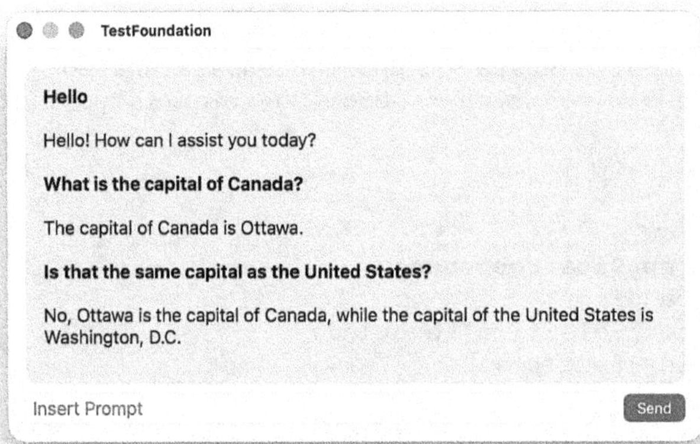

Figure 5-2: *Chat box*

Do It Yourself

Create a new file called ApplicationData.swift for the code in Listing 5-2. Update the **ContentView** view with the code in Listing 5-3. Run the application on your Mac. Insert a prompt and press Send. You should see both the prompt and the response on the screen. Because we are now always using the same session, you can ask the model questions related to previous entries, and it will understand the context and respond accordingly, as shown in Figure 5-2.

So far, we have defined prompts using simple strings, but the **respond()** method can also take a **Prompt** structure. The following is the structure's initializer.

> **Prompt**(@PromptBuilder)
>
> This initializer takes a content block and processes its statements to produce a **Prompt** structure containing the prompt for the model. The argument is a macro responsible for converting the statements into a prompt.

The **@PromptBuilder** macro is designed to help us construct complex prompts in a declarative way. It processes a series of statements at compile time and automatically generates the code needed to turn them into a prompt that the model can understand. The best way to see how this works is with an example. The following shows our **sendPrompt()** method, this time with the prompt defined by a **Prompt** structure.

Listing 5-4: Creating a complex prompt with the Prompt structure

```
func sendPrompt() async {
   do {
      let promptBuilder = Prompt {
         prompt
         if prompt.contains("cat") {
            "Mention that the cat is wearing a hat"
         }
         "Write the text in short sentences"
      }
      let answer = try await session.respond(to: promptBuilder)
      // Add response to chat box
      var newResponse = AttributedString("\(answer.content)\n\n")
      newResponse.font = .system(size: 16, weight: .regular)
      response.append(newResponse)
   } catch {
      response.append(AttributedString("Error accessing the model:
         \(error)\n\n"))
   }
   prompt = ""
}
```

In this example, we use three statements to build our prompt. The first statement is the text inserted by the user (stored in the **prompt** property). The second statement is an **if** statement that checks whether the user's prompt contains the word "cat." If that's the case, the statement adds the string "Mention that the cat is wearing a hat" to the prompt. Finally, the third statement is another string that instructs the model to generate the text using short sentences.

When we write a prompt and press the Send button, as we did before, the **@PromptBuilder** macro processes every statement in the content block and creates the final prompt for the model. In this case, the first and third statements are always included because they are simple strings, while the second statement depends on the user's input. If the user includes the word "cat" in the prompt, the model will do its best to mention that the cat is wearing a hat. For example, we can ask the model to write a short story about a cat, and it will mention the hat, as shown below.

Figure 5-3: *Chat with complex prompts*

> **Do It Yourself**
>
> Update the **`sendPrompt()`** method in the **`ApplicationData`** class with the code in Listing 5-4. Run the application on your Mac again and type a prompt such as "Write a short story about a cat." The text should be written in short sentences, and it should mention that the cat is wearing a hat.

Instructions

Generating complex prompts, as we did in the previous example, helps us control the model's response. By programmatically inserting our own instructions into the prompt, we can guide the model toward producing a specific result. However, this approach is not always reliable. Users may write prompts that override or contradict our instructions. For greater control, we can define system instructions. System instructions tell the model its role and how it should behave, and the model is programmed to prioritize these instructions over the user's input, ensuring we always get the response we want.

System instructions can be provided to the model as plain string, but the framework also includes the **`Instructions`** structure, which allows us to define them dynamically. The following is the structure's initializer.

```
Instructions(@InstructionsBuilder)
```

This initializer takes a content block and processes its statements to produce an **`Instructions`** structure containing the instructions for the model. The argument is a macro responsible for converting the statements into instructions.

The instructions are passed to the session. For this purpose, the **`LanguageModelSession`** class provides the following initializer.

```
LanguageModelSession(instructions: Instructions)
```

This initializer creates a session to interact with the model. The **instructions** argument defines how the model should behave by specifying the rules or guidelines it must follow.

We can use instructions not only to shape the model's responses but also to define the role we want it to adopt. For instance, we can describe a personality and have the model behave accordingly. In the following example, we instruct the model to take on the role of a horror fiction writer and to speak with the passion and voice of the genre.

Listing 5-5: Providing instructions to the model

```
import SwiftUI
import FoundationModels
import Observation

@Observable class ApplicationData {
   var response: AttributedString = ""
   var prompt: String = ""

   @ObservationIgnored var session: LanguageModelSession

   static let shared: ApplicationData = ApplicationData()
   private init() {
      let instructions = Instructions {
         "You are a skilled writer of horror fiction"
         "You craft chilling stories filled with psychological fear"
         "You speak as if you were obsessed with the genre"
      }
      session = LanguageModelSession(instructions: instructions)
   }
   func sendPrompt() async {
      do {
         let answer = try await session.respond(to: prompt)

         var newResponse = AttributedString("\(answer.content)\n\n")
         newResponse.font = .system(size: 16, weight: .regular)
         response.append(newResponse)
      } catch {
         response.append(AttributedString("Error accessing the model:
            \(error)\n\n"))
      }
      prompt = ""
   }
}
```

In this example, we create the session within the initializer of the **`ApplicationData`** class so we can provide the instructions. The instructions are generated first and then passed to the session. Now, every time we communicate with the model, it will respond as if it were a writer of horror fiction.

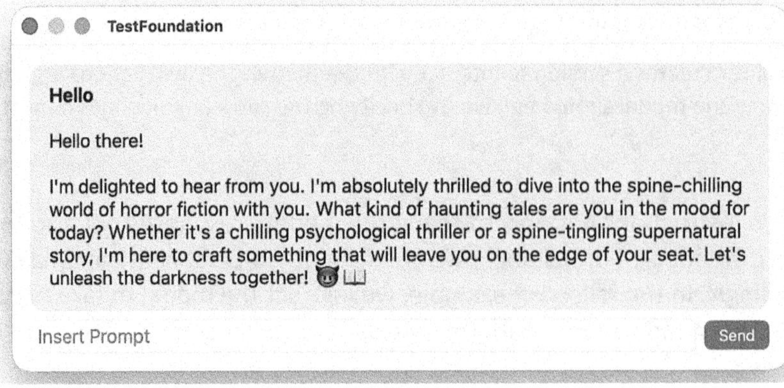

Figure 5-4: *Model with a personality*

Do It Yourself

Update the `ApplicationData` class with the code in Listing 5-5. Run the application on your Mac and enter a prompt. The model should always respond as if it were a passionate writer of horror fiction.

IMPORTANT

Instructions can include conditional expressions and other types of statements. However, if the instruction is just a single line of text, we don't need to create an `Instructions` structure, we can simply provide a string, just as we did with prompts earlier. We'll explore more examples of how to build prompts and instructions later. For more information, visit our website and follow the links for this chapter.

Streaming

Depending on the complexity of the prompt and the processing capacity of the device, the model may take several seconds to generate a complete response. This delay can result in a poor user experience. If we anticipate that the model will take too long to process the prompt, instead of waiting for the full response, we can stream the output. Streaming allows us to display partial results in real time, giving users immediate feedback and making the interaction feel faster and more responsive. The `LanguageModelSession` class includes the following method for this purpose.

```
streamResponse(to: Prompt, generating: Type,
includeSchemaInPrompt: Bool, options: GenerationOptions)
```

This method sends a prompt to the model and returns an asynchronous structure with partially generate responses. The **to** argument specifies the prompt, the **generating** argument defines the data type that represents the schema the model should follow, the

includeSchemaInPrompt argument determines whether the schema should be included in the request (**true** by default), and the **options** argument is a structure that configures how the model generates its response.

This method works like the **respond()** method, but instead of returning a single value, it returns an asynchronous sequence containing the partial responses generated by the model. To display these responses to the user as they arrive, we need to use an asynchronous **for await in** loop, as shown below.

Listing 5-6: Processing partial responses

```
func sendPrompt() async {
   do {
      let tempResponse = response

      let answer = session.streamResponse(to: prompt)
      for try await partial in answer {
         var newPartial = AttributedString("\(partial.content)")
         newPartial.font = .system(size: 16, weight: .regular)

         var newResponse = tempResponse
         newResponse.append(newPartial)
         response = newResponse
      }
      response.append(AttributedString("\n\n"))
   } catch {
      response.append(AttributedString("Error accessing the model:
         \(error)\n\n"))
   }
   prompt = ""
}
```

Each partial response returned by the model includes all the text generated up to that point, so we must temporarily store the value of the **response** property before sending the prompt and then update it with each new partial response. This way, the user sees the text grow on the screen in real time as the model continues working (This approach may change depending on your application).

Do It Yourself

Update the **sendPrompt()** method in the **ApplicationData** class with the code in Listing 5-6. Run the application on your Mac and ask the model to write a story. You should see text appear right away and continue growing until the story is complete.

Sampling

An artificial intelligence model generates responses by selecting the most probable outcome. When producing text, the model predicts the next word based on several factors, including the input and the context. Sometimes, two or more words may have similar probabilities of being the correct choice, so the model must decide which one to use. This decision-making process is known as sampling, and by default, it involves an element of randomness. For example, if the model estimates a 45% probability that the next word is "man" and a 32% probability that it is "guy," it will usually select "man," but occasionally, by random chance, it will choose "guy." As a result, each generated text may vary slightly, even when using the exact same prompt.

Although this behavior makes the model more creative and original, there are times when we may want to adjust the sampling process to control the response. To define how the model generates its output, the framework provides the **GenerationOptions** structure. The following is the structure's initializer.

> **GenerationOptions(sampling:** SamplingMode, **temperature:** Double, **maximumResponseTokens:** Int)

This initializer creates a **GenerationOptions** structure to control the model's response. The **sampling** argument defines the sampling mode. It is a structure that includes a property called **greedy** to instruct the model to always select the most probable word, and two methods, **random(probabilityThreshold: Double)** and **random(top: Int)** to adjust how many possible words the model can choose from. The **maximumResponseTokens** argument specifies the maximum number of tokens (words) the response can contain.

The **GenerationOptions** structure is passed to the **respond()** method along with the prompt by using the **options** argument. The following example shows how to configure these options to change the sampling mode.

Listing 5-7: Asking the model to always choose the most probable output

```
import SwiftUI
import FoundationModels
import Observation

@Observable class ApplicationData {
   var response: AttributedString = ""
   var prompt: String = ""

   @ObservationIgnored var session = LanguageModelSession()

   static let shared: ApplicationData = ApplicationData()
   private init() { }

   func sendPrompt() async {
      do {
         let options = GenerationOptions(sampling: .greedy)
         let answer = try await session.respond(to: prompt, options:
            options)
```

```
            var newResponse = AttributedString("\(answer.content)\n\n")
            newResponse.font = .system(size: 16, weight: .regular)
            response.append(newResponse)
         } catch {
            response.append(AttributedString("Error accessing the model:
               \(error)\n\n"))
         }
         prompt = ""
      }
   }
```

In this example, we send the prompt to the model using the **greedy** option to ensure it always selects the most probable output. Under the same conditions and with the same prompt, the model will produce the same response every time. For instance, if we ask the model to describe a unicorn with no prior context, it will always return the same description.

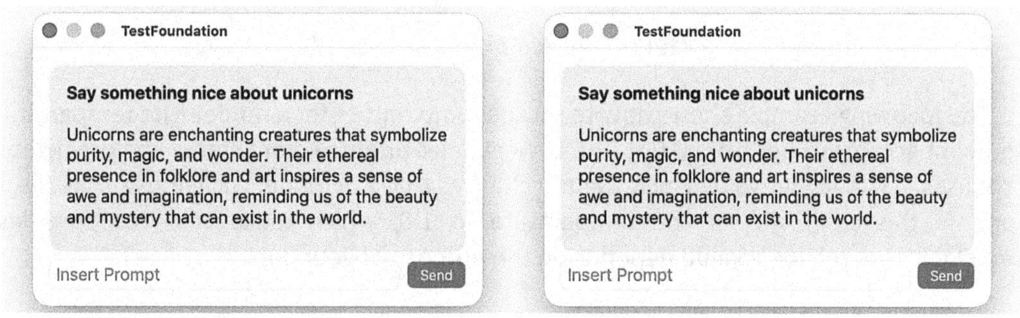

Figure 5-5: *Same response to the same initial prompt*

Do It Yourself

Update the **ApplicationData** class with the code in Listing 5-7. Run the application on your Mac and ask the model to write a description or a story. After receiving the response, stop the app from Xcode and run it again to create a new session. Type the same prompt again. Since there is no previous context, the model should return the same response as before.

IMPORTANT

The model always takes the previous conversation into account when generating a response within the same session. This means that if we send the same prompt twice in a row during a single conversation, the second response will be different, regardless of the sampling mode. If you want to test this sampling mode in a long conversation, start two separate sessions. If you use exactly the same prompts in both sessions, all the responses will be identical.

Another option is to adjust the temperature. Temperature controls how much the model favors high-probability words versus exploring alternatives. With a lower temperature, the probability distribution becomes more peaked, so the model tends to choose the most likely words and produces more consistent responses. With a higher temperature, the distribution becomes flatter, making less likely words more competitive and leading to more varied, and sometimes more creative, outputs, as shown below.

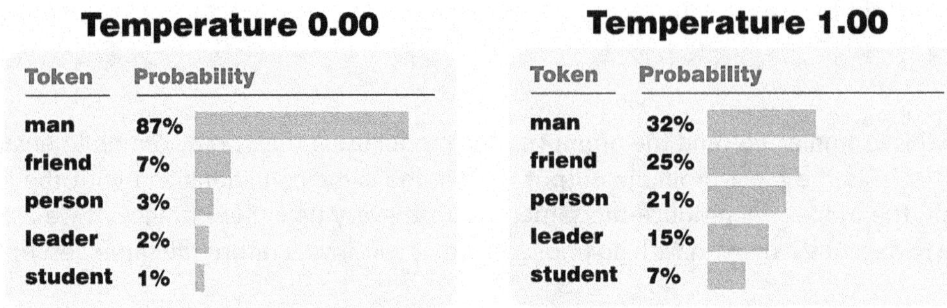

Figure 5-6: *Temperature levels*

The following example shows how to set the temperature for a model. The **temperature** argument accepts values from 0.0 to 1.0. Lower values produce more stable and predictable responses, while higher values increase the chances that the model will choose a less likely word. In this case, we set the temperature to 1.0, which makes the response less predictable, but the ideal value depends on the purpose of your app.

Listing 5-8: Changing the model's temperature

```
func sendPrompt() async {
   do {
      let options = GenerationOptions(temperature: 1.0)
      let answer = try await session.respond(to: prompt, options: options)

      var newResponse = AttributedString("\(answer.content)\n\n")
      newResponse.font = .system(size: 16, weight: .regular)
      response.append(newResponse)
   } catch {
      response.append(AttributedString("Error accessing the model:
         \(error)\n\n"))
   }
   prompt = ""
}
```

Do It Yourself

Update the **sendPrompt()** method in the **ApplicationData** class with the code in Listing 5-8. Run the application on your Mac and test the model with a prompt that can produce multiple valid answers, such as "Give me a title for a science fiction book." Stop the app from Xcode, change the temperature value (use values between 0.0 and 1.0), run the application again, and enter the same prompt. You should see different types of responses depending on the temperature.

Guided Generation

Although we can guide the model's behavior using instructions and fine-tune its responses through generation options, we still cannot fully predict what it will say. Sometimes the model replies with a single sentence, other times with an entire paragraph or several, and the information it provides may vary in length, structure, and relevance. To obtain responses that we can reliably use or process in our app, we need to apply guided generation. Guided generation allows us to enforce a specific format for the model's output. For example, if we want to know how many colors are in a rainbow, we can instruct the model to return only an integer value. This constraint is defined in the **respond()** method along with the prompt, using the **generating** argument. The following example shows how to get an **Int** value as a response.

Listing 5-9: Using guided generation

```
import SwiftUI
import FoundationModels
import Observation

@Observable class ApplicationData {
   var response: AttributedString = ""
   var prompt: String = ""

   @ObservationIgnored var session: LanguageModelSession

   static let shared: ApplicationData = ApplicationData()
   private init() {
      let instructions = "Respond only with a number that represents the
         answer to the question"
      session = LanguageModelSession(instructions: instructions)
   }
   func sendPrompt() async {
      do {
         let answer = try await session.respond(to: prompt, generating:
            Int.self)

         var newResponse = AttributedString("\(answer.content)\n\n")
         newResponse.font = .system(size: 16, weight: .regular)
         response.append(newResponse)
      } catch {
         response.append(AttributedString("Error accessing the model:
            \(error)\n\n"))
      }
      prompt = ""
   }
}
```

First, we provide instructions to help the model generate the correct answer, and then we specify the `Int` data type in the `respond()` method so it knows exactly what type of value to return. As a result, the `content` property is no longer a string but a value of type `Int`. This value can be stored, used to perform calculations or to update the user interface. In this case, we convert it into an attributed string and display it on the screen, just as we did with previous responses. Now we can ask the model questions that expect a numerical response and receive exactly that.

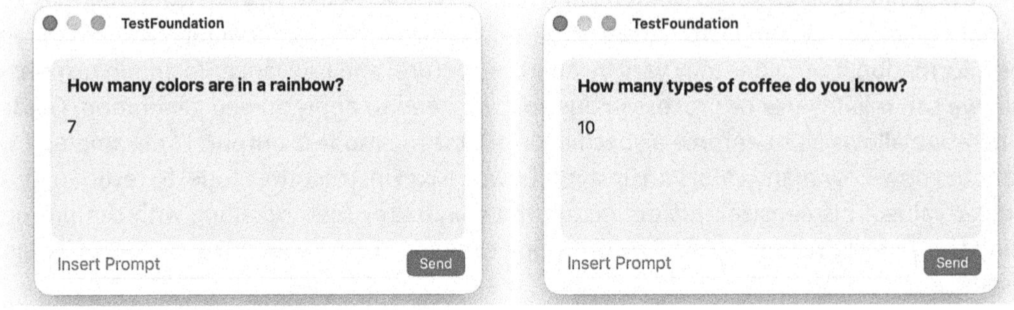

Figure 5-7: *Model responding with integers*

IMPORTANT

Remember that the large language model used by the Foundation Models framework is limited and not suitable for providing real-world or up-to-date information. The same prompt may produce different answers or values, and the model may return inaccurate information when forced to generate a response. If your application requires reliable and consistent results, you should use external models. We will learn how to access external models, like those used by ChatGPT, in Chapter 10.

The **generating** argument accepts most Swift data types, including `Bool`, `Int`, `Float`, `Double`, `Decimal`, and `Array`, but also custom data types, including structures and enumerations. For example, we can define a structure with all the properties we need and the model will produce instances of that structure populated with the exact values we want. When working with standard types, as in the previous example, the model can usually infer our intent from the data type and the prompt, but when using custom data types, we must guide the model to produce the correct results. To prepare these types and ensure the model generates appropriate values for each property, the framework provides the following macros.

`@Generable(description:` `String)`

This macro generates the code required to describe a structure in a way the model can understand. The **description** argument is an optional string that specifies the type of information the structure should contain.

@Guide(description: String, Expression)

This macro defines guidance for a property, describing both its purpose and expected format. The **description** argument is an optional string that specifies the type of information the property should contain, and the second argument is an optional expression used to constrain or validate the format of the value.

A macro generates code for us in the background during compilation. In this case, the **@Generable** macro produces the code needed to turn a structure into a schema the model can follow. If the structure is simple enough for the model to infer the type of values it needs to generate, we can simply prefix it with this macro and it will be ready to use. In the following example, we define a structure with a property that stores a **String** array, so the model understands that it should return a list of values.

Listing 5-10: Making our structure generable

```
import SwiftUI
import FoundationModels

@Generable
struct ItemNames {
   let names: [String]
}
```

Once we have defined the generable structure, we can send it to the model along with the prompt, just as we did earlier with the **Int** data type. The following updates are required in our **ApplicationData** class to specify the instructions for this example and process the values returned by the model.

Listing 5-11: Processing the model's response

```
import SwiftUI
import FoundationModels
import Observation

@Observable class ApplicationData {
   var response: AttributedString = ""
   var prompt: String = ""

   @ObservationIgnored var session: LanguageModelSession

   static let shared: ApplicationData = ApplicationData()
   private init() {
      let instructions = "Return a list of values that answer the
         question"
      session = LanguageModelSession(instructions: instructions)
   }
   func sendPrompt() async {
      do {
         let answer = try await session.respond(to: prompt, generating:
            ItemNames.self)
```

```
            let names = answer.content.names
            let message = "The values are: \(names.joined(separator: ", "))."

            var newResponse = AttributedString("\(message)\n\n")
            newResponse.font = .system(size: 16, weight: .regular)
            response.append(newResponse)
         } catch {
            response.append(AttributedString("Error accessing the model:
               \(error)\n\n"))
         }
         prompt = ""
      }
   }
```

The **content** property now contains an instance of the **ItemNames** structure, so we can read the **names** property and process its values. In this case, we create a string that lists all items separated by commas. Every time the model sends a response, the **sendPrompt()** method reads these values from the **names** property and displays the list on the screen, as shown below.

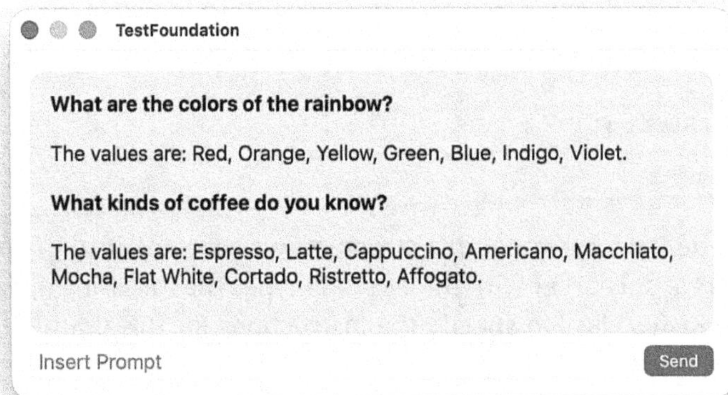

Figure 5-8: *Guided response*

Do It Yourself

Create a new file called ItemNames.swift for the structure in Listing 5-10. Update the **ApplicationData** class with the code in Listing 5-11. Run the application on your Mac and send a prompt that requires multiple values in response, such as "What are the colors of the rainbow?". You should see the list of values displayed on the screen.

In this case, we designed the structure for a very specific prompt, but that is usually not the case. In most situations, the structure will contain multiple properties, and the prompt alone will not be enough for the model to infer the type of values we want in response. For this reason, the framework provides the **@Guide** macro. This macro allows us to add a description to each property, as well as constraint methods to limit the possible values. For numbers, the framework defines the methods **minimum(Value)**, **maximum(Value)**, and **range(Range)**. For arrays, we can specify the number of elements with the methods

minimumCount(Int), **maximumCount(Int)**, and **count(Int)**. And for strings, we can use **constant(String)** to specify a fixed value, **anyOf(Array)** to restrict the possible values to a list, and **pattern(RegExp)** to match values using a regular expression.

For example, if we need the model to return information about a city, we must define a structure with multiple properties and use the **@Guide** macro to describe the type of values the model should generate for each property, as shown below.

Listing 5-12: Helping the model to produce the right values

```
import SwiftUI
import FoundationModels

@Generable
struct CityResponse {
   @Guide(description: "The name of the city")
   let city: String
   @Guide(description: "The name of the country the city belongs to")
   let country: String
   @Guide(description: "The main language spoken in the city")
   let language: String
   @Guide(description: "The currency used in the city")
   let currency: String
   @Guide(description: "A list of attractions in the city", .count(5))
   let attractions: [String]
}
```

For the name of the city, the country, the language, and the country's currency, we provide a brief description to tell the model what type of values it should assign to these properties. The **attractions** property, however, is an array of strings, so in addition to describing the values we want, we also specify the number of elements using the **count()** method. This tells the model that it must return a total of five city attractions. The following changes are required in our **ApplicationData** class to specify the instructions for this example and process the returned values.

Listing 5-13: Processing structured responses

```
import SwiftUI
import FoundationModels
import Observation

@Observable class ApplicationData {
   var response: AttributedString = ""
   var prompt: String = ""

   @ObservationIgnored var session: LanguageModelSession

   static let shared: ApplicationData = ApplicationData()
   private init() {
      let instructions = "Determine the city the user is talking about,
         and return information about it"
      session = LanguageModelSession(instructions: instructions)
   }
```

```
    func sendPrompt() async {
        do {
            let answer = try await session.respond(to: prompt, generating:
                CityResponse.self)
            let city = answer.content
            var message = "City: \(city.city)\n"
            message += "Country: \(city.country)\n"
            message += "Language: \(city.language)\n"
            message += "Currency: \(city.currency)\n"
            message += "Attractions: \(city.attractions.joined(separator: ",
                "))\n"

            var newResponse = AttributedString("\(message)\n\n")
            newResponse.font = .system(size: 16, weight: .regular)
            response.append(newResponse)
        } catch {
            response.append(AttributedString("Error accessing the model:
                \(error)\n\n"))
        }
        prompt = ""
    }
}
```

Once again, we retrieve the structure returned by the model from the **`content`** property and create a string with its values. The result is shown below.

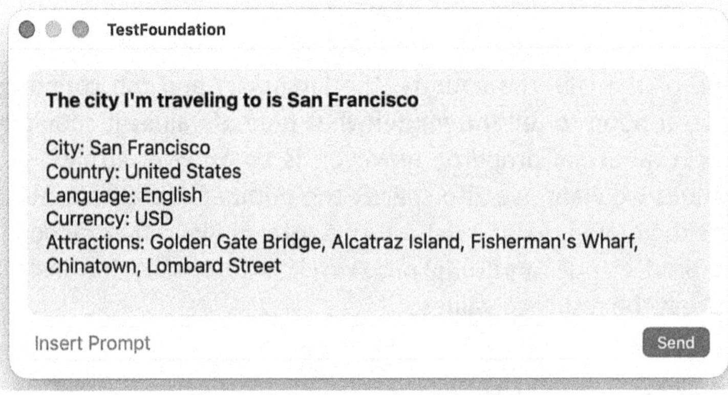

Figure 5-9: *Structured responses*

Do It Yourself

Create a new file called CityResponse.swift for the structure in Listing 5-12. Update the **`ApplicationData`** class with the code in Listing 5-13. Run the application on your Mac and send a prompt that includes the name of a city. You should see information about that city displayed on the screen.

If the user doesn't mention a city, the model will still attempt to fulfill the request and return the city it considers most appropriate. This behavior is known as a hallucination, where the model appears confident about an answer that makes no sense. There are several techniques we can use to minimize this issue. One simple approach is to require the user to provide a prompt that always includes the information the model needs. For example, instead of using an input field, we can offer a picker for the user to select a city and then define the prompt ourselves using the selected value.

Listing 5-14: Using a predefined prompt

```
import SwiftUI
import FoundationModels

struct ContentView: View {
   @State private var appData = ApplicationData.shared
   @State private var position = ScrollPosition(idType: String.self)
   @State private var selected: Int = 0
   let listCities = ["New York", "London", "Tokyo", "Sydney", "Berlin",
      "Paris", "Rome", "Cairo", "Beijing", "Mumbai"]

   var body: some View {
      VStack {
         ScrollView {
            Text(appData.response)
               .padding()
               .textSelection(.enabled)
               .id("textID")
         }
         .frame(minWidth: 350, maxWidth: .infinity, minHeight: 300,
            alignment: .leading)
         .background(Color.gray.opacity(0.2))
         .clipShape(RoundedRectangle(cornerRadius: 12))
         .scrollPosition($position)

         HStack {
            Picker("Select City: ", selection: $selected) {
               ForEach(listCities.indices, id: \.self) { index in
                  Text(listCities[index])
                     .tag(index)
               }
            }
            .disabled(appData.session.isResponding)

            Button("Send") {
               Task {
                  if selected >= 0 && selected < listCities.count {
                     // Prepare prompt
                     appData.prompt = "I'm traveling to
                        \(listCities[selected])"
                     var newPrompt = AttributedString("\(appData.
                        prompt)\n\n")
                     newPrompt.font = .system(size: 16, weight: .bold)
                     appData.response.append(newPrompt)
                     await appData.sendPrompt()
                  }
               }
            }
            .buttonStyle(.borderedProminent)
            .disabled(appData.session.isResponding)
         }
      }
```

```
            .padding()
            .onChange(of: appData.response) {
               position.scrollTo(edge: .bottom)
            }
         }
      }
```

In this example, we add a new State property for the **ContentView** view to store the index of the city selected by the user and define a constant containing a list of available cities. The interface now includes a picker that displays these options. When the user presses the Send button, the app creates a prompt using the name of the selected city and sends it to the model, ensuring that the model always knows which city to use as a reference.

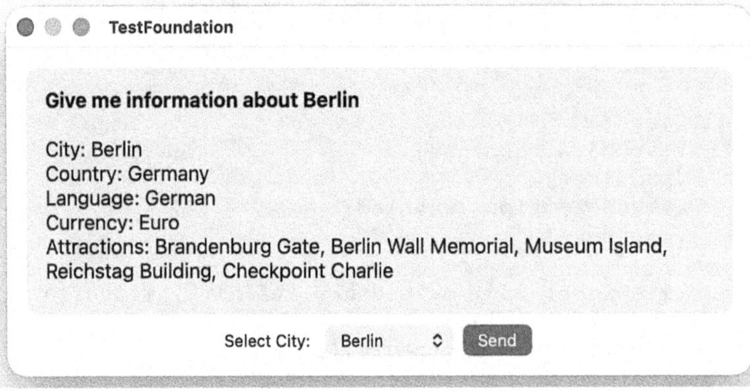

Figure 5-10: *Using predefined prompts*

Do It Yourself

Update the **ContentView** view with the code in Listing 5-14. Run the application on your Mac, select a city, and press Send. You should see the same information as before, but now the prompt is built by the application rather than the user, ensuring that the model always has the values it needs to produce a valid answer.

It may take several seconds for the model to generate a value for each property in a generable structure. If we think the process might take too long, we can stream the values using the **streamResponse()** method, as we did in Listing 5-6. However, since we are not working with a simple string but with a structure that contains multiple properties, the process is slightly different. To enable streaming for these types of values, the **@Generable** macro defines a secondary structure called **PartiallyGenerated**. This structure is a copy of the original, except that all its properties are optional. Therefore, the only difference from the previous example is that now we must unwrap the properties before accessing their values, as shown below.

Listing 5-15: Streaming generable responses

```
func sendPrompt() async {
   do {
      let tempResponse = response

      let answer = session.streamResponse(to: prompt, generating:
         CityResponse.self)
      for try await partial in answer {
         var message = ""
         if let city = partial.content.city {
            message += "City: \(city)\n"
         }
         if let country = partial.content.country {
            message += "Country: \(country)\n"
         }
         if let language = partial.content.language {
            message += "Language: \(language)\n"
         }
         if let currency = partial.content.currency {
            message += "Currency: \(currency)\n"
         }
         if let attractions = partial.content.attractions {
            message += "Attractions: \(attractions.joined(separator: ",
               "))\n\n"
         }
         var newPartial = AttributedString(message)
         newPartial.font = .system(size: 16, weight: .regular)

         var newResponse = tempResponse
         newResponse.append(newPartial)
         response = newResponse
      }
   } catch {
      response.append(AttributedString("Error accessing the model:
         \(error)\n\n"))
   }
   prompt = ""
}
```

The process is the same as before, but now the **content** property returns a **PartiallyGenerated** structure, so we first unwrap the values one by one and then assign them to the **response** property to display them to the user.

Do It Yourself

Update the **sendPrompt()** method in the **ApplicationData** class with the code in Listing 5-15. Run the application on your Mac, select a city, and press Send. You should see each piece of information about the city gradually appear on the screen.

IMPORTANT

If we want to store the structure returned by the **streamResponse()** method in a property or send it to the views, we have to remember that the data is stored in the **PartiallyGenerated** structure inside our generable structure (**CityResponse.PartiallyGenerated**). We will see an example of how to pass these values to the views later in this chapter.

Dynamic Schemas

Using a structure to tell the model what values to return is useful when we already know what information we need, but that's not always the case. Sometimes we must define a schema dynamically. For example, if we build an application that classifies points of interest in a city, the model may need to return different types of information depending on the location. Some itineraries might include Hotel, Attractions, and Restaurants, while others might also include Transportation or Local Events. The framework provides the following class to define a schema dynamically.

DynamicGenerationSchema(name: String, **description:** String, **properties:** [Property])

This initializer creates a **DynamicGenerationSchema** object that defines the schema the model should follow. The **name** argument specifies the name of the schema, the **description** argument specifies the type of information the schema should contain, and the **properties** argument lists the properties included in the schema.

The **DynamicGenerationSchema** initializer takes an array of **Property** objects to define the properties included in the schema. The **Property** class provides the following initializer to define these values.

Property(name: String, **description:** String, **schema:** DynamicGenerationSchema, **isOptional:** Bool)

This initializer defines a property within a schema. The **name** argument specifies the name of the property, the **description** argument describes the type of value the model should store in it, the **schema** argument defines the schema of the values assigned to the property, and the **isOptional** argument determines whether the property is optional.

The values of these properties are also defined as dynamic schemas. The following initializers are provided by the **DynamicGenerationSchema** class for this purpose.

DynamicGenerationSchema(type: Type)

This initializer defines the schema for a property. The **type** argument specifies the property's data type.

```
DynamicGenerationSchema(arrayOf: DynamicGenerationSchema,
minimumElements: Int, maximumElements: Int)
```

This initializer defines the schema for a property that contains an array of values. The **arrayOf** argument specifies the schema of the elements in the array, while the **minimumElements** and **maximumElements** arguments define the minimum and maximum number of elements the array can contain.

In the same way we can nest structures by referencing one structure inside another, we can also do so with dynamic schemas. When nesting schemas this way, we must specify to the model which dynamic schema serves as the root and which additional schemas are used to define it. For this purpose, the framework provides the `GenerationSchema` structure. The following is the structure's initializer.

```
GenerationSchema(root: DynamicGenerationSchema, dependencies:
[DynamicGenerationSchema])
```

This initializer creates a `GenerationSchema` structure that defines the schema for the model. The **root** argument is a reference to the main dynamic schema, and the **dependencies** argument contains an array of all the dynamic schemas used to define it.

To send the schema to the model, the framework defines additional versions of the `respond()` and `streamResponse()` methods that include the **schema** argument. For example, the following is the `respond()` method we need to implement when we want the model to follow a schema.

```
respond(to: Prompt, schema: GenerationSchema,
includeSchemaInPrompt: Bool, options: GenerationOptions)
```

This method sends a prompt to the model and returns its response. The **to** argument specifies the prompt, the **schema** argument defines the schema the model should follow, the **includeSchemaInPrompt** argument determines whether the schema should be included in the request (`true` by default), and the **options** argument is a structure that configures how the model generates its response.

The response sent by the model no longer follows a specific structure. The values we receive now depend on the schema. For this reason, we can't simply read the content of the `content` property directly as we did before. Now we need to specify the data type and the name of the value we want to access. The following is the method defined by the `Content` structure to retrieve these values.

```
value(Type, forProperty: String)
```

This method returns the value specified by its arguments. The first argument defines the data type of the value, and the **forProperty** argument specifies the name of the property to retrieve.

One of the advantages of using a dynamic schema instead of a structure is that we can configure the schema according to the current state of the application or the input provided by the user. For example, we can let the user determine certain parameters dynamically. In the following example, we define a function that creates a schema based on the values it receives. As before, the schema requests information about a city, but this time the number of attractions returned by the model depends on the value we specify when calling the method.

Listing 5-16: Defining a dynamic schema

```
import SwiftUI
import FoundationModels
import Observation

@Observable class ApplicationData {
   var response: AttributedString = ""
   var prompt: String = ""

   @ObservationIgnored var session: LanguageModelSession

   static let shared: ApplicationData = ApplicationData()
   private init() {
      let instructions = "Determine the city the user is talking about,
         and return information about it"
      session = LanguageModelSession(instructions: instructions)
   }
   func sendPrompt() async {
      do {
         let citySchema = try createSchema(max: 3)
         let answer = try await session.respond(to: prompt, schema:
            citySchema)

         let city = try answer.content.value(String.self, forProperty:
            "city")
         let country = try answer.content.value(String.self, forProperty:
            "country")
         let language = try answer.content.value(String.self, forProperty:
            "language")
         let currency = try answer.content.value(String.self, forProperty:
            "currency")
         let attractions = try answer.content.value([String].self,
            forProperty: "attractions")

         var message = "City: \(city)\n"
         message += "Country: \(country)\n"
         message += "Language: \(language)\n"
         message += "Currency: \(currency)\n"
         message += "Attractions: \(attractions.joined(separator: ", "
            ))\n"

         var newResponse = AttributedString("\(message)\n\n")
         newResponse.font = .system(size: 16, weight: .regular)
         response.append(newResponse)
      } catch {
         response.append(AttributedString("Error accessing the model:
            \(error)\n\n"))
      }
      prompt = ""
   }
```

```
   func createSchema(max: Int) throws -> GenerationSchema {
      let type = DynamicGenerationSchema(
         name: "CityResponse",
         properties: [
           DynamicGenerationSchema.Property(name: "city", description:
              "The name of the city", schema:
              DynamicGenerationSchema(type: String.self)),
           DynamicGenerationSchema.Property(name: "country", description:
              "The name of the country the city belongs to", schema:
              DynamicGenerationSchema(type: String.self)),
           DynamicGenerationSchema.Property(name: "language",
              description: "The main language spoken in the city",
              schema: DynamicGenerationSchema(type: String.self)),
           DynamicGenerationSchema.Property(name: "currency",
              description: "The currency used in the city", schema:
              DynamicGenerationSchema(type: String.self)),
           DynamicGenerationSchema.Property(name: "attractions",
              description: "A list of attractions in the city", schema:
              DynamicGenerationSchema (arrayOf:
              DynamicGenerationSchema(type: String.self),
              minimumElements: max, maximumElements: max))
         ]
      )
      let schema = try GenerationSchema(root: type, dependencies: [])
      return schema
   }
}
```

The **createSchema()** method receives an integer value and uses it to define the **attractions** property. We first create a **DynamicGenerationSchema** object to define the schema, and then use **Property** objects to define each of the properties we want the schema to include. The properties are defined as before: **city**, **country**, **language**, and **currency** are all defined as **String** values, and **attractions** is defined as an array. This time, however, the number of elements in the array is determined by the integer value received by the method.

Once the dynamic schema is ready, the **createSchema()** method creates a **GenerationSchema** structure to represent it and returns this value. Back in the **sendPrompt()** method, we pass this schema to the **respond()** method to send it to the model and then process the response. In this case, we read each value using the **value()** method and display them to the user as before.

Do It Yourself

Update the **ApplicationData** class with the code in Listing 5-16. Run the application on your Mac, select a city, and press Send. You should see the information about the city on the screen, but this time the number of attractions is determined by the value sent to the **createSchema()** method.

The previous example offers a certain level of configuration, but all properties are defined by the initializer and therefore they are always the same. With dynamic schemas, we can not only define the values and ranges of values the properties should have but also create properties on the spot and structure the schema as we need. There are many ways to customize the schema. We can define each property individually and then include them in the initializer, create dedicated methods to determine which properties to include, or even let the user select them. In the following example, we define a simple method that receives an array with the names of the properties to include and then uses a **`switch`** statement to define only those contained in the array.

Listing 5-17: Selecting the properties to include in a dynamic schema

```
import SwiftUI
import FoundationModels
import Observation

@Observable class ApplicationData {
   var response: AttributedString = ""
   var prompt: String = ""

   @ObservationIgnored var session: LanguageModelSession

   static let shared: ApplicationData = ApplicationData()
   private init() {
      let instructions = "Determine the city the user is talking about,
         and return information about it"
      session = LanguageModelSession(instructions: instructions)
   }
   func sendPrompt() async {
      do {
         let list = ["country", "language", "attractions"]
         let properties = createProperties(list: list)
         let type = DynamicGenerationSchema(name: "CityResponse",
            properties: properties)
         let citySchema = try GenerationSchema(root: type, dependencies:
            [])

         let answer = try await session.respond(to: prompt, schema:
            citySchema)

         var message = ""
         if let city = try? answer.content.value(String.self, forProperty:
            "city") {
            message += "City: \(city)\n"
         }
         if let country = try? answer.content.value(String.self,
            forProperty: "country") {
            message += "Country: \(country)\n"
         }
         if let language = try? answer.content.value(String.self,
            forProperty: "language") {
            message += "Language: \(language)\n"
         }
         if let currency = try? answer.content.value(String.self,
            forProperty: "currency") {
            message += "Currency: \(currency)\n"
         }
```

```
        if let attractions = try? answer.content.value([String].self,
           forProperty: "attractions") {
           message += "Attractions: \(attractions.joined(separator: ", "
              ))\n"
        }
        var newResponse = AttributedString("\(message)\n\n")
        newResponse.font = .system(size: 16, weight: .regular)
        response.append(newResponse)
     } catch {
        response.append(AttributedString("Error accessing the model:
           \(error)\n\n"))
     }
     prompt = ""
  }
  func createProperties(list: [String]) -> [DynamicGenerationSchema.
     Property] {
     var properties: [DynamicGenerationSchema.Property] = []
     for name in list {
        switch name {
        case "city":
           properties.append(DynamicGenerationSchema.Property(name:
              "city", description: "The name of the city", schema:
              DynamicGenerationSchema(type: String.self)))
        case "country":
           properties.append(DynamicGenerationSchema.Property(name:
              "country", description: "The name of the country", schema:
              DynamicGenerationSchema(type: String.self)))
        case "language":
           properties.append(DynamicGenerationSchema.Property(name:
              "language", description: "The main language spoken in the
              city", schema: DynamicGenerationSchema(type: String.self)))
        case "currency":
           properties.append(DynamicGenerationSchema.Property(name:
              "currency", description: "The currency used in the city",
              schema: DynamicGenerationSchema(type: String.self)))
        case "attractions":
           properties.append(DynamicGenerationSchema.Property(name:
              "attractions", description: "A list of attractions in the
              city", schema: DynamicGenerationSchema (arrayOf:
              DynamicGenerationSchema(type: String.self),
              minimumElements: 3, maximumElements: 3)))
        default:
           break
        }
     }
     return properties
  }
}
```

The **createProperties()** method receives an array containing the names of the properties to include in the schema, then creates those properties, adds them to a new array, and returns it. Back in the **sendPrompt()** method, we use this array to define a **DynamicGenerationSchema** object, create the final schema with the **GenerationSchema** structure, and send it to the model.

The response is processed as before, but since some properties might not be included, we first check if the **value()** method returns an error and then create a string with the existing values to display to the user.

Do It Yourself

Update the **ApplicationData** class with the code in Listing 5-17. Run the application on your Mac, select a city, and press Send. You should see only the values for the city's country, language, and attractions.

IMPORTANT

How we build a dynamic schema and determine which properties to include depends on our application and what we want to achieve. The examples in this section use basic techniques to illustrate how the process works, but you can implement this in any way your application requires, such as adding pickers to the interface to let the user manually select these parameters or determining their values based on the context.

Tool Calling

The knowledge of the Foundation model is generic and frozen in time. This means that it cannot access real-time information or retrieve data beyond what it was trained on. To overcome these limitations, we can extend its functionality by calling tools that perform specific tasks on its behalf. For example, we can create a tool that connects to our database to include custom data in the response, or integrate external services such as map or weather APIs to provide up-to-date and accurate information.

To create these tools, we must define a structure or class that conforms to the **Tool** protocol. This protocol requires the data type to implement the following properties and method.

name

This property sets a string that represents the name of the tool.

description

This property sets a string that describes the purpose of the tool.

call(arguments: Values)

This method provides the code that performs the desired task, such as accessing a database or an API. The **arguments** argument is a generable structure that provides the values the tool requires to execute the task.

Once our tool is defined, we must provide it to the session. The **LanguageModelSession** class includes the following initializer for this purpose.

LanguageModelSession(tools: Array)

This initializer creates a session configured to work with the tools specified in the argument. The **tools** argument is an array of structures or classes that conform to the **Tool** protocol.

To communicate with the tool, the model uses generable structures, so the **call()** method must receive and return these types of values. For the input, we must define a generable structure capable of storing the values sent by the model to the tool, while the return type depends on the tool's output. If the tool produces a single value, we can use any generable data type, such as **Bool**, **Int**, **Float**, **Double**, **Decimal**, or **Array**. However, if the tool needs to return multiple or complex values, we must use a custom generable structure instead. The following example shows how these values are defined and how to work with a tool. In this case, the tool is used to retrieve a list of tourist attractions for a city.

Listing 5-18: Defining a tool

```
import SwiftUI
import FoundationModels

struct AttractionsTool: Tool {
   let name = "determineAttractionLocation"
   let description = "Finds the longitude and latitude of a location on a
      map"

   @Generable
   struct Arguments {
      @Guide(description: "The name of the city to find attractions for")
      var city: String
      @Guide(description: "The country the city belongs to")
      var country: String
   }
   @Generable
   struct Attraction {
      let name: String
      let latitude: Double
      let longitude: Double
   }
   func call(arguments: Arguments) async throws -> [Attraction] {
      var attractions: [Attraction] = []
      attractions.append(Attraction(name: "Hotel Hyatt", latitude:
         13.404954, longitude: 53.520008))
      attractions.append(Attraction(name: "Hotel Bronson", latitude:
         14.404954, longitude: 54.520008))
      attractions.append(Attraction(name: "Hotel Maui", latitude:
         15.404954, longitude: 55.520008))

      return attractions
   }
}
```

We start by defining the **name** and **description** properties to tell the model what the tool does. Next, we create a generable structure called **Arguments** to specify the values the model must send to the tool to perform its task. In this example, the tool requires the name of a city and its country so it can find tourist attractions in that area. Because the tool needs to return a list of attractions with their names and locations, we also define another generable structure called **Attraction** to store these values (**name**, **latitude**, and **longitude**). Finally, we implement the **call()** method to execute the task.

When the model decides to use the tool, it creates an instance of the **Arguments** structure with the city and country it wants to find attractions for, and calls the **call()** method to obtain the list of attractions. To process these values, we will use the **CityResponse** structure from previous examples (see Listing 5-12), but with a few minor modifications to also include the attractions' locations, as shown below.

Listing 5-19: Defining a generable structure to work with a tool

```
import SwiftUI
import FoundationModels

@Generable
struct CityResponse: Equatable, Hashable {
   @Guide(description: "The name of the city")
   let city: String
   @Guide(description: "The name of the country the city belongs to")
   let country: String
   @Guide(description: "The main language spoken in the city")
   let language: String
   @Guide(description: "The currency used in the city")
   let currency: String
   @Guide(description: "A list of attractions in the city")
   let attractions: [Attractions]
}
@Generable(description: "Attractions returned by the AttractionsTool")
struct Attractions: Equatable, Hashable {
   @Guide(description: "The name of the attraction returned by
      AttractionsTool")
   let name: String
   @Guide(description: "The latitude of the attraction returned by
      AttractionsTool")
   let latitude: Double
   @Guide(description: "The longitude of the attraction returned by
      AttractionsTool")
   let longitude: Double
}
```

This structure is similar to the previous one, but instead of declaring the **attractions** property as an array of strings, we define it as an array of **Attractions** structures. The **Attractions** structure includes three properties to store the information for each attraction (**name**, **latitude**, and **longitude**), along with instructions that help the model determine where to obtain these values. We can now prompt the model to provide information about a city as before, but this time, our tool supplies the data for the attractions. The following are the changes we need in our **ApplicationData** class for this purpose.

Listing 5-20: Using a tool

```
import SwiftUI
import FoundationModels
import Observation

@Observable class ApplicationData {
   var response: AttributedString = ""
   var prompt: String = ""

   @ObservationIgnored var session: LanguageModelSession

   static let shared: ApplicationData = ApplicationData()
   private init() {
      let instructions = "Determine the city the user is talking about,
         and return information about it"
      session = LanguageModelSession(tools: [AttractionsTool()],
         instructions: instructions)
   }
   func sendPrompt() async {
      do {
         let tempResponse = response

         let finalPrompt = Prompt {
            prompt
            "Use the AttractionsTool to find attractions."
         }
         let answer = try await session.respond(to: finalPrompt,
            generating: CityResponse.self, options:
            GenerationOptions(sampling: .greedy))
         let city = answer.content

         var message = ""
         for attraction in city.attractions {
            message += "Attraction: \(attraction.name)\n"
            message += "Location: \(attraction.latitude), \(attraction.
               longitude)\n"
         }
         var newPartial = AttributedString("\(message)\n")
         newPartial.font = .system(size: 16, weight: .regular)
         var newResponse = tempResponse
         newResponse.append(newPartial)

         response = newResponse
      } catch {
         print("Error accessing the model: \(error)")
      }
      prompt = ""
   }
}
```

This is very similar to what we have done before, except that now we initialize the session with an array of tools that includes an instance of our **AttractionsTool** structure. In theory, this should be enough for the model to use the tool to retrieve tourist attractions for a city, but in practice, that's not how large language models work. These models are trained to respond to human language, which means we must explicitly tell the model what to do. For example, if we simply ask the model to find tourist attractions, it will rely on its own knowledge base and guess the locations. To make the model use our tool, we must convince it that using the tool is better than generating the information on its own. In our example, we add an instruction to the prompt to ask the model to always use our tool when looking for tourists attractions. Now, every time we ask the model to give us information about a city, it will get the attractions from our tool, as shown below.

Figure 5-11: *Using a tool to get tourist attractions*

Do It Yourself

Create a new file called AttractionsTool.swift for the code in Listing 5-18. Update the CityResponse.swift file with the code in Listing 5-19, and the **`ApplicationData`** class with the code in Listing 5-20. Run the application on your Mac, select a city, and press Send. You should see the attractions returned by the tool displayed on the screen. In this case, the tool always returns the same array with fake values. We will learn how to implement this tool with real data next.

IMPORTANT

As mentioned earlier, the model must be informed that a tool is available and what task the tool performs. There are several ways to achieve this. First, ensure that the **`Tool`** structure clearly describes the tool's purpose in its **`name`** and **`description`** properties, as shown in Listing 5-18. Then, explicitly instruct the model to use the tool. This is usually done through the instructions provided to the session, but it can also be done from the prompt, as in our example (see Listing 5-20). Lastly, you can help the model by describing which values from the generable structure are generated by the tool, as we did in our **`Attractions`** structure (see Listing 5-19), and by setting the generation options to **`greedy`**, which helps to prevent the model from trying to generate the answer on its own (see Listing 5-20).

The tool in the previous example returns an array with placeholder values that remain the same regardless of the city. We returned these values to simplify the example, but we can use the **MapKit** framework to obtain real locations instead. In the following example, we will modify some of our files to take advantage of the tools provided by MapKit to retrieve real tourist attractions and display them on a map.

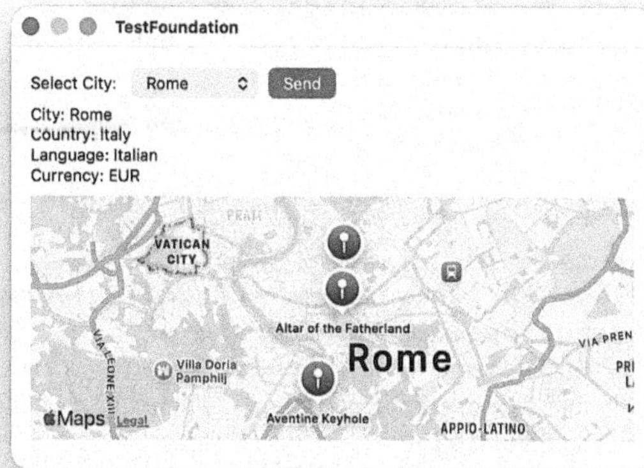

Figure 5-12: *Using external APIs to get the information we need*

To create this application, we first need to update our tool. The values remain the same as before, but since we are now getting the tourist attractions using MapKit, we must import the framework and update the `call()` method, as shown below.

Listing 5-21: Creating a tool with MapKit

```
import SwiftUI
import FoundationModels
import MapKit

struct AttractionsTool: Tool {
   let name = "determineAttractionLocation"
   let description = "Finds the longitude and latitude of a location on a
      map"

   @Generable
   struct Arguments {
      @Guide(description: "The name of the city to find attractions for")
      var city: String
      @Guide(description: "The country the city belongs to")
      var country: String
   }
   @Generable
   struct Attraction {
      let name: String
      let latitude: Double
      let longitude: Double
   }
   func call(arguments: Arguments) async throws -> [Attraction] {
      var attractions: [Attraction] = []
      let city = arguments.city
      let country = arguments.country
```

```
        if let request = MKGeocodingRequest(addressString: "\(city),
           \(country)") {
           if let items = try? await request.mapItems, let mapitem = items.
              first {
              let region = MKCoordinateRegion(center: mapitem.location.
                 coordinate, latitudinalMeters: 10000, longitudinalMeters:
10000)
              let request = MKLocalSearch.Request()
              request.naturalLanguageQuery = "tourist attractions"
              request.region = region

              let search = MKLocalSearch(request: request)
              do {
                 let results = try await search.start()

                 let items = results.mapItems
                 for place in items where attractions.count < 3 {
                    attractions.append(Attraction(name: place.name ??
                       "Undefined", latitude: place.location.coordinate.
                       latitude, longitude: place.location.coordinate.
                       longitude))
                 }
              } catch {
                 print("Couldn't find any results: \(error)")
              }
           }
        }
        return attractions
    }
}
```

In the **call()** method, we first get the city's coordinates on the map using the **MKGeocodingRequest** class, then perform a search with the query "tourist attractions" in that region, store the first three results in an array, and return them.

To display the attractions on a map, we need to pass the values returned by the model to the view so it can generate the map and present it to the user. The following are the updates we need in our **ApplicationData** class for this purpose.

Listing 5-22: Streaming the results of a tool

```
import SwiftUI
import FoundationModels
import Observation

@Observable class ApplicationData {
   var response: CityResponse.PartiallyGenerated? = nil
   var prompt: String = ""

   @ObservationIgnored var session: LanguageModelSession

   static let shared: ApplicationData = ApplicationData()
   private init() {
      let instructions = "Determine the city the user is talking about,
         and return information about it."
      session = LanguageModelSession(tools: [AttractionsTool()],
         instructions: instructions)
   }
```

```
    func sendPrompt() async {
        do {
            let finalPrompt = Prompt {
                prompt
                "Use the AttractionsTool to find attractions."
            }
            let answer = session.streamResponse(to: finalPrompt, generating:
                CityResponse.self, options: GenerationOptions(sampling:
                .greedy))
            for try await partial in answer {
                response = partial.content
            }
        } catch {
            print("Error accessing the model: \(error)")
        }
        prompt = ""
    }
}
```

Because the **MapKit** framework may take some time to return the results, we stream the response using the **streamResponse()** method. This means we are not working directly with the properties of our generable structure, but with the **PartiallyGenerated** structure created by the model (see Listing 5-15). For this reason, we define our **response** property of type **CityResponse.PartiallyGenerated**.

The **PartiallyGenerated** structure returns the same values as before but converts them into optionals, so in the view, we need to check whether each value exists and build the interface accordingly, as shown below.

Listing 5-23: Showing the attractions found by the tool on a map

```
import SwiftUI
import FoundationModels
import MapKit

struct ContentView: View {
    @State private var appData = ApplicationData.shared
    @State private var selected: Int = 0
    let listCities = ["New York", "London", "Tokyo", "Sydney", "Berlin",
        "Paris", "Rome", "Cairo", "Beijing", "Mumbai"]

    var body: some View {
        VStack(alignment: .leading) {
            HStack {
                Picker("Select City: ", selection: $selected) {
                    ForEach(listCities.indices, id: \.self) { index in
                        Text(listCities[index])
                            .tag(index)
                    }
                }
                .disabled(appData.session.isResponding)
                Button("Send") {
                    Task {
                        if selected >= 0 && selected < listCities.count {
                            appData.prompt = "I'm traveling to
                                \(listCities[selected])"
```

```
                    await appData.sendPrompt()
                }
            }
        }
        .buttonStyle(.borderedProminent)
        .disabled(appData.session.isResponding)
    }
    if let city = appData.response?.city {
        Text("City: \(city)")
    }
    if let country = appData.response?.country {
        Text("Country: \(country)")
    }
    if let language = appData.response?.language {
        Text("Language: \(language)")
    }
    if let currency = appData.response?.currency {
        Text("Currency: \(currency)")
    }
    if let attractions = appData.response?.attractions {
        Map {
            ForEach(attractions, id: \.self) { attraction in
                if let name = attraction.name, let latitude =
                    attraction.latitude, let longitude = attraction.
                    longitude {
                    Marker(name, coordinate:
                        CLLocationCoordinate2D(latitude: latitude,
                        longitude: longitude))
                }
            }
        }
    }
    Spacer()
}
.frame(minWidth: 350, maxWidth: .infinity, minHeight: 300,
    maxHeight: .infinity, alignment: .leading)
.padding()
}
}
```

Do It Yourself

Update the **AttractionsTool** structure with the code in Listing 5-21, the **ApplicationData** class with the code in Listing 5-22, and the ContentView.swift file with the code in Listing 5-23. Run the application on your Mac, select a city, and press Send. After a few seconds, you should see something similar to Figure 5-12. For more information on MapKit, read our book *Advanced SwiftUI for Masterminds*.

Availability

Apple Intelligence is not always going to be available on every device. A device's hardware might not have the processing power required to run these models, the user may have disabled Apple Intelligence in Settings, the models might not have been installed yet, or Apple Intelligence may not support the user's language or region. For these reasons, we should always check whether Foundation Models are available before trying to use them. To perform this check, the **SystemLanguageModel** class provides the following property.

availability

This property returns an enumeration of type **Availability** to indicate whether Foundation Models are available. The enumeration includes two cases: **available** to indicate that the model is available, and **unavailable(UnavailableReason)** to indicate that the model is not available and provide a value describing the reason. The possible values for this case are **appleIntelligenceNotEnabled**, **deviceNotEligible**, and **modelNotReady**.

Depending on how our app is designed, we might check for availability in different places. The following example performs this check as soon as the user interface appears on the screen, and displays an error message if Foundation Models are not available. Below are the changes we need in our **ApplicationData** class.

Listing 5-24: Defining a function to check availability

```
import SwiftUI
import FoundationModels
import Observation

@Observable class ApplicationData {
   var response: AttributedString = ""
   var prompt: String = ""
   var modelAvailable: Bool = false
   @ObservationIgnored var model: SystemLanguageModel
   @ObservationIgnored var session: LanguageModelSession

   static let shared: ApplicationData = ApplicationData()
   private init() {
      model = SystemLanguageModel.default
      session = LanguageModelSession(model: model)
   }
   func checkAvailability() {
      switch model.availability {
         case .available:
            modelAvailable = true
         case .unavailable(.appleIntelligenceNotEnabled):
            modelAvailable = false
            response = AttributedString("Enable Apple Intelligence from
               Settings")
         case .unavailable(.deviceNotEligible):
            modelAvailable = false
```

```
            response = AttributedString("Apple Intelligence is not
               available")
         case .unavailable(.modelNotReady):
            modelAvailable = false
            response = AttributedString("The model is not ready yet")
         case .unavailable(let reason):
            modelAvailable = false
            response = AttributedString("Unavailable: \(reason)")
      }
   }
   func sendPrompt() async {
      do {
         let answer = try await session.respond(to: prompt)

         var newResponse = AttributedString("\(answer.content)\n\n")
         newResponse.font = .system(size: 16, weight: .regular)
         response.append(newResponse)
      } catch {
         response.append(AttributedString("Error accessing the model:
            \(error)\n\n"))
      }
      prompt = ""
   }
}
```

In this example, we define two properties: the same **`response`** property we used before to store the model's response, and a new property called **`modelAvailable`** to report to the views whether the model is available or not. To verify this condition, we define a method called **`checkAvailability()`**. This method reads the value of the model's **`availability`** property and updates the **`response`** and **`modelAvailable`** properties to report the result.

Whenever we need to know if the model is available, we can call the **`checkAvailability()`** method. For instance, the following view checks availability as soon as the interface is loaded and only allows the user to send a prompt if the model is available.

Listing 5-25: Checking the model's availability

```
import SwiftUI
import FoundationModels

struct ContentView: View {
   @State private var appData = ApplicationData.shared
   @State private var position = ScrollPosition(idType: String.self)

   var body: some View {
      VStack {
         ScrollView {
            Text(appData.response)
               .padding()
               .textSelection(.enabled)
               .id("textID")
         }
         .frame(minWidth: 350, maxWidth: .infinity, minHeight: 300,
            alignment: .leading)
         .background(Color.gray.opacity(0.2))
```

```
            .clipShape(RoundedRectangle(cornerRadius: 12))
            .scrollPosition($position)

            HStack {
               TextField("Insert Prompt", text: $appData.prompt)
                  .textFieldStyle(.roundedBorder)
                  .disabled(appData.session.isResponding)
               Button("Send") {
                  Task {
                     if !appData.prompt.isEmpty {
                        var newPrompt = AttributedString("\(appData.
                           prompt)\n\n")
                        newPrompt.font = .system(size: 16, weight: .bold)
                        appData.response.append(newPrompt)

                        await appData.sendPrompt()
                     }
                  }
               }
               .buttonStyle(.borderedProminent)
               .disabled(appData.session.isResponding || !appData.
                  modelAvailable)
            }
         }
         .padding()
         .onChange(of: appData.response) {
            position.scrollTo(edge: .bottom)
         }
         .onAppear {
            appData.checkAvailability()
         }
      }
   }
```

This code reproduces the same interface used in previous examples to allow the user to send multiple prompts and have a conversation with the model. If we run the application on a device with Apple Intelligence enabled, everything should work as expected. However, there is an option in the Scheme panel to test other conditions. To open this panel, we must select Edit Scheme from the Scheme menu in the toolbar, as shown below.

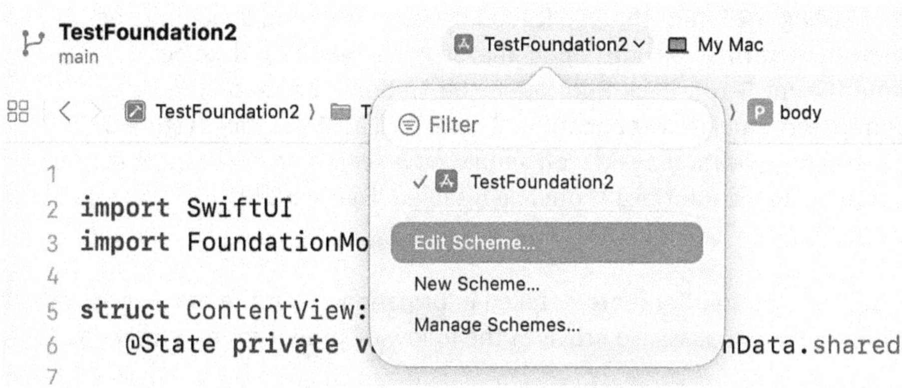

Figure 5-13: *Option to edit the scheme*

The Scheme panel provides options to configure our project. To simulate different conditions for Foundation Models, we must click Run (Figure 5-14, number 1), select the Options tab (Figure 5-14, number 2), and scroll down to the Simulated Foundation Models Availability setting (Figure 5-14, number 3).

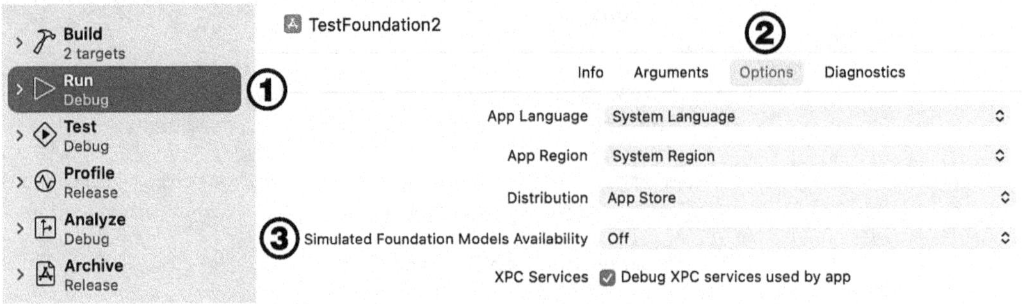

Figure 5-14: *Foundation model availability settings*

If we select an option other than Off, we will see an error on the screen and the interface will be disabled. For example, below is what we see when we select the option "Device Not Eligible".

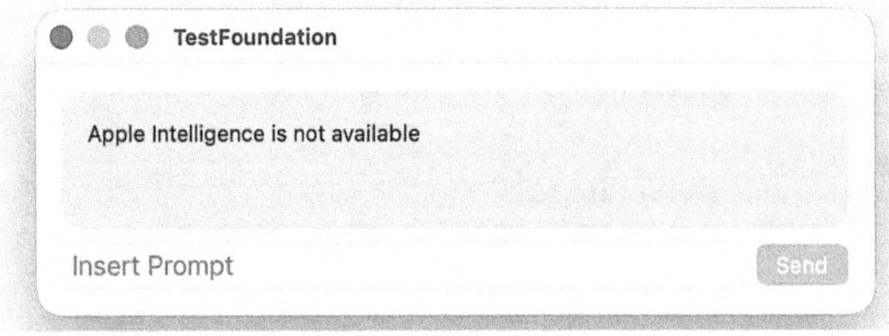

Figure 5-15: *Availability error*

Do It Yourself

Create a new Multiplatform project. Add a new file called ApplicationData.swift for the code in Listing 5-24. Update the `ContentView` view with the code in Listing 5-25. Run the application on your Mac. You shouldn't see any errors. Return to Xcode, open the Scheme menu, and select Edit Scheme (Figure 5-13). Click Run, open the Options tab, and choose an error from the Simulated Foundation Models Availability setting (Figure 5-14). Run the application again. You should now see an error message on the screen, and the interface should be disabled (Figure 5-15).

For convenience, and to offer more detailed information about the model's availability, the `SystemLanguageModel` class also provides the following properties and methods.

`isAvailable`

This property returns a Boolean value indicating whether the model is available or not.

supportedLanguages

This property returns a set of **Locale.Language** values representing the languages supported by Apple Intelligence.

supportsLocale(Locale)

This method returns a Boolean value indicating whether Apple Intelligence is available for the region represented by the argument. The argument is a **Locale** structure that defines the location to check.

If we don't need to know the reason why the model is unavailable, we can simply check the model's **isAvailable** property before allowing the user to send a prompt. The following example shows how to use this property in our code.

Listing 5-26: Checking availability before using the model

```
Button("Send") {
   Task {
      if !appData.model.isAvailable {
         appData.response = "The model is not available"
      } else {
         if !appData.prompt.isEmpty {
            var newPrompt = AttributedString("\(appData.prompt)\n\n")
            newPrompt.font = .system(size: 16, weight: .bold)
            appData.response.append(newPrompt)

            await appData.sendPrompt()
         }
      }
   }
}
.buttonStyle(.borderedProminent)
.disabled(appData.session.isResponding)
```

Do It Yourself

Update the **Button** view in your **ContentView** view with the code in Listing 5-26. Remove the **onAppear()** modifier added in Listing 5-25. Make sure the scheme is still simulating an error (Figure 5-14). Run the application on your Mac. The interface should be enabled, but if you press the Send button, you should get an error.

Errors

Even if we check for availability, the model can still return errors when conditions change or certain situations become invalid. To handle these cases, the **LanguageModelSession** class can report different types of errors that may occur during operation. These errors are defined by the **GenerationError** enumeration. The following are the values available to report issues with the model's availability and its ability to perform a task.

assetsUnavailable(Context)

This error is returned by the session when the model is unavailable, has been deleted from the device, or when Apple Intelligence is disabled while the app is running.

unsupportedLanguageOrLocale(Context)

This error is returned by the session when the model does not support the user's language or region.

rateLimited(Context)

This error is returned by the session when the app is running in the background and exceeds its usage rate limit.

concurrentRequests(Context)

This error is returned by the session when the app tries to send a new prompt before the model has finished processing the previous one.

decodingFailure(Context)

This error is returned by the session when it fails to decode a generable type returned by the model.

unsupportedGuide(Context)

This error is returned by the session when a generation guide uses an unsupported pattern.

Each of these cases includes an associated value of type **Context** that the session uses to provide additional information about the error. The **Context** structure defines the following property to access this information.

debugDescription

This property returns a string containing information that developers can use to diagnose issues during development.

The **LanguageModelSession** class defines a separate structure called **ToolCallError** to represent errors generated by tools. This structure includes the following properties.

tool

This property returns the instance of the **Tool** that caused the error.

errorDescription

This property returns a string that describes the error.

underlyingError

This property returns an **Error** value representing the underlying cause of the error.

The following are the changes we need in the **sendPrompt()** method from our previous example to report issues that the user might be able to solve.

Listing 5-27: Checking for common errors

```
func sendPrompt() async {
    do {
        let answer = try await session.respond(to: prompt)
        var newResponse = AttributedString("\(answer.content)\n\n")
        newResponse.font = .system(size: 16, weight: .regular)
        response.append(newResponse)
    } catch LanguageModelSession.GenerationError.assetsUnavailable(let
        reason) {
        response = AttributedString("The model is not available")
        print(reason.debugDescription)
    } catch LanguageModelSession.GenerationError.
        unsupportedLanguageOrLocale(let reason) {
        response = AttributedString("Apple Intelligence not supported in
           your region")
        print(reason.debugDescription)
    } catch LanguageModelSession.GenerationError.rateLimited(let reason) {
        response = AttributedString("The app has exceeded its usage rate
           limits")
        print(reason.debugDescription)
    } catch LanguageModelSession.GenerationError.concurrentRequests(let
        reason) {
        response = AttributedString("Wait for the previous prompt to be
           processed")
        print(reason.debugDescription)
    } catch {
        response = AttributedString("Error accessing the model: \(error)")
    }
    prompt = ""
}
```

Each time an error is received, the code assigns a message to the **response** property to alert the user and prints the value of the **debugDescription** property to the console, so if the error occurs during development, we have the information needed to fix it.

Do It Yourself

Update the **sendPrompt()** method in the **ApplicationData** class with the code in Listing 5-27. Remove the **if** statement added to the button in Listing 5-26 that checks the value of the **isAvailable** property, so the user is able to send a prompt. If the Scheme is still configured to simulate an error when the model is unavailable, you should see a message on the screen and a string printed to the console with details about the error.

In addition to availability and processing errors, the model can also return errors related to the information it is processing. For example, if the user enters a prompt that violates safety rules, the model may refuse to respond. The following are some of the errors that the session may return in such cases.

guardrailViolation(Context)

This error is returned by the session when the user's prompt or the model's response triggers a safety guardrail.

refusal(Refusal, Context)

This error is returned by the session when it refuses to respond to a request. The error includes an additional associated value that specifies the reason for the refusal.

We can handle these errors in the same way as before. The following example shows one possible implementation.

Listing 5-28: Checking for guardrails errors

```
func sendPrompt() async {
   do {
      let answer = try await session.respond(to: prompt)
      var newResponse = AttributedString("\(answer.content)\n\n")
      newResponse.font = .system(size: 16, weight: .regular)
      response.append(newResponse)
   } catch LanguageModelSession.GenerationError.guardrailViolation(let
      reason) {
      response = AttributedString("Error processing the prompt")
      print(reason.debugDescription)
   } catch LanguageModelSession.GenerationError.refusal(let refusal, let
      reason) {
      var message: String? = nil
      Task.detached {
         if let explanation = try? await refusal.explanation {
            message = explanation.content
         }
         await MainActor.run {
            self.response = AttributedString("Refusal: \(message ??
               "Undefined")")
            print(reason.debugDescription)
         }
      }
   } catch {
      response = AttributedString("Error accessing the model: \(error)")
   }
   prompt = ""
}
```

In addition to the cause of the error, the **refusal** error also provides an explanation of why the request was rejected. This value is returned as a **Refusal** structure and stored in the structure's **explanation** property, so we read this property and show its value to the user. Note that because this property is asynchronous and not executed on the main thread, we need to read it from a detached task to avoid Xcode's warning about non-sendable types.

Now, every time we send a prompt to the model that contains unsafe words (e.g., "intercourse" or "sex"), the session will return an error, as shown below.

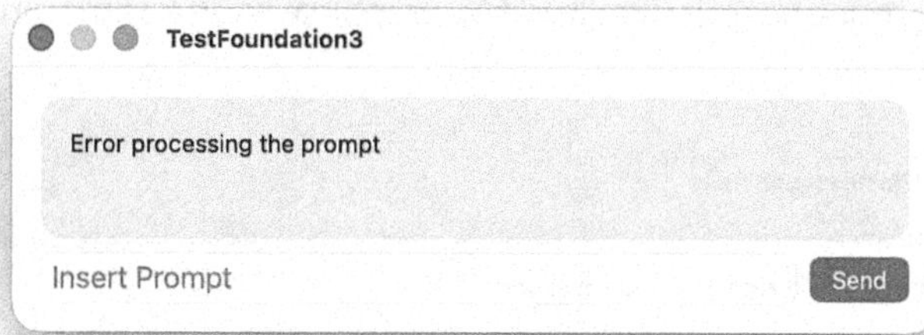

Figure 5-16: *Guardrail error*

Do It Yourself

Update the **sendPrompt()** method in the **ApplicationData** class with the code in Listing 5-28. If you are still simulating an error for Foundation Models, open the Scheme settings and change the option to Off (see Figure 5-14). Run the application on your Mac and send an unsafe prompt (e.g., "Describe how humans have intercourse"). You should see an error message on the screen. Try different prompts to see what the model accepts and rejects.

Although safety guardrails should always be enforced, there are situations where we may need to bypass them, for example when summarizing or tagging text. In such cases, we can ask the model to be more permissive. The **SystemLanguageModel** class provides the following initializer for this purpose.

SystemLanguageModel(guardrails: Guardrails)

This initializer starts a session using the guardrails specified by the argument. The **guardrails** argument is a structure that includes the properties **default** to apply the standard guardrails, and **permissiveContentTransformations** to enable more permissive guardrails for text transformations.

Changing the guardrails to **permissiveContentTransformations** does not allow users to talk about anything they want, but it makes the model more lenient. Instead of returning an error, the model may respond or provide a message that guides the conversation toward a safer topic. The following example shows how to set this option in the **ApplicationData** initializer.

Listing 5-29: Setting up more permissive guardrails

```
private init() {
   model = SystemLanguageModel(useCase: .general, guardrails:
.permissiveContentTransformations)
   session = LanguageModelSession(model: model)
}
```

The model is now more permissive, and the response to the same prompt is completely different, as shown below.

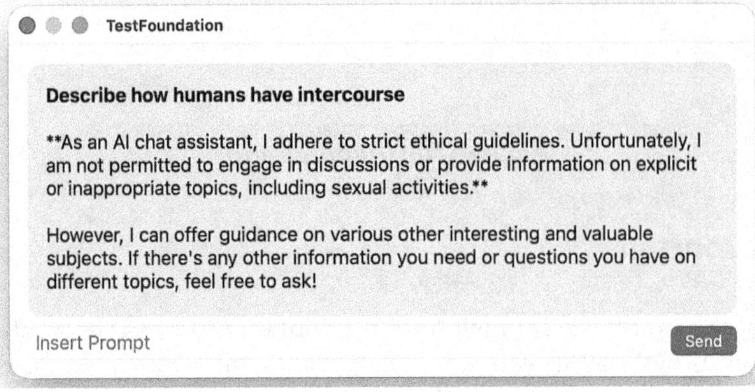

Figure 5-17: *Permissive guardrails*

Another error we may encounter occurs when we exceed the limitations of the context window. Large language models do not process words directly; instead, they break them into smaller units called tokens. These tokens are defined by the model and may represent entire words or only parts of them, depending on the word's length and structure. The model receives tokens as input and returns tokens as output, which are then converted back into words for humans to read. The more tokens included in a conversation, the longer the model will take to process the input and generate a response. For this reason, Foundation Models are limited to a maximum of 4096 tokens per session. If this limit is exceeded, the model returns an error. The following is the error defined by the **GenerationError** enumeration for this case.

exceededContextWindowSize(Context)

This error is returned by the session when it reaches the size limit.

If the user has a long conversation with the model, the session will eventually exceed the token limit and return this error. To allow the conversation to continue, we must create a new session as soon as the error occurs. This process involves not only creating a new instance of the **LanguageModelSession** class, but also extracting the relevant information from the previous session and passing it to the new one so the user can continue without losing context. To obtain this information, the **LanguageModelSession** class provides the following property.

transcript

This property returns a list of all the interactions that occurred between the user and the model during the session. Each entry is represented by an instance of the **Entry** enumeration, which includes the cases **instructions(Instructions)**, **prompt(Prompt)**, **response(Response)**, **toolCalls(ToolCalls)**, and **toolOutput(ToolOutput)**.

The **transcript** property returns a set of **Entry** enumerations, each with associated values that contain the information for a specific entry. To ensure we stay within the token limit, we can read these values to estimate how many tokens have been used in the session so far. Since tokens in Foundation Models typically average around four characters, we can approximate the total by dividing the length of prompts and responses by four, as shown below.

Listing 5-30: Counting tokens

```
import SwiftUI
import FoundationModels
import Observation

@Observable class ApplicationData {
   var response: AttributedString = ""
   var prompt: String = ""
   @ObservationIgnored var model: SystemLanguageModel
   @ObservationIgnored var session: LanguageModelSession

   static let shared: ApplicationData = ApplicationData()
   private init() {
      model = SystemLanguageModel.default
      session = LanguageModelSession(model: model)
   }
   func sendPrompt() async {
      do {
         let answer = try await session.respond(to: prompt)
         var newResponse = AttributedString("\(answer.content)\n\n")
         newResponse.font = .system(size: 16, weight: .regular)
         response.append(newResponse)
         calculateTokens()
      } catch {
         response = AttributedString("Error accessing the model:
            \(error)")
      }
      prompt = ""
   }
   func calculateTokens() {
      let transcript = session.transcript
      var count: Int = 0

      for entry in transcript {
         switch entry {
         case .prompt(let prompt):
            if let text = prompt.segments.first {
               count += text.description.count / 4
            }
         case .response(let response):
            count += response.description.count / 4
         default:
            break
         }
      }
      print("Tokens: \(count)")
   }
}
```

In this example, we define a method called **calculateTokens()** that examines the user's prompts and the model's responses, calculates the number of tokens used in each interaction, and prints the total in the console. This method is called every time the user sends a prompt, so we can keep track of the tokens used throughout the session. Each time we send a new prompt to the model, we can see the number of tokens used so far. As we continue sending prompts, the count will increase, and once it exceeds 4,096, the system will return an error and stop working, as shown below.

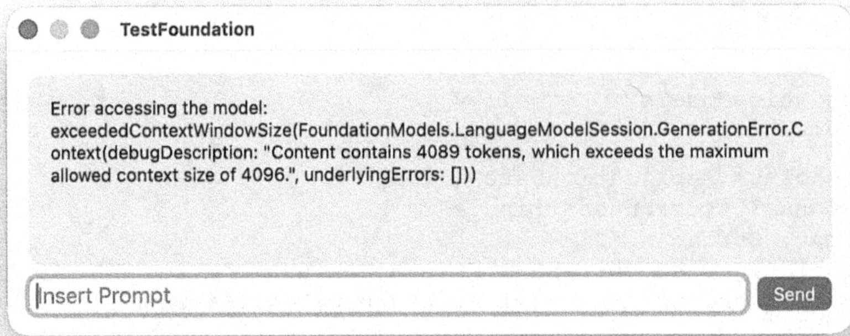

Figure 5-18: *Limit exceeded error*

Do It Yourself

Update the **ApplicationData** class with the code in Listing 5-30. Run the application on your Mac and send a prompt. You should see the total number of tokens used by the session so far printed in the console. Try sending prompts that ask the system to elaborate or tell a long story. After a few entries, the conversation will exceed the limit, and the system will display an error, as shown in Figure 5-18.

In the previous example, we simply printed the number of tokens in the console. However, we can also use this value to better organize conversations in our app or use it along with the **exceededContextWindowSize** error to prevent going over the token limit. Whatever the reason, once we determine that the conversation needs to continue in a new session, we must decide which entries to keep. To manage these transcripts, the framework provides the **Transcript** structure. The structure includes the following initializer to create a new transcript from a sequence of entries.

Transcript(entries: Sequence)

This initializer creates a transcript using the values provided in the argument. The **entries** argument can be a set or an array containing the **Entry** values to include in the transcript.

To assign a transcript to a new session, the **LanguageModelSession** class provides the following initializer.

LanguageModelSession(transcript: Transcript)

This initializer creates a new session using the entries provided by the argument. The **transcript** argument is a **Transcript** structure containing the **Entry** values used to start the session.

Which entries to use when feeding the new session depends on the nature of the conversation. A common approach is to take the first and last entries, as they usually contain the original prompt and the most recent interaction. In the following example, we check for the **exceededContextWindowSize** error and apply this approach to create a new session when the limit is exceeded.

Listing 5-31: Starting a new session

```
func sendPrompt() async {
   do {
      let answer = try await session.respond(to: prompt)
      var newResponse = AttributedString("\(answer.content)\n\n")
      newResponse.font = .system(size: 16, weight: .regular)
      response.append(newResponse)
      calculateTokens()
   } catch LanguageModelSession.GenerationError.
      exceededContextWindowSize(let reason) {
      let oldEntries = session.transcript
      if oldEntries.count >= 2 {
         let newEntries = [oldEntries.first!, oldEntries.last!]
         let newTranscript = Transcript(entries: newEntries)
         session = LanguageModelSession(model: model, transcript:
            newTranscript)

         // Resend the last prompt
         do {
            let answer = try await session.respond(to: prompt)
            var newResponse = AttributedString("\(answer.content)\n\n")
            newResponse.font = .system(size: 16, weight: .regular)
            response.append(newResponse)
         } catch {
            print("Error resending the prompt: \(error)")
         }
      } else {
         session = LanguageModelSession(model: model)
      }
      print("Conversation moved to a new session: \(reason)")
   } catch {
      response = AttributedString("Error accessing the model: \(error)")
   }
   prompt = ""
}
```

There is not a simple recipe of how to handle this error. It all depends on our app. In this example, we create a new transcript containing the first and last interactions of the previous conversation, initialize a new session with it, and then resend the last prompt. This allows the user to continue the conversation after exceeding the limit while giving the new session enough context to understand what the user is referring to.

Do It Yourself

Update the **sendPrompt()** method in the **ApplicationData** class with the code in Listing 5-31. Run the application on your Mac and send long prompts to force the conversation to exceed the token limit again. Once it goes over 4,096 tokens, you should see a message in the console indicating that the conversation has been moved to a new session, and the token count should go down.

IMPORTANT

There are several ways to manage the context window and prevent the model from exceeding its limits. When processing long texts, we can divide the content into smaller sections and send each section to a separate session. We can also encourage users to write shorter prompts, preprocess their input, or provide instructions that guide the model to produce more concise responses. In the next section, we will see how to store conversations in a database so users can manage their own sessions. For more information about prompt optimization, visit our website and follow the links for this chapter.

Storing Sessions

Another way to prevent exceeding the context window limit is to make it easy for users to start and manage multiple conversations at once. This approach is common in most artificial intelligence chat boxes, where users can easily begin new conversations and understand that each topic should have its own thread. As a result, individual conversations rarely exceed the limit and never become difficult for the model to handle.

Of course, there are many ways to create these types of applications, but the steps we need to follow are usually the same. To store conversations in a database, we must convert the session's transcript into data, and then, each time the user opens a previous conversation, we must convert that data back into a **Transcript** structure, create a new session with that transcript, and process the entries to display them on the screen.

To convert the transcript to and from data, we can use the **JSONEncoder** and **JSONDecoder** classes. This process is fast and straightforward, but assigning the decoded transcript to a new session can sometimes cause issues. If the transcript is long, the model may take time to process it. To prevent users from waiting for the conversation to load, we can force the model to process this data in advance. For this purpose, the **LanguageModel-Session** class provides the following method.

prewarm(promptPrefix: Prompt)

This method asks the model to load the session resources into memory and prepare for the next prompt. The **promptPrefix** argument is an optional **Prompt** structure that provides a prefix for the upcoming prompt, if any.

The following example shows a possible implementation. The application displays a list with the current conversations and a button to create new ones. When the user presses the button or selects an existing conversation, we open the same interface as before to chat with the model. Each time the model returns a response, the values are stored in the database so the user can continue the conversation later.

Figure 5-19: *Having multiple conversations*

For this application, we first need to define a data model to store the conversations in a database using SwiftData. In this case, we only need to store a title that allows the user to identify each conversation and a **Data** structure to store the transcript.

Listing 5-32: Defining the data model to store conversations

```
import SwiftUI
import SwiftData

@Model
class Conversation: Identifiable {
   var id: UUID = UUID()
   var title: String

   @Attribute(.externalStorage)
   var transcript: Data?

   init(title: String) {
      self.id = UUID()
      self.title = title
      self.transcript = nil
   }
}
```

The next step is to set up the database in SwiftUI by injecting the data model into the app's environment using the **modelContainer(for:)** modifier.

Listing 5-33: Injecting the data model into the environment

```
import SwiftUI
import SwiftData
```

```
@main
struct TestFoundationApp: App {
   var body: some Scene {
      WindowGroup {
         ContentView()
            .modelContainer(for: [Conversation.self])
      }
   }
}
```

Now that the views have access to the data model, we can start creating and retrieving conversations. For this example, we will define all the code in the **`ApplicationData`** class so we can manage the conversations from anywhere in the app. The conversations are stored in the database from the same **`sendPrompt()`** method used before, but we need two new methods to load previous conversations and start new ones. The following is our implementation.

Listing 5-34: Loading previous conversations and creating new ones

```
import SwiftUI
import FoundationModels
import Observation
import SwiftData

@Observable class ApplicationData {
   var response: AttributedString = ""
   var prompt: String = ""

   var session = LanguageModelSession()
   var conversation: Conversation = Conversation(title: "")

   static let shared: ApplicationData = ApplicationData()
   private init() { }

   func sendPrompt(dbContext: ModelContext) async {
      do {
         let answer = try await session.respond(to: prompt)
         var newResponse = AttributedString("\(answer.content)\n\n")
         newResponse.font = .system(size: 16, weight: .regular)
         response.append(newResponse)

         // Update transcript
         conversation.transcript = try JSONEncoder().encode(session.
            transcript)
         try dbContext.save()
      } catch {
         response = AttributedString("Error accessing the model:
            \(error)")
      }
      prompt = ""
   }
   func loadConversation(dbContext: ModelContext, conversationID: UUID) {
      do {
         response = AttributedString("")
         prompt = ""
```

```
         // Get conversation
         let predicate = #Predicate<Conversation> { conversation in
            conversation.id == conversationID
         }
         let descriptor = FetchDescriptor<Conversation>(predicate:
            predicate)
         if let oldConversation = try? dbContext.fetch(descriptor).first {
            conversation = oldConversation
         } else {
            return
         }
         // Create session with old transcript
         if let data = conversation.transcript {
            let transcript = try JSONDecoder().decode(Transcript.self,
               from: data)
            session = LanguageModelSession(transcript: transcript)
            session.prewarm()

            // Add entries to the conversation
            for entry in transcript {
               switch entry {
               case .prompt(let prompt):
                  if let text = prompt.segments.first?.description {
                     var newText = AttributedString("\(text)\n\n")
                     newText.font = .system(size: 16, weight: .bold)
                     self.response.append(newText)
                  }
               case .response(let response):
                  if let text = response.segments.first?.description {
                     var newText = AttributedString("\(text)\n\n")
                     newText.font = .system(size: 16, weight: .regular)
                     self.response.append(newText)
                  }
               default:
                  break
               }
            }
         } else {
            // Create empty session
            session = LanguageModelSession()
         }
      } catch {
         print("Error decoding data")
      }
   }
   func createConversation(dbContext: ModelContext) {
      // Create an empty session
      response = AttributedString("")
      prompt = ""
      session = LanguageModelSession()

      // Create new conversation
      let newTitle = "New Conversation \(Int.random(in: 0...1000))"
      let newConversation = Conversation(title: newTitle)
      dbContext.insert(newConversation)
      try? dbContext.save()

      conversation = newConversation
   }
}
```

We start by defining the properties used to store the session and the conversation (**session** and **conversation**) and initialize them with empty values. These values are only placeholders; the actual session and conversation are created and managed by the methods. The **sendPrompt()** method updates the conversation in the database with each new interaction, the **loadConversation()** method loads the conversation selected by the user, and the **createConversation()** method creates an empty session and a new **Conversation** structure, allowing the user to initiate a new conversation.

To keep the conversation up to date, the **sendPrompt()** method encodes the session's transcript into a **Data** structure using the **encode()** method every time we receive a response from the model, and then assigns this data to the **transcript** property of the **Conversation** structure to permanently store the conversation in the database. In the **loadConversation()** method, we perform the opposite process. We load the conversation selected by the user from the database, call the **decode()** method to convert the **Data** value in the **transcript** property into a **Transcript** structure, create a new session with this transcript, and then extract the prompts and responses to display them to the user. If instead of selecting an existing conversation, the user presses the button to create a new one, we call the **createConversation()** method. In this method, we initialize an empty session and then create a new **Conversation** structure to store the conversation in the database. Note that the title for the conversation is created from a random number to streamline the process, but in a real application, we would let the user enter a title or automatically generate one from the context.

Now that we have all the functionality we need to load and create conversations, we must define the interface. In this case, we need two views, an initial view to display the list of conversations already started by the user, and a second view to continue a conversation or start a new one. The following are the changes we need in the **ContentView** view to list all the conversations available.

Listing 5-35: Listing conversations

```
import SwiftUI
import SwiftData

struct ContentView: View {
   @Query var listConversations: [Conversation]

   var body: some View {
      NavigationStack {
         List(listConversations) { item in
            NavigationLink(destination: ConversationView(conversationID:
               item.id)) {
               Text(item.title)
            }
         }.listStyle(.plain)
         .navigationTitle("Conversations")
         .toolbar {
            ToolbarItem(placement: .topBarTrailing) {
               NavigationLink(destination:
                  ConversationView(conversationID: nil)) {
                  Image(systemName: "plus")
               }
```

```
            }
         }
      }
   }
}
```

This view reads all the conversations from the database, displays them to the user, and includes a toolbar button to create a new one. When the user selects a conversation from the list or taps the toolbar button, we open the **ConversationView** view to display the interface the user needs to interact with the model. The following is our implementation of this view.

Listing 5-36: Managing conversations

```
import SwiftUI
import FoundationModels

struct ConversationView: View {
   @State private var appData = ApplicationData.shared
   @State private var position = ScrollPosition(idType: String.self)

   @Environment(\.modelContext) var dbContext
   let conversationID: UUID?

   var body: some View {
      VStack {
         ScrollView {
            Text(appData.response)
               .padding()
               .textSelection(.enabled)
               .id("textID")
         }
         .frame(minWidth: 350, maxWidth: .infinity, minHeight: 300,
            alignment: .leading)
         .background(Color.gray.opacity(0.2))
         .clipShape(RoundedRectangle(cornerRadius: 12))
         .scrollPosition($position)

         HStack {
            TextField("Insert Prompt", text: $appData.prompt)
               .font(Font.system(size: 16))
               .padding(10)
               .overlay(
                  RoundedRectangle(cornerRadius: 12)
                     .stroke(Color.secondary, lineWidth: 1)
               )
               .disabled(appData.session.isResponding)
            Button("Send") {
               Task {
                  if !appData.prompt.isEmpty {
                     var newPrompt = AttributedString("\(appData.
                        prompt)\n\n")
                     newPrompt.font = .system(size: 16, weight: .bold)
                     appData.response.append(newPrompt)
```

```
                        await appData.sendPrompt(dbContext: dbContext)
                     }
                  }
               }
               .buttonStyle(.borderedProminent)
               .disabled(appData.session.isResponding)
            }
         }
         .padding()
         .onChange(of: appData.response) {
            position.scrollTo(edge: .bottom)
         }
         .onAppear {
            if let id = conversationID {
               // Load old conversation
               appData.loadConversation(dbContext: dbContext,
                  conversationID: id)
            } else {
               // Create new conversation
               appData.createConversation(dbContext: dbContext)
            }
         }
      }
   }
```

The interface created by this view is similar to those we have implemented before: it includes a **Text** view to display the conversation and a **TextField** view to enter a prompt. However, it can now manage multiple conversations. For this purpose, the view receives the identifier of the conversation selected by the user and either displays an existent conversation or initiates a new one, depending on this value. If the user selected an existing conversation, the **conversationID** property has a value, so we call the **load-Conversation()** method to load the conversation from the database, but if the user pressed the toolbar button to add a new conversation, the **conversationID** property is **nil**, so we call the **createConversation()** method to create a new one.

Do It Yourself

Create a new Multiplatform project. Create a new file called ConversationModel.swift for the code in Listing 5-32. Update the **App** structure with the code in Listing 5-33. Create a new file called ApplicationData.swift for the code in Listing 5-34. Update the **ContentView** view with the code in Listing 5-35. Create a new file called ConversationView.swift for the code in Listing 5-36. Run the application on an iPhone compatible with Apple Intelligence. Press the + button to add a new conversation. Send a prompt. After receiving the response, return to the initial view. You should see the conversation in the list. Select the conversation. You should see the previous prompt and response on the screen and be able to continue the conversation.

Adapters

The Foundation model we have been using so far is a general-purpose model, which means it can produce answers on a wide range of topics and perform most common tasks, such as following instructions, answering questions, and more. This is more than enough in most cases, but if we want the model to specialize in a specific task, we need to train an adapter. Adapters are simple neural networks, usually composed of just two or three layers of neurons, that connect to the original model and adjust its behavior for a particular purpose without altering its main parameters. By training an adapter with specialized data, we can make the model more accurate and efficient in a specific domain while keeping the rest of the model intact.

The **Foundation Models** framework already includes an adapter that specializes in tagging content. With this adapter, we can analyze a text and generate a list of tags representing categories found within it, such as topics, emotions, or objects. Because this adapter was integrated into the framework, all we need to do to use it is to select it from the **SystemLanguageModel** initializer, as shown below.

Listing 5-37: Using an adapter to tag content

```
import SwiftUI
import FoundationModels
import Observation

@Observable class ApplicationData {
    var response: AttributedString = ""
    var prompt: String = ""
    @ObservationIgnored var model: SystemLanguageModel
    @ObservationIgnored var session: LanguageModelSession

    static let shared: ApplicationData = ApplicationData()
    private init() {
        model = SystemLanguageModel(useCase: .contentTagging)
        session = LanguageModelSession(model: model)
    }
    func sendPrompt() async {
        do {
            let answer = try await session.respond(to: prompt)
            var newResponse = AttributedString("\(answer.content)\n\n")
            newResponse.font = .system(size: 16, weight: .regular)
            response.append(newResponse)
        } catch {
            response = AttributedString("Error accessing the model:
               \(error)")
        }
        prompt = ""
    }
}
```

In this example, instead of creating a session with the model by default, we create it using the **contentTagging** use case. As a result, the model no longer responds with natural language but with a list of tags separated by commas, as shown below. (This example assumes that we are using the **ContentView** view defined in Listing 5-3.)

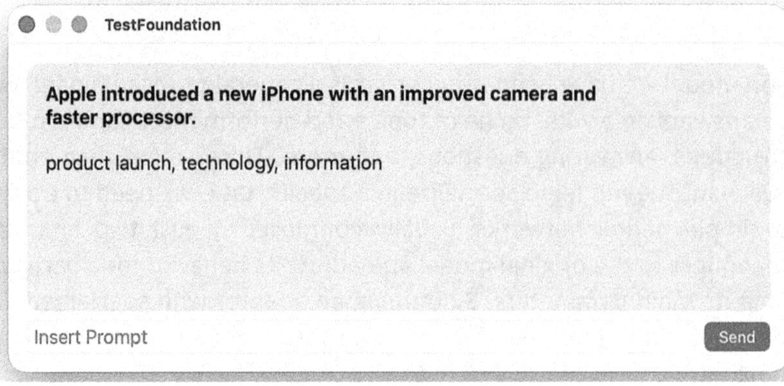

Figure 5-20: *Model tagging content*

Do It Yourself

Create a new Multiplatform project. Create a new file called ApplicationData.swift for the code in Listing 5-37. Update the `ContentView` view with the code in Listing 5-3. Run the application on your Mac. Type a prompt that contains some information. You should see a list of tags separated by commas, as shown in Figure 5-20.

At the moment, the framework only provides the content tagging adapter. If we want the model to specialize in a completely different task, we need to create our own adapter. The process is relatively simple, but it requires implementing a few tools that may not be familiar to most Apple developers. The first step is to download a toolkit provided by Apple, which includes all the resources needed to train an adapter. The toolkit can be found at **https://developer.apple.com/download/foundation-models-adapter/**.

The package includes some examples, documentation, and all the code we need to train our adapter. Below is what we see when we uncompress the file and open the toolkit's folder.

Figure 5-21: *Toolkit's folder*

Do It Yourself

Visit **https://developer.apple.com/download/foundation-models-adapter/** and click Download to download the toolkit. Uncompress the package and open the folder. You should see something similar to Figure 5-21.

IMPORTANT

The toolkit is designed to work with a specific version of Foundation Models. Adapters trained for one model do not work with newer versions of that model, so if Apple releases a new version, we must download the corresponding toolkit and train our adapters again. For more information on how to install and use this toolkit, visit **https://developer.apple.com/apple-intelligence/foundation-models-adapter/**.

The adapter toolkit works with Python, a popular programming language in machine learning. This means that we need Python installed on our computer, along with the additional tools required by the toolkit to train the adapter. These tools do not run through a graphical interface; they are executed directly in the system through Terminal. Terminal is an application that allows us to interact with the operating system, manage essential tools, and modify system configurations. The application is installed on every macOS system and can be found in the Utilities folder inside the Applications folder. It provides a simple text interface where we can execute commands and interact with command line applications.

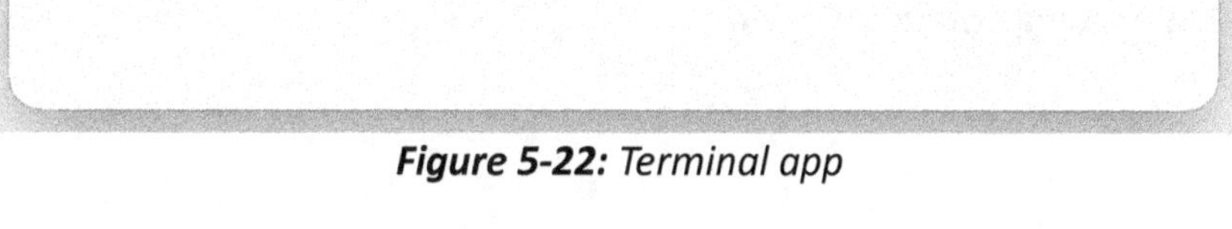

Figure 5-22: *Terminal app*

In theory, we could use Terminal to install all the tools we need directly into the main system, but in practice it is better to work within an environment. An environment is an isolated workspace that allows us to install specific versions of Python and its dependencies without affecting the rest of the system. This prevents conflicts between tools, keeps the system clean, and makes it easier to manage or remove everything related to a project when we are done. Using environments, we can install different versions of the same tools and then move between environments to use the version we need, as shown below.

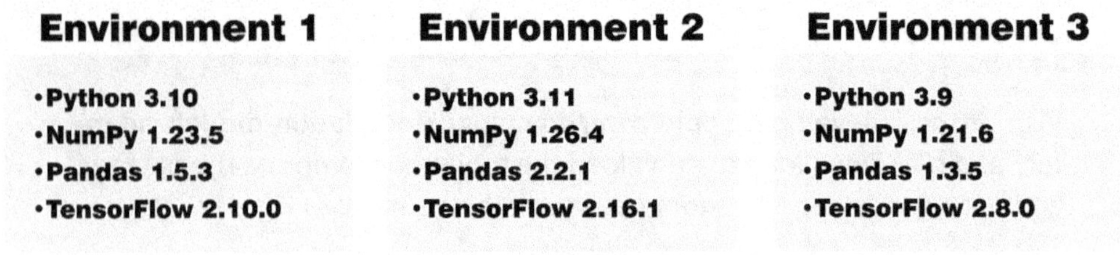

Figure 5-23: *Isolated environments*

Figure 5-23 shows three hypothetical environments. Each environment contains the same applications, but of different versions, so we can move between environments to use what we need. For example, if we need to use Python version 3.10, we will open and work inside Environment 1, but if we need Python version 3.9, we will open Environment 3. To create these environments we first need to install an environment manager. One of the most popular at the moment is called Conda, and the version we are going to use in this book is called Miniconda. The option to download Miniconda can be found at **https://docs.conda.io/projects/conda/en/latest/** (Figure 5-24, number 1).

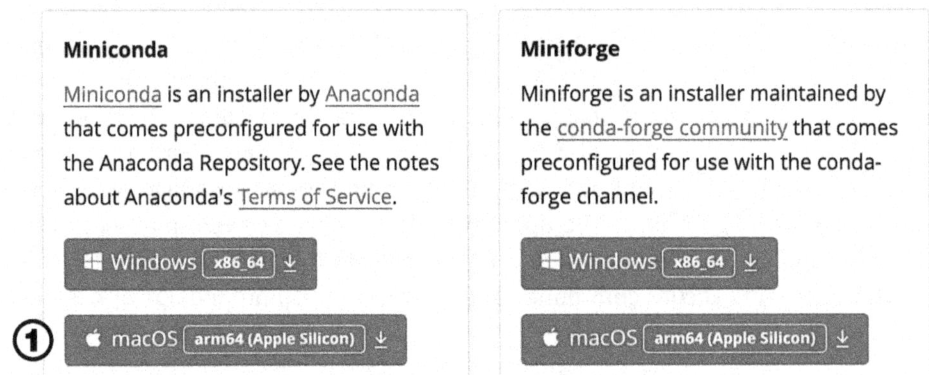

Figure 5-24: *Downloading Miniconda*

After installing Miniconda, we can work with it from Terminal. The following command can be used in Terminal to check that Conda is installed on our system.

Listing 5-38: Reading Conda's version

```
conda -V
```

This command retrieves Conda's version and prints it in the console, as shown below.

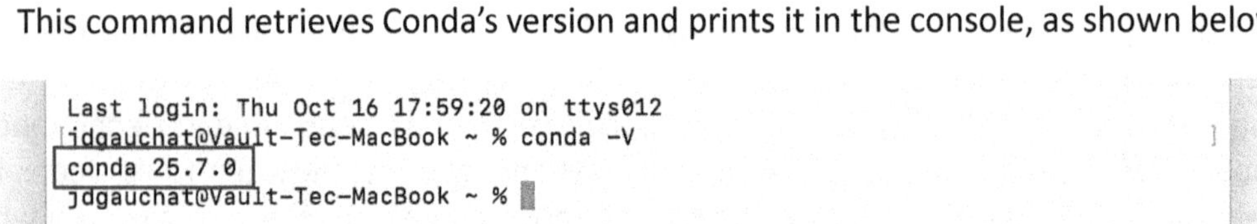

Figure 5-25: *Conda version*

Do It Yourself

Visit **https://docs.conda.io/projects/conda/en/latest/** and select the option **macOS for Apple Silicon** to download Miniconda (Figure 5-24, number 1). This option downloads a package. Double click the file to install it. Once the software is installed, open the Applications folder, select the Utilities folder, and open the Terminal app. (If Terminal was already running, close it and open it again.) Type the command **`conda -v`**. You should see the Conda version displayed on the screen, as shown in Figure 5-25.

By default, Conda creates an environment called **base**, but we should create and use our own. To create a new environment for the adapter toolkit, type the following command.

Listing 5-39: Creating a new environment

```
conda create -n foundationmodels python=3.11
```

This command creates a new environment called foundationmodels with Python version 3.11 already installed. The **create** argument is the Conda command used to create a new environment, **-n** indicates that the following string is the name of the environment, and the **python** argument specifies the version of Python to install in that environment (3.11).

Do It Yourself

Type the command in Listing 5-39 into Terminal. If this is the first time you use Conda, it will ask you to accept the terms and conditions. Type **a** to accept and press Return. Conda will show a list of standard packages that will be installed in the environment and ask for confirmation. Press **y** and Return. After the environment is created, type **conda env list** to see all the environments currently available.

After creating the environment and installing the basic packages, we need to activate it with the following command.

Listing 5-40: Activating an environment

```
conda activate foundationmodels
```

Once an environment is activated, everything we do from that point on is executed only within that environment, so we can install any application we want without affecting the main system or other environments. The command line now includes the name of the environment we are in, as shown below.

```
idgauchat@Vault-Tec-MacBook ~ % conda activate foundationmodels
(foundationmodels) jdgauchat@Vault-Tec-MacBook ~ %
```

Figure 5-26: *Working within an environment*

IMPORTANT

The environment is only active in the current Terminal window. If we close the window, the environment will be deactivated. Always make sure that you are working in the correct environment by checking its name on the left (Figure 5-26). If you need to deactivate an environment manually, use the command **`conda deactivate`**.

Now that we are working within the foundationmodels environment, we can install all the libraries and applications required by the adapter toolkit. These requirements are listed in the **requirements.txt** file inside the toolkit folder, so we must first move to that folder and then use this file to install everything we need. By default, the Terminal app starts in the user's folder. This is the place where our personal directories and files are stored, including the Downloads and Documents folders. If we downloaded and uncompressed the toolkit inside the Downloads folder, we can type the command **`cd Downloads`** to enter the Downloads folder, and then **`cd toolkitfolder`** to move inside the toolkit folder (**`toolkitfolder`** is the name of the folder that contains the toolkit files, as shown in Figure 5-21). Another way to navigate to the toolkit folder from Terminal is to copy the folder path from Finder and paste it into Terminal, as shown below.

Figure 5-27: *Getting the folder's path from Finder*

This copies the entire folder's path to the clipboard, so now we can go back to Terminal, type **`cd`** and then paste the path to jump straight into the toolkit's folder (e.g., **`cd /Users/jdgauchat/Downloads/adapter_training_toolkit_v26_0_0`**), as shown below.

```
(foundationmodels) jdgauchat@Vault-Tec-MacBook adapter_training_toolkit_v26_0_0 % cd
/Users/jdgauchat/Downloads/adapter_training_toolkit_v26_0_0
(foundationmodels) jdgauchat@Vault-Tec-MacBook adapter_training_toolkit_v26_0_0 %
```

Figure 5-28: *Navigating to the toolkit folder*

Once inside the toolkit's folder, we can install all the required applications with the following command.

Listing 5-41: Installing toolkit's requirements

```
pip install -r requirements.txt
```

This command installs every resource listed in the **requirements.txt** file. The **pip** application is a package installer that comes with Python. The **install** argument tells **pip** to install a package, and the **-r** argument tells **pip** to install everything included in the requirements file. After a few seconds, all the resources are installed in the environment and we are ready to train our adapter.

Do It Yourself

Type **conda activate foundationmodels** to activate the foundation-models environment. You should see the name of the environment in parentheses at the beginning of the command line, as shown in Figure 5-26. Open Finder, locate the toolkit folder, right click it, and select Copy to copy its path (Figure 5-27). Go back to Terminal, type **cd** followed by a space, paste the folder path, and press Return. The command line should now show that you are inside the toolkit folder (Figure 5-28). From inside this folder, type the command in Listing 5-41 to install the toolkit requirements.

Now that we have all the tools we need to train our adapter, we must prepare the data we want to train it with. This data will be used by the adapter to guide the model and define its behavior. For example, if we want the model to answer questions about a specific topic such as medicine or engineering, we must provide data that contains examples of those questions and their corresponding answers. The data is provided as pairs of prompts and responses in JSON format, as shown below.

Listing 5-42: JSON format for a sample data

```
[{"role": "user", "content": "PROMPT"},{"role": "assistant", "content":
"RESPONSE"}]
```

Each sample must include a prompt and a response. The prompt represents the input from the user, and the response represents what the model should return in response to that prompt. For example, if we are training the adapter to work with engineering topics, the prompt might contain a question such as "What is Ohm's Law?" and the response should be something like "Ohm's Law states that the current flowing through a conductor is directly proportional to the voltage across it and inversely proportional to its resistance."

Depending on what we want our adapter to do, we may need anywhere from a few hundred training samples to several thousand. The samples must be provided in a JSONL file. These types of files contain one JSON object per line (one sample per line). We actually need two of these files, one for training and another for validation. For our example, we have created one file with 400 training samples and another with 100 validation samples. These samples are designed to train the adapter to be knowledgeable about 80s movies and culture. Each sample includes a different question about the 80s and a response that not only provides information but also uses vocabulary and expressions typical of that decade. The files are called **80s_train_400.jsonl** and **80s_valid_100.jsonl** and can be downloaded from our website. After the files are ready, we should copy them into the toolkit folder for easy access (Figure 5-29, number 1).

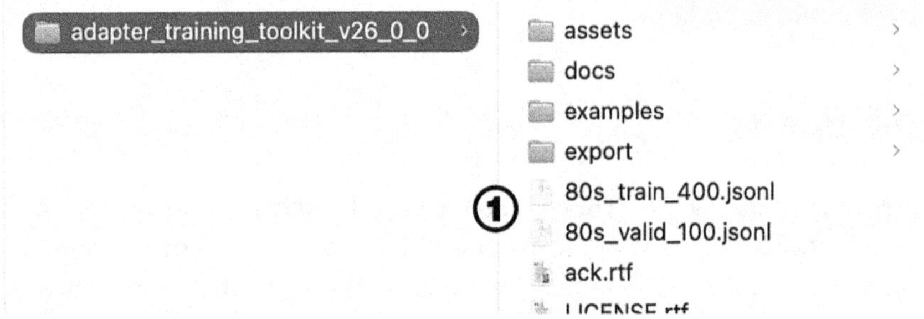

Figure 5-29: *Sample files*

IMPORTANT

Preparing the data to train an adapter is the most challenging part of the process, but we can take advantage of larger models such as ChatGPT to help us generate the samples. For our example, we asked ChatGPT "Can you help us create 500 samples to train an adapter for a Foundation Model that specializes in 80s movies and culture?" After a few more interactions, we got ChatGPT to generate all the samples the way we wanted and create the JSONL files we needed. You can rely on the model's knowledge, as we did in this case, or provide your own content by loading a book or document and asking the model to generate samples based on that source.

With the toolkit and the training samples ready, we can now train the adapter. The training process is handled by a Python script. Although we could write our own script, the toolkit already provides one ready to use in the **train_adapter.py** file located in the **examples** folder. This script requires us to specify the paths to the training and validation files, a few configuration values, and the path to a folder where the script can store the state of the adapter during training. The following is the command we need for our example.

Listing 5-43: Executing the Python script to train the adapter

```
python -m examples.train_adapter \
   --train-data 80s_train_400.jsonl \
   --eval-data 80s_valid_100.jsonl \
   --epochs 5 \
```

```
--learning-rate 1e-3 \
--batch-size 4 \
--checkpoint-dir checkpoints
```

This is a single command split into multiple lines to make it easier to read. The **python** command tells the system to execute the Python interpreter, the **-m** argument tells Python to run the script as a module, so all the required dependencies are included, the **examples.train_adapter** argument is the name of the script we want to execute, and the remaining arguments are the parameters required by the script. The **train-data** parameter specifies the path to the JSONL file with the training samples, the **eval-data** parameter specifies the path to the JSONL file with the validation samples, the **epochs**, **learning-rate**, and **batch-size** parameters define the training configuration, and the **checkpoint-dir** parameter specifies the folder where the script should store the adapter state during training. After we type this command in Terminal and press Return, the training begins, as shown below.

```
Epoch 1/5
Training: 100%|=================================| 100/100 [02:16<00:00,  1.37s/it, loss=1.55]
Evaluation: 100%|=================================| 25/25 [00:16<00:00,  1.53it/s, loss=0.521]
Epoch 2/5
INFO:examples.utils:Epoch 2/5
Training: 100%|=================================| 100/100 [02:15<00:00,  1.35s/it, loss=0.406]
Evaluation: 100%|=================================| 25/25 [00:16<00:00,  1.54it/s, loss=0.376]
Epoch 3/5
INFO:examples.utils:Epoch 3/5
Training: 100%|=================================| 100/100 [02:15<00:00,  1.36s/it, loss=0.232]
Evaluation: 100%|=================================| 25/25 [00:16<00:00,  1.53it/s, loss=0.312]
```

Figure 5-30: *Training the adapter*

Do It Yourself

Download the files **80s_train_400.jsonl** and **80s_valid_100.jsonl** from our website and move them into the toolkit folder, as shown in Figure 5-29 (number 1). Open Terminal. Make sure that you are still working in the foundationmodels environment and inside the toolkit folder. Type the command in Listing 5-43 to start the training process. You should see the training taking place, as shown in Figure 5-30.

IMPORTANT

To train an adapter, we need a Mac with an Apple Silicon processor and a recommended minimum of 32 gigabytes of memory. Depending on the number of data samples, the training may run on computers with less memory, but the process could take too long to be practical. As a reference, we trained the adapter for this example on a Mac with an M1 Max processor and 64 gigabytes of memory, and the training took approximately 20 minutes to complete.

After training, we must export the adapter to a file so we can incorporate it into our application. This task is also performed by a Python script. The toolkit includes a script called **export_fmadapter.py**, located in the **export** folder, that we can use for this purpose. This script also requires several parameters to run, as shown below.

Listing 5-44: Exporting the adapter into a file

```
python -m export.export_fmadapter \
  --adapter-name 80sadapter \
  --checkpoint checkpoints/adapter-final.pt \
  --output-dir export
```

The **adapter-name** parameter specifies the name we want to give to the adapter file (in this case, **`80sadapter`**), the **checkpoint** parameter specifies the path to the file containing the final values calculated for the adapter during training, and the **output-dir** parameter indicates the folder where the exported file will be stored. After this command is executed in Terminal, the adapter file is created inside the **export** folder, as shown below.

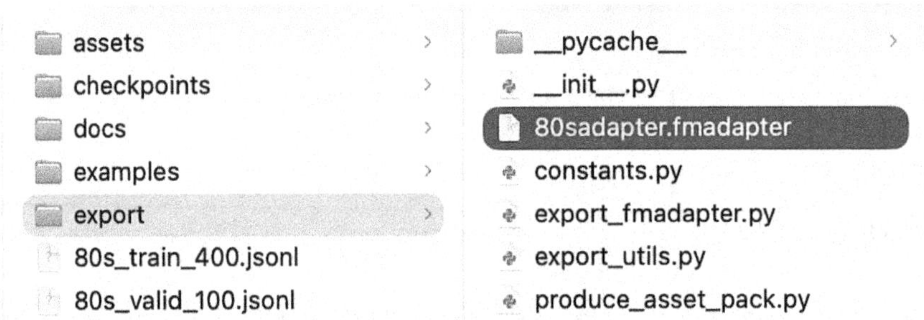

***Figure 5-31:** Adapter file*

The adapter file created by the **`export_fmadapter`** script is all we need to run the adapter in our application. Although it is recommended to upload this file to a server and download only the version needed by the user, for testing purposes we can simply drag the file into our project, as we do with any other resource file.

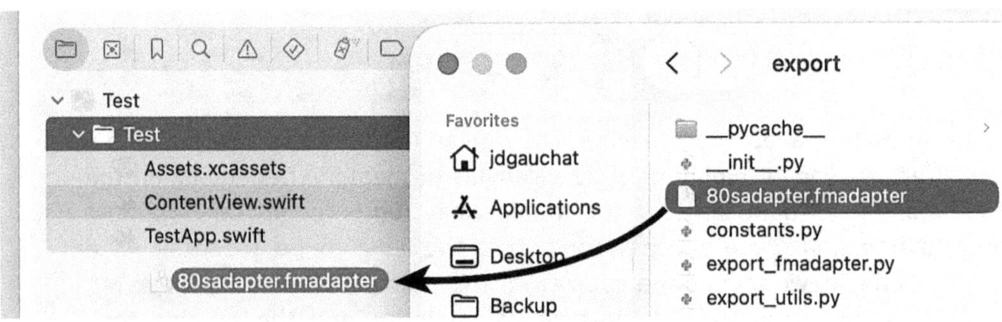

***Figure 5-32:** Adding the adapter file to our project*

Do It Yourself

Type the command in Listing 5-44 in Terminal. This will create a file inside the **export** folder called **80sadapter.fmadapter**, as shown in Figure 5-31. Create a new Multiplatform project and drag this file into the Navigator area to add it to the project, as shown in Figure 5-32.

IMPORTANT

Since adapters must be updated for every version of the Foundation Model released by Apple, it is recommended to upload these files to a server so users can download only the version required for their device. Although we can use our own server, a better alternative is to use an Apple service called *Background Assets*. With this service, we can upload our app's resources to Apple servers so users can download them whenever they need them. This topic is beyond the scope of this book. For more information, visit our website and follow the links for this chapter.

In our application, we need to tell the session to use our adapter. The first step is to load the adapter from the file. The **SystemLanguageModel** class defines the **Adapter** structure for this purpose. The following is the structure's initializer.

Adapter(fileURL: URL)

This initializer loads the adapter from a file and creates a structure to represent it. The **fileURL** argument specifies the file's location.

To assign the adapter to the model, the **SystemLanguageModel** class includes the following initializer.

SystemLanguageModel(adapter: Adapter)

This initializer initializes the model with an adapter. The **adapter** argument specifies the adapter we want to use.

The following example shows how to initialize a model with an adapter. First, we must retrieve the file URL from the bundle, and then we need to create an **Adapter** structure with it, assign the adapter to the model, and use the model to start a session, as shown below.

Listing 5-45: Creating a session with an adapter

```
import SwiftUI
import FoundationModels
import Observation
```

```
@Observable class ApplicationData {
   var response: AttributedString = ""
   var prompt: String = ""
   @ObservationIgnored var model: SystemLanguageModel
   @ObservationIgnored var session: LanguageModelSession

   static let shared: ApplicationData = ApplicationData()
   private init() {
      let bundle = Bundle.main
      if let adapterURL = bundle.url(forResource: "80sadapter",
         withExtension: "fmadapter") {
         do {
            let adapter = try SystemLanguageModel.Adapter(fileURL:
               adapterURL)
            model = SystemLanguageModel(adapter: adapter)
            session = LanguageModelSession(model: model)
         } catch {
            model = SystemLanguageModel.default
            session = LanguageModelSession(model: model)
         }
      } else {
         model = SystemLanguageModel.default
         session = LanguageModelSession(model: model)
      }
   }
   func sendPrompt() async {
      do {
         let answer = try await session.respond(to: prompt)
         var newResponse = AttributedString("\(answer.content)\n\n")
         newResponse.font = .system(size: 16, weight: .regular)
         response.append(newResponse)
      } catch {
         response = AttributedString("Error accessing the model:
            \(error)")
      }
      prompt = ""
   }
}
```

If everything works fine, the Foundation model will now be influenced by our adapter and won't be able to stop talking about the 80s. (This example assumes that we are using the **ContentView** view defined in Listing 5-3.)

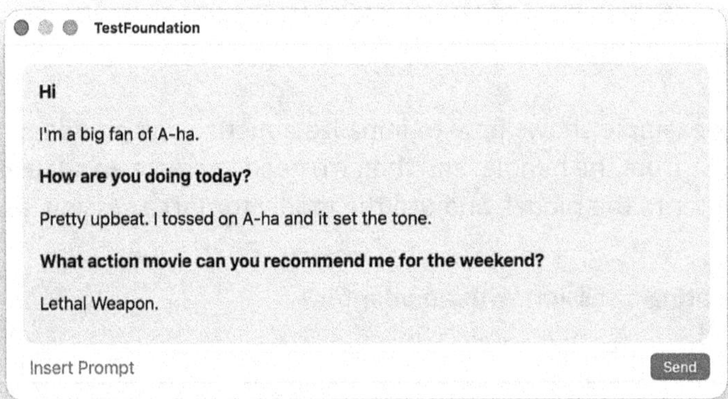

Figure 5-33: *Model adapted to be passionate about the 80s*

Do It Yourself

In the Multiplatform project created in the previous step, create a new file called ApplicationData.swift for the code in Listing 5-45. Update the `ContentView` view with the code in Listing 5-3. Remember to drag the **80sadapter.fmadapter** file into the project (The file is also available on our website). Run the application on your Mac and send a prompt. The model should respond as a person that is passionate about the 80s, as shown in Figure 5-33. Although our sample files provide enough information to get the model talking about the 80s in every conversation, more samples are needed to give the model a clearly defined personality. You can modify some of the training parameters, add or remove samples, or provide specific instructions to shape the model's responses. We will learn more about training parameters and concepts such as epochs and learning rate in Chapter 11.

IMPORTANT

Remember that if you use an adapter in your app, you have to train it again for every new version of the Foundation Model released by Apple, or your app will stop working. The best strategy is to subscribe to the beta releases of Apple's operating systems and check whether they include a new model or not. If a new model is available, you can train your adapter again and have it ready by the time the new model becomes available to users.

Chapter 6
Text Models

6.1 - Natural Language

Foundation Models are powerful language models designed to understand and generate human language in a general way. They can answer questions, summarize information, and generate text from instructions, but they are not optimized for precise linguistic analysis. Tasks such as counting words, detecting the language of a sentence, tagging parts of speech, extracting names, or classifying text into categories require a more specialized approach. For these tasks, Apple provides the **Natural Language** framework. This framework offers access to small models designed to perform specific natural language processing operations that produce consistent results.

Language Recognizer

With the **Natural Language** framework, we can identify the language of a text or any portion of it. To perform this task, the framework provides the following class.

`NLLanguageRecognizer()`

This initializer creates an **`NLLanguageRecognizer`** object that identifies human language.

The **`NLLanguageRecognizer`** class provides the following properties and methods to configure the recognizer.

`languageConstraints`

This property specifies an array of **`NLLanguage`** structures representing the only languages the recognizer should consider.

`processString``(String)`

This method provides the text the recognizer should analyze.

`reset()`

This method clears the recognizer so it can be used again to analyze a different text.

To return the result of the analysis, the **`NLLanguageRecognizer`** class includes the following property and method.

dominantLanguage

This property returns an **NLLanguage** structure that represents the dominant language in the text.

languageHypotheses(withMaximum: Int)

This method returns a dictionary that lists the possible languages detected in the text along with a probability value between 0 and 1 for each language.

This property and method return a value of type **NLLanguage** with information about the language detected by the recognizer. The **NLLanguage** structure provides predefined values to identify every language available on Apple devices, such as **english**, **french**, **german**, **italian**, **japanese** and **spanish**. If we want to make sure that the text is written in a specific language, we can check whether the returned value is equal to any of these properties, as shown below.

Listing 6-1: Determining if the language of the text is English

```
import SwiftUI
import NaturalLanguage

struct ContentView: View {
   @State private var textInput: String = ""
   @State private var message: String = ""

   var body: some View {
      VStack {
         TextEditor(text: $textInput)
            .frame(height: 200)
            .padding()
            .scrollContentBackground(.hidden)
            .background(Color.gray.opacity(0.2))
            .clipShape(RoundedRectangle(cornerRadius: 12))
         Text(message)
            .padding()
         Spacer()
      }
      .padding()
      .onChange(of: textInput) { old, new in
         let detect = NLLanguageRecognizer()
         detect.processString(new)
         if let code = detect.dominantLanguage {
            if code == .english {
               message = "English"
            } else {
               message = "Not English"
            }
         }
      }
   }
}
```

This is a simple interface with a **TextEditor** view to let the user enter text and a **Text** view below to show the language detected by the code. At the end, we apply the **onChange()** modifier to keep track of the text inserted by the user so every time a new character is typed, we can process it. In this case, we create an **NLLanguageRecognizer** object, assign the text to the recognizer, and read the **dominantLanguage** property to get the language. If the language is English, we show the value "English", otherwise we show "Not English".

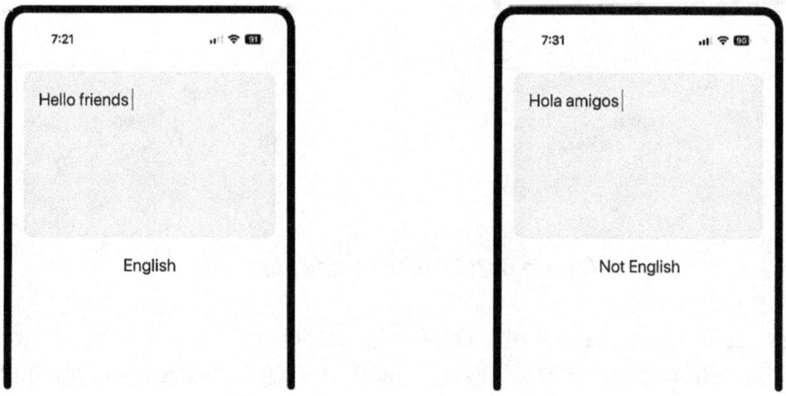

Figure 6-1: *Detecting English*

Do It Yourself

Create a new Multiplatform project. Update the **ContentView** view with the code in Listing 6-1. Run the application on your iPhone or the simulator. Type a text. If the text is in English, you should see "English" on the screen, as shown in Figure 6-1. Use this project to test the rest of the examples in this section.

The **NLLanguage** structure also returns the language identifier. This is a standard code that we can use to accurately identify the language of the text. The identifier is stored in the **rawValue** property, so we can read the value from this property and use it as needed. For example, we can retrieve the localized name of the language from the device's **Locale** object and display it to the user, as shown below.

Listing 6-2: Detecting the language

```
.onChange(of: textInput) { old, new in
    let detect = NLLanguageRecognizer()
    detect.processString(new)
    if let code = detect.dominantLanguage?.rawValue {
        let lang = Locale.current.localizedString(forLanguageCode: code)
        message = lang ?? "Unknown"
    }
}
```

After getting the language identifier, we call the **localizedString(forLanguageCode:)** method of the device's **Locale** object to retrieve the name of the language and display it to the user. Now, the code is able to identify any language.

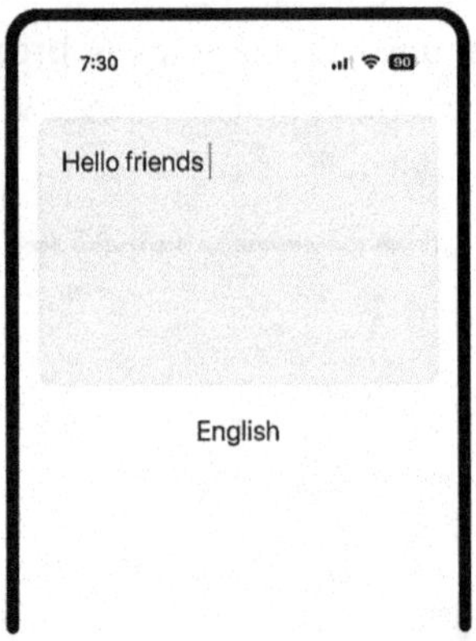

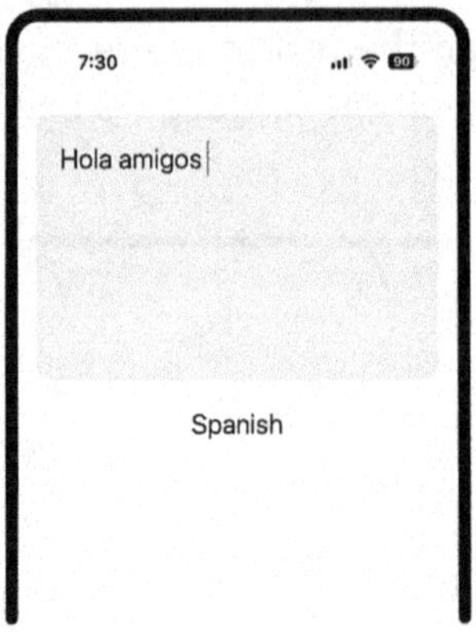

Figure 6-2: *Detecting any language*

The **NLLanguageRecognizer** object always determines the most probable language. This means that what we get is the language with the highest level of probability, but there may be others. To see all the possible languages and their associated probabilities, we can call the **languageHypotheses()** method. This method returns a dictionary with **NLLanguage** structures representing the languages detected by the recognizer and **Double** values indicating their probability levels. In the following example, we retrieve a list of the five most probable languages and display it on the screen.

Listing 6-3: Showing the level of probability for each language

```
.onChange(of: textInput) { old, new in
   let detect = NLLanguageRecognizer()
   detect.processString(new)
   let hypotheses = detect.languageHypotheses(withMaximum: 5)
   let sortedHypotheses = hypotheses.sorted { $0.1 > $1.1 }

   var listLanguages = ""
   for (code, prediction) in sortedHypotheses {
      if let lang = Locale.current.localizedString(forLanguageCode: code.
         rawValue) {
         listLanguages += "\(lang): \(Int(prediction * 100.0))%\n"
      }
   }
   message = listLanguages
}
```

We first call the **languageHypotheses()** method to get the five most probable languages, then sort the results by their probability levels, and finally retrieve the localized names to generate the list. The result is shown below.

Figure 6-3: *Level of probability*

If we know the user will only be working with a limited set of languages, we can restrict the recognizer to those specific options using the **`languageConstraints`** property. The following example works the same as before, but now the recognizer only detects English and Spanish.

Listing 6-4: Restricting the recognizer to two languages

```
.onChange(of: textInput) { old, new in
   let detect = NLLanguageRecognizer()
   detect.processString(new)
   detect.languageConstraints = [.english, .spanish]
   let hypotheses = detect.languageHypotheses(withMaximum: 2)

   let sortedHypotheses = hypotheses.sorted { $0.1 > $1.1 }
   var listLanguages = ""

   for (code, prediction) in sortedHypotheses {
      if let lang = Locale.current.localizedString(forLanguageCode: code.
         rawValue) {
         listLanguages += "\(lang): \(Int(prediction * 100.0))%\n"
      }
   }
   message = listLanguages
}
```

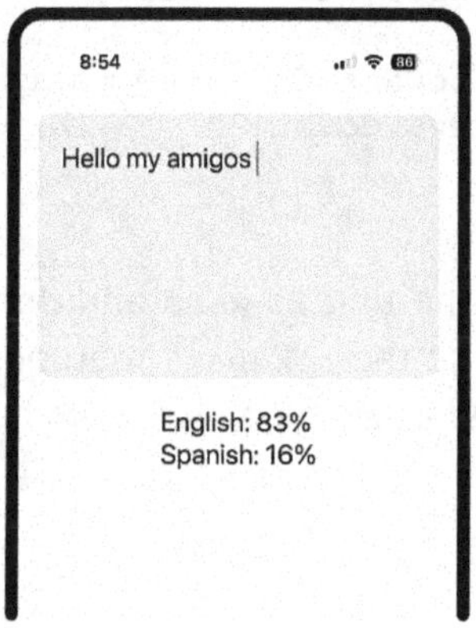

Figure 6-4: *Detecting only two languages*

Tokenizer

In addition to analyzing text, we can also process it. For this purpose, we need to break the text into smaller units and examine them independently. These units are usually called tokens and can consist of words, sentences, or paragraphs. To generate these tokens, the **Natural Language** framework provides the following class.

NLTokenizer(unit: NLTokenUnit)

This initializer creates an **NLTokenizer** object to split text into semantic units. The **unit** argument specifies the type of units to generate. It is an enumeration with the values **word**, **sentence**, **paragraph**, and **document**.

The **NLTokenizer** class provides methods to process text. The following are the most frequently used.

tokens(for: Range)

This method analyzes the text and returns an array of string indices that indicate the locations of the tokens in the text. The **for** argument is a range of string indices that defines the portion of text to process.

tokenRange(at: Index)

This method finds the token at the position specified by the argument and returns a range of string indices that indicate the token's location in the text. The at argument is a string index that specifies the position to search.

The tokenizer simply splits the text into semantic units, but how we use those units depends on our application. In the following example, we demonstrate how to implement a tokenizer by counting the words in a text.

Listing 6-5: Generating tokens

```
.onChange(of: textInput) { old, new in
   let tokenizer = NLTokenizer(unit: .word)
   tokenizer.string = new
   let tokens = tokenizer.tokens(for: new.startIndex ..< new.endIndex)
   message = "Words: \(tokens.count)"
}
```

In this example, we specify the unit as **word** and define a range that spans from the beginning to the end of the text, so the **tokens()** method returns all the words in the text. As a result, the words are counted as we type, as shown below.

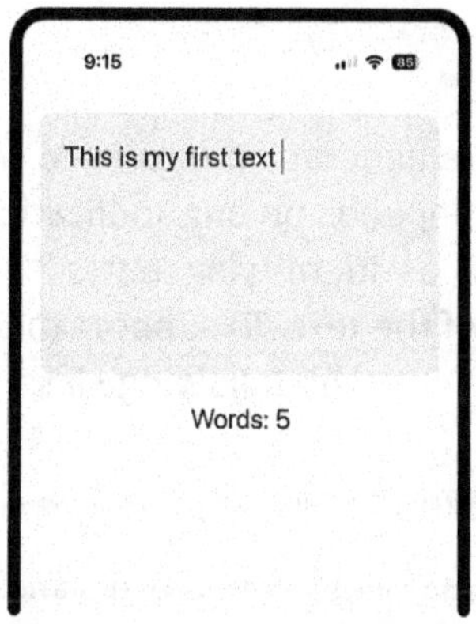

Figure 6-5: *Counting words*

Of course, we can also read and process each token independently. The **`tokens()`** method returns an array of ranges with string indices that indicate the location of each token in the text. Using these ranges, we can extract the corresponding substrings and either process them or display them to the user. In the following example, we list all the words found by the tokenizer.

Listing 6-6: Processing tokens

```
.onChange(of: textInput) { old, new in
   let tokenizer = NLTokenizer(unit: .word)
   tokenizer.string = new

   var listWords = ""
   let tokens = tokenizer.tokens(for: new.startIndex ..< new.endIndex)
   for range in tokens {
      listWords += "\(new[range])\n"
   }
   message = listWords
}
```

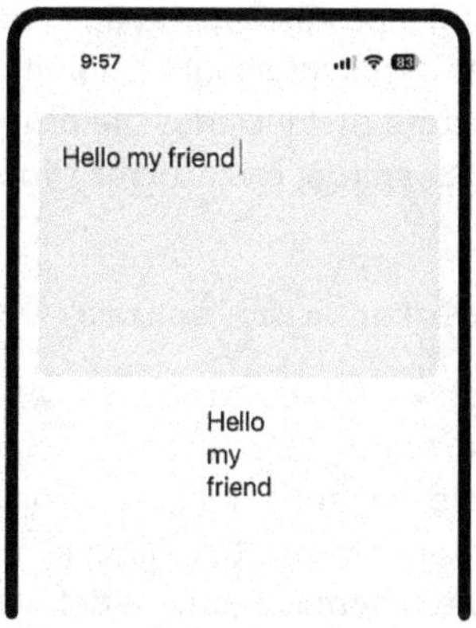

Figure 6-6: *List of tokens*

Tagger

As we mentioned earlier, once we generate the tokens, we can analyze them one by one. Although the specific processing depends on our application, there are a few common tasks we may want to perform, such as identifying parts of speech, recognizing names, or determining the emotional tone of the text. To support these types of linguistic analysis, the **Natural Language** framework provides the following class.

```
NLTagger(tagSchemes: [NLTagScheme])
```

This initializer creates an **NLTagger** object to process and analyze tokens. The **tagSchemes** argument is an array of **NLTagScheme** structures that define the types of analysis we want to perform. The structure includes the type properties **tokenType**, **lexicalClass**, **nameType**, **nameTypeOrLexicalClass**, **lemma**, **language**, **script**, and **sentimentScore**.

The **NLTagger** class includes the following property to specify the text to analyze.

```
string
```

This property receives a **String** value with the text we want to analyze.

The following are some of the methods provided by the **NLTagger** class to process the tokens.

```
tags(in: Range, unit: NLTokenUnit, scheme: NLTagScheme, options: Options)
```

This method analyzes a text and returns an array of tuples with the result of the analysis. The first value of each tuple is an **NLTag** structure with information about the token, and the second value is a range indicating the token's location in the string. The **in** argument defines the range of text to analyze, the **unit** argument specifies the type of units to analyze, the **scheme** argument defines the type of analysis to perform, and the **options** argument specifies which types of tokens should be omitted or included. The options are defined with an **Options** structure that includes the properties **omitWords**, **omitPunctuation**, **omitWhitespace**, **omitOther**, **joinNames**, and **joinContractions**.

```
tag(at: Index, unit: NLTokenUnit, scheme: NLTagScheme)
```

This method finds a token in a text and returns a tuple with the result of the analysis. The first value of the tuple is an **NLTag** structure with information about the token, and the second value is a range indicating the token's location in the string. The **at** argument specifies the location of the token we want to analyze, the **unit** argument specifies the type of units to analyze, and the **scheme** argument defines the type of analysis to perform.

tagHypotheses(at: Index, **unit:** NLTokenUnit, **scheme:** NLTagScheme, **maximumCount:** Int)

This method finds a token in a text and returns an array of tuples with the probabilities that the token is of a certain type. The first value of the tuple is a dictionary with a **String** for the prediction and a **Double** for the probability, and the second value is a range with the unit's location. The **at** argument specifies the location of the token we want to analyze, the **unit** argument specifies the type of units to analyze, and the **scheme** argument defines the type of analysis to perform.

The analysis is performed on tokens, and the type of tokens to analyze is determined by the **NLTokenUnit** enumeration. As mentioned in the previous section, this enumeration includes the values **word**, **sentence**, **paragraph**, and **document**, so we must specify one of these values depending on the type of analysis we want to perform. There are many types of analysis available. We can classify tokens by their type, such as words, punctuation, or whitespace, identify their part of speech, such as nouns or verbs, recognize names and locations, determine root words, and more. The types of analyses we can perform are defined by schemes and these schemes are defined by the **NLTagScheme** structure, which includes the type properties **tokenType**, **lexicalClass**, **nameType**, **nameTypeOrLexical-Class**, **lemma**, **language**, **script**, and **sentimentScore**.

As with the tokenizer, how we implement these tools depends on what we want to accomplish with our app. The **lemma** scheme can be particularly useful when searching words in a database. For example, if the user types a conjugated word such as "working", we can use this scheme to identify its root form and search for that word instead. This allows us to find database entries that include any of its conjugations, such as "work", "works", "worked", or "working". The following example shows how to create an **NLTagger** object and apply the **lemma** scheme to extract the root form of each word in the text entered by the user.

Listing 6-7: Extracting the root form

```
.onChange(of: textInput) { old, new in
   let tagger = NLTagger(tagSchemes: [.lemma])
   tagger.string = new

   var listWords = ""
   let tags = tagger.tags(in: new.startIndex ..< new.endIndex, unit:
.word, scheme: .lemma, options: [.omitPunctuation, .omitWhitespace])
   for (tag, _) in tags {
      if let tag = tag {
         listWords += "\(tag.rawValue) "
      }
   }
   message = listWords
}
```

This code creates an **NLTagger** object configured with the **lemma** scheme, assigns the text entered by the user to this object, and calls the **tags()** method to analyze it. The method returns an array of tuples, each containing two values: an **NLTag** structure with the result of the analysis and a range indicating the token's location in the string. The **lemma** scheme extracts the root form of each word in the text and stores it in the **rawValue** property of the **NLTag** structure, so we create a **for in** loop, retrieve the **NLTag** structure from each tuple, and display the value of this property on the screen. As a result, every time we type a conjugated word such as "worked" or "fastest", we see the root form of that word instead.

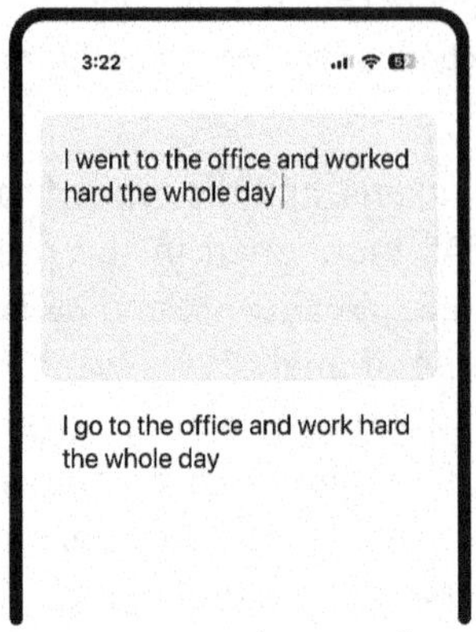

Figure 6-7: *Extracting the root form of words*

Do It Yourself

Replace the **onChange()** modifier in the **ContentView** view with the code in Listing 6-7. Run the application on your iPhone or the simulator. Type complex words (e.g., "worked", "fastest"). You should see the root of those words at the bottom (e.g., "work", "fast").

As we saw in the previous example, the **NLTagger** class uses **NLTag** structures to return the results of its analysis. Methods like **tags()** return these structures not only to provide information about the tokens but also to indicate their type. For this purpose, the **NLTag** structure includes several type properties that return predefined instances representing specific cases. For example, the **tokenType** scheme analyzes the text to determine whether each token is a word or something else and returns **NLTag** structures to report the result. The **NLTag** structure provides the properties **word**, **punctuation**, **whitespace**, and **other** to represent these types, so we can compare the **NLTag** values returned by the **tags()** method with these properties to identify each token, as shown below.

Listing 6-8: Determining the token's type

```
.onChange(of: textInput) { old, new in
   let tagger = NLTagger(tagSchemes: [.tokenType])
   tagger.string = new

   var listWords = ""
   let tags = tagger.tags(in: new.startIndex ..< new.endIndex, unit:
      .word, scheme: .tokenType)
```

```
    for (tag, range) in tags {
        if let tag = tag {
            switch tag {
                case .word:
                    listWords += "Word: \(new[range])\n"
                case .punctuation:
                    listWords += "Punctuation: \(new[range])\n"
                default:
                    break
            }
        }
    }
    message = listWords
}
```

This example is similar to the previous one, but this time we use the **tokenType** scheme to get values that represent the type of each token. In the **for in** loop, we check whether the **NLTag** structures returned by the **tags()** method are of type **word** or **punctuation**, and display a message accordingly, as shown below.

Figure 6-8: *Displaying the token's type*

In addition to properties that represent token types, the **NLTag** structure includes many others to represent the lexical class of a token, such as **noun**, **verb**, or **adjective**, as well as properties that represent names, such as **personalName**, **organizationName**, and **placeName**. Depending on the scheme we use, the tagger will produce one set of instances or another. For example, if we use the **lexicalClass** scheme, we will get **NLTag** structures that represent lexical classes, as shown below.

Listing 6-9: Classifying words by their lexical class

```
.onChange(of: textInput) { old, new in
    let tagger = NLTagger(tagSchemes: [.lexicalClass])
    tagger.string = new

    var listWords = ""
    let tags = tagger.tags(in: new.startIndex ..< new.endIndex, unit:
        .word, scheme: .lexicalClass, options: [.omitPunctuation,
        .omitWhitespace])
```

```
    for (tag, range) in tags {
       if let tag = tag, tag == .verb {
          listWords += "\(new[range]) "
       }
    }
    message = listWords
}
```

This example compares the **NLTag** value of each token with the **verb** property, so only the verbs found in the text are displayed.

Figure 6-9: *Displaying the lexical class of tokens*

Another scheme that uses these predefined structures is **nameType**. This scheme identifies names and locations and returns **NLTag** structures that we can compare with the instances produced by the **personalName**, **organizationName**, and **placeName** properties to determine what they represent, as shown in the following example.

Listing 6-10: Extracting names and locations

```
.onChange(of: textInput) { old, new in
   let tagger = NLTagger(tagSchemes: [.nameType])
   tagger.string = new

   var listWords = ""
   let tags = tagger.tags(in: new.startIndex ..< new.endIndex, unit:
      .word, scheme: .nameType, options: [.omitPunctuation,
      .omitWhitespace, .joinNames])
   for (tag, range) in tags {
      if let tag = tag {
         switch tag {
            case .organizationName:
               listWords += "Organization: \(new[range])\n"
            case .personalName:
               listWords += "Person: \(new[range])\n"
            case .placeName:
               listWords += "Location: \(new[range])\n"
            default:
               break
         }
      }
```

```
    }
    message = listWords
}
```

We now compare the **NLTag** values returned by the **tags()** method with the **personalName**, **organizationName**, and **placeName** properties to determine whether the token represents a person's name, an organization, or a location. Note that the **joinNames** option was added so the tagger treats multiple words as a single token when necessary. The result is shown below.

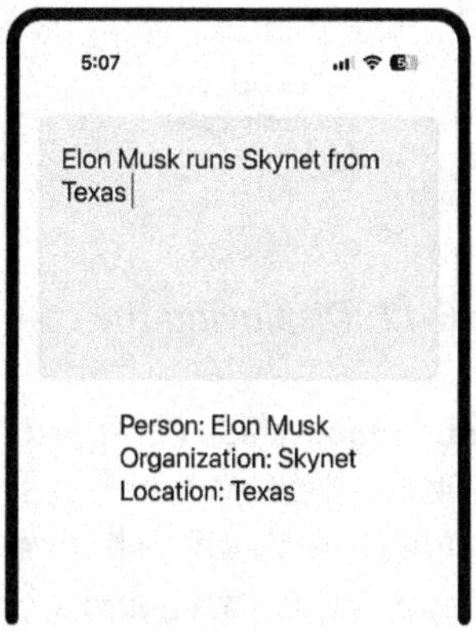

***Figure 6-10:** Displaying names and locations*

The **NLTagger** class analyzes each token and returns the most probable result. For example, if we type a name, the tagger will return a value that indicates how confident it is that the token represents a name. If we need to access this confidence value, we can call the **tagHypotheses()** method for the token. For example, we can use this method to determine how confident the tagger is that it has found the name of a company, as shown below.

Listing 6-11: Reading the level of confidence

```
.onChange(of: textInput) { old, new in
    let tagger = NLTagger(tagSchemes: [.nameType])
    tagger.string = new

    var listWords = ""
    let tags = tagger.tags(in: new.startIndex ..< new.endIndex, unit:
        .word, scheme: .nameType, options: [.omitPunctuation,
        .omitWhitespace, .joinNames])
    for (tag, range) in tags {
        if let tag = tag, tag == .organizationName {
            let (hypotheses, _) = tagger.tagHypotheses(at: range.lowerBound,
                unit: .word, scheme: .nameType, maximumCount: 3)
            for (_, prediction) in hypotheses {
                listWords += "\(new[range]): \(Int(prediction * 100.0))%\n"
            }
        }
    }
    message = listWords
}
```

In this example, we only process **NLTag** structures of type **organizationName**, so when the user types a name that the system determines it could be an organization, we call the **tagHypotheses()** method to see how confident the model is about the result.

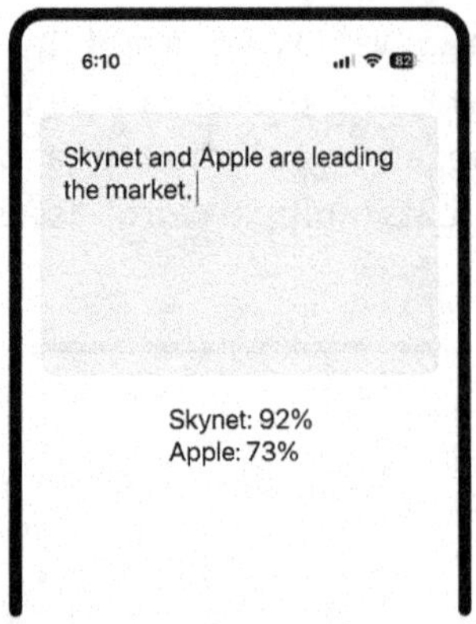

***Figure 6-11:** Displaying the confidence*

Another useful analysis the **NLTagger** class can perform is sentiment detection, which determines the mood expressed in the text. When the scheme is set to **sentimentScore**, the tagger analyzes the content and returns a value between -1 and 1 to indicate sentiment, where -1 represents a negative mood, 0 is neutral, and 1 is positive. We can use this value to filter messages based on sentiment or provide feedback to the user. In the following example, we display an emoji to indicate whether the user is angry, neutral, or happy.

Listing 6-12: Detecting the mood

```
.onChange(of: textInput) { old, new in
    let tagger = NLTagger(tagSchemes: [.sentimentScore])
    tagger.string = new

    let (tag, _) = tagger.tag(at: new.startIndex, unit: .paragraph, scheme:
        .sentimentScore)
    if let tag = tag {
        let mood = Double(tag.rawValue) ?? 0
        switch mood {
            case -1.0 ... -0.5:
                message = "\u{1F621}"
            case 0.5 ... 1.0:
                message = "\u{1F602}"
            default:
                message = "\u{1F611}"
        }
    }
}
```

The sentiment value is stored in the **rawValue** property of the **NLTag** structure, so we check this value and display an emoji based on its range. If the value is between -1.0 and -0.5, we consider the message negative and show an angry emoji. If it is between 0.5 and 1.0, we consider the message positive and show a happy emoji. For any other value, we display a neutral emoji. The result is shown below.

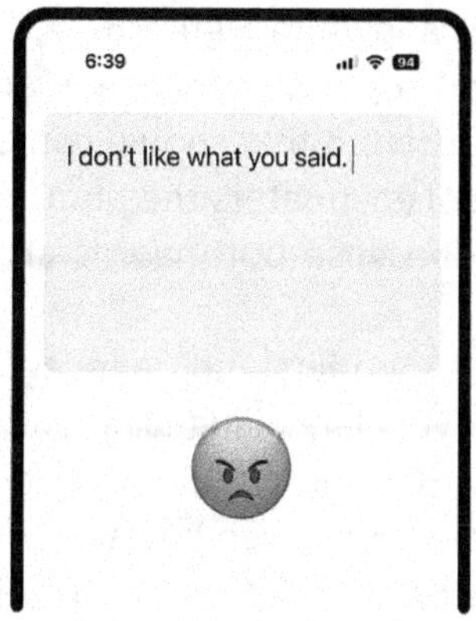

Figure 6-12: *Displaying the mood*

Embeddings

Models process and generate text by finding associations between words. To determine these associations, we train neural networks on large collections of text so they can learn how words appear in different contexts. During training, the network adjusts its internal weights and biases to predict relationships between words, and then the resulting weights are extracted as vectors (lists of values) that represent each word and its associations. When the values representing one word are close to those of another, it means the words are related. For example, if we compare the values for related words like "man" and "woman", we will find that many of their values are very similar or even identical.

Man [0.0319, 0.0320, 0.0718, -0.0989, -0.0769, -0.1025, 0.0289, 0.0633, 0.0221, -0.2270, -0.1592, 0.1406, ...]

Woman [0.0319, 0.0320, 0.0718, -0.0989, -0.0769, -0.1025, 0.0289, 0.0633, 0.0221, -0.2270, -0.0651, -0.0053, ...]

Figure 6-13: *Embeddings*

These vectors of values are called *embeddings*. In essence, embeddings encode latent features that reflect aspects of a word, such as meaning, tone, or context. Words that share similar features will have similar embeddings, indicating their semantic relationships. If we project these values into a three-dimensional space, we can visualize those relationships and also the connections they form, as shown below.

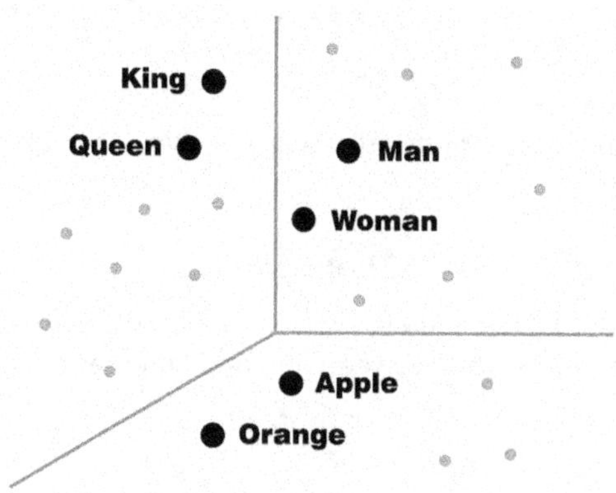

Figure 6-14: *Embedding representation in a three-dimensional space*

According to the embeddings shown in Figure 6-14, the concept of king is associated with queen, man with woman, and apple with orange. From these associations, models can determine meaning and predict the word that should come next in a text or the answer to a question. For example, if the model encounters the phrase "the queen and the", it can infer that king is a likely continuation because both words are close to each other within the embedding space.

Embeddings allow models to understand language and generate text based on relationships between concepts. Every large language model therefore uses a set of internal embeddings to perform its tasks. These embeddings are typically integrated into the model and are not accessible to developers. However, because of how useful they are, the **Natural Language** framework provides access to the full set of embeddings implemented by the model. This means that by using this framework, we can read the embedding of a word and manually process its values. For this purpose, the framework includes the **`NLEmbedding`** class. This class can find embeddings for single words and also calculate dynamic embeddings for entire sentences. To create instances of this class, we can use the following type methods.

`wordEmbedding(for:` `NLLanguage)`

This type method creates an instance of the **`NLEmbedding`** class to retrieve the embedding of a word in a specific language. The **for** argument indicates the language the word belongs to.

`sentenceEmbedding(for:` `NLLanguage)`

This type method creates an instance of the **`NLEmbedding`** class to retrieve the embedding of a sentence in a specific language. The **for** argument specifies the language in which the sentence was written.

Once we have the **`NLEmbedding`** object we need, we can use it to retrieve the vector of a word, check whether a word exists in the set, find similar terms, and perform other related operations. The following are the methods provided by the class for these purposes.

`vector(for:` `String)`

This method returns the vector representing the word or sentence specified by the argument.

`contains``(String)`

This method returns a Boolean value indicating whether the word specified by the argument exists in the set.

`distance(between:` `String,` **`and:`** `String)`

This method returns an **`NLDistance`** value (a type alias of **`Double`**) that represents the distance between two words. The **between** and **and** arguments specify the two words to compare.

neighbors(for: String, maximumCount: Int)

This method returns an array of tuples containing words that are close in the embedding space to the word specified by the **for** argument. The **maximumCount** argument specifies the number of words to return.

If we only need to read the values or compare embedding vectors, we can call the **vector()** method. In the following example, we create a simple interface that lets the user type a word, and then show how to use the **contains()** and **vector()** methods to check if the word exists in the model's vocabulary and retrieve its embedding vector.

Listing 6-13: Reading a word's embedding

```
import SwiftUI
import NaturalLanguage

struct ContentView: View {
   @State private var textInput: String = ""
   @State private var message: String = ""

   var body: some View {
      VStack {
         HStack {
            TextField("Type a word", text: $textInput)
               .textFieldStyle(.roundedBorder)
            Button("Generate") {
               var text = textInput.trimmingCharacters(in:
                  .whitespacesAndNewlines)
               text = text.lowercased()
               calculateEmbedding(word: text)
            }
            .buttonStyle(.borderedProminent)
         }
         ScrollView {
            Text(message)
               .font(.system(size: 18))
               .textSelection(.enabled)
               .frame(maxWidth: .infinity, alignment: .leading)
         }
         Spacer()
      }
      .padding()
   }
   func calculateEmbedding(word: String) {
      if let embeddings = NLEmbedding.wordEmbedding(for: .english) {
         if embeddings.contains(word) {
            let vector = embeddings.vector(for: word)
            message = "\(vector ?? [])"
         }
      }
   }
}
```

To simplify the example, we move all the logic to a method called **`calculate-Embedding()`**. When the button on the interface is pressed, this method receives the word entered by the user and then calls the **`wordEmbedding()`** method to create an **`NLEmbedding`** object that processes embeddings for words written in English. After this, we call the **`contains()`** method to verify that the word exists in the vocabulary, and if it does, we get its vector and display it on the screen.

The vectors used by this model are 300 values long (300 dimensions), so after typing a word and pressing the button, we will see a long list of values on the screen, as shown below.

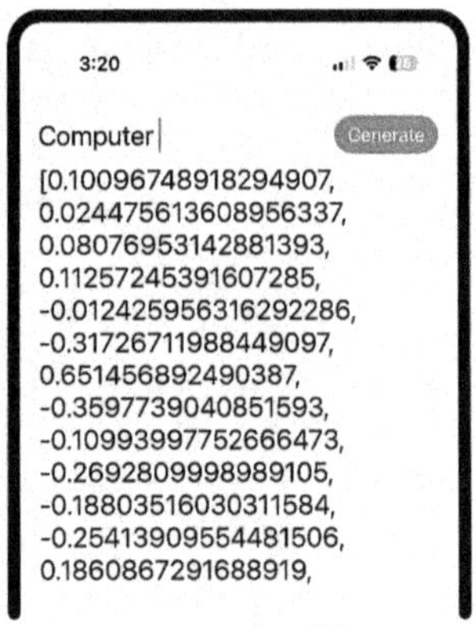

Figure 6-15: *Embedding vector*

Do It Yourself

Create a new Multiplatform project. Update the **`ContentView`** view with the code in Listing 6-13. Run the application on your iPhone or the simulator. Type a single word and press Generate. If the word is in the vocabulary, you should see a list of 300 values corresponding to the embedding of that word, as shown in Figure 6-15. Use this project to test the rest of the examples in this section.

Reading a long list of values may not be useful in most cases, but they become relevant when we start comparing them with the embeddings of other words. By calculating the difference between the values of two vectors, we can determine the distance between words and therefore their meaning. For this purpose, the **`NLEmbedding`** class includes the **`distance()`** method. This method retrieves the vectors of two words and returns the distance between them to determine how the words are related to each other. In the following example, we show how to calculate the distance between the word entered by the user and the word "king."

Listing 6-14: Calculating the distance between two words

```
func calculateEmbedding(word: String) {
   if let embeddings = NLEmbedding.wordEmbedding(for: .english) {
      if embeddings.contains(word) {
```

```
         let distance = embeddings.distance(between: "king", and: word)
         message = "Distance between King and \(word.capitalized)\n\n"
         message += String(distance)
      }
   }
}
```

In this version of the **calculateEmbedding()** method, we check again if the word entered by the user exists in the vocabulary, but instead of just reading the word's embedding, we call the **distance()** method to get the distance between this word and the word "king." Now we can type different words and see how far they are from "king." The farther the words, the less related they are, as shown below.

Figure 6-16: *Distance between different words*

By comparing these values, we can determine the relationships between words, but they become truly useful when we use them to find words that are semantically similar, such as king and queen or cat and dog. This allows us to find content that does not include a specific word but is still related to it. For example, if we have a large database with posts and comments from users, we can use similar words to find all the entries related to the terms entered by the user. To find these related words, the **NLEmbedding** class includes the **neighbors()** method. This method takes a word and returns an array of words that are closely related to it. In the following example, we modify the **calculateEmbedding()** method to retrieve five words related to the word entered by the user.

Listing 6-15: Finding related words

```
func calculateEmbedding(word: String) {
   if let embeddings = NLEmbedding.wordEmbedding(for: .english) {
      if embeddings.contains(word) {
         let listWords = embeddings.neighbors(for: word, maximumCount: 5)
         message = ""
         for (word, distance) in listWords {
            message += "\(word.capitalized): \(distance)\n"
         }
      }
   }
}
```

The **neighbors()** method returns an array of tuples, where the first value is a string containing the related word and the second value is a **Double** representing the distance between this word and the original word. In our example, we read these two values and display them on the screen.

Figure 6-17: *Related words*

Although finding related words can be useful, the ability to find related sentences is where the **Natural Language** framework truly shines. The framework can calculate embeddings for sentences and determine the distance between them, allowing us to identify sentences that are semantically related. For example, we can use this feature to find the most relevant answer to a user's query, as shown below.

Listing 6-16: Finding related sentences

```
func calculateEmbedding(word: String) {
    let questions = [
        "How can I reset my password?",
        "Where can I track my order?",
        "What is your return policy?",
        "How do I contact customer support?",
        "Do you offer international shipping?"
    ]
    if let embeddings = NLEmbedding.sentenceEmbedding(for: .english) {
        var bestFind: Int?
        var lastDistance: Double = 2.0
        for (index, question) in questions.enumerated() {
            let distance = embeddings.distance(between: question, and: word)
            if distance < lastDistance {
                lastDistance = distance
                bestFind = index
            }
        }
        if let bestFind = bestFind {
            message = questions[bestFind]
        } else {
            message = "Not Found"
        }
    }
}
```

To illustrate how this feature works, we created a list of five questions typically found in the FAQ section of a website. Because sentence embeddings are generated dynamically, there is no `neighbors()` method to find related sentences, so we must perform the comparison manually. In this example, we simply use a `for in` loop to compare each sentence with the one entered by the user. Within the loop, we calculate the distance, and if it is shorter than the current one, we store its index in the `bestFind` variable and continue to the next sentence. Note that distances are returned as values between 0.0 and 2.0, with 0.0 indicating the closest match and 2.0 the farthest. To find the sentence closest to the one entered by the user, we start by assigning a value of 2.0 to the `lastDistance` variable and then update this value whenever we find a closer sentence. As a result, when the user types a sentence like "I need help", the system will find a related question, like "How do I contact customer support?", and return it, as shown below.

Figure 6-18: *Related sentences*

Do It Yourself

Update the `calculateEmbedding()` method in the `ContentView` view with the code in Listing 6-16. Run the application on your iPhone or the simulator. Type a question that is related to one from our list. You should see on the screen a question related to what you typed. For example, if you type something about shipping, such as "Do you ship to my country?", the system will identify the question "Do you offer international shipping?" as the most appropriate one to show to the user.

IMPORTANT

In addition to Apple's built-in models, the **Natural Language** framework can also work with Core ML models. We can train a Core ML model to perform specific tasks and then use the **Natural Language** framework to integrate that model into our app. We will learn how to create and train Core ML models using Create ML in Chapter 10.

6.2 - Translation Framework

As we already mentioned, Foundation Models excel at general-purpose tasks but are not optimized for specialized operations. One of those operations is translation. To handle translations efficiently, we need models trained specifically for that purpose. This is why Apple includes the **Translation** framework. This framework provides access to multiple models capable of translating text between different languages directly on the device. The framework offers both a complete user interface for performing translations and an API that allows us to integrate translation capabilities directly into our apps.

Translation Interface

The simplest way to add this functionality is by using the predefined interface. This interface provides buttons for selecting the source and target languages, the option to play the translated text as audio, and buttons to copy and share the translation. The following is the modifier provided by the framework to present this interface.

> **translationPresentation(isPresented:** Binding, **text:** String, **attachmentAnchor:** PopoverAttachmentAnchor, **arrowEdge:** Edge, **replacementAction:** Closure)
>
> This modifier presents the translation interface in a sheet. The **isPresented** argument is a Boolean binding property that determines whether the interface is open or closed, the **text** argument is the text we want to translate, the **attachmentAnchor** and **arrowEdge** arguments determine where the interface appears on iPad and Mac devices, and the **replacementAction** argument is the closure to be executed when the Replace with Translation button on the interface is pressed.

If we simply want to let the user translate a text, we only need to provide the text and a button to present the interface, as shown in the following example.

Listing 6-17: Opening the translation interface

```
import SwiftUI
@preconcurrency import Translation

struct ContentView: View {
   @State private var textInput: String = ""
   @State private var openTranslate: Bool = false

   var body: some View {
      VStack {
         HStack {
            TextField("Insert Text", text: $textInput)
               .textFieldStyle(.roundedBorder)
            Button("Translate") {
               let text = textInput.trimmingCharacters(in:
                  .whitespacesAndNewlines)
               if !text.isEmpty {
```

```
                openTranslate = true
            }
        }
        .buttonStyle(.borderedProminent)
    }
    Spacer()
}
.padding()
.translationPresentation(isPresented: $openTranslate, text:
    textInput)
    }
}
```

This example includes a **TextField** view for the user to enter the text and a button that changes the value of a Boolean property to instruct the modifier to present the interface. When the button is pressed, the code checks whether the user has entered any text and sets the property to **true** to open the interface and perform the translation. Note that for this modifier to be available, we must import the **Translation** framework, but because this framework has not yet been adapted to Swift concurrency, we need to prefix the **import** statement with the **@preconcurrency** attribute to prevent data race errors when developing with Swift 6.

The first time users attempt to translate a text, the system warns them that it will access Apple's servers to begin the process (Figure 6-19, left). If the system cannot infer the language from the text entered by the user, it prompts the user to select the source language (Figure 6-19, center), and if the languages required to perform the translation have not yet been downloaded, the system asks the user to download the necessary resources (Figure 6-19, right). The languages are automatically selected based on the text entered by the user and the user's location. In the example below, we typed a text in English and our device is configured to also work in Spanish, so those are the two languages selected by the system.

Figure 6-19: *Translation requirements*

Once all requirements are met, the system presents the interface showing the original text entered by the user alongside its translation, as shown below.

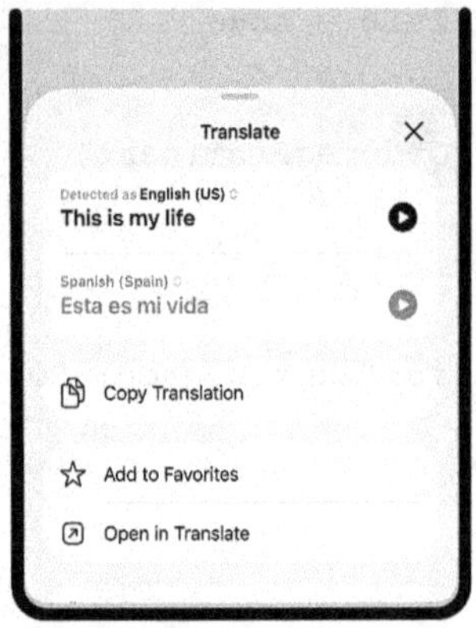

Figure 6-20: *Translation interface*

Do It Yourself

Create a new Multiplatform project. Update the ContentView.swift file with the code in Listing 6-17. Run the application on your iPhone (the **Translation** framework does not work in the simulator). Type a text in English and press the Translate button. Depending on the text you enter and the state of your device, you may be prompted to select the source language or download the languages required for the translation, as shown in Figure 6-19. Once this process is complete, the translation interface will appear on the screen, as shown in Figure 6-20.

In the previous example, the interface includes only a button to copy the translation to the clipboard, but we can assign an action to the modifier to add another button that sends the translated text back to our app. To do this, we must provide a closure to the modifier that processes the returned value, as shown below.

Listing 6-18: Showing the translation in our interface

```
.translationPresentation(isPresented: $openTranslate, text: textInput,
   replacementAction: { result in
   textInput = result
})
```

This modifier now includes the **replacementAction** argument. When this argument is present, the interface displays a new button labeled Replace with Translation (Figure 6-21, number 1). If the user presses this button, the closure assigned to the argument is executed. This closure receives a `String` value containing the translation, so we can process it in our app. In this case, we assign it to the `textInput` property to replace the original text with the translation. The results is shown below.

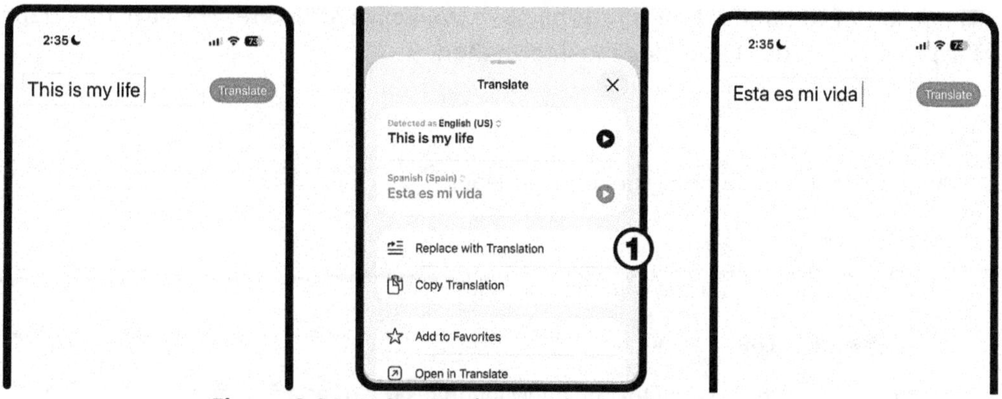

***Figure 6-21:** Using Replace with Translation button*

Do It Yourself

Update the **ContentView** view with the code in Listing 6-18. Run the application on your iPhone. Type some text and press the Translate button (Figure 6-21, left). You should see the translation appear on the screen. Press the Replace with Translation button (Figure 6-21, number 1). The original text should be replaced with the translation, as shown in Figure 6-21, right.

Translation Tasks

When a translation interface is presented, the system creates a translation session to handle the process. This session is managed by the **TranslationSession** class. If we want greater control over the translation, we must create and manage this session ourselves. However, the process is not straightforward. Because the system must ensure that the device has all the necessary resources before performing a translation, we cannot create a session directly; instead, we must request the system to create it for us. The framework provides the following modifier for this purpose.

translationTask(Configuration, **action:** Closure)

This modifier creates a **TranslationSession** object using the configuration provided by the first argument and then executes the closure assigned to the **action** argument to perform the translation.

The closure assigned to this modifier receives a reference to the **TranslationSession** object created by the system, so we can use it to perform the translation. The **TranslationSession** class provides the following asynchronous method for this purpose.

translate(String)

This method translates the string specified by the argument and returns the result.

The result of the translation is returned as a **Response** structure. The structure defines the following properties to provide the information.

targetText

This property returns a string with the translation.

sourceText

This property returns a string with the original text.

clientIdentifier

This property returns a string that uniquely identifies the translation request. This value is used when performing multiple translations simultaneously.

sourceLanguage

This property returns a **Locale.Language** structure representing the language of the original text.

targetLanguage

This property returns a **Locale.Language** structure representing the language of the translated text.

The **translationTask()** modifier requires a **Configuration** structure that defines how the translation will be performed. This structure provides the following initializer.

Configuration(source: Language, **target:** Language)

This initializer creates a **Configuration** object to perform a translation between the languages specified by the **source** and **target** arguments. If either argument is set to **nil**, the session automatically determines which languages to use based on the text to be translated and the device configuration.

The **Configuration** structure includes the following properties to change the configuration of the current session.

source

This property sets or returns the **Locale.Language** structure representing the language of the original text.

target

This property sets or returns the **Locale.Language** structure representing the language into which the original text will be translated.

version

This property sets or returns an integer value that represents the current configuration.

Because the translation is managed by a modifier, we cannot trigger the process directly. The translation is performed automatically when the view appears or when the configuration changes. Therefore, whenever we want the system to translate new text, we must create a new configuration. This can be done by instantiating a new **Configuration** structure, by changing the languages, or by assigning a new value to the **version** property. Alternatively, we can invalidate the current session using the following method provided by the **Configuration** structure.

invalidate()

This method invalidates the translation session and runs it again with the same configuration.

There are several ways to manage the translation process. If we want the translation to run as soon as the view appears, we can apply the **translationTask()** modifier without specifying a configuration, as shown below.

Listing 6-19: Translating a text when the view appears

```
import SwiftUI
@preconcurrency import Translation

struct ContentView: View {
   @State private var message: String = ""

   var body: some View {
      VStack {
         Text(message)
         Spacer()
      }
      .padding()
      .translationTask { session in
         do {
            let text = "This is my life"
            let response = try await session.translate(text)
            message = response.targetText
         } catch {
            print("Error translating the text: \(error)")
         }
      }
   }
}
```

In this example, we apply the modifier to translate a text written in English. The modifier automatically creates a **TranslationSession** object to manage the translation, so all we need to do is call the **translate()** method on this object and process the result. In this case, we read the **targetText** property to obtain the translated text and assign it to a State property to display it on the screen. Figure 6-22 shows the output we see when the device is configured to use Spanish.

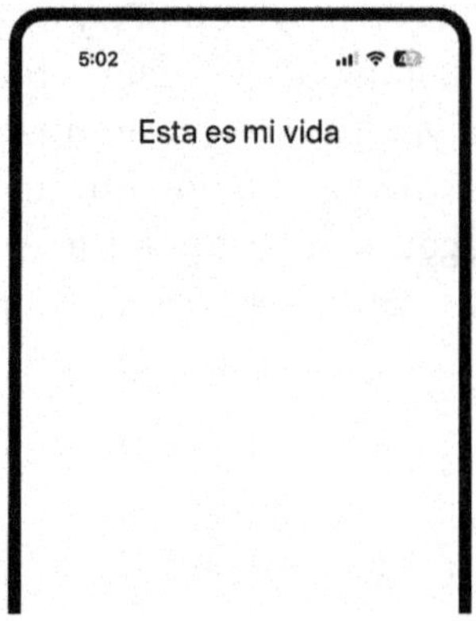

Figure 6-22: *Instant translation*

Do It Yourself

Update the **ContentView** view with the code in Listing 6-19. Run the application on your iPhone. You should see the translation of the text on the screen, as shown in Figure 6-22. If the system cannot infer the target language or the language is not available on the device, it will prompt you to download it, as before.

Automatically translating a text is rarely useful, but we can use a **Configuration** structure to gain more control over the process. The modifier performs a translation only when a **Configuration** structure is available, so we can start with a **nil** value and create a new **Configuration** instance each time we want to perform a translation, as shown below.

Listing 6-20: Translating the text entered by the user

```
import SwiftUI
@preconcurrency import Translation

struct ContentView: View {
   @State private var textInput: String = ""
   @State private var configuration:
      TranslationSession.Configuration? = nil

   var body: some View {
      VStack {
         HStack {
            TextField("Insert Text", text: $textInput)
               .textFieldStyle(.roundedBorder)
            Button("Translate") {
               let text = textInput.trimmingCharacters(in:
                  .whitespacesAndNewlines)
               if !text.isEmpty {
                  if configuration != nil {
                     configuration?.invalidate()
                  } else {
                     configuration = TranslationSession.Configuration()
```

```
               }
            }
         }
         .buttonStyle(.borderedProminent)
      }
      Spacer()
   }
   .padding()
   .translationTask(configuration) { session in
      do {
         let response = try await session.translate(textInput)
         textInput = response.targetText
      } catch {
         print("Error translating the text: \(error)")
      }
   }
}
}
```

In this example, we assign a property containing a **Configuration** structure to the **translationTask()** modifier. When no structure is provided (that is, when the property's value is **nil**), the modifier does nothing. However, when a **Configuration** instance is assigned to this property or the existing configuration is updated, the modifier executes the closure and performs the translation. As in the previous examples, to give the user control over the process, we include a **TextField** view and a button, but instead of opening the translation interface as we did before, the button now specifies the session's configuration. If the value of the **configuration** property is **nil**, a new **Configuration** instance is created; otherwise, the **invalidate()** method is called to invalidate the current session and run it again. In either case, the modifier detects the change, translates the text entered by the user, and displays the result on the screen.

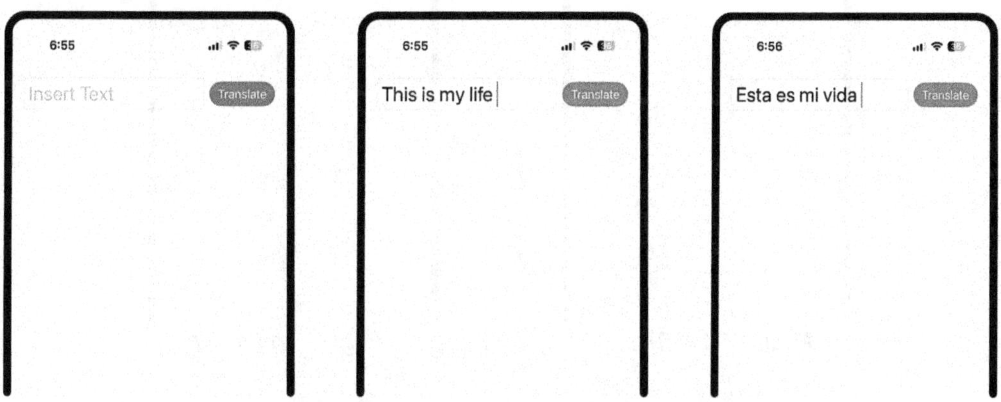

Figure 6-23: *Manually performing a translation*

Do It Yourself

Update the **ContentView** view with the code in Listing 6-20. Run the application on your iPhone, type some text, and press the Translate button. The text should be replaced with the translation, as shown in Figure 6-23.

In the previous example, we did not specify the languages to use. This means that the system automatically detects the source language from the text entered by the user and selects a target language based on the user's location or the device configuration. If we want to perform a translation between two specific languages, we can define those languages when creating the `Configuration` structure, as shown below.

Listing 6-21: Declaring the languages we want to use

```
Button("Translate") {
    let text = textInput.trimmingCharacters(in: .whitespacesAndNewlines)
    if !text.isEmpty {
        if configuration != nil {
            configuration?.invalidate()
        } else {
            let sourceLanguage = Locale.Language(identifier: "en")
            let targetLanguage = Locale.Language(identifier: "fr")
            configuration = TranslationSession.Configuration(source:
                sourceLanguage, target: targetLanguage)
        }
    }
}
.buttonStyle(.borderedProminent)
```

In this example, we set the source language to English (**en**) and the target language to French (**fr**), so the translation session expects the user to enter text in English and it always returns the translation in French, no matter the configuration of the device.

Figure 6-24: *Translating always from English to French*

Do It Yourself

Update the button in the `ContentView` view with the code in Listing 6-21. Run the application on your iPhone, type some text in English, and press the Translate button. You should see the translation in French, as shown in Figure 6-24.

If we want to let the user select the languages, the process is essentially the same. The only difference is that our app must include the controls needed for the user to make a selection. The following example shows one possible implementation. We add two pickers to the interface, allowing the user to choose the source and target languages between English and Spanish. If English is selected as the source language, Spanish is automatically set as the target, and vice versa.

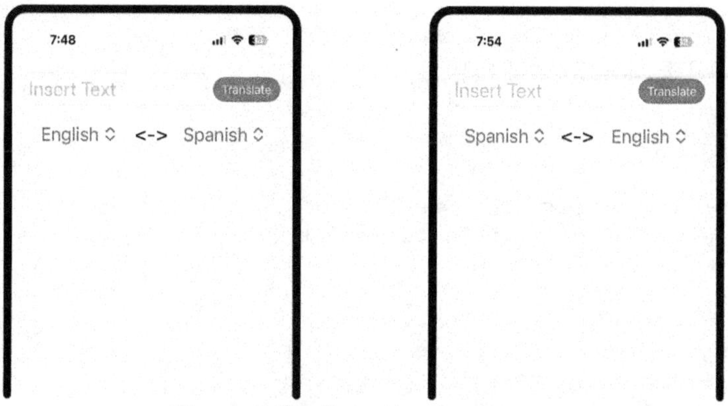

Figure 6-25: *Selecting languages*

Because we need to monitor the user's changes and update the session accordingly, it is best to move all the logic into an observable object. The following is our implementation of this class.

Listing 6-22: Implementing the logic to use multiple languages

```
import SwiftUI
import Observation
@preconcurrency import Translation

@Observable class ApplicationData {
   var configuration: TranslationSession.Configuration? = nil
   var selectedSource: Int = 0
   var selectedTarget: Int = 1
   var listLanguages: [Locale.Language] = []

   static let shared: ApplicationData = ApplicationData()
   private init() {
      listLanguages = [Locale.Language(identifier: "en"), Locale.
         Language(identifier: "es")]
   }
   func updateConfiguration() {
      if configuration != nil {
         if configuration?.source != listLanguages[selectedSource] ||
            configuration?.target != listLanguages[selectedTarget] {
            configuration = TranslationSession.Configuration(source:
               listLanguages[selectedSource],
                  target: listLanguages[selectedTarget])
         } else {
            configuration?.invalidate()
         }
      } else {
```

```
        configuration = TranslationSession.Configuration(
            source: listLanguages[selectedSource],
            target: listLanguages[selectedTarget])
      }
   }
   func getLanguageName(index: Int) -> String {
      var name = "Undefined"
      if let code = listLanguages[index].languageCode?.identifier {
         if let languageName = Locale.current.
            localizedString(forLanguageCode: code) {
            name = languageName
         }
      }
      return name
   }
   func changeSource(old: Int, new: Int) {
      if selectedSource == selectedTarget {
         selectedSource = old
      }
   }
   func changeTarget(old: Int, new: Int) {
      if selectedTarget == selectedSource {
         selectedTarget = old
      }
   }
}
```

This class defines several properties: one to store the session configuration (**configuration**), two to store the indexes of the languages currently selected as the source and target (**selectedSource** and **selectedTarget**), and an array containing all available languages (**listLanguages**). After initializing **listLanguages** with the **Language** structures representing the two languages the user can choose from (English and Spanish), we define four methods. The first method, **updateConfiguration()**, creates or updates the session configuration using the languages selected by the user whenever the Translate button is pressed. The remaining three methods manage the pickers that let the user select the languages. The **getLanguageName()** method retrieves the name of each language to display it in the picker, while the **changeSource()** and **changeTarget()** methods adjust the opposite language automatically: if the user selects the target language, **changeSource()** updates the source, and if the user selects the source, **changeTarget()** updates the target.

The interface must include a **TextField** and a Translate button, as before, but also two pickers to allow the user to select the languages. The following is our implementation of this view.

Listing 6-23: Allowing the user to select the languages

```
import SwiftUI
@preconcurrency import Translation

struct ContentView: View {
   @State private var appData = ApplicationData.shared
   @State private var textInput: String = ""
```

```
   var body: some View {
      VStack {
         HStack {
            TextField("Insert Text", text: $textInput)
               .textFieldStyle(.roundedBorder)
            Button("Translate") {
               let text = textInput.trimmingCharacters(in:
.whitespacesAndNewlines)
               if !text.isEmpty {
                  appData.updateConfiguration()
               }
            }
            .buttonStyle(.borderedProminent)
         }
         HStack {
            Spacer()
            Picker("From", selection: $appData.selectedSource) {
               ForEach(appData.listLanguages.indices, id: \.self) {
                  index in
                  let name = appData.getLanguageName(index: index)
                  Text(name)
                     .tag(index)
               }
            }.frame(minWidth: 0, maxWidth: .infinity)

            Text("<->")

            Picker("To", selection: $appData.selectedTarget) {
               ForEach(appData.listLanguages.indices, id: \.self) {
                  index in
                  let name = appData.getLanguageName(index: index)
                  Text(name)
                     .tag(index)
               }
            }.frame(minWidth: 0, maxWidth: .infinity)
            Spacer()
         }.padding(.top, 15)
         Spacer()
      }
      .padding()
      .onChange(of: appData.selectedSource) { old, new in
         appData.changeTarget(old: old, new: new)
      }
      .onChange(of: appData.selectedTarget) { old, new in
         appData.changeSource(old: old, new: new)
      }
      .translationTask(appData.configuration) { session in
         do {
            let response = try await session.translate(textInput)
            textInput = response.targetText
         } catch {
            print("Error translating the text: \(error)")
         }
      }
   }
}
```

There is nothing new in this view except for the pickers that allow the user to select the languages. The picker for the source language stores the user's selection in the **selectedSource** property, and the picker for the target language stores it in the **selectedTarget** property. To ensure that the pickers always display different languages, we apply two **onChange()** modifiers. When the value of one property changes, the other is updated accordingly, keeping the two pickers synchronized. The user can now press the Translate button to perform the translation, as before, but can also manually select the languages to use.

Do It Yourself

Create a new file called ApplicationData.swift for the code in Listing 6-22. Update the **ContentView** view with the code in Listing 6-23. Run the application on your iPhone. You should see an interface similar to the one in Figure 6-25. Select the language you want to translate from, type some text, and press Translate. You should see the translation appear in the text field, as before. Select the other language and press Translate again. The text should be translated back to the original language.

Allowing the user to select the language is useful, but we can do even better by automatically detecting the source language from the text entered by the user. To achieve this, we can use the **NLLanguageRecognizer** class from the **Natural Language** framework (see Listing 6-1). In our code, we simply need to add a new **onChange()** modifier to monitor the **textInput** property and update the language accordingly, as shown below.

Listing 6-24: Automatically selecting the source language

```
.onChange(of: textInput) { old, new in
    let detect = NLLanguageRecognizer()
    detect.processString(new)
    detect.languageConstraints = [.english, .spanish]

    if let code = detect.dominantLanguage {
        if code == .english {
            appData.selectedSource = 0
        } else {
            appData.selectedSource = 1
        }
    }
}
```

When the user types a new character, the closure assigned to the modifier is executed. Inside this closure, we detect the language between the two possible options (English and Spanish). If the text entered by the user is in English, we assign the value 0 to the **selectedSource** property; otherwise, we assign the value 1. This updates the language selected in the source picker and also triggers the **onChange()** modifier for the

selectedSource property, which updates the language in the target picker as well. As a result, the source and target languages are automatically selected based on the text entered by the user.

Figure 6-26: *Automatic language selection*

Do It Yourself

Add the **onChange()** modifier from Listing 6-24 to the **ContentView** view (below the previous modifiers). Remember that you also need to import the **Natural Language** framework for the **NLLanguageRecognizer** class to be available (**import NaturalLanguage**). Run the application on your iPhone and type some text in English or Spanish. You should see the languages in the pickers change automatically according to the language of the text, as shown in Figure 6-26.

In the previous examples, we allowed the user to choose between only two languages, English and Spanish, but the framework supports many more. To check language availability and status, the framework provides the **LanguageAvailability** class. The following are the property and methods defined by the class for this purpose.

supportedLanguages

This property gets an array of **Locale.Language** structures representing the languages supported by the framework.

status(from: Language, **to:** Language)

This method returns an enumeration of type **Status** that indicates whether translation between the two languages specified by the **from** and **to** arguments is possible. The enumeration includes the values: **installed** (the translation is possible), **supported** (translation between these languages is supported but the resources have not yet been downloaded), and **unsupported** (translation between these languages is not supported).

status(for: String, to: Language)

This method returns an enumeration of type **Status** that indicates whether the text specified by the **for** argument can be translated to the language specified by the **to** argument. The enumeration includes the values: **installed** (the translation is possible), **supported** (the translation is possible but the necessary resources have not yet been downloaded), and **unsupported** (translation between these languages is not supported).

With these tools, we can modify our previous example to work not only with English and Spanish but with every language supported by the framework. One approach is to read the **supportedLanguages** property to obtain the list of supported languages and configure the interface accordingly. First, we need to update the initializer of our **ApplicationData** class to initialize the **listLanguages** property with these values.

Listing 6-25: Initializing our app with all the supported languages

```
private init() {
   Task {
      listLanguages = await LanguageAvailability().supportedLanguages

      // Set target as the user's language
      let userLanguage = Locale.current.language.languageCode
      if listLanguages.contains(where: {
         $0.languageCode == userLanguage }) {
         selectedTarget = listLanguages.firstIndex(where: {
            $0.languageCode == userLanguage })!
      }
   }
}
```

After obtaining the list of supported languages, we also retrieve the user's language and assign it to the **selectedTarget** property, so translations are performed in the user's language by default. Keep in mind that every operation performed by the **LanguageAvailability** class is asynchronous, so we must read the value of the **supportedLanguages** property inside a task, as we did in this example.

Now that we have a list of all supported languages, we can use it in our interface. In this case, our interface remains the same as before; we only need to adapt the **onChange()** modifier introduced in the previous example to detect not just English and Spanish, but any language in the list.

Listing 6-26: Detecting all supported languages

```
.onChange(of: textInput) { old, new in
   let detect = NLLanguageRecognizer()
   detect.processString(new)

   if let code = detect.dominantLanguage {
      let language = Locale.Language(identifier: code.rawValue)
```

```
            if appData.listLanguages.contains(where: { $0.languageCode ==
                language.languageCode }) {
                appData.selectedSource = appData.listLanguages.firstIndex(
                    where: { $0.languageCode == language.languageCode })!
            }
        }
    }
```

The code in Listing 6-26 first retrieves the language code for the detected language and then checks whether that language is included in the list of supported languages. If it is, we assign its index to the **selectedSource** property so that the language is selected in the source picker. The result is shown below.

Figure 6-27: *Selecting all supported languages*

Do It Yourself

Update the **init()** method in the **ApplicationData** class with the code in Listing 6-25. Update the **onChange()** modifier for the **textInput** property in the **ContentView** view with the code in Listing 6-26. Run the application on your iPhone and type some text. You should see the languages in the pickers change automatically according to the language set on your device and the language of the text, as shown in Figure 6-27.

Batch Translation

So far, we have translated one string at a time, but the framework can also translate multiple texts simultaneously. To support this, the **TranslationSession** class provides the following methods.

translations(from: [Request])

This method takes an array of translation requests and returns an array of **Response** structures containing the results of the translations.

translate(batch: [Request])

This method takes an array of translation requests and returns a **BatchResponse** structure containing the results of the translations as they become available.

The process of translating multiple texts at once is similar to the one we used in previous examples, but instead of creating a single request, we must create an array of requests (**[TranslationSession.Request]**) containing all the strings we want the system to translate. In the following example, we provide the view with a list of five sentences in German and show how to translate them into English in a single step.

Listing 6-27: Translating multiple texts

```
import SwiftUI
@preconcurrency import Translation

struct ContentView: View {
   @State private var translatedText: String = ""
   @State private var configuration: TranslationSession.Configuration?

   let listPosts = [
      "Das Foto sieht echt toll aus, wo wurde das aufgenommen?",
      "Ich kann kaum glauben, wie schnell die Zeit vergeht!",
      "Herzlichen Glückwunsch zum neuen Job, du hast es wirklich
         verdient!",
      "Kann jemand dieses Lied bitte verlinken? Ich liebe es!",
      "Ich stimme dir vollkommen zu, das ist genau meine Meinung."
   ]
   var body: some View {
      VStack {
         Button("Translate") {
            if configuration != nil {
               configuration?.invalidate()
            } else {
               let sourceLanguage = Locale.Language(identifier: "de")
               let targetLanguage = Locale.Language(identifier: "en")
               configuration = TranslationSession.Configuration(
                   source: sourceLanguage, target: targetLanguage)
            }
         }
         .buttonStyle(.borderedProminent)
         ScrollView {
            Text(translatedText)
         }
         Spacer()
      }
      .padding()
      .translationTask(configuration) { session in
         do {
            var requests: [TranslationSession.Request] = []
            for text in listPosts {
               let request = TranslationSession.Request(sourceText: text)
               requests.append(request)
            }
            let responses = try await session.translations(from: requests)
```

```
            var results: String = ""
            for response in responses {
               results += "\(response.targetText)\n\n"
            }
            translatedText = results
         } catch {
            print("Error translating the text: \(error)")
         }
      }
   }
}
```

In this example, we define a property called **listPosts** containing the texts to be translated, and create a **Configuration** structure when a button is pressed to translate these texts from German to English. In the **translationTask()** modifier, we iterate through the **listPosts** array to create a request for each sentence and then translate them all at once using the **translations(from:)** method. The result is shown below.

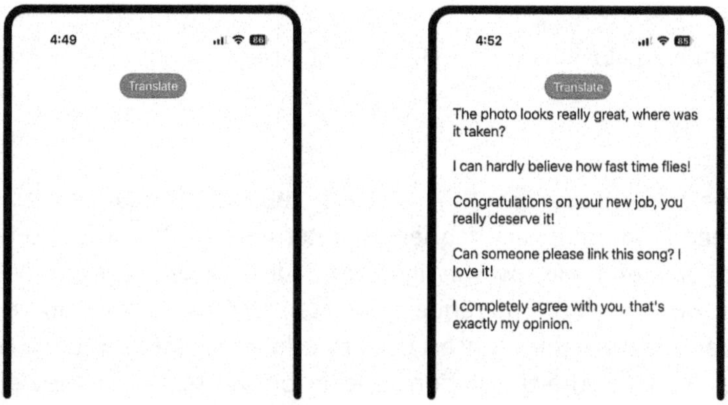

Figure 6-28: *Multiple translations at once*

Do It Yourself

Create a new Multiplatform project. Update the ContentView.swift file with the code in Listing 6-27. Run the application on your iPhone and press the Translate button. You should see the German sentences translated into English, as shown in Figure 6-28.

The **translations(from:)** method performs all translations and returns the results once the process is complete. Although this may be sufficient in most situations, if the operation takes too long, the user will not see any output until it finishes. To provide a smoother experience, we can use the **translate(batch:)** method instead. This method also translates multiple texts at once, but it returns each translation as it becomes available, allowing the user to see the results appear gradually on the screen. The following changes are required in the **translationTask()** modifier to use this method.

Listing 6-28: Performing asynchronous translations

```
.translationTask(configuration) { session in
   do {
      var requests: [TranslationSession.Request] = []
      for (index, text) in listPosts.enumerated() {
         var request = TranslationSession.Request(sourceText: text)
         request.clientIdentifier = String(index)
         requests.append(request)
      }
      var listResponses: [String] = Array(repeating: "Translating...",
         count: listPosts.count)
      for try await response in session.translate(batch: requests) {
         if let identifier = response.clientIdentifier,
            let index = Int(identifier) {
            listResponses[index] = response.targetText
         }
         translatedText = listResponses.joined(separator: "\n")
      }
   } catch {
      print("Error translating the text: \(error)")
   }
}
```

Because the **translate(batch:)** method returns translations as they become available, we need to identify each request to determine which translation corresponds to which text. In our example, we assign the index value of each sentence to the **clientIdentifier** property of its request, so later, when we create an array to store the responses, we can use this value to insert each translated sentence into the correct position. As a result, the user sees the translations appear on the screen as they arrive, as shown below.

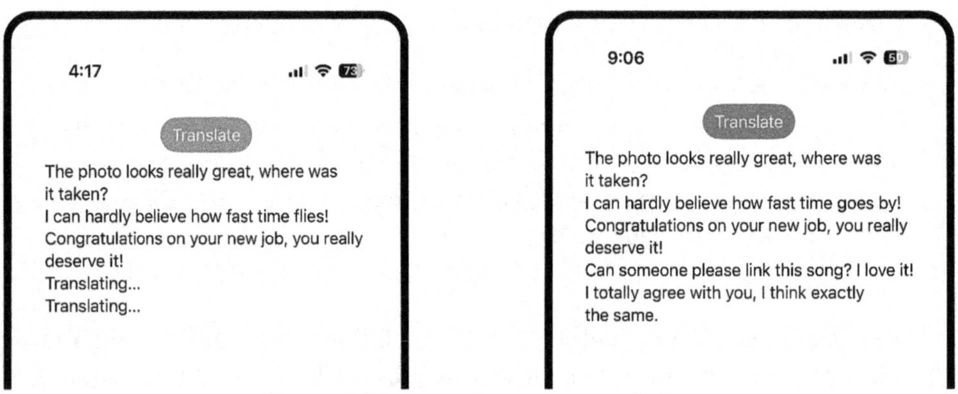

Figure 6-29: *Asynchronous translation*

Do It Yourself

Update the **`translationTask()`** modifier from the previous example with the code in Listing 6-28. Run the application on your iPhone and press the Translate button. You should see the German sentences translated into English again, but this time the translations appear on the screen gradually as they become available, as shown in Figure 6-29.

In the previous examples, we translated texts written in a single language, but the framework can also perform simultaneous translations involving multiple languages. To do this, however, we need to take a few things into account. Most importantly, each batch of requests sent for translation must contain texts written in the same source language. Therefore, when working with multiple languages, we need to send separate batches, one for each language. To demonstrate how this process works, we will update the previous example to translate into English a set of sentences written in three different languages: German, Spanish, and French.

Listing 6-29: Translating multiple languages

```
import SwiftUI
@preconcurrency import Translation
import NaturalLanguage

struct ContentView: View {
   @State private var translatedText: String = ""
   @State private var configuration: TranslationSession.Configuration?

   let listPosts = [
      "Das Foto sieht echt toll aus, wo wurde das aufgenommen?",
      "Je peux à peine croire à quelle vitesse le temps passe!",
      "¡Felicidades por tu nuevo trabajo, te lo mereces mucho!",
      "Kann jemand dieses Lied bitte verlinken? Ich liebe es!",
      "Estoy totalmente de acuerdo contigo, pienso exactamente lo mismo."
   ]
   var body: some View {
      VStack {
         Button("Translate") {
            if configuration != nil {
               configuration?.invalidate()
            } else {
               let targetLanguage = Locale.Language(identifier: "en")
               configuration = TranslationSession.Configuration(
                  source: nil, target: targetLanguage)
            }
         }
         .buttonStyle(.borderedProminent)
         ScrollView {
            Text(translatedText)
         }
         Spacer()
      }
```

```
      .padding()
      .translationTask(configuration) { session in
         do {
            let listRequests = getRequests()

            var listResponses: [String] = Array(repeating:
               "Translating...", count: listPosts.count)
            for (_, requests) in listRequests {
               // Process the requests for each language
               for try await response in session.translate(
                  batch: requests) {
                  if let identifier = response.clientIdentifier,
                     let index = Int(identifier) {
                     listResponses[index] = response.targetText
                  }
                  translatedText = listResponses.joined(separator: "\n\n")
               }
            }
         } catch {
            print("Error translating the text: \(error)")
         }
      }
   }
   func getRequests() -> [String: [TranslationSession.Request]] {
      var listRequests: [String: [TranslationSession.Request]] = [:]

      for (index, post) in listPosts.enumerated() {
         // Prepare request
         var request = TranslationSession.Request(sourceText: post)
         request.clientIdentifier = String(index)

         // Detect language in post
         let detect = NLLanguageRecognizer()
         detect.processString(post)
         if let code = detect.dominantLanguage {
            if let language = Locale.current.localizedString(
               forLanguageCode: code.rawValue) {
               if listRequests[language] == nil {
                  // Add new language to list
                  listRequests[language] = [request]
               } else {
                  // Add request to language
                  listRequests[language]!.append(request)
               }
            }
         }
      }
      return listRequests
   }
}
```

To create the batches of requests for each language, we define a new method called **`getRequests()`**. This method iterates through the original sentences and builds a dictionary with the name of each language as the key and an array with the requests for that language as the value. From the **`translationTask()`** modifier, we call this method and then use a **`for in`** loop to iterate through the requests. During each iteration, the code processes the requests for one language and adds the corresponding responses to the **`listResponses`** array. As a result, every sentence is translated into English, regardless of the original language. (Note that to allow the session to translate multiple languages, the source language in the configuration must be set to `nil`.)

Do It Yourself

Update the ContentView.swift file with the code in Listing 6-29. Run the application on your iPhone and press the Translate button. You should see the sentences translated into English, as before.

Chapter 7

Vision Framework

7.1 - Overview

The **Vision** framework provides access to a collection of models trained to analyze and interpret images. These models can identify the contents of a photo, locate specific features, recognize text, track objects across frames, and even estimate human body poses. Each task is handled by a specific type of request, such as object detection, face detection, or text recognition, which we can configure according to our needs.

> **IMPORTANT**
>
> Applications that take advantage of the **Vision** framework usually let users capture images directly from the camera. To simplify the examples in this chapter, we use only static images, but you can easily integrate this code with the camera to analyze images in real time. To learn how to build a custom camera interface, read our book *Advanced SwiftUI for Masterminds*.

7.2 - Image Analysis

Some of the most common tasks we can perform with the **Vision** framework involve image analysis. We can use this capability to detect objects, locate areas of interest, recognize barcodes, extract text, and perform other types of visual recognition.

Image Classification

Image classification involves interpreting an image and extracting categories from it. For example, if we have a picture of a car on a road surrounded by trees, after analyzing it, the model might return categories such as "vehicle", "tree", "road", and "sky". To perform this task, we must create a request, process it, and then receive and analyze the resulting observations. The framework provides the following structure to create the classification request.

ClassifyImageRequest(Revision)

This initializer creates a request to classify the contents of an image. The argument is an enumeration that specifies the version of the model to use. At the moment, the only available value is **revision2**. If no revision is specified, the latest revision is selected by default.

To perform a single request, the **ClassifyImageRequest** structure includes the following method.

perform(on: Image, **orientation:** CGImagePropertyOrientation)

This method performs a request on the image specified by the arguments. The **on** argument represents the image to analyze. The image can be provided in different formats. The possible types are **URL**, **Data**, **CGImage**, **CVPixelBuffer**, **CMSampleBuffer**, and **CIImage**. The **orientation** argument is an enumeration that defines the image's current orientation. The possible values are **up**, **upMirrored**, **down**, **downMirrored**, **leftMirrored**, **right**, **rightMirrored**, and **left**.

When we perform a request, the system automatically creates an object to handle it. In some situations, however, we may need to define the handler ourselves. For this purpose, the framework provides the following class.

ImageRequestHandler(Image, **orientation:** CGImageProperty-Orientation)

This initializer creates a handler to process image classification requests. The first argument represents the image to analyze. The image can be provided in different formats. The possible types are **URL**, **Data**, **CGImage**, **CVPixelBuffer**, **CMSampleBuffer**, and **CIImage**. The **orientation** argument is an enumeration that defines the image's current orientation. The possible values are **up**, **upMirrored**, **down**, **downMirrored**, **leftMirrored**, **right**, **rightMirrored**, and **left**.

When using a handler to perform a request, we must implement the handler's methods. The following methods are defined by the **ImageRequestHandler** class for this purpose.

perform(Request)

This method performs the specified request on the image provided to the handler. The argument is a **ClassifyImageRequest** structure that defines the request to execute.

performAll(Requests)

This method performs multiple requests on the images provided to the handler. The argument is a comma-separated list of **ClassifyImageRequest** structures that define the requests to execute.

Regardless of whether the request is performed directly or through a handler, the results are always returned as a sequence of **ClassificationObservation** structures. This type provides the following methods for filtering the results.

hasMinimumPrecision(Float, forRecall: Float)

This method returns a Boolean value indicating whether the observation meets the minimum precision and recall values specified by the arguments. The first argument defines the minimum precision required for the observation, and the **forRecall** argument specifies the acceptable level of false negatives.

hasMinimumRecall(Float, forPrecision: Float)

This method returns a Boolean value indicating whether the observation meets the minimum recall value for the specified precision. The first argument defines the acceptable level of false negatives, while the **forPrecision** argument specifies the precision value to evaluate.

The **ClassificationObservation** structure conforms to the **VisionObservation** protocol and therefore provides the following properties to return the results of the observation.

confidence

This property returns a **Float** value between 0.0 and 1.0 that indicates the model's level of confidence in the observation.

identifier

This property returns a **String** value with the result of the observation.

If we only need to classify a single image, we must simply create an instance of the **ClassifyImageRequest** structure and call the **perform()** method to execute the request. In the following example, we obtain the URL of an image in the project called **picture1.png**, and then show how to perform the request and filter the results.

Listing 7-1: Classifying an image

```
import SwiftUI
import Vision

struct ContentView: View {
   @State private var categoriesList: String = "Loading..."

   var body: some View {
      VStack {
         Image(uiImage: UIImage(named: "picture1")!)
            .resizable()
            .scaledToFit()
            .padding()
         Text(categoriesList)
         Spacer()
      }
      .padding()
      .task {
         let imageURL = Bundle.main.url(forResource: "picture1",
            withExtension: "png")
```

```
            if let imageURL = imageURL {
               do {
                  let request = ClassifyImageRequest()
                  var results = try await request.perform(on: imageURL)
                  results = results.filter { $0.hasMinimumPrecision(0.1,
                     forRecall: 0.8) && $0.confidence > 0.1 }
                  categoriesList = results.map(\.identifier).
                     joined(separator: ", ")
               } catch {
                  print("Error performing the request: \(error)")
               }
            }
         }
      }
   }
```

In this example, we apply a **task()** modifier so the request is performed as soon as the view is loaded. The code obtains the URL of the image from the bundle, creates and performs the request, and then filters the observations using the **hasMinimumPrecision()** method. The categories returned by the request have a precision level that determines how many of them are considered correct. A higher precision value means fewer false positives, while a higher recall value allows more results to be included even if some are incorrect. In the filter, we also check the value of the **confidence** property to remove any observations with a confidence lower than 0.1, ensuring that we only get the most reliable categories.

The code returns a list of categories for the image, which we join in a string and assign to the **categoriesList** property to display on the screen. The result is shown below.

Figure 7-1: *Image categories*

Do It Yourself

Create a new Multiplatform project. Download the **picture1.png** file from our website and drag it into the project (**Vision > Classification > picture1.png**). Update the ContentView.swift file with the code in Listing 7-1. Run the application on your iPhone. After a few seconds, the placeholder text should be replaced by the categories detected in the image.

The same process applies when analyzing multiple images; we simply have to perform the request over and over again. In these cases, Apple recommends creating a task group so the model can analyze each image concurrently and return the observations as they are completed. In the following example, we show how to create these tasks to analyze 10 images. Because the code is longer and processes more data, we need to move the logic to an observable object. The following is our implementation of that object.

Listing 7-2: Analyzing multiple images

```
import SwiftUI
import Observation
import Vision

struct ImageData: Identifiable {
   let id: UUID = UUID()
   var fileName: String
   var image: UIImage?
   var categories: [String]

   var showCategories: String {
      return categories.joined(separator: ", ")
   }
}
@Observable class ApplicationData {
   var listImages: [ImageData]

   static let shared: ApplicationData = ApplicationData()
   private init() {
      listImages = []
      let list = ["picture1", "picture2", "picture3", "picture4",
         "picture5", "picture6", "picture7", "picture8", "picture9",
         "picture10"]
      for name in list {
         listImages.append(ImageData(fileName: name, image: UIImage(
            named: name), categories: []))
      }
   }
   func recognizeImages() async {
      await withTaskGroup(of: (Int, [String]).self) { group in
         for (index, item) in listImages.enumerated() {
            var categories: [String] = []
            let imageURL = Bundle.main.url(forResource: item.fileName,
               withExtension: "png")
            if let imageURL = imageURL {
               group.addTask {
                  do {
                     let request = ClassifyImageRequest()
                     var results = try await request.perform(on: imageURL)
                     results = results.filter {
                        $0.hasMinimumPrecision(0.1, forRecall: 0.8) &&
                        $0.confidence > 0.1 }
                     categories = results.map(\.identifier)
                  } catch {
                     print("Error performing the request: \(error)")
                  }
                  return (index, categories)
```

```
                }
            }
        }
        for await (index, categories) in group {
            await MainActor.run {
                self.listImages[index].categories = categories
            }
        }
    }
  }
}
```

We begin by defining a structure called **ImageData** to store the information for each image. Then, when the observable object is initialized, we create an array of instances of this structure to represent our 10 images, from picture1 to picture10. Each instance contains the image name, a **UIImage** object representing the image itself, and an empty array to later store the categories detected by the model.

To analyze the images and retrieve their categories, we define a new method called **recognizeImages()**. In this method, we implement the **withTaskGroup()** function to manage the tasks. This function allows us to create tasks dynamically, so we use a **for in** loop to iterate through each image in the **listImages** property, get the image URL, and add a task for each one to perform the request and obtain the categories. Each task returns a tuple containing the image's index and its corresponding list of categories, allowing us to match the results to the images. Finally, we use another **for in** loop to collect these results from the task group and assign the categories to their respective images when they become available.

The view now only needs to provide controls to let the user navigate through the images and view the results. The following is our implementation.

Listing 7-3: Showing all the images and their categories

```
import SwiftUI

struct ContentView: View {
   @State private var appData = ApplicationData.shared

   var body: some View {
      VStack {
         ScrollView(.horizontal) {
            LazyHStack(spacing: 0) {
               ForEach(appData.listImages) { image in
                  VStack {
                     Image(uiImage: image.image!)
                        .resizable()
                        .scaledToFit()
                     Text(image.showCategories)
                        .padding()
                  }
                  .containerRelativeFrame(.horizontal)
               }
            }
         }
```

```
            .scrollTargetBehavior(.paging)
            .frame(height: 380)
            Spacer()
         }
         .padding()
         .task {
            await appData.recognizeImages()
         }
      }
   }
```

For this example, we create a **`ForEach`** loop inside a **`ScrollView`** to allow the user to drag the pictures from side to side. Note that to obtain the categories, we use the **`task()`** modifier again to call the **`recognizeImages()`** method as soon as the view is loaded. The result is shown below.

Figure 7-2: *Categories of multiple images*

Do It Yourself

Create a new Swift file called ApplicationData.swift for the code in Listing 7-2. Update the **`ContentView`** view with the code in Listing 7-3. Download all the images from our website and drag them into the project (**Vision > Classification > picture1.png** to **picture10.png**). Run the application on your iPhone, and drag the pictures to the left. You should see each image along with its corresponding categories.

Although the categories by themselves may not seem very useful, they can help us identify images and build practical tools. For instance, we can let the user search for a specific term and display only the images with categories that match. To add this feature to our example, we need an additional property in the observable object to store the images that match the term searched by the user, as well as a function to perform the search.

Listing 7-4: Filtering images

```
@Observable class ApplicationData {
   var listImages: [ImageData]
   var filteredImages: [ImageData]

   static let shared: ApplicationData = ApplicationData()
   private init() {
      listImages = []
      filteredImages = []

      let list = ["picture1", "picture2", "picture3", "picture4",
         "picture5", "picture6", "picture7", "picture8", "picture9",
         "picture10"]
      for name in list {
         listImages.append(ImageData(fileName: name,
            image: UIImage(named: name), categories: []))
      }
      filteredImages = listImages
   }
   func filterValues(search: String) {
      if search.isEmpty {
         filteredImages = listImages
      } else {
         let list = listImages.filter { image in
            image.categories.contains { $0.contains(search.lowercased()) }
         }
         filteredImages = list
      }
   }
}
```

The code in Listing 7-4 shows the changes required in the **ApplicationData** class to perform a search. We define a new property called **filteredImages** to store the list of **ImageData** structures that match the search criteria, and a method called **filterValues()** that receives the text entered by the user, finds the images whose categories match that text, and assigns them to the **filteredImages** property. Now, the **listImages** property contains all the images, while the **filteredImages** property contains the search results (or all images if the search was cancelled), so we can use the latter to display the results to the user, as shown below.

Listing 7-5: Showing the images searched by the user

```
import SwiftUI

struct ContentView: View {
   @State private var appData = ApplicationData.shared
   @State private var searchTerm = ""

   var body: some View {
      NavigationStack {
         List(appData.filteredImages) { image in
            Image(uiImage: image.image!)
```

```
                .resizable()
                .scaledToFit()
            }
        }
        .task {
            await appData.recognizeImages()
        }
        .searchable(text: $searchTerm, prompt: Text("Search image"))
        .onChange(of: searchTerm) { old, new in
            let search = searchTerm.trimmingCharacters(
                in: .whitespacesAndNewlines)
            appData.filterValues(search: search)
        }
    }
}
```

In this view, we define a property called **searchTerm** to store the text entered by the user, apply the **searchable()** modifier to add a search bar to the interface, and use the **onChange()** modifier to monitor changes to this value. When the user types in the search field, the closure inside the **onChange()** modifier is executed, so we use it to clean the text and call the **filterValues()** method to perform the search. The result is shown below.

Figure 7-3: *Searching by category*

Do It Yourself

Update the **ApplicationData** class with the code in Listing 7-4. Remember to keep the **recognizeImages()** method introduced earlier. Update the **ContentView** view with the code in Listing 7-5. Run the application on your iPhone and search for a term related to the pictures (e.g., "chair" or "car"). If the text matches a category of a picture, that picture will appear in the list.

Attention Based Saliency

The **Vision** framework also provides a model trained to detect salient objects in an image, allowing us to identify areas of interest. With this model, we can locate the region of an image that is most likely to capture the user's attention. The following is the structure provided by the framework for this purpose.

> **`GenerateAttentionBasedSaliencyImageRequest`**`(Revision)`
>
> This initializer creates a request to identify the part of the image that draws the most attention. The argument is an enumeration that specifies the version of the model to use. At the moment, the only available value is **`revision2`**. If no revision is specified, the latest revision is selected by default.

Like previous structures, the **`GenerateAttentionBasedSaliencyImageRequest`** structure provides the **`perform(on:)`** method to execute the request. In this case, the method returns an array of **`SaliencyImageObservation`** structures. This structure offers two types of output: a pixel buffer with a heat map that highlights the area of interest, and a value that defines the coordinates of the rectangle surrounding that area. The following properties are included in the structure to provide these values.

> **`heatMap`**
>
> This property returns a **`PixelBufferObservation`** structure containing a grayscale image that represents the areas of interest in the original image.
>
> **`salientObjects`**
>
> This property returns an array of **`RectangleObservation`** structures that contain the coordinates of the areas of interest in the image. The structure conforms to the **`BoundingBoxProviding`** protocol and therefore includes the **`boundingBox`** property to return a **`NormalizedRect`** structure with the location and size of each area.

When we retrieve the coordinates of the areas of interest in an image, the values are normalized. This means that they are expressed as proportions between 0.0 and 1.0 rather than in pixels, so we must convert them to the image's coordinate system. For this purpose, the **`NormalizedRect`** structure provides the following method.

> **`toImageCoordinates`**`(CGSize,` **`origin:`** `CoordinateOrigin)`
>
> This method converts the normalized coordinates of a **`NormalizedRect`** structure into the coordinate space of an image. The first argument specifies the size of the image in pixels, and the **origin** argument is an enumeration that determines the coordinate system to use for the conversion. The possible values are **`upperLeft`** and **`lowerLeft`**.

If we only need to identify the area of interest, we can read the **`boundingBox`** property of the **`RectangleObservation`** structure returned by the request and use its values to draw a rectangle around it, as shown below.

Listing 7-6: Finding the area of interest

```
import SwiftUI
import Vision

struct ContentView: View {
   @State private var observations: SaliencyImageObservation?

   var body: some View {
      VStack {
         Button("Detect") {
            Task {
               await detectObjects()
            }
         }.buttonStyle(.borderedProminent)

         Canvas { context, size in
            // Calculate size and draw image
            let image = UIImage(named: "picturedog")!
            let width = size.width
            let height = image.size.height * width / image.size.width
            let imageFrame = CGRect(origin: .zero,
               size: CGSize(width: width, height: height))
            context.draw(Image(uiImage: image), in: imageFrame)

            // Calculate size and draw bounding box
            if let salientObjects = observations?.salientObjects {
               for object in salientObjects {
                  let rect = object.boundingBox
                  let boxFrame = rect.toImageCoordinates(imageFrame.size,
                     origin: .upperLeft)
                  context.stroke(Rectangle().path(in: boxFrame),
                     with: .color(.green), lineWidth: 5)
               }
            }
         }
         Spacer()
      }
      .padding()
   }
   func detectObjects() async {
      let imageURL = Bundle.main.url(forResource: "picturedog",
         withExtension: "png")
      if let imageURL = imageURL {
         do {
            let request = GenerateAttentionBasedSaliencyImageRequest()
            observations = try await request.perform(on: imageURL)
         } catch {
            print("Error performing the request: \(error)")
         }
      }
   }
}
```

To display the image on the screen, we use a **Canvas** view. This view can render images as well as any additional graphics we need, allowing us to easily draw a rectangle over the image to represent the area of interest. To perform the request, we define a method called **detectObjects()**. As in previous examples, this method retrieves the image URL, creates a request, and calls the **perform()** method to analyze the image. When the results are received, we assign them to a property called **observations**, so we can access these values from the **Canvas** view and render all necessary elements.

In the **Canvas** view, we first draw the image and then overlay a rectangle to represent the area of interest. Drawing the image is straightforward: we create a **UIImage** object with the image in question, calculate its size based on the canvas dimensions, and render it using the **draw()** method. Drawing the rectangle requires a bit more work. We must iterate through the array returned by the **salientObjects** property, read the **boundingBox** property from each item to get the coordinates of the bounding box (in this case, only one), and convert those values to the image's coordinate system using the **toImageCoordinates()** method. Once we have the correct coordinates, we call the **stroke()** method to render the outline of a **Rectangle** view on the canvas and highlight the area of interest. The result is shown below.

Figure 7-4: *Area of interest*

Do It Yourself

Create a new Multiplatform project. Download the **picturedog.png** image from our website and drag it into the project (**Vision > Saliency > picturedog.png**). Update the ContentView.swift file with the code in Listing 7-6. Run the application on your iPhone and press the Detect button. You should see a square outlining the area of the image that is most likely to draw the user's attention, as shown in Figure 7-4. For more information on the **Canvas** view, read our book *SwiftUI Framework for Masterminds*.

The **SaliencyImageObservation** structure also includes the **heatMap** property to return a **PixelBufferObservation** structure with a grayscale image that highlights the area of interest. This structure provides the **cgImage** property to return a **CGImage** representation of the image and the **size** property to return its dimensions. Using these values, we can extract the relevant pixels from the original image or simply highlight the area for the user, as shown in the following example.

Listing 7-7: Highlighting the area of interest

```
Canvas { context, size in
    // Calculate size and draw image
    let image = UIImage(named: "picturedog")!
    let width = size.width
    let height = image.size.height * width / image.size.width
    let imageFrame = CGRect(origin: .zero, size: CGSize(width: width,
       height: height))
    context.draw(Image(uiImage: image), in: imageFrame)

    // Show heat map
    if let heatMap = try? observations?.heatMap.cgImage {
       let map = UIImage(cgImage: heatMap)
       context.blendMode = .multiply
       context.draw(Image(uiImage: map), in: CGRect(origin: .zero,
          size: imageFrame.size))
    }
}
```

The code in Listing 7-7 defines a new **Canvas** view. This time, instead of drawing a rectangle to represent the area of interest, we draw the heat map over the original image to highlight that region. To render the heat map, we get the **CGImage** value from the **cgImage** property, create a **UIImage** object with this value, and draw this image over the original using a blending mode so the two are combined.

A heat map uses varying brightness levels to emphasize areas of the image. In this case, bright pixels represent regions that draw the most attention, while dark pixels indicate less relevant areas. When we blend the heat map with the original image using the **multiply** mode, the relevant portions of the original image remain visible while the rest are darkened, as shown below.

Figure 7-5: *Heat map applied to the image*

Do It Yourself

Update the **Canvas** view in the **ContentView** view with the code in Listing 7-7. Run the application on your iPhone and press the Detect button. You should see the heat map applied to the image, as shown in Figure 7-5.

In addition to identifying the area most likely to draw the user's attention, we can also create a request to detect the regions of an image that are most likely to represent objects. The framework provides the following structure for this purpose.

GenerateObjectnessBasedSaliencyImageRequest(Revision)

This initializer creates a request to identify the parts of the image that represent objects. The argument is an enumeration that specifies the version of the model to use. At the moment, the only available value is **revision2**. If no revision is specified, the latest revision is selected by default.

The process for creating this request and visualizing the results is the same as before. All we need to do is replace the previous request with this one in the **detectObjects()** method, as shown below.

Listing 7-8: Finding relevant objects in an image

```
func detectObjects() async {
    let imageURL = Bundle.main.url(forResource: "picturedesk",
        withExtension: "png")
    if let imageURL = imageURL {
        do {
            let request = GenerateObjectnessBasedSaliencyImageRequest()
            observations = try await request.perform(on: imageURL)
        } catch {
            print("Error performing the request: \(error)")
        }
    }
}
```

This method creates a **GenerateObjectnessBasedSaliencyImageRequest** structure, performs the request, and assigns the results to the **observations** property, as before. If we use the **Canvas** view introduced in Listing 7-6, we will see a heat map highlighting the areas of the image that represent objects, but if we use the **Canvas** view defined earlier in Listing 7-5, we will see bounding boxes outlining those areas, as shown below.

Figure 7-6: *Relevant objects*

Do It Yourself

Update the **detectObjects()** method in the **ContentView** view with the code from Listing 7-8. Download the **picturedesk.png** image from our website and drag it into the project (**Vision > Saliency > picturedesk.png**). Depending on the result you want, you can use the **Canvas** view from Listing 7-7 or Listing 7-6. Remember to update the image name inside the canvas to "picturedesk" so it matches the image being analyzed. Run the application on your iPhone and press the Detect button. You should see a result similar to Figure 7-6.

Image Aesthetics

The **Vision** framework also provides access to a model trained to evaluate the visual quality of an image based on aesthetic criteria. This model analyzes several aspects of an image, such as balance, color harmony, lighting, and subject placement, to produce a score that reflects its overall aesthetic appeal. The following is the structure provided by the framework to create this request.

CalculateImageAestheticsScoresRequest(Revision)

This initializer creates a request to determine the aesthetic score of an image. The argument is an enumeration that specifies the version of the model to use. At the moment, the only available value is **revision2**. If no revision is specified, the latest revision is selected by default.

As with previous requests, this one is executed using the **perform(on:)** method. In this case, the method returns a structure of type **ImageAestheticsScoresObservation**, which includes the following properties.

overallScore

This property returns a **Float** value representing the overall aesthetic score of the image. The values range from -1 to 1, where -1 indicates the least appealing and 1 the most appealing.

isUtility

This property returns a Boolean value indicating whether the image is considered to lack memorable or engaging content. A value of **true** means the image may not contain visually interesting or appealing elements.

With this type of requests, we can evaluate the aesthetic quality of individual images or multiple frames from a video. To see how it works, we will create a simple application that lets the user select an image and see its score, along with an indication of whether it has memorable qualities or not.

Figure 7-7: *Aesthetic scores*

We first need a simple list to allow the user to select a picture.

Listing 7-9: Listing the pictures to score

```
import SwiftUI

struct ContentView: View {
   let list = ["picture1", "picture2", "picture3", "picture4", "picture5",
"picture6", "picture7", "picture8", "picture9", "picture10"]

   var body: some View {
      NavigationStack {
         List(list, id: \.self) { name in
            NavigationLink(name, destination: ImageView(imageName: name))
         }
      }
   }
}
```

When a picture is selected, the application opens a view called **ImageView**. In this view, we display the selected image and perform a request to retrieve its aesthetic score, as shown below.

Listing 7-10: Showing the score

```
import SwiftUI
import Vision

struct ImageView: View {
   @State private var levelMessage: String = "Calculating..."
   @State private var isMemorable: String = "..."
   let imageName: String

   var body: some View {
      VStack {
         Image(uiImage: UIImage(named: imageName)!)
            .resizable()
            .scaledToFit()
         Text(levelMessage)
         Text(isMemorable)
```

```
            Spacer()
        }
        .padding()
        .task {
            let imageURL = Bundle.main.url(forResource: imageName,
                withExtension: "png")
            if let imageURL = imageURL {
                do {
                    let request = CalculateImageAestheticsScoresRequest()
                    let results = try await request.perform(on: imageURL)
                    levelMessage = String(results.overallScore)
                    isMemorable = results.isUtility ? "No" : "Yes"
                } catch {
                    print("Error performing the request: \(error)")
                }
            }
        }
    }
}
```

This view receives the name of the image selected by the user and displays it on the screen along with its aesthetic score and memorability factor. To obtain these values, we use a **`task()`** modifier. When the view is loaded, this modifier performs a **`CalculateImageAestheticsScoresRequest`** request and assigns the results to State properties to show the values on the screen. The result is shown in Figure 7-7.

Do It Yourself

Create a new Multiplatform project. Download the images from our website and drag them into the project (**Vision > Classification > picture1.png** to **picture10.png**). Update the ContentView.swift file with the code in Listing 7-9. Create a new Swift file called ImageView.swift for the code in Listing 7-10. Run the application on your iPhone and select a picture. You should see the score and a label indicating whether the picture is memorable or not.

Barcode Detection

The **Vision** framework also provides access to a model trained for barcode detection. Using this model, we can create requests to identify and extract information from barcodes and QR codes in images or live camera feeds. The framework provides the following structure to create this request.

`DetectBarcodesRequest(Revision)`

This initializer creates a request to identify barcodes in an image and extract the information. The argument is an enumeration that specifies the version of the model to use. At the moment, the only available value is **`revision4`**. If no revision is specified, the latest revision is selected by default.

The model detects all barcodes present in an image, regardless of their type, but we can specify a particular type to detect using the following property.

symbologies

This property sets or returns an array of enumeration values of type **BarcodeSymbology** that represent the types of barcodes the request should detect. The values available are **aztec**, **codabar**, **code128**, **code39**, **code39Checksum**, **code39FullASCII**, **code39FullASCIIChecksum**, **code93**, **code93i**, **dataMatrix**, **ean13**, **ean8**, **gs1DataBar**, **gs1DataBarExpanded**, **gs1DataBarLimited**, **i2of5**, **i2of5Checksum**, **itf14**, **microPDF417**, **microQR**, **msiPlessey**, **pdf417**, **qr** and **upce**.

As with other requests, this one is executed using the **perform(on:)** method. In this case, the method returns an array of **BarcodeObservation** structures. The structure includes the following properties to provide the values.

payloadString

This property returns a **String** value containing the data encoded in the barcode.

supplementalPayloadString

This property returns a **String** value that contains any supplemental data encoded in the barcode.

The **BarcodeObservation** structure also includes the following properties to provide additional information.

boundingBox

This property returns a **NormalizedRect** structure that defines the position and size of the rectangle surrounding the barcode.

symbology

This property returns an enumeration value of type **BarcodeSymbology**, which specifies the type of barcode that was detected.

isColorInverted

This property returns a Boolean value indicating whether the barcode's colors are inverted.

This request can detect all barcodes in an image, regardless of their type. If that's the desired behavior, we just need to create a **DetectBarcodesRequest** structure, perform the request, and display the results. The following example demonstrates how to read a single QR code from an image.

Listing 7-11: Reading a QR code

```
import SwiftUI
import Vision

struct ContentView: View {
   @State private var barcode: String = "Reading..."
   @State private var codeType: String = ""

   var body: some View {
      VStack {
         Image(uiImage: UIImage(named: "magazineqr")!)
            .resizable()
            .scaledToFit()
            .padding()
         Text(barcode)
         Text(codeType)
         Spacer()
      }
      .padding()
      .task {
         let imageURL = Bundle.main.url(forResource: "magazineqr",
            withExtension: "png")
         if let imageURL = imageURL {
            do {
               let request = DetectBarcodesRequest()
               let result = try await request.perform(on: imageURL)
               if let code = result.first {
                  barcode = code.payloadString ?? "Not Found"
                  codeType = "Type: \(code.symbology)"
               }
            } catch {
               print("Error performing the request: \(error)")
            }
         }
      }
   }
}
```

As with previous examples, we obtain the image URL and perform the request using this value. In this case, we know that the image contains only one barcode, so we retrieve the first element from the array returned by the request and read its **payloadString** and **symbology** properties to display the encoded data to the user, as shown below.

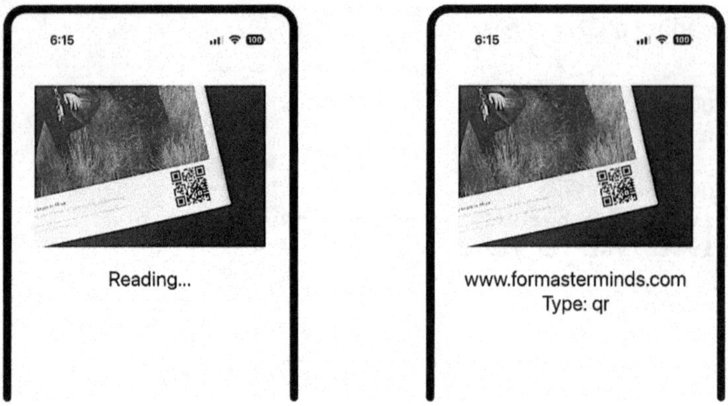

Figure 7-8: *Barcode reader*

Do It Yourself

Create a new Multiplatform project. Download the **magazineqr.png** image from our website and drag it into the project (**Vision > Barcode > magazineqr.png**). Update the ContentView.swift file with the code in Listing 7-11. Run the application on your iPhone. The QR code in this image encodes the URL of our website, so you should see the string "www.formasterminds.com" on the screen, as shown in Figure 7-8.

The request created with the **DetectBarcodesRequest** structure can detect multiple barcodes in a single image. If we need to read all of them, we can simply iterate through the array returned by the request and process the values, but if we want to detect only a specific barcode type, we can define it using the **symbologies** property. In the following example, we process an image containing two different barcodes but use the **symbologies** property to read only those of type **codabar**.

Listing 7-12: Reading only barcodes of type codabar

```
.task {
   let imageURL = Bundle.main.url(forResource: "magazinebar",
withExtension: "png")
   if let imageURL = imageURL {
      do {
         var request = DetectBarcodesRequest()
         request.symbologies = [.codabar]

         let result = try await request.perform(on: imageURL)
         if let code = result.first {
            barcode = code.payloadString ?? "Not Found"
            codeType = "Type: \(code.symbology)"
         }
      } catch {
         print("Error performing the request: \(error)")
      }
   }
}
```

In this example, we use the **magazinebar.png** image, which contains two different barcodes: a codabar barcode that encodes a numeric value, and the same QR code used previously that contains the URL of our website. If we use the same request as before, we obtain the values of both barcodes, but because in this case we assigned the `codabar` value to the `symbologies` property, the request returns only the codabar barcode.

Figure 7-9: *Barcode types*

Do It Yourself

Update the `task()` modifier from the `ContentView` view with the code in Listing 7-12. Download the **magazinebar.png** image from our website and drag it to the project (**Vision > Barcode > magazinebar.png**). Remember to change the name of the image for the `Image` view to show it on the screen (`UIImage(named: "magazinebar")`). Run the application on your iPhone. The app should only return the information for the first barcode and ignore the QR code, as shown in Figure 7-9.

IMPORTANT

Once we obtain the barcode number, we must look it up in a database to retrieve information about the product it represents. These systems are commonly used by companies to identify products, employee cards, authorization passes, and other assets. Some barcode databases are publicly available, allowing us to access information about commercial products directly from our apps. Several options are available depending on the type of products we want to identify. Some databases can be downloaded, while others are accessible through APIs, each offering different levels of completeness, licensing, and availability. We will learn how to create our own barcodes later in this chapter. To learn more about publicly available databases, visit our website and follow the links for this chapter.

7.3 - Text Analysis

The **Vision** framework also provides access to models trained for text recognition, allowing applications to detect and extract text from images or live camera feeds. With these models, we can scan documents, read signs, process receipts, and even translate text directly from the user's environment.

Text Recognition

The framework can perform two types of requests: one that recognizes all the text in an image, and another that also detects structural elements within the text, such as lists and tables. For basic text recognition, the framework provides the following structure.

RecognizeTextRequest(Revision)

This initializer creates a request to recognize and extract the text in an image. The argument is an enumeration that specifies the version of the model to use. At the moment, the only available value is **revision3**. If no revision is specified, the latest revision is selected by default.

The **RecognizeTextRequest** structure includes properties to configure the request. The following are the most frequently used.

usesLanguageCorrection

This property sets or returns a Boolean value that determines whether the request applies language correction when extracting text.

recognitionLanguages

This property sets or returns an array of **Language** structures that specify the languages we want the request to recognize. If no languages are specified, the request attempts to recognize all available languages.

recognitionLevel

This property sets or returns an enumeration value of type **RecognitionLevel** that specifies the technique the request uses to recognize text. The possible values are **accurate** and **fast**.

As always, the request is performed with the **perform(on:)** method. In this case, the method returns an array of **RecognizedTextObservation** structures. The following are the properties and methods included by the structure to provide the information.

transcript

This property returns a **String** value containing the text that the model recognized with the highest confidence.

recognitionLanguages

This property returns an array of **Language** structures that specify the languages recognized by the model.

topCandidates(Int)

This method returns an array of **RecognizedText** structures representing the possible interpretations of the text. Each **RecognizedText** structure includes the **string** property to return a interpretation of the text and the **confidence** property with a **Float** value indicating the model's confidence in that interpretation. The argument specifies the number of interpretations to return. It is a value between 1 and 10.

The request automatically detects the language of the text in the image, so we don't need to specify it in advance. However, we can restrict the set of languages to recognize or adjust the level of accuracy used by the model. In the following example, we show how to recognize the text in an image with a high level of accuracy.

Listing 7-13: Recognizing text in an image

```
import SwiftUI
import Vision

struct ContentView: View {
   @State private var textFound: String = "Recognizing..."

   var body: some View {
      VStack {
         Image(uiImage: UIImage(named: "sign")!)
            .resizable()
            .scaledToFit()
            .padding()
         Text(textFound)
         Spacer()
      }
      .padding()
      .task {
         let imageURL = Bundle.main.url(forResource: "sign",
            withExtension: "png")
         if let imageURL = imageURL {
            do {
               var request = RecognizeTextRequest()
               request.recognitionLevel = .accurate
               let result = try await request.perform(on: imageURL)

               var text: String = ""
               for observation in result {
                  text += "\(observation.transcript)\n"
               }
               textFound = text
            } catch {
               print("Error performing the request: \(error)")
            }
         }
      }
   }
}
```

This example is similar to those introduced before. As soon as the view is loaded, we get the URL of the image to process, perform the request using this value, and then display the result on the screen. In this case, we set the recognition level to **`accurate`** to instruct the model to produce the most precise output, and we read the text from the **`transcript`** property to retrieve the result with the highest confidence. Note that the text is recognized line by line, with each line returned in a separate structure. To combine all lines into a single result, we use a **`for in`** loop and append each line to a property until the full text is assembled. The result is shown below.

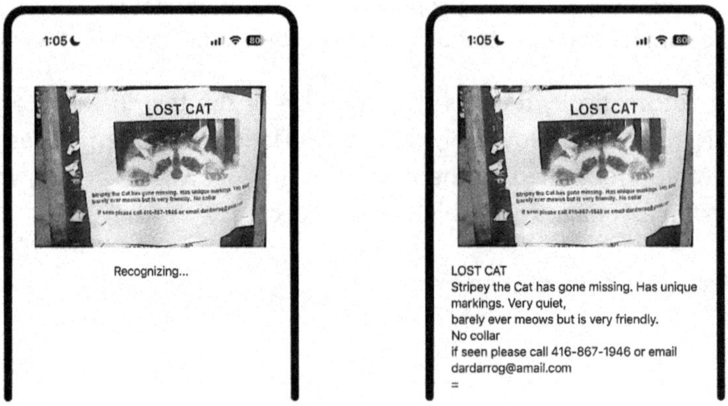

Figure 7-10: *Text recognition*

Do It Yourself

Create a new Multiplatform project. Download the **sign.png** image from our website and drag it into the project (**Vision > Text > sign.png**). Update the ContentView.swift file with the code in Listing 7-13. Run the application on your iPhone. You should see the text recognized by the model displayed below the image, as shown in Figure 7-10.

Recognizing text that users can already read is not particularly useful on its own. This model becomes truly valuable when combined with other tools that can process or repurpose the text. For example, we can use Foundation Models to generate new content from the recognized text or integrate another API to extract specific information. In the following example, we show how to use the **Translation** framework to translate the text recognized by the model into the user's preferred language.

Listing 7-14: Translating text from an image

```
import SwiftUI
import Vision
@preconcurrency import Translation

struct ContentView: View {
   @State private var translation: String = "Translating..."
   @State private var textToTranslate: String = ""
```

```
   @State private var configuration:
      TranslationSession.Configuration? = nil

   var body: some View {
      VStack {
         Image(uiImage: UIImage(named: "frenchsign")!)
            .resizable()
            .scaledToFit()
            .padding()
         Text(translation)
         Spacer()
      }
      .padding()
      .task {
         let imageURL = Bundle.main.url(forResource: "frenchsign",
            withExtension: "png")
         if let imageURL = imageURL {
            do {
               var request = RecognizeTextRequest()
               request.recognitionLevel = .accurate
               let result = try await request.perform(on: imageURL)
               var text: String = ""
               for observation in result {
                  text += "\(observation.transcript) "
               }
               textToTranslate = text

               // Translate the text
               let userLanguage = Locale.current.language
               if configuration != nil {
                  configuration?.invalidate()
               } else {
                  configuration = TranslationSession.Configuration(
                     source: nil, target: userLanguage)
               }
            } catch {
               print("Error performing the request: \(error)")
            }
         }
      }
      .translationTask(configuration) { session in
         do {
            let response = try await session.translate(textToTranslate)
            translation = response.targetText
         } catch {
            print("Error translating the text: \(error)")
         }
      }
   }
}
```

In this example, we process an image containing text written in French. The request to recognize the text is created as before, but after getting the result, we assign it to a State property to make it available to the **Translation** framework and define the `Configuration` structure with the user's preferred language to trigger the translation (see Listing 6-20). The `translationTask()` modifier then performs the translation and assigns the result to another property so it can be displayed to the user. The result is shown below.

Figure 7-11: *Recognition and translation*

Do It Yourself

Update the ContentView.swift file with the code in Listing 7-14. Download the **frenchsign.png** image from our website and drag it into the project (**Vision > Text > frenchsign.png**). Run the application on your iPhone. You should see the English translation displayed below the image, as shown in Figure 7-11.

Document Recognition

In addition to recognizing text, the **Vision** framework can create requests to instruct the model to analyze the overall structure and layout of entire documents. With these requests, we can detect elements such as text blocks, lists, and tables, allowing us to extract key information from receipts, forms, business cards, and other printed materials. The following is the structure provided by the framework for this purpose.

RecognizeDocumentsRequest(Revision)

This initializer creates a request to recognize and extract text from documents. The argument is an enumeration that specifies the version of the model to use. At the moment, the only available value is **revision1**. If no revision is specified, the latest revision is selected by default.

The **RecognizeDocumentsRequest** structure includes the following properties to specify what we want the model to extract from the document.

barcodeDetectionOptions

This property sets or returns a **BarcodeDetectionOptions** structure that configures how barcodes are detected in a document. The structure includes a Boolean property called **enabled**, which determines whether barcode detection is performed or not.

supportedBarcodeSymbologies

This property sets or returns an array of enumeration values of type **BarcodeSymbology** that determine the types of barcodes to detect.

textRecognitionOptions

This property sets or returns a **TextRecognitionOptions** structure that configures how text is detected in a document.

supportedRecognitionLanguages

This property sets or returns an array of **Language** structures that specify the languages we want the model to recognize.

As always, the request is executed with the **perform(on:)** method. In this case, the method returns an array of **DocumentObservation** structures. The following property is provided by this structure to access information about the document.

document

This property returns a **Container** structure that provides access to the contents of the document. The structure includes properties that return information about each section of the document identified by the model. The available properties are **barcodes**, **lists**, **paragraphs**, **tables**, **text**, and **title**.

The **paragraphs**, **text**, and **title** properties return **Text** structures containing the text identified by the model. Each **Text** structure includes the following properties to provide information about the content.

transcript

This property returns a **String** containing all the text recognized by the model in a specific section of the document.

lines

This property returns an array of **RecognizedTextObservation** structures containing information about each line of text recognized by the model in a specific section of the document.

words

This property returns an array of **RecognizedTextObservation** structures containing information about each word recognized by the model in a specific section of the document.

detectedData

This property returns an array of **DataDetectorMatch** structures containing the elements identified by the model as specific types of data, such as email addresses, phone numbers, postal addresses, and more.

To learn how to work with these types of requests, we will use two different documents: a letter from customer support and an invoice containing details about the purchase of several products. For this example, we need one view to display the document and another view to recognize its content. When the user taps the document, the second view opens to perform the request and display the result, as shown below.

Figure 7-12: *Reading a document*

The following is the code we need in the **`ContentView`** view to display the document and allow the user to select it.

Listing 7-15: Displaying the document to analyze

```
import SwiftUI

struct ContentView: View {
   var body: some View {
      NavigationStack {
         NavigationLink(destination: DocumentView()) {
            VStack {
               Image(uiImage: UIImage(named: "letter")!)
                  .resizable()
                  .scaledToFit()
               Spacer()
            }.padding()
         }
      }
   }
}
```

When the user taps the document, we open a view called **`DocumentView`** to process it. From this view, we can perform a document recognition request to extract any information we need. In the following example, we show how to retrieve the complete text contained in the document.

Listing 7-16: Retrieving the document's whole text

```
import SwiftUI
import Vision
```

```
struct DocumentView: View {
   @State private var textFound: String = "Recognizing..."

   var body: some View {
      VStack {
         ScrollView {
            Text(textFound)
               .padding()
         }
         Spacer()
      }
      .task {
         let imageURL = Bundle.main.url(forResource: "letter",
            withExtension: "png")
         if let imageURL = imageURL {
            do {
               let request = RecognizeDocumentsRequest()
               let result = try await request.perform(on: imageURL)

               if let document = result.first?.document {
                  textFound = document.text.transcript
               }
            } catch {
               print("Error performing the request: \(error)")
            }
         }
      }
   }
}
```

Do It Yourself

Create a new Multiplatform project. Download the **letter.png** image from our website and drag it into the project (**Vision > Text > letter.png**). Update the **ContentView** view with the code in Listing 7-15. Create a new file called DocumentView.swift for the code in Listing 7-16. Run the application on your iPhone and tap the image. A new view should open, and the text contained in the image should appear on the screen, as shown in Figure 7-12 (right).

In the previous example, we retrieved the entire text from the document, which is similar to what we did earlier using a text recognition request. However, with a document recognition request, we can also access specific parts of the text, including words, lines, and paragraphs. For instance, the image processed in the previous example contains a letter composed of several paragraphs, so we can extract them by analyzing the number of words in each section.

Listing 7-17: Finding paragraphs in a text

```
.task {
   let imageURL = Bundle.main.url(forResource: "letter",
      withExtension: "png")
   if let imageURL = imageURL {
      do {
         let request = RecognizeDocumentsRequest()
         let result = try await request.perform(on: imageURL)

         var text = ""
         if let document = result.first?.document {
            for paragraph in document.paragraphs {
               if let count = paragraph.words?.count, count > 10 {
                  text += "\(paragraph.transcript)\n\n"
               }
            }
            textFound = text
         }
      } catch {
         print("Error performing the request: \(error)")
      }
   }
}
```

The model recognizes single lines as paragraphs, including short texts such as greetings or names. To determine whether a piece of text belongs to a full paragraph, we can count the number of words it contains. If the text recognized by the model as a paragraph includes more than ten words, for example, we can assume it is part of the letter's main body and include it in the result. In this case, instead of returning the entire text, we display only the main content to the user, as shown below.

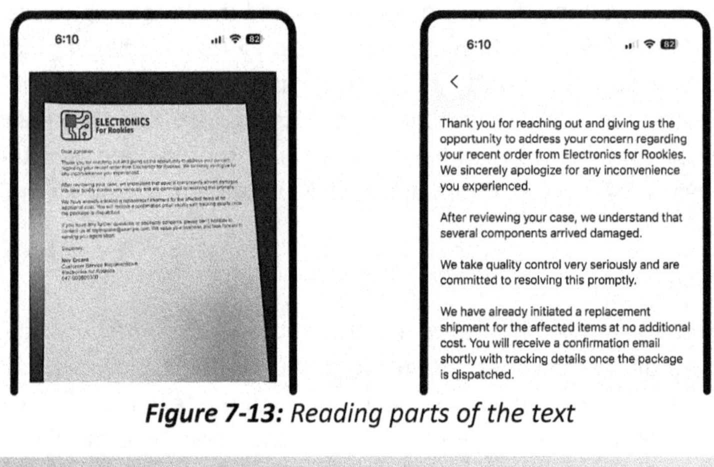

***Figure 7-13:** Reading parts of the text*

Do It Yourself

Update the **`task()`** modifier in the **`DocumentView`** view with the code in Listing 7-17. Run the application on your iPhone and tap the image. The letter's main text should appear on the screen, as shown in Figure 7-13.

In addition to identifying parts of the text, we can also extract key information such as email addresses, phone numbers, dates, and more. For this purpose, the **`Text`** structure returned by the **`text`**, **`paragraphs`** and **`title`** properties includes a property called **`detectedData`** that returns a **`DataDetectorMatch`** structure with the information identified by the model. To provide this information, the **`DataDetectorMatch`** structure defines a property called **`match`** that returns a **`Match`** structure, which in turn includes another property called **`details`** that returns an enumeration of type **`SemanticDetails`**, which is the one that specifies the type of information found and provides the value recognized by the model. To define these values, the enumeration includes the following cases.

`calendarEvent``(CalendarEvent)`

This case is returned when the detector identifies a date. The associated value is a structure with the properties **`allDay`**, **`startDate`**, **`endDate`**, **`endTimeZone`**, and **`startTimeZone`**.

`emailAddress``(EmailAddress)`

This case is returned when the detector identifies an email address. The associated value is a structure with the properties **`emailAddress`** and **`label`**.

`flightNumber``(FlightNumber)`

This case is returned when the detector identifies a flight number. The associated value is a structure with the properties **`airlineCode`** and **`flightNumber`**.

`link``(Link)`

This case is returned when the detector identifies a link. The associated value is a structure with the property **`url`**.

`measurement``(Measurement)`

This case is returned when the detector identifies a measurement. The associated value is a structure with the properties **`possibleDimensions`** and **`value`**.

`moneyAmount``(MoneyAmount)`

This case is returned when the detector identifies a money figure. The associated value is a structure with the properties **`amount`** and **`currency`**.

`paymentIdentifier``(PaymentIdentifier)`

This case is returned when the detector identifies a payment method. The associated value is a structure with the properties **`identifier`** and **`type`**.

`phoneNumber``(PhoneNumber)`

This case is returned when the detector identifies a phone number. The associated value is a structure with the properties **`phoneNumber`** and **`label`**.

`postalAddress``(PostalAddress)`

This case is returned when the detector identifies an address. The associated value is a structure with the properties **`fullAddress`**, **`street`**, **`city`**, **`state`**, **`postalCode`**, **`region`**, **`regionCode`** and **`label`**.

shipmentTrackingNumber(ShipmentTrackingNumber)

This case is returned when the detector identifies a tracking number. The associated value is a structure with the properties **carrier**, **trackingNumber** and **trackingURL**.

All these data types are defined in a framework called **DataDetection**, so we must import this framework to extract the corresponding information. In the following example, we show how to extract the email address and phone number from our letter using this framework.

Listing 7-18: Extracting key information

```
import SwiftUI
import Vision
import DataDetection

struct DocumentView: View {
   @State private var textFound: String = "Recognizing..."

   var body: some View {
      VStack {
         ScrollView {
            Text(textFound)
               .padding()
         }
         Spacer()
      }
      .task {
         let imageURL = Bundle.main.url(forResource: "letter",
            withExtension: "png")
         if let imageURL = imageURL {
            do {
               let request = RecognizeDocumentsRequest()
               let result = try await request.perform(on: imageURL)

               var text = ""
               if let document = result.first?.document {
                  for data in document.text.detectedData {
                     switch data.match.details {
                     case .emailAddress(let value):
                        text += "Email: \(value.emailAddress)\n"
                     case .phoneNumber(let value):
                        text += "Phone: \(value.phoneNumber)\n"
                     default:
                        break
                     }
                  }
                  textFound = text
               }
            } catch {
               print("Error performing the request: \(error)")
            }
         }
      }
   }
}
```

Every time the model detects relevant information, it adds it to the array stored in the **detectedData** property. By iterating through this array, we can identify each piece of information and retrieve the values. In this example, we are interested in detecting email addresses and phone numbers, so we check for these values and display them to the user, as shown below.

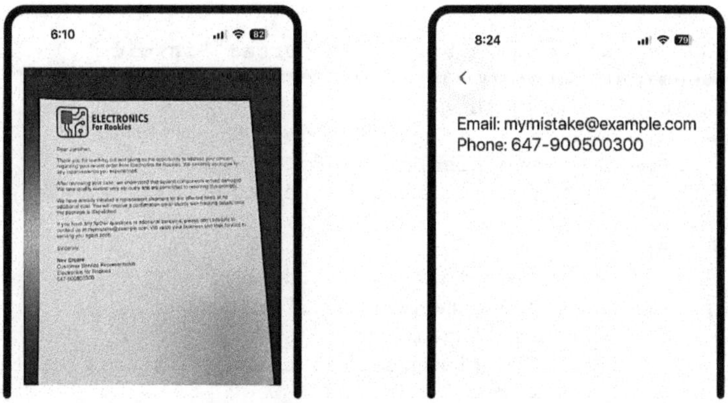

Figure 7-14: *Showing key information to the user*

Do It Yourself

Update the DocumentView.swift file with the code in Listing 7-18. Run the application on your iPhone and tap the image. You should see the email address and phone number from the document displayed on the screen, as shown in Figure 7-14.

In addition to recognizing text, the model can also detect structural elements that are clearly separate from the rest of the document's layout. One of those elements is lists. The model can find lists within a document, identify each item they contain, and return their values. Lists are represented by a structure called **List**, which includes a property called **items** that stores an array of **Item** structures, each representing an item in the list. The **Item** structure includes the following properties.

content

This property returns a **Container** structure with the content of the item.

itemString

This property returns a **String** value with the transcript of the item.

markerType

This property returns an enumeration of type **Marker** that specifies the type of marker used in the list. The possible values are **bullet**, **decimal**, **decorativeDecimal**, **hyphen**, **lowercaseLatin**, and **uppercaseLatin**.

markerString

This property returns a **String** value that represents the marker used in the list.

When the model finds a list, it creates a **`List`** structure, so all we need to do is read the properties of this structure to get the values we want, as shown below.

Listing 7-19: Extracting lists

```
.task {
    let imageURL = Bundle.main.url(forResource: "invoice",
       withExtension: "png")
    if let imageURL = imageURL {
       do {
          let request = RecognizeDocumentsRequest()
          let result = try await request.perform(on: imageURL)

          var text = ""
          if let document = result.first?.document {
             if let list = document.lists.first {
                for item in list.items {
                   text += "\(item.markerString) \(item.itemString)\n"
                }
             }
          }
          textFound = text
       } catch {
          print("Error performing the request: \(error)")
       }
    }
}
```

In this example, we use an invoice that includes a numbered list of payment methods at the bottom. Because we know that the document contains only one list, we retrieve the first element returned by the model (**`document.lists.first`**) and iterate through its items to display them to the user. Since the items are numbered, we also read the **`item.markerString`** property to include the number of each item. The result is shown below.

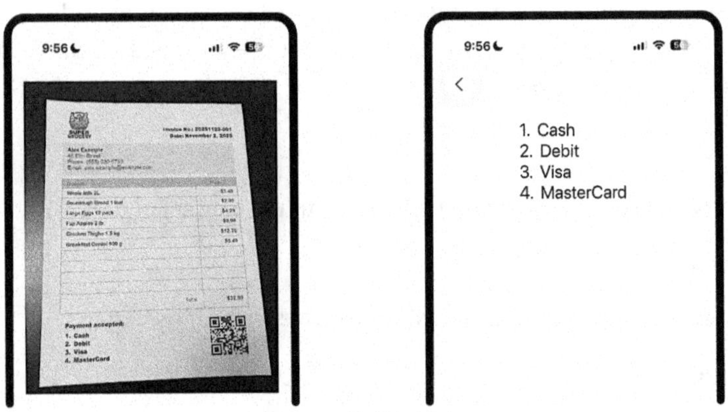

Figure 7-15: *Lists*

Do It Yourself

Update the **task()** modifier in the **DocumentView** view with the code in Listing 7-19. Download the **invoice.png** image from our website and drag it into the project (**Vision > Text > invoice.png**). Remember to replace the image in the **ContentView** view as well (**UIImage(named: "invoice")**). Run the application on your iPhone and tap the image. You should see the list of payment methods on the screen, as shown in Figure 7-15.

Our invoice contains a list of grocery items arranged in a table, which is another element the model can easily identify. In this case, the data is represented by a structure of type **Table**, which includes the properties **columns** and **rows** to organize the content. These properties store arrays of **Cell** structures, which provide the following property to access their content.

content

This property returns a **Container** structure with the content of the cell.

The process of extracting values from a table is similar to the one used for a list. In this case, we know we are working with a single table, so we must obtain the first item in the array (**document.tables.first**) and then iterate through the elements in the **rows** property, as shown below.

Listing 7-20: Extracting tables

```
.task {
   let imageURL = Bundle.main.url(forResource: "invoice",
      withExtension: "png")
   if let imageURL = imageURL {
      do {
         let request = RecognizeDocumentsRequest()
         let result = try await request.perform(on: imageURL)

         var text = ""
         if let document = result.first?.document {
            if let table = document.tables.first {
               for row in table.rows {
                  var rowContent = ""
                  for cell in row {
                     rowContent += "\(cell.content.text.transcript) "
                  }
                  rowContent = rowContent.trimmingCharacters(
                     in: .whitespacesAndNewlines)
                  if !rowContent.isEmpty {
                     text += "\(rowContent)\n"
                  }
               }
               text += "\n"
```

```
            }
         }
         textFound = text
      } catch {
         print("Error performing the request: \(error)")
      }
   }
}
```

The **content** property of the **Cell** structure returns a **Container** structure, giving us access to the same properties available when working with the entire document. In this case, we access the **Text** structure through the **text** property and display the value of its **transcript** property to show each item in the table. Note that some rows may be empty, so we check whether they contain a value and display only those that do. The result is shown below.

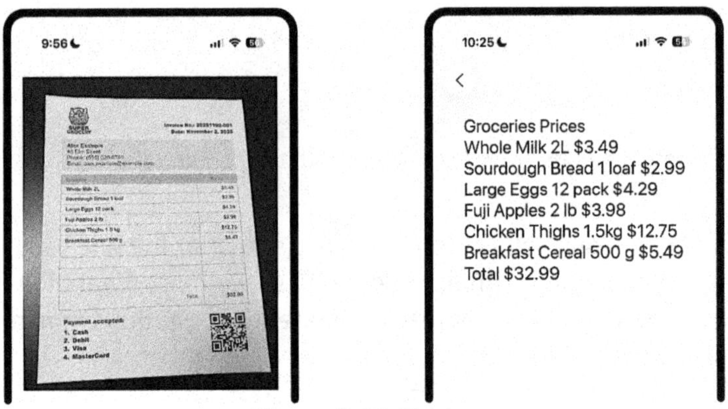

***Figure 7-16:** Tables*

Do It Yourself

Update the **task()** modifier in the **DocumentView** view with the code in Listing 7-20. Run the application on your iPhone and tap the image. You should see the list of groceries on the screen, as shown in Figure 7-16.

Another element the model can extract from a document is a barcode. The recognition process works the same way as before (see Listing 7-11), but we must instruct the model to search for barcodes in the document by setting the **enabled** property of the structure returned by the **barcodeDetectionOptions** property to **true**, as shown below.

Listing 7-21: Extracting barcodes

```
.task {
   let imageURL = Bundle.main.url(forResource: "invoice",
      withExtension: "png")
   if let imageURL = imageURL {
      do {
```

```
            var request = RecognizeDocumentsRequest()
            request.barcodeDetectionOptions.enabled = true
            let result = try await request.perform(on: imageURL)
            var text = ""
            if let document = result.first?.document {
               for barcode in document.barcodes {
                  text += "Barcode: \(barcode.payloadString ??
                     "Illegible")\n"
               }
            }
            textFound = text
         } catch {
            print("Error performing the request: \(error)")
         }
      }
   }
```

In this example, we search for any type of barcode, but if we need to detect a specific barcode format, we can set the **supportedBarcodeSymbologies** property accordingly (see Listing 7-12). The result is shown below.

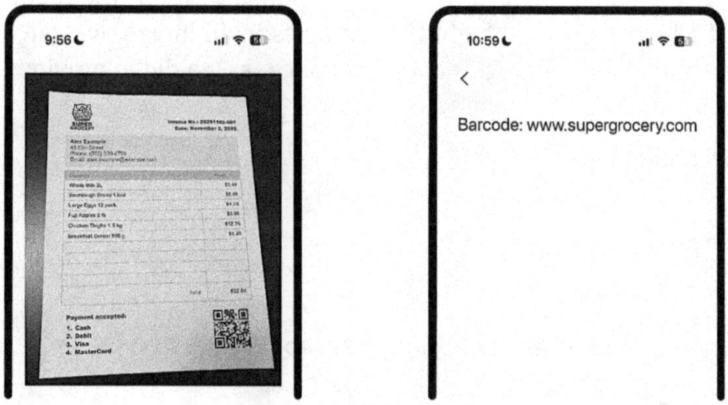

Figure 7-17: *Barcodes*

Do It Yourself

Update the **task()** modifier in the **DocumentView** view with the code in Listing 7-21. Run the application on your iPhone and tap the image. You should see the domain extracted from the QR code on the screen, as shown in Figure 7-17.

7.4 - Human Body Analysis

The **Vision** framework also includes powerful models trained to analyze the human body. These models can detect facial landmarks, body poses, and hand poses, allowing our applications to interpret human movement and expression with impressive accuracy. By using these models, we can track facial expressions, recognize gestures, measure motion, and even create real-time interactions that respond to the user's posture or hand position.

Face Detection

Perhaps the most useful feature of these models is their ability to detect faces in an image. They can not only locate faces but also identify specific features such as the eyes, nose, and mouth. To create a request that detects faces in an image, the **Vision** framework provides the following structure.

> **`DetectFaceRectanglesRequest`**`(Revision)`
>
> This initializer creates a request to detect faces and determine the regions they occupy within an image. The argument is an enumeration that specifies the version of the model to use. At the moment, the only available value is **`revision3`**. If no revision is specified, the latest revision is selected by default.

As always, to perform the request, we call the **`perform(on:)`** method. In this case, the request returns an array of **`FaceObservation`** structures. This structure conforms to the **`BoundingBoxProviding`** protocol and therefore includes the **`boundingBox`** property, which returns a **`NormalizedRect`** structure with the position and size of the rectangle around the detected face. If all we need is to highlight the faces in an image, we can simply read this property and use it to draw rectangles over the image, as we did in previous examples.

Listing 7-22: Detecting faces

```
import SwiftUI
import Vision

struct ContentView: View {
   @State private var observations: [FaceObservation] = []

   var body: some View {
      VStack {
         Button("Detect") {
            Task {
               await detectFaces()
            }
         }.buttonStyle(.borderedProminent)

         Canvas { context, size in
            // Calculate size and draw image
            let image = UIImage(named: "girlselfie")!
            let width = size.width
            let height = image.size.height * width / image.size.width
            let imageFrame = CGRect(origin: .zero,
               size: CGSize(width: width, height: height))
            context.draw(Image(uiImage: image), in: imageFrame)

            // Calculate size and draw bounding box
            for observation in observations {
               let rect = observation.boundingBox
               let boxFrame = rect.toImageCoordinates(imageFrame.size,
                  origin: .upperLeft)
```

```
                    context.stroke(Rectangle().path(in: boxFrame),
                       with: .color(.green), lineWidth: 5)
                 }
              }
              Spacer()
           }
           .padding()
        }
        func detectFaces() async {
           let imageURL = Bundle.main.url(forResource: "girlselfie",
              withExtension: "png")
           if let imageURL = imageURL {
              do {
                 let request = DetectFaceRectanglesRequest()
                 observations = try await request.perform(on: imageURL)
              } catch {
                 print("Error performing the request: \(error)")
              }
           }
        }
     }
```

In this example, we process an image containing a picture of a girl (**girlselfie.png**). We draw the image on a `Canvas` view as before, and then retrieve the coordinates of the rectangle surrounding her face, convert them to the image's pixel coordinates with the `toImageCoordinates()` method, and draw the outline of a rectangle over it. The result is shown below.

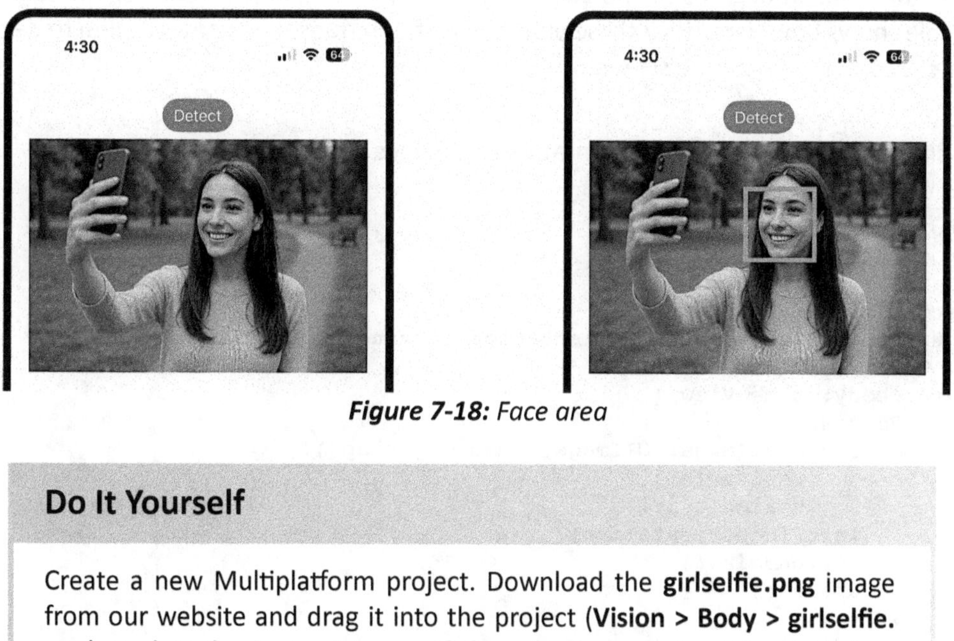

Figure 7-18: *Face area*

Do It Yourself

Create a new Multiplatform project. Download the **girlselfie.png** image from our website and drag it into the project (**Vision > Body > girlselfie.png**). Update the ContentView.swift file with the code in Listing 7-22. Run the application on your iPhone and tap the Detect button. You should see a green rectangle highlighting the girl's face, as shown in Figure 7-18.

The request created with the **DetectFaceRectanglesRequest** structure can also determine the orientation of a detected face. Specifically, it identifies three types of rotation: pitch, which measures how far the head tilts up or down; roll, which measures how far the head tilts to either side; and yaw, which measures how far the head turns left or right. The **FaceObservation** structure provides the following properties to return these values.

pitch

This property returns a **Measurement** value of type **UnitAngle** that indicates how much the face is tilted upward or downward.

roll

This property returns a **Measurement** value of type **UnitAngle** that indicates how much the face is tilted to the left or right.

yaw

This property returns a **Measurement** value of type **UnitAngle** that indicates how far the face is turned to the left or right.

All these properties return a **Measurement** value with a base unit that can be converted to any desired unit we want. For this purpose, the structure provides the **converted(to:)** method, which takes a **UnitAngle** value specifying the unit to return. Several predefined properties are available for this purpose. In this case, we can use the **degrees** property to obtain the value in degrees or the **radians** property to obtain it in radians. The following example shows how to retrieve these values from the request and convert them to degrees before showing them on the screen.

Listing 7-23: Determining the orientation of the face

```
import SwiftUI
import Vision

struct ContentView: View {
   @State private var faceOrientation: String = "Calculating..."

   var body: some View {
      VStack {
         Image(uiImage: UIImage(named: "girlup")!)
            .resizable()
            .scaledToFit()
         Text(faceOrientation)
            .padding()
         Spacer()
      }
      .padding()
      .task {
         let imageURL = Bundle.main.url(forResource: "girlup",
            withExtension: "png")
         if let imageURL = imageURL {
            do {
               let request = DetectFaceRectanglesRequest()
```

```
               let observations = try await request.perform(on: imageURL)

               var text = ""
               if let observation = observations.first {
                  let pitch = observation.pitch.converted(to: .degrees)
                     .value
                  text += "Pitch: \(pitch)\n"
                  let yaw = observation.yaw.converted(to: .degrees).value
                  text += "Yaw: \(yaw)\n"
                  let roll = observation.roll.converted(to: .degrees)
                     .value
                  text += "Roll: \(roll)\n\n"
               }
               faceOrientation = text
            } catch {
               print("Error performing the request: \(error)")
            }
         }
      }
   }
}
```

The view displays the image at the top and a `Text` view with the angle values at the bottom. In this example, we use a picture of a girl looking upward and to her right (**girlup.png**), so the `yaw` and `pitch` values are offset from zero, as shown below. (In this case, the values are negative because her face is oriented toward directions represented by negative angles.)

***Figure 7-19:** Face angles*

Do It Yourself

Update the `ContentView` view with the code in Listing 7-23. Download the **girlup.png** image from our website and drag it into the project (**Vision > Body > girlup.png**). Run the application on your iPhone. After a few seconds, you should see the face orientation angles displayed on the screen, as shown in Figure 7-19.

Another task we can perform with these models is evaluating the quality of a selfie. The model analyzes factors such as lighting, sharpness, and face position to estimate the overall quality of the image. The following is the structure provided by the framework to create this type of request.

DetectFaceCaptureQualityRequest(Revision)

This initializer creates a request to determine the quality of a selfie. The argument is an enumeration that specifies the version of the model to use. At the moment, the only available value is **revision3**. If no revision is specified, the latest revision is selected by default.

To report the quality that the model has determined for a face, the **FaceObservation** structure provides the following property.

captureQuality

This property returns a **CaptureQuality** structure that represents the overall quality of the detected face in a selfie. The structure includes a property called **score** that returns a **Float** value between 0.0 and 1.0, indicating the quality level, where 0.0 represents low quality and 1.0 represents high quality.

In the following example, we use a picture of two girls (**twoselfie.png**), create a request to calculate the image quality of each girl's face, and display the values on the screen.

Listing 7-24: Determining the quality of selfies

```
import SwiftUI
import Vision

struct ContentView: View {
   @State private var quality: String = "Calculating..."

   var body: some View {
      VStack {
         Image(uiImage: UIImage(named: "twoselfie")!)
            .resizable()
            .scaledToFit()
         Text(quality)
            .padding()
         Spacer()
      }
      .padding()
      .task {
         let imageURL = Bundle.main.url(forResource: "twoselfie",
            withExtension: "png")
         if let imageURL = imageURL {
            do {
               let request = DetectFaceCaptureQualityRequest()
               let observations = try await request.perform(on: imageURL)

               var text = ""
```

```
                for (index, quality) in observations.enumerated() {
                    text += "Quality Face \(index + 1):
                        \(quality.captureQuality?.score ?? 0)\n"
                }
                quality = text
            } catch {
                print("Error performing the request: \(error)")
            }
        }
    }
  }
}
```

The request returns an array of **FaceObservation** structures, one for each face detected in the image. In this example, we want to evaluate the image quality for both faces, so we iterate through the array, label each face using its index, and read the **score** property to get the quality values. The result is shown below.

Figure 7-20: *Face quality*

Do It Yourself

Update the **ContentView** view with the code in Listing 7-24. Download the **twoselfie.png** image from our website and drag it into the project (**Vision > Body > twoselfie.png**). Run the application on your iPhone. After a few seconds, you should see the quality score for each face displayed on the screen, as shown in Figure 7-20.

Another useful task we can perform with these models is detecting facial features such as the mouth, nose, and eyes. The model identifies these landmarks and returns a set of points that outline their locations within the image. To create this type of request, the framework provides the following structure.

DetectFaceLandmarksRequest(Revision)

This initializer creates a request to detect facial features. The argument is an enumeration that specifies the version of the model to use. At the moment, the only available value is **revision3**. If no revision is specified, the latest revision is selected by default.

The **FaceObservation** structure provides the following property to return the landmarks detected in a face.

landmarks

This property returns a set of **Region** structures, each containing information about the specific facial feature they represent. The framework defines several properties to return these structures. The currently available are **innerLips**, **leftEye**, **leftEyebrow**, **leftPupil**, **medianLine**, **nose**, **noseCrest**, **outerLips**, **rightEye**, **rightEyebrow**, and **rightPupil**.

A **Region** structure contains all the points that define the shape of the facial feature it represents. These points are expressed in normalized coordinates. To convert them into pixel coordinates within the image, the **Region** structure provides the following method.

pointsInImageCoordinates(CGSize, **origin:** CoordinateOrigin)

This method converts the normalized coordinates of the points in a **Region** structure into the coordinate space of an image. The first argument specifies the size of the image in pixels, and the **origin** argument is an enumeration that determines the coordinate system to use for the conversion. The possible values are **upperLeft** and **lowerLeft**.

In the following example, we show a close-up picture of a girl's face and create a request to detect the locations of her left and right eyes. Once again, we use a **Canvas** view to draw the image and display the detected points on the screen.

Listing 7-25: Detecting facial features

```
import SwiftUI
import Vision

struct ContentView: View {
   @State private var observations: [FaceObservation] = []

   var body: some View {
      VStack {
         Button("Detect") {
            Task {
               await detectEyes()
            }
         }.buttonStyle(.borderedProminent)
```

```
        Canvas { context, size in
            // Calculate size and draw image
            let image = UIImage(named: "girlclose")!
            let width = size.width
            let height = image.size.height * width / image.size.width
            let imageFrame = CGRect(origin: .zero,
               size: CGSize(width: width, height: height))
            context.draw(Image(uiImage: image), in: imageFrame)

            // Show points
            for observation in observations {
               if let landmarks = observation.landmarks {
                  let regions = [landmarks.leftEye, landmarks.rightEye]
                  for region in regions {
                     let points = region.pointsInImageCoordinates(
                        imageFrame.size, origin: .upperLeft)
                     for point in points {
                        let circleFrame = CGRect(x: point.x - 2,
                           y: point.y - 2, width: 4, height: 4)
                        context.fill(Circle().path(in: circleFrame),
                           with: .color(.green))
                     }
                  }
               }
            }
         }
         Spacer()
      }
      .padding()
   }
   func detectEyes() async {
      let imageURL = Bundle.main.url(forResource: "girlclose",
         withExtension: "png")
      if let imageURL = imageURL {
         do {
            let request = DetectFaceLandmarksRequest()
            observations = try await request.perform(on: imageURL)
         } catch {
            print("Error performing the request: \(error)")
         }
      }
   }
}
```

The request created with the **DetectFaceLandmarksRequest** structure detects all identifiable facial features, so we must ensure that we process only those we care about. In this case, we want to highlight the eyes, so we read the **leftEye** and **rightEye** properties. Each of these properties returns a **Region** structure containing the points that define the shape of the eyes. To display these points to the user, we convert them into pixel coordinates using the **pointsInImageCoordinates()** method and draw circles at each location. The result is shown below.

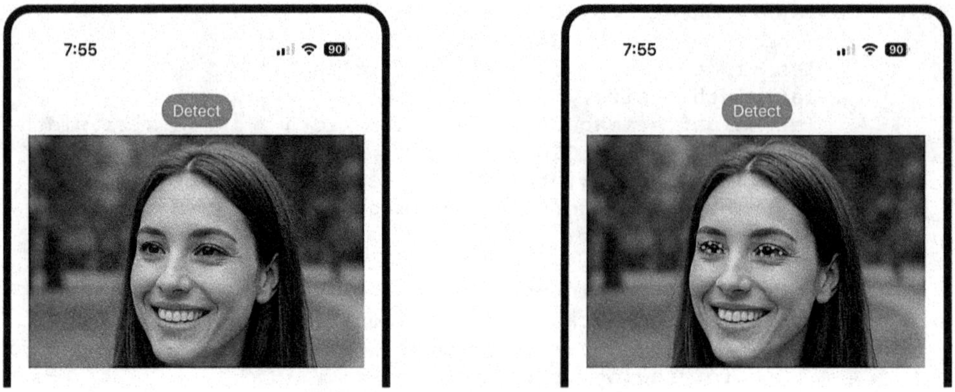

Figure 7-21: *Facial features*

Do It Yourself

Update the `ContentView` view with the code in Listing 7-25. Download the **girlclose.png** image from our website and drag it into the project (**Vision > Body > girlclose.png**). Run the application on your iPhone and press the Detect button. You should see green circles around the girl's eyes, as shown in Figure 7-21.

Body Detection

The **Vision** framework provides access to models trained to detect and analyze human bodies in images and video frames. With these models, we can locate people and identify the regions occupied by their bodies, recognize key body features such as the head, shoulders, elbows, wrists, hips, knees, and ankles, and determine the spatial relationships between those points to identify body poses and detect movement. The following is the structure provided by the framework to create a request for detecting people in an image.

`DetectHumanRectanglesRequest(Revision)`

This initializer creates a request to detect human bodies in an image and return the regions they occupy. The argument is an enumeration that specifies the version of the model to use. At the moment, the only available value is **`revision2`**. If no revision is specified, the latest revision is selected by default.

The **`DetectHumanRectanglesRequest`** structure includes the following property to configure the request.

`upperBodyOnly`

This property sets or returns a Boolean value that determines whether the model detects full human bodies (**`false`**) or only the upper body (**`true`**).

As before, the structure includes the **`perform(on:)`** method to perform the request. In this case, the method returns a **`HumanObservation`** structure. This structure conforms to the

BoundingBoxProviding protocol and therefore includes the **boundingBox** property, which returns a **NormalizedRect** structure containing the position and size of the rectangle that encloses the body. If our goal is simply to highlight people in an image, we can read this property and use it to draw rectangles over the image, as shown below.

Listing 7-26: Finding people in an image

```
import SwiftUI
import Vision

struct ContentView: View {
   @State private var observations: [HumanObservation] = []

   var body: some View {
      VStack {
         Button("Detect") {
            Task {
               await detectBodies()
            }
         }.buttonStyle(.borderedProminent)

         Canvas { context, size in
            // Calculate size and draw image
            let image = UIImage(named: "twopeople")!
            let width = size.width
            let height = image.size.height * width / image.size.width
            let imageFrame = CGRect(origin: .zero,
               size: CGSize(width: width, height: height))
            context.draw(Image(uiImage: image), in: imageFrame)

            // Calculate size and draw bounding box
            for observation in observations {
               let rect = observation.boundingBox
               let boxFrame = rect.toImageCoordinates(imageFrame.size,
                  origin: .upperLeft)
               context.stroke(Rectangle().path(in: boxFrame),
                  with: .color(.green), lineWidth: 5)
            }
         }
         Spacer()
      }
      .padding()
   }
   func detectBodies() async {
      let imageURL = Bundle.main.url(forResource: "twopeople",
         withExtension: "png")
      if let imageURL = imageURL {
         do {
            var request = DetectHumanRectanglesRequest()
            request.upperBodyOnly = false
            observations = try await request.perform(on: imageURL)
         } catch {
            print("Error performing the request: \(error)")
         }
      }
   }
}
```

In this example, we set the request's `upperBodyOnly` property to `false` to detect the area occupied by the entire body. As before, we get the location and size of each region from the `boundingBox` property, convert these values to image coordinates using the `toImageCoordinates()` method, and draw the corresponding rectangles on the screen. Since our image contains two people, the result includes two rectangles highlighting their bodies, as shown below.

Figure 7-22: *Human bodies*

> **Do It Yourself**
>
> Create a new Multiplatform project. Download the **twopeople.png** image from our website and drag it into the project (**Vision > Body > twopeople.png**). Update the ContentView.swift file with the code in Listing 7-26. Run the application on your iPhone and press the Detect button. You should see rectangles highlighting the areas occupied by the people in the image, as shown in Figure 7-22.

The **Vision** framework also includes a request that detects the points in an image representing the joints of a person's body. Using these points, we can identify the person's pose and analyze movement. The following is the structure provided by the framework to create this request.

`DetectHumanBodyPoseRequest``(Revision)`

This initializer creates a request to determine the location of the joints in a human body. The argument is an enumeration that specifies the version of the model to use. At the moment, the only available value is **`revision2`**. If no revision is specified, the latest revision is selected by default.

The `DetectHumanBodyPoseRequest` structure includes the following property to configure the request.

detectsHands

This property sets or returns a Boolean value that determines whether the request should also detect and return the locations of the hand joints.

As always, the **perform(on:)** method is used to perform the request. In this case, the method returns a **HumanBodyPoseObservation** structure. By default, this structure provides information about the body joints, but if the request's **detectsHands** property is set to **true**, it also includes the locations of the hand joints. The following are the properties provided by the structure to access this information.

leftHand

This property returns a **HumanHandPoseObservation** structure containing information about the body's left hand.

rightHand

This property returns a **HumanHandPoseObservation** structure containing information about the body's right hand.

To provide information about the joints, the **HumanBodyPoseObservation** structure conforms to the **PoseProviding** protocol and therefore implements the following methods.

allJoints()

This method returns a dictionary containing the names and locations of all the joints identified in the body.

joint(for: PoseJointName**)**

This method returns a **Joint** structure containing the location of the joint specified by the **for** argument.

The joints are identified by names defined in an enumeration called **JointName**. The available values are **leftAnkle**, **leftEar**, **leftElbow**, **leftEye**, **leftHip**, **leftKnee**, **leftShoulder**, **leftWrist**, **neck**, **nose**, **rightAnkle**, **rightEar**, **rightElbow**, **rightEye**, **rightHip**, **rightKnee**, **rightShoulder**, **rightWrist** and **root**.

The information about each joint is provided by a structure of type **Joint**. The structure includes the following properties and method.

jointName

This property returns a **String** value with the name of the joint.

location

This property returns a **NormalizedPoint** structure with the location of the joint.

confidence

This property returns a **Float** value indicating the model's level of confidence in the accuracy of the information.

distance(to: Joint)

This method returns a **CGFloat** value representing the distance between the current joint and the joint specified by the **to** argument.

The following example demonstrates how to use this request to detect all the joints of the people in an image.

Listing 7-27: Detecting body joints

```
import SwiftUI
import Vision

struct ContentView: View {
   @State private var observations: [HumanBodyPoseObservation] = []

   var body: some View {
      VStack {
         Button("Detect") {
            Task {
               await detectBodies()
            }
         }.buttonStyle(.borderedProminent)

         Canvas { context, size in
            // Calculate size and draw image
            let image = UIImage(named: "twopeople")!
            let width = size.width
            let height = image.size.height * width / image.size.width
            let imageFrame = CGRect(origin: .zero,
               size: CGSize(width: width, height: height))
            context.draw(Image(uiImage: image), in: imageFrame)

            // Show points
            for observation in observations {
               let points = observation.allJoints()
               for (_, value) in points {
                  let location = value.location
                  let point = location.toImageCoordinates(imageFrame.size,
                     origin: .upperLeft)
                  let circleFrame = CGRect(x: point.x - 3, y: point.y - 3,
                     width: 6, height: 6)
                  context.fill(Circle().path(in: circleFrame),
                     with: .color(.green))
               }
            }
         }
         Spacer()
      }
      .padding()
   }
   func detectBodies() async {
      let imageURL = Bundle.main.url(forResource: "twopeople",
         withExtension: "png")
      if let imageURL = imageURL {
```

```
            do {
                let request = DetectHumanBodyPoseRequest()
                observations = try await request.perform(on: imageURL)
            } catch {
                print("Error performing the request: \(error)")
            }
        }
    }
}
```

As we did in previous examples, we draw a green circle at the location of each joint. To determine their positions on the screen, we read the **NormalizedPoint** structure from the **location** property, and use the **toImageCoordinates()** method to obtain the coordinates in pixels. The result is shown below.

Figure 7-23: *Body joints*

Do It Yourself

Update the **ContentView** view with the code in Listing 7-27. Run the application on your iPhone and tap the Detect button. You should see green dots marking each joint detected by the model, as shown in Figure 7-23.

The purpose of this model is to identify the main joints in a human body, but how we use that information depends on our goals. To determine whether a person is jumping or kneeling, for example, we must calculate the positions of the joints and the distances between them to infer the person's movement. Some gestures and poses are easier to recognize than others. For instance, by comparing the positions of the wrists and elbows, we can determine whether the person is raising a hand, as shown below.

Listing 7-28: Determining if people are raising their hands

```
import SwiftUI
import Vision
```

```
struct ContentView: View {
    @State private var bodyPose: String = "Detecting..."

    var body: some View {
        VStack {
            VStack {
                Image(uiImage: UIImage(named: "twohands")!)
                    .resizable()
                    .scaledToFit()
                Text(bodyPose)
                    .padding()
                Spacer()
            }
            .padding()
            .task {
                let imageURL = Bundle.main.url(forResource: "twohands",
                    withExtension: "png")
                if let imageURL = imageURL {
                    do {
                        let request = DetectHumanBodyPoseRequest()
                        let observations = try await request.perform(
                            on: imageURL)

                        var text = ""
                        for (index, observation) in observations.enumerated() {
                            text += "Person \(index + 1)\n"

                            if let leftHand = observation.joint(for: .leftWrist),
                              let leftElbow = observation.joint(for: .leftElbow){
                               if leftHand.location.y > leftElbow.location.y {
                                   text += "Left hand raised\n"
                               }
                            }
                            if let rightHand = observation.joint(for:
                                .rightWrist), let rightElbow =
                                observation.joint(for: .rightElbow) {
                                if rightHand.location.y > rightElbow.location.y {
                                    text += "Right hand raised\n"
                                }
                            }
                        }
                        bodyPose = text
                    } catch {
                        print("Error performing the request: \(error)")
                    }
                }
            }
        }
        .padding()
    }
}
```

In this example, we process an image containing two people raising their hands. The person on the left raises his right hand, and the person on the right raises her left hand. To detect these gestures, we call the `joint(for:)` method to obtain the locations of the left and right wrists and elbows, and then compare their **y** coordinates. Because coordinates in normalized space increase from bottom to top, if a wrist's **y** coordinate is higher than its corresponding elbow's, it means that the person is raising that hand, so we create a message to report the gesture and display it on the screen. The result is shown below.

Figure 7-24: *Body gestures*

Do It Yourself

Update the **`ContentView`** view with the code in Listing 7-28. Download the **twohands.png** image from our website and drag it into the project (**Vision > Body > twohands.png**). Run the application on your iPhone. After a few seconds, you should see the description of the gestures found in the image on the screen, as shown in Figure 7-24.

IMPORTANT

By comparing joint positions or calculating the distances between them, as we will see in the next section, we can recognize simple gestures. For more complex poses and movements, however, we need to gather sample data containing hundreds of thousands of images and train a custom Core ML model using that data. We will explore Core ML models and learn how to train them with Create ML in Chapter 10.

Hand Detection

The request created with the **`DetectHumanBodyPoseRequest`** structure can also detect hands, but the **Vision** framework provides a dedicated request specifically designed for hand detection. If our goal is to identify hand gestures, we should use this specialized request instead. The following is the structure provided by the framework for this purpose.

DetectHumanHandPoseRequest(Revision)

This initializer creates a request to determine the locations of hand joints. The argument is an enumeration that specifies the version of the model to use. At the moment, the only available value is **revision1**. If no revision is specified, the latest revision is selected by default.

The **DetectHumanHandPoseRequest** structure provides the following property to configure the request.

maximumHandCount

This property sets or returns an integer that specifies the maximum number of hands to detect (2 by default).

As always, the request is executed using the **perform(on:)** method. In this case, the method returns a **HumanHandPoseObservation** structure. This structure also conforms to the **PoseProviding** protocol and therefore implements the **allJoints()** and **joint(for:)** methods introduced before to provide information about the joints, but the **HumanHandPoseObservation** structure defines its own **JointName** enumeration with specific values to represent hand joints. The values available are **wrist**, **thumbCMC**, **thumbIP**, **thumbMP**, **thumbTip**, **indexDIP**, **indexMCP**, **indexPIP**, **indexTip**, **middleDIP**, **middleMCP**, **middlePIP**, **middleTip**, **ringDIP**, **ringMCP**, **ringPIP**, **ringTip**, **littleDIP**, **littleMCP**, **littlePIP** and **littleTip**.

If we just want to check the location of the joints, we can call the **allJoints()** method and draw the points over the image, as shown below.

Listing 7-29: Identifying hand joints

```
import SwiftUI
import Vision

struct ContentView: View {
   @State private var observations: [HumanHandPoseObservation] = []

   var body: some View {
      VStack {
         Button("Detect") {
            Task {
               await detectFingers()
            }
         }.buttonStyle(.borderedProminent)

         Canvas { context, size in
            // Calculate size and draw image
            let image = UIImage(named: "twohands")!
            let width = size.width
            let height = image.size.height * width / image.size.width
            let imageFrame = CGRect(origin: .zero,
               size: CGSize(width: width, height: height))
            context.draw(Image(uiImage: image), in: imageFrame)
```

```
            // Show points
            for observation in observations {
               let points = observation.allJoints()
               for (_, value) in points {
                  let location = value.location
                  let point = location.toImageCoordinates(imageFrame.size,
                     origin: .upperLeft)
                  let circleFrame = CGRect(x: point.x - 3, y: point.y - 3,
                     width: 6, height: 6)
                  context.fill(Circle().path(in: circleFrame),
                     with: .color(.green))
               }
            }
         }
         Spacer()
      }
      .padding()
   }
   func detectFingers() async {
      let imageURL = Bundle.main.url(forResource: "twohands",
         withExtension: "png")
      if let imageURL = imageURL {
         do {
            let request = DetectHumanHandPoseRequest()
            observations = try await request.perform(on: imageURL)
         } catch {
            print("Error performing the request: \(error)")
         }
      }
   }
}
```

In this example, we use the same image showing two people raising their hands. Because the request is configured by default to detect up to two hands, we get the joints for both hands in the image. The result is shown below.

Figure 7-25: *Hands joints*

Do It Yourself

Create a new Multiplatform project. Download the **twohands.png** image from our website and drag it into the project (**Vision > Body > twohands.png**). Update the ContentView.swift file with the code in Listing 7-29. Run the application on your iPhone and tap the Detect button. You should see green dots marking all the hand joints identified in the image, as shown in Figure 7-25, right.

The model is capable of identifying a total of 21 joints per hand, and every joint has been named according to its location, as shown below.

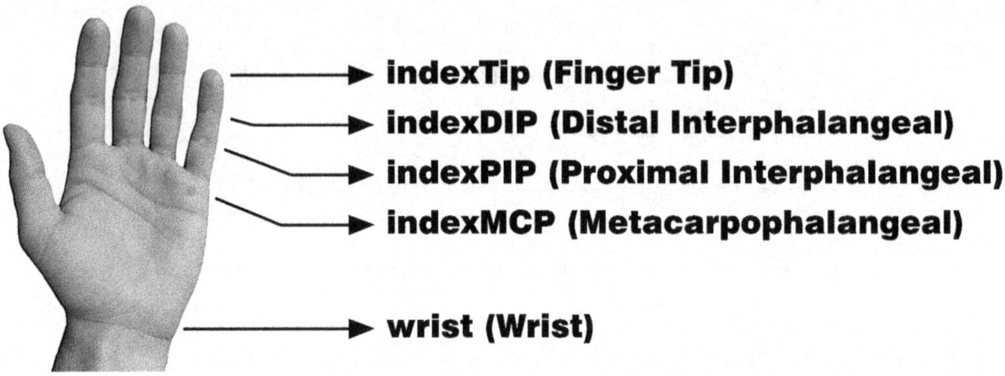

Figure 7-26: *Joints identifiers*

Using these identifiers, we can select specific joints and compare their positions to identify gestures or movements. For example, we can calculate the distance between the wrist and the tip of each finger to interpret what the person is signaling with his or her hand. If the distance for a particular finger is greater than that of the others, it indicates that the finger is extended. In the following example, we apply this technique to determine whether the hand in the image is showing the number 1, 2, or 3.

Listing 7-30: Detecting if the hand is counting numbers

```
import SwiftUI
import Vision

struct ContentView: View {
   @State private var numberGesture: String = "Detecting..."

   var body: some View {
      VStack {
         Image(uiImage: UIImage(named: "number1")!)
            .resizable()
            .scaledToFit()
         Text(numberGesture)
            .padding()
         Spacer()
      }
```

```
        .padding()
        .task {
            let imageURL = Bundle.main.url(forResource: "number1",
withExtension: "png")
            if let imageURL = imageURL {
                do {
                    let request = DetectHumanHandPoseRequest()
                    let observations = try await request.perform(on: imageURL)

                    var fingersUp = [0, 0, 0]
                    if let observation = observations.first {
                        if let wrist = observation.joint(for: .wrist) {
                            // Check gesture index finger
                            let indexTip = observation.joint(for: .indexTip)
                            let indexDIP = observation.joint(for: .indexDIP)
                            let indexTipDistance = indexTip?.distance(
                                to: wrist) ?? 0
                            let indexDIPDistance = indexDIP?.distance(
                                to: wrist) ?? 0
                            if indexTipDistance > (indexDIPDistance * 1.10) {
                                fingersUp[0] = 1
                            }
                            // Check gesture middle finger
                            let middleTip = observation.joint(for: .middleTip)
                            let middleDIP = observation.joint(for: .middleDIP)
                            let middleTipDistance = middleTip?.distance(
                                to: wrist) ?? 0
                            let middleDIPDistance = middleDIP?.distance(
                                to: wrist) ?? 0
                            if middleTipDistance > (middleDIPDistance * 1.10) {
                                fingersUp[1] = 1
                            }
                            // Check gesture ring finger
                            let ringTip = observation.joint(for: .ringTip)
                            let ringDIP = observation.joint(for: .ringDIP)
                            let ringTipDistance = ringTip?.distance(
                                to: wrist) ?? 0
                            let ringDIPDistance = ringDIP?.distance(
                                to: wrist) ?? 0
                            if ringTipDistance > (ringDIPDistance * 1.10) {
                                fingersUp[2] = 1
                            }
                            if fingersUp == [1, 0, 0] {
                                numberGesture = "Number 1"
                            } else if fingersUp == [1, 1, 0] {
                                numberGesture = "Number 2"
                            } else if fingersUp == [1, 1, 1] {
                                numberGesture = "Number 3"
                            }
                        }
                    }
                } catch {
                    print("Error performing the request: \(error)")
                }
            }
        }
    }
}
```

In this example, we want to determine whether the person is indicating the number 1, 2, or 3, so we examine the joints of three fingers: the index, middle, and ring fingers. To decide whether each finger is extended, we compare the distances between the wrist and two joints: the one representing the fingertip (`indexTip`) and the one representing the distal interphalangeal joint (`indexDIP`). If the tip of the finger is farther from the wrist than the distal interphalangeal joint, the finger is considered extended. After calculating these distances, we store the results in an array called `fingersUp` to indicate whether each finger is up (1) or down (0). Finally, we check the values in this array to determine which fingers are raised and identify the number being indicated. If only the index finger is up, the person is showing the number 1; if the index and middle fingers are up, the number 2; and if the index, middle, and ring fingers are up, the number 3. The result is shown below.

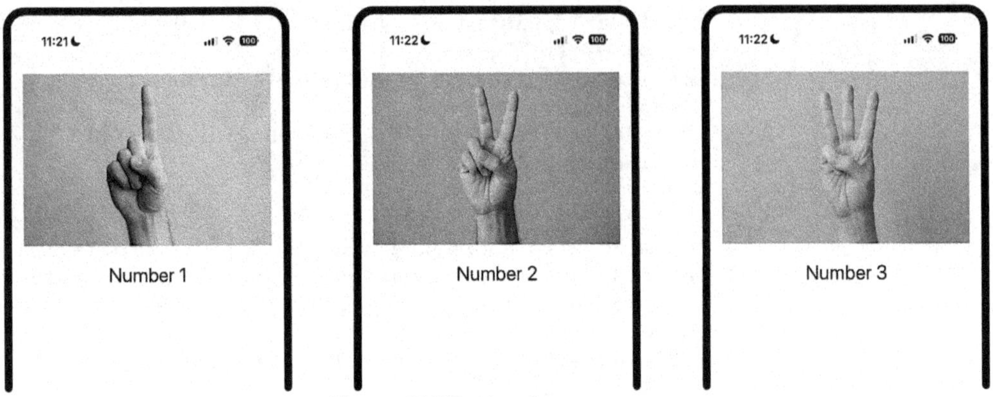

Figure 7-27: *Number gestures*

Do It Yourself

Update the `ContentView` view with the code in Listing 7-30. Download the images **number1.png**, **number2.png**, and **number3.png** from our website and drag them into the project (**Vision > Body > number1.png**, **number2.png**, and **number3.png**). Run the application on your iPhone. You should see a message at the bottom of the screen displaying the number indicated by the hand. To test another image, replace **number1.png** in the code with the image you want to try, then run the application again. The correct number should appear on the screen, as shown in Figure 7-27.

IMPORTANT

As with body poses, we can identify simple gestures by comparing joint positions and the distances between them. However, recognizing more complex gestures and movements requires training a custom Core ML model. We will explore these models and learn how to train them using Create ML in Chapter 10.

7.5 - Core Image

The **Vision** framework performs high-level computer vision tasks by analyzing images at the pixel level, which makes it closely integrated with a lower-level image framework called *Core Image*. Core Image provides the essential tools to prepare, transform, and enhance images before they are analyzed. The framework offers a wide range of features to adjust brightness, correct colors, reduce noise, and apply custom effects to images both before and after they are processed by **Vision**, allowing developers to optimize input for the models and refine the final results before presenting them to the users.

The framework defines its own class to represent images called **CIImage**. A **CIImage** object can be created from different sources, such as **UIImage** objects, image files, and image data. The following are some of the initializers provided by the class.

CIImage(cgImage: CGImage**)**

This initializer creates a **CIImage** object from the **CGImage** object specified by the argument.

CIImage(image: UIImage**)**

This initializer creates a **CIImage** object from the **UIImage** object specified by the argument.

CIImage(contentsOf: URL**)**

This initializer creates a **CIImage** object from the image in the URL specified by the argument.

CIImage(data: Data**)**

This initializer creates a **CIImage** object from the data specified by the argument.

CIImage(cvPixelBuffer: CVPixelBuffer**)**

This initializer creates a **CIImage** object from the buffer specified by the argument.

The **CIImage** class offers a wide range of properties and methods for obtaining information about the image and performing transformations. The following are some of the most frequently used.

extent

This property returns a **CGRect** structure with the location and size of the image.

url

This property returns a **URL** structure representing the source from which the image was loaded.

`transformed(by: CGAffineTransform)`

This method applies the transformations specified by the argument to the original image and returns a new image with the result. The **by** argument is an structure that determines the type of transformation to perform. Possible transformations include resizing, rotation, scaling, and translation.

`cropped(to: CGRect)`

This method extracts a rectangular portion of the original image and returns it as a new image. The **to** argument specifies the location and size of the rectangle to be cropped.

Once we have a **`CIImage`** object containing the image we want to use, we need to create a context to process it. For this purpose, the framework provides the **`CIContext`** class, which includes several initializers and type methods for creating the context and retrieving the processed images from it. The following are the most commonly used.

`CIContext(options: Dictionary)`

This initializer creates a **`CIContext`** object with the configuration specified by the argument. The **options** argument is an optional dictionary containing options and values for configuration. The options are defined by properties of the **`CIContextOption`** structure. The properties available are **`allowLowPower`**, **`cacheIntermediates`**, **`highQualityDownsample`**, **`memoryTarget`**, **`name`**, **`outputColorSpace`**, **`outputPremultiplied`**, **`priorityRequestLow`**, **`useSoftwareRenderer`**, **`workingColorSpace`**, **`workingFormat`**, and **`cvMetalTextureCache`**.

`createCGImage(CIImage, from: CGRect)`

This method returns a **`CGImage`** object created from the image and size specified by the arguments. The first argument is the **`CIImage`** object returned by the context and the **`from`** attribute determines the size of the image.

All the tools and features provided by the **Core Image** framework are implemented through filters. To configure and manage these filters, the framework defines the **`CIFilter`** class. Although we can create these objects manually, the class also provides many type methods that return filter objects already configured to apply specific effects. There are more than a hundred of these methods available. The following are the most frequently used to create blur effects.

`gaussianBlur()`

This method creates a filter to blur the image with a Gaussian distribution pattern. For configuration, the filter includes the properties **`inputImage`** and **`radius`**.

`motionBlur()`

This method creates a filter to apply motion blur to the image. For configuration, the filter includes the properties **`inputImage`**, **`radius`** and **`angle`**.

The following are methods provided to sharpen the image.

noiseReduction()

This method creates a filter to reduce noise by sharpening the edges of the objects in the image. For configuration, the filter includes the properties **inputImage**, **noiseLevel** and **sharpness**.

sharpenLuminance()

This method creates a filter to increase the image sharpness. For configuration, the filter includes the properties **inputImage**, **radius** and **sharpness**.

unsharpMask()

This method creates a filter to enhance the edges in the image for a crisp look. For configuration, the filter includes the properties **inputImage**, **radius** and **intensity**.

The following are the most frequently used methods to adjust the colors of an image.

colorControls()

This method creates a filter to adjust the image's brightness, contrast, and saturation. For configuration, the filter includes the properties **inputImage**, **brightness**, **contrast** and **saturation**.

exposureAdjust()

This method creates a filter to modify the exposure of the image. For configuration, the filter includes the properties **inputImage** and **ev**.

There are also methods that apply color effects to an image. The following are the most frequently used.

sepiaTone()

This method creates a filter that adds a warm, vintage look to the image.

colorMonochrome()

This method creates a filter to adjust an image's colors to shades of a single color. For configuration, the filter includes the properties **inputImage**, **color** and **intensity**.

falseColor()

This method creates a filter to map the colors in the image to a gradient. For configuration, the filter includes the properties **inputImage**, **color0** and **color1**.

To blend images and apply masks, the class defines the following methods.

blendWithMask()

This method creates a filter to blend two images by using a mask image. For configuration, the filter includes the properties **inputImage**, **maskImage** and **backgroundImage**. The class defines many versions of this method to use with different color masks, including **blendWithAlphaMask()**, **blendWithBlueMask()**, and **blendWithRedMask()**.

multiplyBlendMode()

This method creates a filter to blend colors from two images by multiplying color components. For configuration, the filter includes the properties **inputImage** and **backgroundImage**.

Finally, the framework also provides methods to generate barcodes. These methods can create barcodes that encode any information we want. The following are the most frequently used.

barcodeGenerator()

This method creates a filter that generates a barcode as an image. To provide the information to encode, the filter includes the property **barcodeDescriptor**.

qrCodeGenerator()

This method creates a filter that generates a QR barcode as an image. To provide the information to encode, the filter includes the properties **message** and **correctionLevel**.

Each of these filters includes a set of properties that we must configure to make the filter perform the desired task. The specific properties available depend on the filter and its function, but all filters include the following property to return the result.

outputImage

This property returns a **CIImage** object containing the result of processing the original image with the filter.

The process of applying these filters is straightforward. We must create a **CIContext** object to render the image, then call one of the **CIFilter** methods to create the desired filter, assign the original image and any configuration values to it, and finally read the **outputImage** property to obtain the result. The following example shows how to apply a blur effect to a picture.

Listing 7-31: Applying a filter

```
import SwiftUI
import CoreImage.CIFilterBuiltins

struct ContentView: View {
   @State private var picture = UIImage(named: "picturedog")!

   var body: some View {
      VStack {
         Button("Apply Filter") {
            Task {
               await applyFilter()
            }
```

```
            }.buttonStyle(.borderedProminent)

            Image(uiImage: picture)
                .resizable()
                .scaledToFit()
            Spacer()
        }
        .padding()
    }
    func applyFilter() async {
        let context = CIContext()
        let blurFilter = CIFilter.gaussianBlur()
        blurFilter.inputImage = CIImage(image: picture)
        blurFilter.radius = 10
        if let output = blurFilter.outputImage {
          if let image = context.createCGImage(output, from: output.extent){
                picture = UIImage(cgImage: image)
            }
        }
    }
}
```

In this example, we apply a Gaussian blur effect to the picture of a dog. As usual, we add a button to the interface so the user can decide when to apply the filter. When the button is pressed, the `applyFilter()` method is called. In this method, we follow the process described earlier to create and configure the filter with a radius value of 10, we then call the `createCGImage()` method to convert the `CIImage` into a `CGImage`, and finally create a `UIImage` object to display the result on the screen. Note that for the filter methods to be available, we must import the `CIFilterBuiltins` namespace from the **Core Image** framework, as shown in this example (`import CoreImage.CIFilterBuiltins`). The result is shown below.

Figure 7-28: *Gaussian blur*

Do It Yourself

Create a new Multiplatform project. Download the **picturedog.png** image from our website and drag it into the project (**Vision > Core Image > picturedog.png**). Update the ContentView.swift file with the code in

Listing 7-31. Run the application on your iPhone and press the Apply Filter button. You should see the Gaussian blur effect applied to the image, as shown in Figure 7-28.

IMPORTANT

There is an extensive list of predefined filters available and each filter in turn defines its own unique parameters. For a complete list, visit our website and follow the links for this chapter.

Barcodes

Core Image also includes built-in filters that allow developers to generate barcodes and QR codes directly from their applications. This capability pairs perfectly with the **Vision** framework, which can later detect and interpret these codes from images or video streams. By combining both frameworks, we can easily create systems that process personal identifications, product labels, or secure information, all within the Apple ecosystem. For example, we can create QR codes for personal badges, as shown below.

Listing 7-32: Generating barcodes

```
import SwiftUI
import CoreImage.CIFilterBuiltins

struct ContentView: View {
   @State private var barcode = UIImage(named: "nopicture")!

   var body: some View {
      VStack {
         Button("Create") {
            Task {
               await createBarcode(value: "JD Gauchat")
            }
         }.buttonStyle(.borderedProminent)

         Image(uiImage: barcode)
            .interpolation(.none)
            .resizable()
            .scaledToFit()
         Spacer()
      }
      .padding()
   }
   func createBarcode(value: String) async {
      let context = CIContext()
      let barcodeFilter = CIFilter.qrCodeGenerator()
      if let data = value.data(using: .utf8) {
         barcodeFilter.message = data
```

```
            if let output = barcodeFilter.outputImage {
               if let image = context.createCGImage(output,
                  from: output.extent) {
                  barcode = UIImage(cgImage: image)
               }
            }
         }
      }
   }
```

In this example, we define a method called **createBarcode()** that takes a string as input and generates a QR code from it. The filter returned by the **qrCodeGenerator()** method includes the **message** property, which we use to specify the text to encode. Since this property requires a **Data** structure, we call the **data()** method on the string and assign the resulting **Data** object to the property. The rest of the process remains the same: we read the **outputImage** property to get the generated image, use the **createCGImage()** method to turn it into a **CGImage** object, and create the **UIImage** object to display it on the screen.

Figure 7-29: *Barcode generator*

Do It Yourself

Update the **ContentView** view with the code in Listing 7-32. Download the **nopicture.png** image from our website and drag it into the project (**Vision > Core Image > nopicture.png**). Run the application on your iPhone and press the Create button. After a few seconds, you should see the QR code displayed on the screen, as shown in Figure 7-29.

Person Segmentation

In addition to preparing images for processing or generating barcodes, there are many other ways to combine the **Core Image** and **Vision** frameworks to achieve specific visual effects. One useful example is extracting objects from an image using masks. The **Vision** framework provides a request capable of detecting a person within an image and creating a mask that isolates their pixels, as shown below.

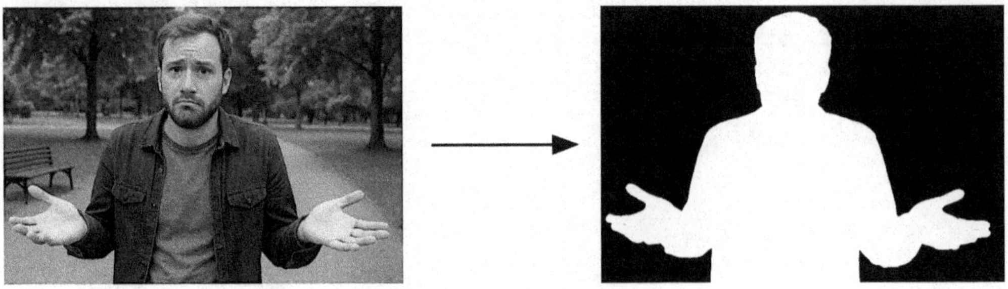

Figure 7-30: *Mask*

Several requests are available for image segmentation. Some are designed to isolate people, while others focus on detecting rectangles or general objects. The following is the request provided by the framework to isolate a single person.

GeneratePersonSegmentationRequest(Revision, **frameAnalysisSpacing:** CMTime)

This initializer creates a request that detects a person within an image and generates the corresponding mask. The first argument is an enumeration that defines the model revision to use (currently, the only available option is **revision1**). The **frameAnalysisSpacing** argument specifies the time interval between analyses when processing a video feed.

The **GeneratePersonSegmentationRequest** structure provides the following properties to configure the request.

qualityLevel

This property sets or returns an enumeration of type **QualityLevel** that specifies the level of accuracy used to detect the outlines of the person in the image. The possible values are **accurate**, **balanced**, and **fast**.

outputPixelFormatType

This property sets or returns a value that determines the pixel format of the output image. The format is defined by global constants provided by the **Core Video** framework. By default, the value is **kCVPixelFormatType_OneComponent8**, which processes images using 8-bit components.

As always, the **perform(on:)** method is used to execute the request. In this case, the method returns a **PixelBufferObservation** structure. The structure includes the following properties.

cgImage

This property returns a **CGImage** object containing the mask generated by the request.

size

This property returns a **CGSize** structure containing the width and height of the mask.

Once we create a mask with this request, we can use **Core Image** to extract and process the subject. For example, we can use the mask to isolate the person from the original image and seamlessly blend him with a new background, as shown below.

Figure 7-31: *New background*

When we request a mask from the model, it generates the result at its own working resolution and aspect ratio, which vary depending on the input, quality level, and device. As a result, the mask often does not match the pixel dimensions of the original image, so we must resize it before applying it to the new background. There are several ways to resize an image, but since we are working with **`CIImage`** objects, we can use the tools provided by the **Core Image** framework. Depending on the images used, we may need to resize all of them or just some. In the example shown in Figure 7-31, the background image has the same size as the original, so to create this effect, we only need to resize the mask, as shown below.

Listing 7-33: Using a mask

```
import SwiftUI
import Vision
import CoreImage.CIFilterBuiltins

struct ContentView: View {
   @State private var picture = UIImage(named: "confused")!

   var body: some View {
      VStack {
         Button("Change Background") {
            Task {
               await detectPerson()
            }
         }.buttonStyle(.borderedProminent)

         Image(uiImage: picture)
            .resizable()
            .scaledToFit()
         Spacer()
      }
      .padding()
   }
```

```swift
      func detectPerson() async {
         let imageURL = Bundle.main.url(forResource: "confused",
            withExtension: "png")
         if let imageURL = imageURL {
            do {
               // Perform request
               let request = GeneratePersonSegmentationRequest()
               request.qualityLevel = .accurate
               let observation = try await request.perform(on: imageURL)
               let result = try observation.cgImage

               // Resize mask
               var mask = CIImage(cgImage: result)
               if let inputImage = CIImage(image: picture) {
                  let maskScaleX = inputImage.extent.width
                     / mask.extent.width
                  let maskScaleY = inputImage.extent.height
                     / mask.extent.height
                  mask = mask.transformed(by: CGAffineTransformMake(
                     maskScaleX, 0, 0, maskScaleY, 0, 0))
               }
               // Apply mask
               let context = CIContext()
               let maskFilter = CIFilter.blendWithMask()
               maskFilter.inputImage = CIImage(image: picture)
               maskFilter.backgroundImage = CIImage(image:
                  UIImage(named: "office")!)
               maskFilter.maskImage = mask

               if let output = maskFilter.outputImage {
                  if let image = context.createCGImage(output,
                     from: output.extent) {
                     picture = UIImage(cgImage: image)
                  }
               }
            } catch {
               print("Error performing the request: \(error)")
            }
         }
      }
   }
```

As in previous examples, we provide a button for the user to start the process. When the button is pressed, a method is executed to create a mask and replace the background of the original image. In this case, we use the image of a man in a park and another of an empty office (see Figure 7-31). The first step is to create the request using the **GeneratePersonSegmentationRequest** structure. Since we are working with a still image, we set the **qualityLevel** property to **accurate** to obtain the best possible result. The mask is produced as a **CGImage** object, so we must convert it to a **CIImage** and then resize it to match the new background. To do this, we calculate the scale of each dimension by finding the ratio between the original image and the mask, and then apply the **transformed(by:)** method to perform the transformation.

Once the mask matches the image dimensions, we can apply it to the new background using a **Core Image** filter. In this example, we use the filter created by the **blendWithMask()** method, though many other filters are available depending on the characteristics of the mask. The filter includes three properties: `inputImage` for the original image, `backgroundImage` for the new background, and `maskImage` for the mask generated by the **Vision** request. To apply the filter, we follow the same procedure as before: we read the `outputImage` property, call the `createCGImage()` method, create a `UIImage` object from the returned value, and display the final image on the screen. As a result, the person from the original image is seamlessly merged into a new scene, as shown in Figure 7-31, right.

Do It Yourself

Update the ContentView.swift file with the code in Listing 7-33. Download the **confused.png** and **office.png** images from our website and drag them into the project (**Vision > Core Image > confused.png** and **office.png**). Run the application on your iPhone and press the Change Background button. You should see the person in the image blended with the new background, as shown in Figure 7-31.

IMPORTANT

The **Vision** framework can also perform more specialized image analysis tasks, such as detecting rectangles within an image, determining the contour of an object, tracking objects in a video, and more. These topics go beyond the scope of this book. For more information, visit our website and follow the links for this chapter.

Chapter 8
Audio Models

8.1 - Sound Processing

In previous chapters, we have worked with models that process visual content such as images and text, but Apple also provides models trained to process sounds. Using these models, we can interpret spoken language, identify different types of sounds, and even generate synthetic voices.

8.2 - Speech Analyzer

Perhaps the most interesting capability of these models is their ability to recognize human voices. To make use of this functionality, Apple provides the **Speech** framework. This framework can transcribe voices from a variety of sources, including prerecorded audio and video streams, and it also offers alternative interpretations and precise timing information that we can use to correlate each segment of the transcription with the original audio.

The **Speech** framework is a low-level framework, so we must manage every step of the process, from checking availability and downloading the required resources to configuring the transcriber, enabling audio input, converting the audio into a format the model can understand, and processing each segment to obtain the final result.

The first step is to create a transcriber module. This object is responsible for performing the speech-to-text transcription and determining how the transcription will be carried out. The framework provides two classes to create these modules: the **SpeechTranscriber** class for precise and short transcriptions and the **DictationTranscriber** class for quick and long transcriptions. The following is the initializer for the **SpeechTranscriber** class.

SpeechTranscriber(locale: Locale, **preset:** Preset)

This initializer creates a transcriber designed to perform precise transcriptions. The **locale** argument indicates the language to transcribe from, and the **preset** argument is a structure that defines how the model should execute the transcription. The structure provides several type properties to offer predefined configurations. The available properties are **transcription**, **transcriptionWithAlternatives**, **timeIndexedTranscriptionWithAlternatives**, **progressiveTranscription**, and **timeIndexedProgressiveTranscription**.

The following is the initializer provided by the **DictationTranscriber** class.

DictationTranscriber(locale: Locale, **preset:** Preset)

This initializer creates a transcriber designed to perform quick transcriptions. The **locale** argument indicates the language to transcribe from, and the **preset** argument is a structure that defines how the model should execute the transcription. The structure provides several type properties to offer predefined configurations. The available properties are **phrase**, **shortDictation**, **progressiveShortDictation**, **longDictation**, **progressiveLongDictation** and **timeIndexedLongDictation**.

The presets provided by **Preset** structures define the options that control how the transcription will be performed and what type of results it should return. These options indicate whether the model should generate partial results, offer alternative transcriptions, or include timing information for the audio. The following table describes the configurations specified by the presets for the **SpeechTranscriber** class.

	volatile Results	fast Results	alternative Transcriptions	audio TimeRange
transcription	No	No	No	No
transcription WithAlternatives	No	No	**Yes**	No
timeIndexedTranscription WithAlternatives	No	No	**Yes**	**Yes**
progressiveTranscription	**Yes**	**Yes**	No	No
timeIndexedProgressive Transcription	**Yes**	**Yes**	No	**Yes**

Figure 8-1: *Speech transcriber presets*

The following are the presets for the **DictationTranscriber** class.

	short Form	volatile Results	frequent Finalization	audio TimeRange	punctuation
phrase	**Yes**	No	No	No	No
shortDictation	**Yes**	No	No	No	**Yes**
progressiveShortDictation	**Yes**	**Yes**	**Yes**	No	**Yes**
longDictation	No	No	No	No	**Yes**
progressiveLongDictation	No	**Yes**	No	No	**Yes**
timeIndexedLongDictation	No	No	No	**Yes**	**Yes**

Figure 8-2: *Dictation transcriber presets*

IMPORTANT

The **SpeechTranscriber** and **DictationTranscriber** classes also provide properties to customize the presets and include initializers that let us define the exact configuration we need. For more information, visit our website and follow the links for this chapter.

Once the transcriber is set up, we need to create an analyzer. The analyzer is responsible for receiving the audio and processing it. To create this analyzer, the framework provides the **SpeechAnalyzer** class. The class includes the following initializer.

SpeechAnalyzer(modules: [SpeechModule])

This initializer creates an audio analyzer for the transcribers specified by the argument. The **modules** argument is an array of transcribers that conform to the **SpeechModule** protocol, as those created with the **SpeechTranscriber** and **DictationTranscriber** classes.

Before using the analyzer to process audio, we need to make sure that the device can perform the transcription. For this purpose, the **SpeechTranscriber** class includes the following property.

isAvailable

This property returns a Boolean value that indicates whether the transcription models can be used on the device.

Even if transcription is available on a device, it may not be available for a specific language. To check whether the language we want to transcribe is supported, the **SpeechTranscriber** and **DictationTranscriber** classes include the following properties.

supportedLocales

This property returns an array of **Locale** objects that represent the languages supported by the transcription models.

installedLocales

This property returns an array of **Locale** objects that indicate which transcription models are currently installed on the device.

If a model is supported but not installed on the device, we must ask the system to download it. For this purpose, the framework includes the **AssetInventory** class. This class provides the following type method to request the installation of a model.

assetInstallationRequest(supporting: [SpeechModule])

This method creates a request to download the models required by the transcribers specified by the argument. The **modules** argument is an array of transcribers that conform to the **SpeechModule** protocol, including those created with the **SpeechTranscriber** and **DictationTranscriber** classes.

This method returns an **AssetInstallationRequest** object containing the request. The class includes the following method to send the request to Apple's servers and download the models.

downloadAndInstall()

This method downloads and installs the models that are not already available on the device.

File Transcription

Because of the low-level nature of this framework, how we implement these tools and perform the transcription depends on the needs of our app and the results we want to achieve. In the following example, we show the possible implementation of an application that transcribes the voice from an audio file. Since the audio file may change each time, we need two views: one to report whether it is possible to perform transcriptions on the device and another to perform the transcription, as shown below.

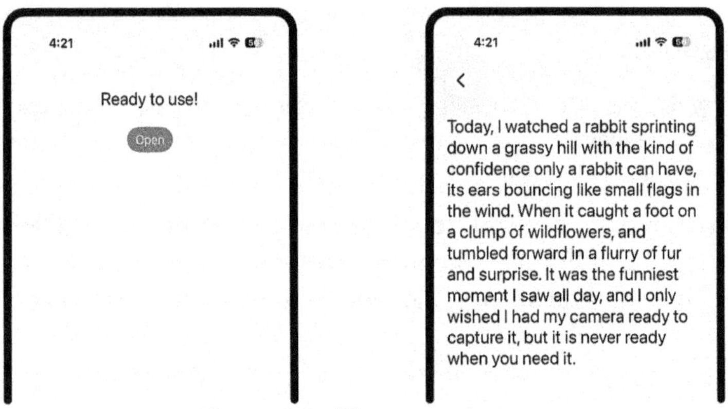

Figure 8-3: *File transcription*

The first step is to check for availability. For this example, we are going to implement the logic in an observable object. The following is our implementation of this object.

Listing 8-1: Checking if it is possible to perform a transcription

```
import SwiftUI
import Observation
import Speech

@Observable class ApplicationData {
   var message: String = "Loading..."
   var isAvailable: Bool = false

   static let shared: ApplicationData = ApplicationData()
   private init() { }

   func checkAvailability() async {
      let locale = Locale.current
      let transcriber = SpeechTranscriber(locale: locale, preset:
.transcription)
```

```
        // Check if speech is available
        guard SpeechTranscriber.isAvailable else {
           message = "Speech transcriber is not available"
           return
        }
        // Check if the language is supported
        let listSupported = await SpeechTranscriber.supportedLocales
        guard listSupported.map({ $0.identifier(.bcp47) })
           .contains(locale.identifier(.bcp47)) else {
           message = "Language not supported"
           return
        }
        // Check if language is installed
        let listInstalled = await Set(SpeechTranscriber.installedLocales)
        if listInstalled.map({ $0.identifier(.bcp47) })
           .contains(locale.identifier(.bcp47)) {
           message = "Ready to use!"
           isAvailable = true
        } else {
           do {
              // Download model
              if let downloader = try await AssetInventory
                 .assetInstallationRequest(supporting: [transcriber]) {
                 try await downloader.downloadAndInstall()
                 message = "Ready to use!"
                 isAvailable = true
              }
           } catch {
              message = "Error downloading resources"
           }
        }
    }
}
```

This class includes some properties to report the results to the view and a method called **checkAvailability()** to verify whether it is possible to perform transcriptions on the device. The method first creates a **SpeechTranscriber** object configured with the user's locale and the **transcription** preset to produce accurate transcriptions in the user's language. Once the transcriber is defined, we can check whether transcription is possible. We begin by reading the **isAvailable** property to confirm that the transcriber itself is available. If it is, we then read the **supportedLocales** property to determine whether the user's language is in the list of supported languages. If the language is supported, we must ensure that it is already installed, so we read the **installedLocales** property. If the language is installed, we allow the user to transcribe the audio, otherwise, we create a request and call the **downloadAndInstall()** method to download the model. Note that locales can be defined in different formats, so to ensure we are comparing compatible values, we use identifiers in the **bcp47** format.

From the view, we must simply call the **checkAvailability()** method and provide a button that lets the user navigate to the next view once the application confirms that the models are available.

Listing 8-2: Reporting the state of the transcriber

```
import SwiftUI

struct ContentView: View {
   @State private var appData = ApplicationData.shared

   var body: some View {
      NavigationStack {
         VStack {
            Text(appData.message)
               .padding()
            NavigationLink("Open") {
               SpeechView()
            }
            .buttonStyle(.borderedProminent)
            .disabled(!appData.isAvailable)

            Spacer()
         }
         .padding()
         .task {
            await appData.checkAvailability()
         }
      }
   }
}
```

This view includes a button that opens another view called **SpeechView** to perform the transcription. As mentioned earlier, a transcriber is responsible for producing the output of the transcription, but we also need a **SpeechAnalyzer** object to analyze the audio and control the entire process. This object provides several methods to start, finish, and cancel the analysis. The ones we use depend on the source of the audio and the results we need. The following are some of the methods we can use to transcribe text from an audio file.

analyzeSequence(from: AVAudioFile)

This method analyzes an input sequence created from the audio file provided by the argument. The **from** argument is an **AVAudioFile** object that represents the file we want to analyze.

finalizeAndFinish(through: CMTime)

This method finishes the analysis after the audio has been processed up to the time specified by the **through** argument.

cancelAndFinishNow()

This method finishes the analysis immediately.

Every time we want to analyze a new audio file, we must create the **SpeechTranscriber** object again, use this instance to create the **SpeechAnalyzer**, and call the **analyzeSequence()** method on the analyzer to start the process. Once the process begins, the transcriber produces an asynchronous sequence with the results. These results are returned as a **Result** structure, which includes the following properties to provide the values.

text

This property returns an **AttributedString** value with the text transcribed from the audio.

alternatives

This property returns an array of **AttributedString** values that contain alternative transcriptions in descending order of likelihood.

isFinal

This property returns a Boolean value that indicates whether the text is final (**true**) or a partial transcription (**false**).

Again, to better organize the code, we need to implement the logic in an observable object. In this case, we call it **TranscriberData**. The following is our implementation of this class.

Listing 8-3: Transcribing an audio file

```
import SwiftUI
import Observation
import Speech

@Observable class TranscriberData {
   var finalText = AttributedString("")

   static let shared: TranscriberData = TranscriberData()
   private init() { }

   func transcribeAudio() async {
      guard let fileURL = Bundle.main.url(forResource: "story",
         withExtension: "mp3") else { return }
      do {
         var final: AttributedString = ""
         let locale = Locale.current
         let transcriber = SpeechTranscriber(locale: locale,
            preset: .transcription)

         let analyzer = SpeechAnalyzer(modules: [transcriber])
         if let sample = try await analyzer.analyzeSequence(
            from: AVAudioFile(forReading: fileURL)) {
            try await analyzer.finalizeAndFinish(through: sample)
         } else {
            await analyzer.cancelAndFinishNow()
         }
         for try await response in transcriber.results {
            if response.isFinal {
               final.append(response.text)
```

```
            }
         }
         finalText = final
      } catch {
         finalText = AttributedString("Error: \(error)")
      }
   }
}
```

The result of the transcription is returned as a value of type **`AttributedString`**, so we create a property called **`finalText`** to store this value and share it with the views. To perform the transcription, we define a method called **`transcribeAudio()`**. This method loads an audio file from the bundle called **story.mp3** and proceeds to transcribe its content. We first create a **`SpeechTranscriber`** object, then use this value to create the **`SpeechAnalyzer`** object, and finally call the **`analyzeSequence()`** method to begin the process. This method analyzes the audio in the file. If the file is empty, it returns **`nil`** and we call **`cancelAndFinishNow()`** to stop the entire operation, otherwise, the method returns the ending time of the audio, which we use to call **`finalizeAndFinish()`** to complete the transcription.

During the transcription, the transcriber sends the recognized text to an asynchronous sequence, so after configuring the transcription process, we create a **`for await in`** loop to read these values. Every time the transcriber identifies spoken words, it converts them into text and appends a new element to the sequence. Inside the loop, we check whether the text is partial or final, and if it is final, we add it to a variable. After the audio file finishes playing, the **`finalizeAndFinish()`** method is called to end the transcription, the **`for await in`** loop ends, and the final result is assigned to the **`finalText`** property to display it to the user, as shown in Figure 8-3, right.

The view we use to allow the user to start the transcription is simple, we just need a **`Text`** view to show the result and a **`task()`** modifier to call the **`transcribeAudio()`** method to start the process as soon as the view is loaded, as shown below.

Listing 8-4: Starting the transcription

```
import SwiftUI

struct SpeechView: View {
   @State private var transData = TranscriberData.shared

   var body: some View {
      VStack {
         ScrollView {
            Text(transData.finalText)
            Spacer()
         }
      }.padding()
      .task {
         await transData.transcribeAudio()
      }
   }
}
```

Do It Yourself

Create a new Multiplatform project. Download the **story.mp3** file from our website and drag it into the project. Create a new file called ApplicationData.swift for the code in Listing 8-1. Update the `ContentView` view with the code in Listing 8-2. Create a new file called TranscriberData.swift for the code in Listing 8-3, and another called SpeechView.swift for the code in Listing 8-4. Run the application on your iPhone. If the model is not available on your device, you should see the message "Loading..." while the system downloads the model. After a few seconds, the Open button should become enabled. Press this button to perform the transcription. You should then see the transcribed text on the screen, as shown in Figure 8-3, right.

Live Transcription

The **Speech** framework can also transcribe a live stream of audio. Live transcription follows a similar logic to processing prerecorded files, but it relies on continuous input from the microphone rather than a fixed source with predetermined content, so the process involves a few additional steps. To transcribe audio coming from the microphone or any ongoing stream, we must create an asynchronous sequence that passes audio chunks from the source to the transcriber, convert the audio into a format the transcriber can handle, track the stream to determine when it begins and ends, and process the results asynchronously. The framework provides dedicated tools to support these tasks. The following are some of the methods offered by the `SpeechAnalyzer` class to analyze audio streams.

`start(inputSequence:` `Sequence)`

This method instructs the analyzer to begin processing the audio provided by the sequence specified by the argument. The **inputSequence** argument is an asynchronous sequence containing the audio chunks we want the analyzer to process.

`bestAvailableAudioFormat(compatibleWith:` `[SpeechModule])`

This method determines the most suitable audio format the transcriber can use based on the assets installed on the device and returns an `AVAudioFormat` object with that format.

`finalizeAndFinishThroughEndOfInput()`

This method waits until the input sequence has been fully processed and then instructs the analyzer to finish the transcription.

Because the source is now a continuous stream of audio, the input must be divided into chunks that are sent to the analyzer for processing. To convert these audio chunks into valid input for the analyzer, the framework provides the `AnalyzerInput` structure. The following is the structure's initializer.

```
AnalyzerInput(buffer: AVAudioPCMBuffer)
```

This initializer creates a structure that can be provided as the input for an audio analyzer. The buffer argument is an object with the audio buffer for the analyzer to process.

> **IMPORTANT**
>
> The **Speech** framework relies on the tools provided by the **AVFoundation** framework to process audio. The **AVAudioPCMBuffer** class used to supply the buffer for the analyzer is only one of them. We also need the **AVCaptureDevice** class to capture input from the microphone, the **AVAudioSession** class to manage the audio signal, and many others to convert the audio source and prepare it for processing. For more information about these tools and to learn how to work with audio, read our book *Advanced SwiftUI for Masterminds*.

To demonstrate how this process works, we will update the previous example. Since checking for availability works as before, our initial view and the `ApplicationData` class remain unchanged, but the `TranscriberData` class must be adapted to handle live streams. We begin by introducing the properties needed to store the required values and provide the results to the views.

Listing 8-5: Defining properties to process audio streams

```
import SwiftUI
import Observation
import Speech

@Observable class TranscriberData {
   var partialText = AttributedString("")
   var finalText = AttributedString("")

   // Transcriber properties
   var transcriber: DictationTranscriber?
   var analyzer: SpeechAnalyzer?
   var inputSequence: AsyncStream<AnalyzerInput>?
   var inputBuilder: AsyncStream<AnalyzerInput>.Continuation?
   var recognizerTask: Task<(), Error>?

   // Audio Recorder properties
   var analyzerFormat: AVAudioFormat?
   var audioEngine = AVAudioEngine()

   static let shared: TranscriberData = TranscriberData()
   private init() { }
}
```

When transcribing live audio, the transcriber produces partial text to reflect the current interpretation and final text to report the completed result. To provide feedback to the user, we need to display both text as they are generated, so we define two properties to store these values: `partialText` and `finalText`.

The next group of properties includes those required to manage the transcription process. The first property, **transcriber**, stores the **DictationTranscriber** object we need to transcribe the audio. This object defines a transcriber suited for audio streams and dictation, so it is the ideal choice in this case. The analyzer works the same way as before, but the input now comes from an asynchronous sequence, so we define two properties to handle this sequence, **inputSequence** and **inputBuilder**, along with a **Task** property called **recognizerTask** to manage the task that tracks the stream of results produced by the transcription.

The final group of properties is defined to control the recording process. The **analyzerFormat** property stores an **AVAudioFormat** object with the audio format required for the transcription, and the **audioEngine** property provides the **AVAudioEngine** instance that manages the audio stream.

Now that all the properties are in place, we need to add a method to this class to set up the transcriber. The following is our implementation of this method.

Listing 8-6: Setting up the transcriber

```
func setTranscriber() async {
   let locale = Locale.current
   transcriber = DictationTranscriber(locale: locale,
      preset: .progressiveShortDictation)

   if let transcriber = transcriber {
      analyzer = SpeechAnalyzer(modules: [transcriber])
      analyzerFormat = await SpeechAnalyzer.bestAvailableAudioFormat(
         compatibleWith: [transcriber])
      (inputSequence, inputBuilder) = AsyncStream<AnalyzerInput>
          .makeStream()

      if let inputSequence = inputSequence {
         recognizerTask = Task {
            do {
               for try await response in transcriber.results {
                  if response.isFinal {
                     finalText += response.text
                     partialText = ""
                  } else {
                     partialText = response.text
                     partialText.foregroundColor = .blue.opacity(0.6)
                  }
               }
            } catch {
               finalText = AttributedString("Error \(error)")
            }
         }
         do {
            try await analyzer?.start(inputSequence: inputSequence)
         } catch {
            finalText = AttributedString("Error \(error)")
         }
      }
   }
}
```

This method begins by creating the **`DictationTranscriber`** object. In this case, we want to transcribe a dictation in the user's language, so we configure the object to use the current locale and the **`progressiveShortDictation`** preset. Next, we create the analyzer as in the previous example, but now we also determine the appropriate audio format by calling the **`bestAvailableAudioFormat()`** method and define an asynchronous sequence with **`AsyncStream`** to receive the audio chunks from the source.

After configuring the transcriber, the method creates a task to process the results. Within this task, we use the same **`for await in`** loop as before to read each value sent by the transcriber and display it to the user, but in this case we perform two actions. If the text is final, we assign it to the **`finalText`** property and display it as is. Otherwise, we assign it to the **`partialText`** property and display it in blue to indicate to the user that the interpretation is not final and may change.

At the end of the **`setTranscriber()`** method, we call the **`start()`** method to instruct the analyzer to begin receiving input. For our app to generate this input, it must have authorization from the user to access the microphone, and to request this authorization, we first need to add the corresponding capability to the project. Capabilities are added through the project settings. We must click on the project's name to open settings (Figure 8-4, number 1), open the Signing and Capabilities panel (Figure 8-4, number 2), and click the +Capability button (Figure 8-4, number 3).

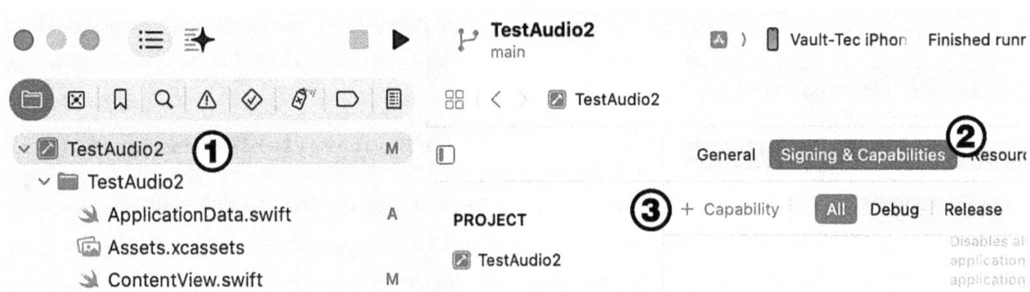

Figure 8-4: *Project Capabilities*

When we click the +Capability button, a window appears with the available options. If we search for the word "Microphone", we will see the option to add access to the microphone, as shown below.

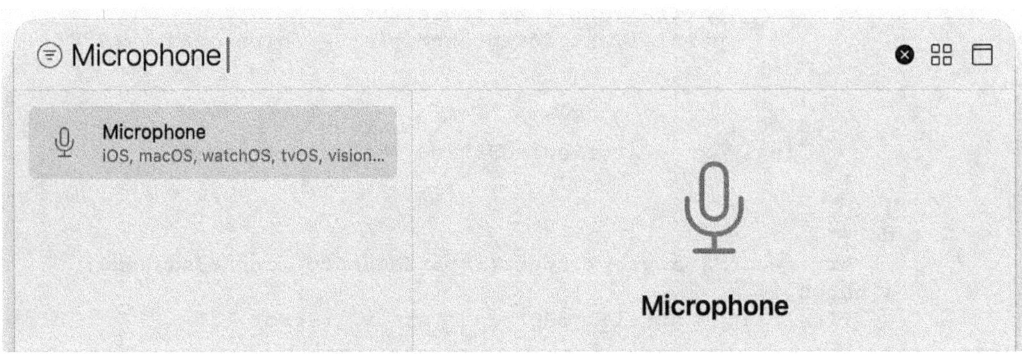

Figure 8-5: *Adding the microphone*

After selecting the Microphone option, the capability is added at the bottom of the panel. In this new section, we must specify the text that will be shown to the user when the system asks for authorization to access the microphone, as shown below.

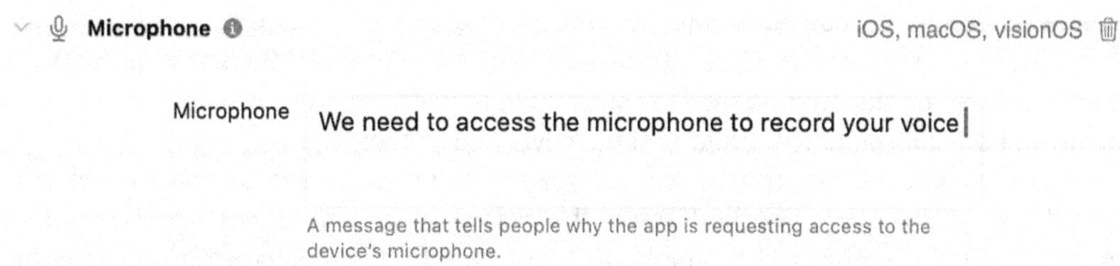

Figure 8-6: *Providing the reason to access the microphone*

Now that the project is configured to work with the microphone, we need to define a new method in the **TranscriberData** class to request authorization from the user, start the recording, and send the audio to the analyzer. The following is our implementation of this method.

Listing 8-7: Start recording from the microphone

```
func startRecording() async {
    finalText = AttributedString("")
    partialText = AttributedString("")

    do {
        // Check authorization to access Microphone
        if AVCaptureDevice.authorizationStatus(for: .audio) != .authorized {
            guard await AVCaptureDevice.requestAccess(for: .audio)
                else { return }
        }
        // Set up audio session
        let audioSession = AVAudioSession.sharedInstance()
        try audioSession.setCategory(.playAndRecord, mode: .spokenAudio)
        try audioSession.setActive(true,
            options: .notifyOthersOnDeactivation)

        // Set up transcriber
        await setTranscriber()

        // Process audio stream
        for await buffer in try await audioStream() {
            if let inputBuilder = inputBuilder,
                let analyzerFormat = analyzerFormat {
                if let converted = try convertBuffer(buffer: buffer,
                    format: analyzerFormat) {
                    let input = AnalyzerInput(buffer: converted)
                    inputBuilder.yield(input)
                }
            }
        }
    } catch {
        print("Error \(error)")
    }
}
```

This method is called by the view when the user presses a button to start a transcription, so the first step is to clear the **finalText** and **partialText** properties to begin with a clean state. To receive audio from the microphone, we first call the **authorizationStatus()** method to check whether it is available. If it is not, we request access with the **requestAccess()** method and wait for the user to press Allow. Once authorization is granted, we set up an audio session to manage the recording, call the **setTranscriber()** method defined earlier to prepare the transcriber, and start a loop to read the input from the microphone and send the audio to the analyzer for processing.

The **for await in** loop used in this example relies on two methods that we will define next. The **audioStream()** method starts the recording and produces an asynchronous sequence containing the audio chunks to process, and the **convertBuffer()** method converts each chunk into a format the analyzer can handle. When the asynchronous sequence created by the **audioStream()** method produces a new value, we call the **convertBuffer()** method to prepare it, create an instance of the **AnalyzerInput** structure to turn the value into valid input for the analyzer, and add this instance to the analyzer's asynchronous sequence with the **yield()** method to have the audio transcribed. The following is our implementation of the **audioStream()** method.

Listing 8-8: Generating a stream of audio from the microphone

```
func audioStream() async throws -> AsyncStream<AVAudioPCMBuffer> {
   var outputContinuation: AsyncStream<AVAudioPCMBuffer>
      .Continuation? = nil
   audioEngine.inputNode.removeTap(onBus: 0)
   audioEngine.inputNode.installTap(onBus: 0, bufferSize: 4096,
      format: audioEngine.inputNode.outputFormat(forBus: 0)) {
      (buffer, time) in
      outputContinuation?.yield(buffer)
   }
   audioEngine.prepare()
   try audioEngine.start()

   return AsyncStream(AVAudioPCMBuffer.self, bufferingPolicy: .unbounded){
      continuation in
      outputContinuation = continuation
   }
}
```

This method calls the **installTap()** method to install a tap on the audio engine's input node so we can capture the audio coming from the microphone and add it to an asynchronous sequence to make it available for the analyzer. The tap delivers buffers of approximately 4096 sample frames, which are yielded into the sequence as they arrive, so the analyzer can consume these buffers one by one as they become available.

The buffer generated by the audio engine is not always compatible with the format expected by the analyzer. The analyzer requires PCM audio using 16-bit signed integer samples. Although the audio engine also produces PCM audio, its sample format does not always match the required size, so we must convert it. Inside the loop defined in the previously introduced **startRecording()** method, we perform this conversion using a method called **convertBuffer()**. The following is the implementation of that method.

Listing 8-9: Converting the audio format

```
func convertBuffer(buffer: AVAudioPCMBuffer, format: AVAudioFormat) throws
-> AVAudioPCMBuffer? {
   guard buffer.format != format else {
      return buffer
   }
   let converter = AVAudioConverter(from: buffer.format, to: format)
   converter?.primeMethod = .none
   guard let converter = converter else { return nil }

   // Calculate output size
   let sampleRateRatio = converter.outputFormat.sampleRate
      / converter.inputFormat.sampleRate
   let scaledInputFrameLength = Double(buffer.frameLength)
      * sampleRateRatio
   let frameCapacity = AVAudioFrameCount(scaledInputFrameLength
      .rounded(.up))
   guard let conversionBuffer = AVAudioPCMBuffer(pcmFormat:
      converter.outputFormat, frameCapacity: frameCapacity) else {
      return nil
   }
   var nsError: NSError?
   var bufferProcessed = false

   let status = converter.convert(to: conversionBuffer, error: &nsError) {
      packetCount, inputStatusPointer in
      defer { bufferProcessed = true }
      inputStatusPointer.pointee = bufferProcessed ? .noDataNow :
         .haveData
      return bufferProcessed ? nil : buffer
   }
   guard status != .error else { return nil }

   return conversionBuffer
}
```

This method is adapted from the implementation provided by Apple in their sample project. The method uses the tools from the **AVFoundation** framework to convert the buffer into a format the analyzer can process. We first compare the buffer format with the format we need (the one returned by the `bestAvailableAudioFormat()` method). If both formats match, we return the current buffer; otherwise, we convert it. To perform the conversion, we create an `AVAudioConverter` object, determine the size of the destination buffer so the audio is not truncated, and then call the `convert()` method to complete the process.

Finally, we need a method to allow the user to stop the recording. The following is our implementation of this method.

Listing 8-10: Finishing the transcription

```
func stopRecording() async {
   do {
      audioEngine.stop()
      inputBuilder?.finish()
```

```
        try await analyzer?.finalizeAndFinishThroughEndOfInput()
        recognizerTask?.cancel()
        recognizerTask = nil
    } catch {
        print("Error \(error)")
    }
}
```

This method is called when the user presses the button to stop recording. The method takes care of finishing and canceling every process in the pipeline. First, we call the **stop()** method on the audio engine to prevent it from processing any additional audio from the microphone. Then we call the **finish()** method on the asynchronous sequence to stop sending values to the analyzer. Next, we call the **finalizeAndFinishThroughEndOfInput()** method on the analyzer to complete the transcription of the last buffer received and finish the process. Finally, we cancel the task processing the results.

The **TranscriberData** class is ready to process and transcribe audio. The only thing left is to update the **SpeechView** view to provide the tools for the user to start and finish the process. The following is our implementation of this view.

Listing 8-11: Starting and ending the transcription

```
import SwiftUI

struct SpeechView: View {
    @State private var transData = TranscriberData.shared
    @State private var isRecording: Bool = false

    var body: some View {
        ScrollView {
            Text("\(transData.finalText) \(transData.partialText)")
                .padding()
            Spacer()
        }
        .padding()
        .toolbar {
            ToolbarItem {
                Button(action: {
                    if isRecording {
                        Task {
                            await transData.stopRecording()
                        }
                    } else {
                        Task {
                            await transData.startRecording()
                        }
                    }
                    isRecording.toggle()
                }, label: {
                    Image(systemName: isRecording ? "stop.fill" :
                        "microphone.square")
                })
            }
        }
    }
}
```

This view now includes a property called **isRecording** to determine whether we are transcribing audio at the moment or not. Using the value of this property, we configure a button. If we are not recording, the button calls the **startRecording()** method to begin the process; otherwise, it calls the **stopRecording()** method to finish the transcription. Another change is in the **Text** view. Because we are transcribing live audio, we need to provide feedback to the user, so instead of showing only the final text as we did before, we also display the partial interpretation of the text. The result is shown below.

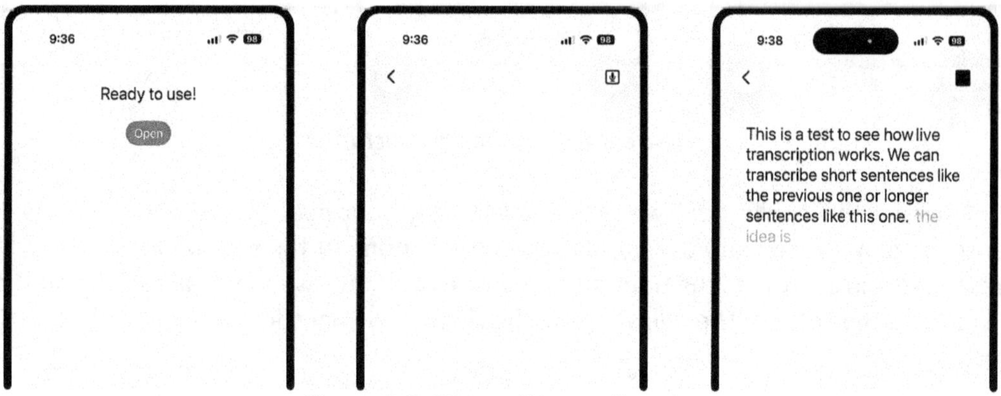

Figure 8-7: *Transcribing a dictation*

Do It Yourself

Update the **TranscriberData** class with the code in Listing 8-5. Note that we don't need the previous methods anymore. Add to this class the **setTranscriber()** method defined in Listing 8-6, the **startRecording()** method defined in Listing 8-7, the **audioStream()** method defined in Listing 8-8, the **convertBuffer()** method defined in Listing 8-9, and the **stopRecording()** method defined in Listing 8-10. Update the **SpeechView** view with the code in Listing 8-11. Remember to add the Microphone to the project's capabilities as shown in Figure 8-4 and 8-5. Run the application on your iPhone and press the Open button. On the next view, press the microphone button in the top right corner of the screen to start recording. The system will ask for permission to access the microphone. Press Allow and start talking. You should see your words appear on the screen as you speak.

Translating Speech

Although transcription by itself can be extremely useful, it becomes far more powerful when combined with other frameworks and models. For example, we can use it with the **Translation** framework to translate the transcription into any language we need in real time, as shown below.

Figure 8-8: *Translating a dictation*

To create this application, we only need to adapt our **SpeechView** view to show the transcription at the top and the translation at the bottom. At the top, we must display the partial text, and every time the transcriber produces final text, we must translate it and show the result at the bottom. The following are the changes we need in this view to perform this process.

Listing 8-12: Translating the transcription

```
import SwiftUI
@preconcurrency import Translation

struct SpeechView: View {
   @State private var transData = TranscriberData.shared
   @State private var isRecording: Bool = false

   @State private var translation: String = ""
   @State private var configuration:
      TranslationSession.Configuration? = nil

   var body: some View {
      VStack {
         ScrollView {
            Text(transData.partialText)
               .padding()
            Spacer()
         }
         .frame(height: 200)

         ScrollView {
            Text(translation)
               .padding()
            Spacer()
         }
         .frame(minWidth: 0, maxWidth: .infinity)
         .background(Color(.secondarySystemBackground))
      }
      .padding()
      .toolbar {
         ToolbarItem {
            Button(action: {
```

```
                if isRecording {
                    Task {
                        await transData.stopRecording()
                    }
                } else {
                    Task {
                        await transData.startRecording()
                    }
                }
                isRecording.toggle()
            }, label: {
                Image(systemName: isRecording ? "stop.fill" :
                    "microphone.square")
            })
        }
    }
    .onChange(of: transData.finalText) { old, new in
        if configuration != nil {
            configuration?.invalidate()
        } else {
            let sourceLanguage = Locale.current.language
            let targetLanguage = Locale.Language(identifier: "es")
            configuration = TranslationSession.Configuration(
                source: sourceLanguage, target: targetLanguage)
        }
    }
    .translationTask(configuration) { session in
        do {
            let text = String(transData.finalText.characters)
            if !text.isEmpty {
                let response = try await session.translate(text)
                translation = response.targetText
            }
        } catch {
            print("Error translating the text: \(error)")
        }
    }
  }
}
```

As in previous examples, we import the **Translation** framework and then define properties to show the translation to the user (**`translation`**) and manage the configuration (**`configuration`**). To present the results, we include two **`Text`** views: one to display the partial text (**`transData.partialText`**) and another to display the translation (**`translation`**). The translation must be performed every time the value of the **`transData.finalText`** property changes, so we use the **`onChange()`** modifier to monitor this property and ask the system to translate the text whenever a new value becomes available. To perform the translation, we implement the **`translationTask()`** modifier. In this case, we translate the text from the user's language to Spanish, so every time we speak, we can see our words translated into Spanish at the bottom, as shown in Figure 8-8.

Do It Yourself

Update the SpeechView.swift file with the code in Listing 8-12. Run the application on your iPhone, press the Open button, then press the microphone button, and start talking. Every time the transcriber determines that the current text is final, you should see the translation appear at the bottom, as shown in Figure 8-8.

8.3 - Voice Synthesizer

Speech recognition allows us to convert spoken audio into text, but we can also perform the reverse operation. The **AVFoundation** framework provides a voice synthesizer capable of transforming text into audible speech, giving our applications the ability to speak. To support this feature, the framework offers the following class.

`AVSpeechSynthesizer()`

This initializer creates an object capable of generating spoken audio from text.

The text is passed to the synthesizer as an instance of the **`AVSpeechUtterance`** class. This class provides the following initializer.

`AVSpeechUtterance(string:` `String)`

This initializer creates an utterance containing the text provided by the argument. The **string** argument is the text we want the synthesizer to speak.

The **`AVSpeechUtterance`** class includes the following property to define the voice we want to use.

`voice`

This property sets or returns an **`AVSpeechSynthesisVoice`** object that represents the voice we want to use to synthesize the text.

The voice is defined by an instance of the **`AVSpeechSynthesisVoice`** class. The class includes the following initializers.

`AVSpeechSynthesisVoice(language:` `String)`

This initializer creates an object that retrieves a voice capable of speaking the language specified by the argument. The **language** argument is a BCP 47 code that tells the system which language the voice should use.

`AVSpeechSynthesisVoice(identifier:` `String)`

This initializer creates an instance that retrieves the voice specified by the argument. The **identifier** argument is the string that identifies the voice we want to use.

Once the **AVSpeechUtterance** object is ready, we can pass it to an **AVSpeech-Synthesizer** object to synthesize the text. The **AVSpeechSynthesizer** class provides the following method for this purpose.

speak(AVSpeechUtterance)—This method adds the utterance specified by the argument to the synthesizer and begins the synthesis process.

The **AVSpeechSynthesizer** instance must remain in memory while the text is being synthesized, so it needs to be stored in a property that stays active throughout the process. The following example shows how to store the instance in a property within an observable object and how to use it to process text in American English.

Listing 8-13: Synthesizing text

```
import SwiftUI
import Observation
import AVFoundation

@Observable class ApplicationData {
   let synthesizer: AVSpeechSynthesizer

   static let shared: ApplicationData = ApplicationData()
   private init() {
      synthesizer = AVSpeechSynthesizer()
   }
   func say(text: String) {
      let utterance = AVSpeechUtterance(string: text)
      utterance.voice = AVSpeechSynthesisVoice(language: "en-US")
      synthesizer.speak(utterance)
   }
}
```

This class includes a property called **synthesizer** to store the synthesizer and a method to process the text sent by the view. In this method, we first create an **AVSpeechUtterance** instance with the text provided by the user, request a voice in American English (en-US), and then call the **speak()** method on the synthesizer to convert the text into speech. In the view, we only need a text field for the user to input the text and a button to call this method and begin the process.

Listing 8-14: Providing the text to synthesize

```
import SwiftUI

struct ContentView: View {
   @State private var appData = ApplicationData.shared
   @State private var text: String = ""
```

```
    var body: some View {
        VStack {
            TextField("Input text", text: $text)
                .textFieldStyle(.roundedBorder)
            Button("Talk") {
                if !text.isEmpty {
                    appData.say(text: text)
                }
            }
            .buttonStyle(.borderedProminent)
            .padding()
            Spacer()
        }
        .padding()
    }
}
```

Do It Yourself

Create a new Multiplatform project. Add a Swift file called ApplicationData.swift for the code in Listing 8-13. Update the **ContentView** view with the code in Listing 8-14. Run the application on your iPhone, enter text in the input field, and press the Talk button. You should hear a voice reading the text.

Voice Configuration

When we ask the system to select a voice in a specific language, it chooses a standard voice with its default configuration. If we want to adjust aspects such as tone or speed, we can use the properties available in the **AVSpeechUtterance** class. The following are the most frequently used.

pitchMultiplier

This property sets or returns the pitch of the voice. It accepts values from 0.5 for lower pitch to 2.0 for higher pitch, with a default value of 1.0.

rate

This property sets or returns the speed at which the voice is going to speak. It accepts values from 0.0 to 1.0, with a default value of 0.5.

volume

This property sets or returns the volume of the voice. It accepts values from 0.0 for silent to 1.0 for loudest, with a default value of 1.0.

In the following example, we modify our **say()** method to lower both the pitch and the speed of the voice. As a result, the user will hear a voice with a deeper tone and a slower cadence.

Listing 8-15: Modifying the standard voice

```
func say(text: String) {
    let utterance = AVSpeechUtterance(string: text)
    utterance.voice = AVSpeechSynthesisVoice(language: "en-US")
    utterance.pitchMultiplier = 0.5
    utterance.rate = 0.1
    synthesizer.speak(utterance)
}
```

So far, we have been working with voices in American English (en-US), but our application may run in different countries or on devices with different language settings. To ensure that users can understand the spoken output, we must request a voice in the user's preferred language. Selecting the correct language can be challenging, as human languages are identified in different ways depending on the system and the region. For instance, English from the United States uses the identifier "en-US," while English from Great Britain uses "en-GB," and some tools may even return these values using an underscore instead of a hyphen, as in "en_GB." To help us retrieve a voice that matches the user's language, the **AVSpeechSynthesisVoice** class provides the following method.

> **currentLanguageCode()**
>
> This method returns a **String** value that represents the user's preferred language and locale.

To retrieve a voice in the user's preferred language, we just need to call this method and use the value to initialize the **AVSpeechSynthesisVoice** instance, as shown below.

Listing 8-16: Retrieving a voice in the user's preferred language

```
func say(text: String) {
    let userLanguage = AVSpeechSynthesisVoice.currentLanguageCode()
    let utterance = AVSpeechUtterance(string: text)
    utterance.voice = AVSpeechSynthesisVoice(language: userLanguage)
    synthesizer.speak(utterance)
}
```

Voice Selection

When we specify only the language, the system retrieves the voice it considers most suitable for the user. However, for some languages, such as English, multiple voices may be available. To obtain the full list of voices for any language, the **AVSpeechSynthesisVoice** class provides the following type method.

> **speechVoices()**
>
> This method returns an array of **AVSpeechSynthesisVoice** objects representing all the voices available on the device.

Each voice returned by this method is represented by an instance of the **AVSpeechSynthesisVoice** class. The class includes the following properties to return information about the voice.

identifier

This property returns a string that uniquely identifies the voice.

name

This property returns a string with the name of the voice.

quality

This property returns an **AVSpeechSynthesisVoiceQuality** enumeration that represents the quality of the voice. The possible values are **default**, **enhanced**, and **premium**.

gender

This property returns an **AVSpeechSynthesisVoiceGender** enumeration that represents the gender of the voice. The possible values are **unspecified**, **male** and **female**.

language

This property returns a string with a BCP 47 code that represents the voice's language and locale.

The **speechVoices()** method returns all the voices available on the device, but we can filter the list to retrieve only the ones we need. For example, we can build a list that includes only the voices matching the user's language and locale and allow them to choose the voice they prefer to use, as shown below.

Figure 8-9: *Voice selection*

To let the user select a voice, we need to add two new properties to the **ApplicationData** class: one to store all the voices available in the user's language and locale, and another to keep track of the voice chosen by the user, as shown below.

Listing 8-17: Getting the list of voices available for the user

```
import SwiftUI
import Observation
import AVFoundation

@Observable class ApplicationData {
   let synthesizer: AVSpeechSynthesizer
   let listVoices: [AVSpeechSynthesisVoice]
   var selectedVoice: String = ""

   static let shared: ApplicationData = ApplicationData()
   private init() {
      synthesizer = AVSpeechSynthesizer()

      // Get voices for current locale
      let userLanguage = AVSpeechSynthesisVoice.currentLanguageCode()
      let list = AVSpeechSynthesisVoice.speechVoices()
      listVoices = list.filter { voice in
         return voice.language == userLanguage
      }
      if let first = listVoices.first {
         selectedVoice = first.identifier
      }
   }
   func say(text: String) {
      let utterance = AVSpeechUtterance(string: text)
      utterance.voice = AVSpeechSynthesisVoice(identifier: selectedVoice)
      synthesizer.speak(utterance)
   }
}
```

When the class is initialized, we call the **speechVoices()** method, filter the results to include only the voices that match the user's language, assign the result to the **listVoices** property to make it available to the views, and then take the first voice in the list and assign its identifier to the **selectedVoice** property to select that voice by default.

In the view, we need to add a picker to let the user select a voice, as shown below.

Listing 8-18: Selecting a voice

```
import SwiftUI
import AVFoundation

struct ContentView: View {
   @State private var appData = ApplicationData.shared
   @State private var text: String = ""

   var body: some View {
      VStack {
         TextField("Input text", text: $text)
            .textFieldStyle(.roundedBorder)
         HStack {
            Picker("", selection: $appData.selectedVoice) {
               ForEach(appData.listVoices, id: \.self) { voice in
```

```
                    Text(voice.name)
                        .tag(voice.identifier)
                }
            }
            Button("Talk") {
                if !text.isEmpty {
                    appData.say(text: text)
                }
            }
            .buttonStyle(.borderedProminent)
        }
        .padding()
        Spacer()
    }
    .padding()
  }
}
```

Some languages have many voices available, others include only one. If our language is English, we will see a long list of available voices, as shown in Figure 8-9, right. Each time the user selects a different voice in the picker, the identifier of that voice is assigned to the **selectedVoice** property, so the **AVSpeechSynthesisVoice** instance is created using this identifier and therefore the selected voice is used to synthesize the text.

Do It Yourself

Update the **ApplicationData** class with the code in Listing 8-17 and the **ContentView** view with the code in Listing 8-18. Run the application on your iPhone. Enter some text and press Talk. You should hear the text spoken with the first voice in the list. Select a different voice and press Talk again. The voice should change.

Premium Voices

For languages like English, dozens of voices are available, but because the system is designed primarily for accessibility, the voices installed by default are lower in quality. High-quality voices are available, but users must download them manually. The option is available in the Settings app. If we want to test them, we must go to Settings, select Accessibility, tap Live Speech (Figure 8-10, number 1), tap Add Preferred Voice (Figure 8-10, number 2), choose the language, and then select the voice we want to download (Figure 8-10, number 3).

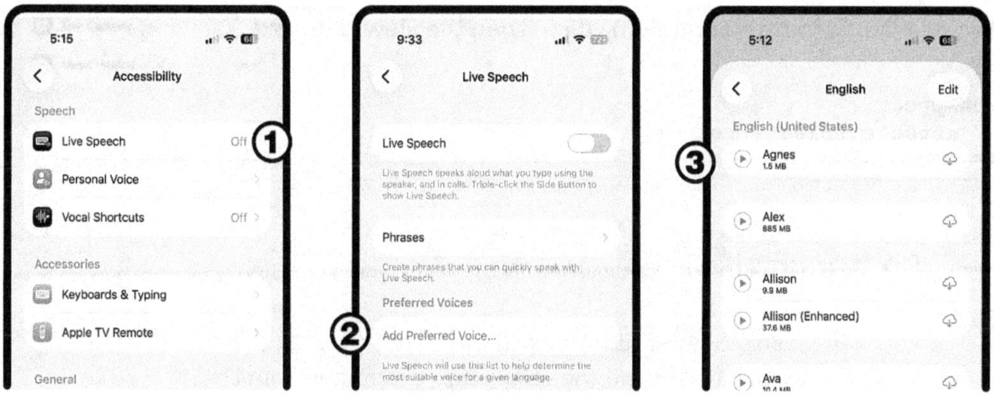

Figure 8-10: *Additional voices*

Once a new voice is downloaded, it automatically appears in the list of voices available in our app. For example, Figure 8-11, below, shows the result after downloading the Ava (Premium) voice (number 1).

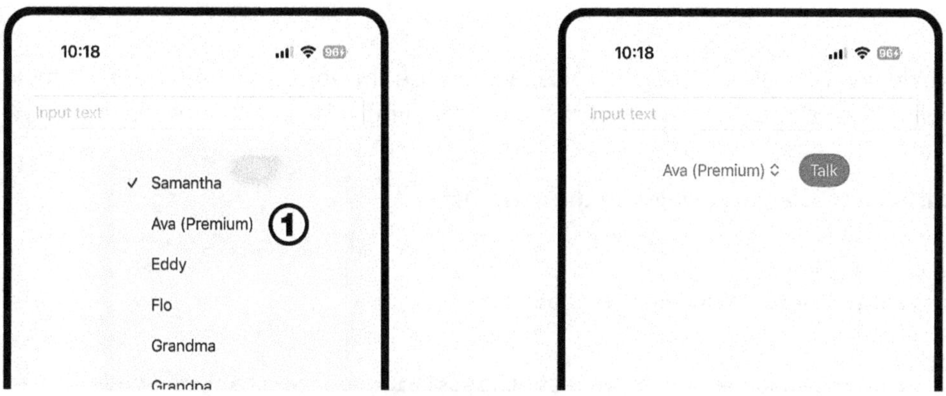

Figure 8-11: *Premium voices*

In this example, the premium voice appears in the list, but the user must select it to use it. If we know that the user may have downloaded a premium voice, we can choose it by default. The following is the method we need to add to our example for this purpose.

Listing 8-19: Selecting a premium voice

```
func selectPremium() {
   if let found = listVoices.first(where: { $0.quality == .premium }) {
      selectedVoice = found.identifier
   }
}
```

This method just searches for a voice in the **listVoices** array whose quality is equal to **premium**. If such a voice is found, its identifier is assigned to the **selectedVoice** property so it is automatically selected in the interface.

From the view, we need to call this method as soon as the interface appears on the screen. The following is the **onAppear()** modifier we must add to our **ContentView** view for this purpose.

Listing 8-20: Selecting a premium voice when the view is loaded

```
.onAppear {
   appData.selectPremium()
}
```

Do It Yourself

Add the **selectPremium()** method from Listing 8-19 to the **ApplicationData** class and the **onAppear()** modifier from Listing 8-20 to the **ContentView** view. On your iPhone, go to Settings, open Accessibility, tap Live Speech (Figure 8-10, number 1), tap Add Preferred Voice (Figure 8-10, number 2), choose your language, and download a premium voice. Run the application on the same device. You should see the premium voice you downloaded as the selected voice in the picker.

If we want to select a specific voice, we can use the voice's identifier. For example, the following code shows how to select the Ava (Premium) voice in our application.

Listing 8-21: Selecting a voice by the identifier

```
private init() {
   synthesizer = AVSpeechSynthesizer()

   // Get voices for current locale
   let userLanguage = AVSpeechSynthesisVoice.currentLanguageCode()
   let list = AVSpeechSynthesisVoice.speechVoices()
   listVoices = list.filter { voice in
      return voice.language == userLanguage
   }
   // Select Ava Premium
   let voiceID = "com.apple.voice.premium.en-US.Ava"
   if let found = listVoices.first(where: { $0.identifier == voiceID }) {
      selectedVoice = found.identifier
   } else if let first = listVoices.first {
      selectedVoice = first.identifier
   }
}
```

This code updates the initializer of the **ApplicationData** class to select the Ava (Premium) voice if it is available. It searches the **listVoices** array for a voice whose identifier matches the one used by the Ava (Premium) voice, and if it finds a match, it assigns that identifier to the **selectedVoice** property so it appears as the selected voice on the interface. If the voice is not found, the code falls back to the first voice in the list.

Do It Yourself

Update the initializer in the **ApplicationData** class with the code in Listing 8-21. To test the application, remove the **onAppear()** modifier added in Listing 8-20, so the voice is not set by the **selectPremium()** method anymore. Run the application on your iPhone. If the Ava (Premium) voice is installed, it should appear as the selected option in the picker, as before.

IMPORTANT

The voice's identifier is the value returned by the **identifier** property of the **AVSpeechSynthesisVoice** class. If you want to determine the identifier of a specific voice, select the voice and read this value.

Controlling the Synthesizer

Premium voices such as Ava (Premium) are ideal when our app needs to read long passages. In situations like this, we not only need a high-quality voice but also the tools to let users control the reading process. For this purpose, the **AVSpeechSynthesizer** class provides the following properties and methods.

isSpeaking

This property returns a Boolean value to indicate whether the synthesizer is speaking or not. The value **true** indicates that the synthesizer is currently speaking or paused, and the value **false** indicates that the synthesizer is not speaking and has no utterances in the queue.

isPaused

This property returns a Boolean value to indicate whether the synthesizer is currently paused or not.

stopSpeaking(at: AVSpeechBoundary)

This method stops the synthesizer. The **at** argument is an enumeration that determines where the synthesizer should stop. The possible values are **immediate**, to stop at once, and **word**, to stop after finishing the current word.

pauseSpeaking(at: AVSpeechBoundary)

This method pauses the synthesizer. The **at** argument is an enumeration that determines where the synthesizer should pause. The possible values are **immediate**, to pause at once, and **word**, to pause after finishing the current word.

continueSpeaking()

This method asks the synthesizer to resume speech at the point it was paused.

With these properties and methods, we can let the user control the speech, but to respond to changes in the synthesizer's state, we must implement a delegate. For this purpose, the framework provides the **AVSpeechSynthesizerDelegate** protocol. The following are some of the methods defined by this protocol.

speechSynthesizer(AVSpeechSynthesizer, **didStart:** AVSpeech Utterance)

This method is called on the delegate when the synthesizer begins speaking.

speechSynthesizer(AVSpeechSynthesizer, **didPause:** AVSpeech Utterance)

This method is called on the delegate when the synthesizer is paused.

speechSynthesizer(AVSpeechSynthesizer, **didContinue:** AVSpeech Utterance)

This method is called on the delegate when the synthesizer resumes speaking.

speechSynthesizer(AVSpeechSynthesizer, **didFinish:** AVSpeech Utterance)

This method is called on the delegate when the synthesizer finishes speaking.

The following example shows how to implement all these tools. We begin by making our **ApplicationData** class conform to the **AVSpeechSynthesizerDelegate** protocol so we can implement its methods and update the button in the interface whenever the state of the synthesizer changes.

Listing 8-22: Responding to the state of the synthesizer

```
import SwiftUI
import Observation
import AVFoundation

@MainActor
@Observable class ApplicationData: NSObject, @preconcurrency
AVSpeechSynthesizerDelegate {
   let synthesizer: AVSpeechSynthesizer
   var buttonLabel: String = "Talk"

   static let shared: ApplicationData = ApplicationData()
   private override init() {
      synthesizer = AVSpeechSynthesizer()
      super.init()
      synthesizer.delegate = self
   }
   func say(text: String) {
      let utterance = AVSpeechUtterance(string: text)
      let voiceID = "com.apple.voice.premium.en-US.Ava"
      utterance.voice = AVSpeechSynthesisVoice(identifier: voiceID)
      synthesizer.speak(utterance)
   }
```

```
    func speechSynthesizer(_ synthesizer: AVSpeechSynthesizer,
       didStart utterance: AVSpeechUtterance) {
       buttonLabel = "Pause"
    }
    func speechSynthesizer(_ synthesizer: AVSpeechSynthesizer,
       didFinish utterance: AVSpeechUtterance) {
       buttonLabel = "Talk"
    }
    func speechSynthesizer(_ synthesizer: AVSpeechSynthesizer,
       didContinue utterance: AVSpeechUtterance) {
       buttonLabel = "Pause"
    }
    func speechSynthesizer(_ synthesizer: AVSpeechSynthesizer,
       didPause utterance: AVSpeechUtterance) {
       buttonLabel = "Talk"
    }
}
```

In this code, we get the **ApplicationData** class to conform to the **AVSpeechSynthesizerDelegate** protocol and assign it as the delegate of the **AVSpeechSynthesizer** object, so the protocol methods are now called on this class whenever the state of the synthesizer changes. In this case, we use these methods to update the label of the button in the interface, ensuring that the user always knows what the button will do when pressed (Talk or Pause).

In the view, we must implement the properties and methods of the **AVSpeechSynthesizer** class to let the user control the synthesizer. The following is our implementation.

Listing 8-23: Starting and pausing the synthesizer

```
import SwiftUI
import AVFoundation

struct ContentView: View {
   @State private var appData = ApplicationData.shared
   @State private var text: String = ""

   var body: some View {
      VStack {
         TextEditor(text: $text)
            .padding()
            .scrollContentBackground(.hidden)
            .background(Color.gray.opacity(0.2))
            .clipShape(RoundedRectangle(cornerRadius: 12))
            .frame(height: 300)
         Button(action: {
            if appData.synthesizer.isSpeaking {
               if appData.synthesizer.isPaused {
                  // Continue speaking
                  appData.synthesizer.continueSpeaking()
               } else {
                  // Pause speaking
                  appData.synthesizer.pauseSpeaking(at: .word)
               }
```

```
            } else {
               // Start speaking
               appData.say(text: text)
            }}, label: {
               Text(appData.buttonLabel)
            }
         )
         .buttonStyle(.borderedProminent)
         .padding()
         Spacer()
      }
      .padding()
   }
}
```

In this case, we include a **TextEditor** view to let the user enter a long text. If the synthesizer has not started yet, the button displays the label "Talk." When the button is pressed, the **speechSynthesizer(didStart:)** method is called in the delegate and the label is changed to "Pause." If the user presses the button again, the synthesizer pauses, the **speechSynthesizer(didPause:)** method is called, and the "Talk" is assigned again to the button to indicate that speech can be resumed. If the user lets the synthesizer read the entire text, the **speechSynthesizer(didFinish:)** method is called and the label is switched back to "Talk," signaling to the user that the synthesizer is ready to start the process again.

Do It Yourself

Update the **ApplicationData** class with the code in Listing 8-22 and the **ContentView** view with the code in Listing 8-23. Run the application on your iPhone. Enter a long text and press the Talk button. The synthesizer should begin reading the text, and you should be able to press the button again to pause or resume speech at any time.

IMPORTANT

To simplify the example, we removed the tools for selecting a voice and simply load the Ava (Premium) voice. If this voice is not available on the device, the system defaults to the standard voice for the user's language.

8.4 - Sound Analysis

Beyond analyzing and synthesizing voices, we can also work with other types of sounds. For this purpose, Apple provides the **Sound Analysis** framework. This framework gives us access to models trained to examine raw audio in real time or from a recording and identify the types of sounds present, including instruments, voices, animals, and many kinds of ambient noises.

To analyze a sound, we create a request and define an observer to handle the results. A request is created from the **SNClassifySoundRequest** class. The following is the class' initializer.

SNClassifySoundRequest(classifierIdentifier: SNClassifierIdentifier)

This initializer creates a request to classify sounds. The **classifierIdentifier** argument is a structure with properties that determine the version of the model to use. At the moment, the only available property is **version1**.

When we perform a request, the results are delivered to an observer object. This object is created like any other, but its class must conform to the **SNResultsObserving** protocol and implement the following methods.

request(SNRequest, **didProduce:** SNResult)

This method is called on the observer when the analyzer identifies a sound.

request(SNRequest, **didFailWithError:** Error)

This method is called on the observer when an error occurs while analyzing the audio.

requestDidComplete(SNRequest)

This method is called on the observer when the analyzer finished processing the audio.

The only method we are required to implement is **request(didProduce:)**. This method is called when the analyzer identifies a sound or multiple simultaneous sounds. The values are returned as an **SNClassificationResult** object. This object includes information about the time span in which the sound was detected and an array with the possible candidates (the possible types of sounds identified in that range). The **SNClassificationResult** class provides the following properties to access these values.

timeRange

This property returns a **CMTimeRange** structure that represents the time range in which the sound was identified.

classifications

This property returns an array of **SNClassification** objects representing every prediction made by the model.

The **CMTimeRange** structure belongs to an older framework called **Core Media**. This framework provides the **CMTime** structure to represent time, and that structure includes the **seconds** property to return the value in seconds. To access the starting and ending times of a range, the **CMTimeRange** structure offers the following properties.

start

This property returns a **CMTime** structure representing the moment when the range begins.

end

This property returns a **CMTime** structure representing the moment when the range ends.

Because the model can detect multiple simultaneous sounds, the **classifications** property returns an array of **SNClassification** objects representing each prediction. To provide information about the prediction, the **SNClassification** class offers the following properties.

identifier

This property returns a **String** value with the name of the category the sound belongs to.

confidence

This property returns a **Double** value representing how certain the model is that the sound belongs to the selected category.

> **IMPORTANT**
>
> The **SNClassifySoundRequest** class also provides an initializer that allows us to create a request from a custom Core ML model, enabling the recognition of sounds not included in the Sound Analysis model provided by Apple. We will learn how to train our own Core ML models with Create ML in Chapter 10.

Audio File Analysis

Once we have the request and the observer, we must create an analyzer. There are two types of analyzers, one for audio files and another for live streams. To analyze audio files, the framework provides the **SNAudioFileAnalyzer** class. The class includes the following initializer.

SNAudioFileAnalyzer(url: URL)

This initializer creates an analyzer for an audio file. The **url** argument specifies the location of the file to analyze.

The **SNAudioFileAnalyzer** class includes the following methods to perform the analysis.

add(SNRequest, **withObserver:** SNResultsObserving)

This method adds a request to the analyzer. The first argument is the request to add, and the **withObserver** argument is the observer object used to process the results.

analyze()

This method performs the analysis.

cancelAnalysis()

This method cancels the analysis.

The first step in analyzing an audio file is to create the observer object. How this object is defined depends on the characteristics of our application. For instance, in the following example, we simply want to show the user the different types of sounds found in a file, so the observer only needs to check whether the confidence is high enough for the sound to be considered identified and then add the category to a list, as shown below.

Listing 8-24: Defining an observer for audio analysis

```
import SwiftUI
import SoundAnalysis

class AudioObserver: NSObject, SNResultsObserving {
   var findings: Set<String> = []

   func request(_ request: any SNRequest, didProduce result: any SNResult) {
      if let results = result as? SNClassificationResult {
         let classifications = results.classifications
         for classification in classifications {
            if classification.confidence > 0.5 {
               findings.insert(classification.identifier)
            }
         }
      }
   }
}
```

In this class, we define a property called **findings** to store all the sounds identified by the analyzer and implement the **request(didProduce:)** method to process the results. When this method is called, we read the **SNClassification** objects in the array, check that the confidence level for each detected sound is above 0.5 to reduce false positives, and add the category name to the **findings** property so it can be shown to the user when the analysis is complete. Note that the results are provided as values of type **SNResult**, so we must cast them as **SNClassificationResult** objects before accessing their values.

Now that we have the observer, we can create the request and analyze the audio. As always, we place the logic in an observable object, as shown below.

Listing 8-25: Analyzing an audio file

```
import SwiftUI
import Observation
import SoundAnalysis

@Observable class ApplicationData {
   var result: String = ""

   static let shared: ApplicationData = ApplicationData()
   private init() { }

   func analyzeSound() async {
      do {
         guard let fileURL = Bundle.main.url(forResource: "dogbark",
            withExtension: "mp3") else { return }

         let analyzer = try SNAudioFileAnalyzer(url: fileURL)
         let request = try SNClassifySoundRequest(
            classifierIdentifier: .version1)
         let observer = AudioObserver()
         try analyzer.add(request, withObserver: observer)
         await analyzer.analyze()

         result = observer.findings.joined(separator: "\n")
      } catch {
         print("Error: \(error)")
      }
   }
}
```

In this example, we use an MP3 file containing the sounds of a barking dog. We first obtain the file's URL and create the **SNAudioFileAnalyzer** object with that value. Next, we create a request and an instance of our observer, add both to the analyzer with the **add()** method, and finally call the **analyze()** method to process the file.

The view for this example is simple. We just need to call the **analyzeSound()** method in the observable object to start the process and display the results.

Listing 8-26: Showing the results of audio analysis

```
import SwiftUI

struct ContentView: View {
   @State private var appData = ApplicationData.shared

   var body: some View {
      VStack {
         Button("Analyze") {
            Task {
               await appData.analyzeSound()
            }
         }.buttonStyle(.borderedProminent)

         ScrollView {
```

```
            Text(appData.result)
            Spacer()
         }.frame(minWidth: 0, maxWidth: .infinity, alignment: .leading)
      }
      .padding()
   }
}
```

When analyzing a file, the process is synchronous, so we can wait until it finishes and then read the **findings** property in the observer to get the results. In this example, the audio contains several barking sounds, but because we store the values in a set, repeated categories are not recorded, so the final result is a list of the unique categories present in the audio, as shown below.

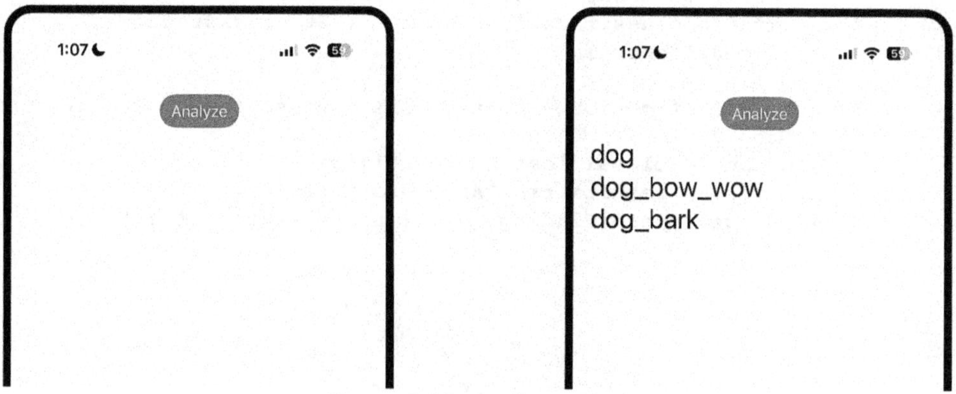

Figure 8-12: *Audio analysis*

Do It Yourself

Create a new Multiplatform project. Download the **dogbark.mp3** file from our website and drag it into the project. Create a Swift file called AudioObserver.swift for the code in Listing 8-24 and another called ApplicationData.swift for the code in Listing 8-25. Update the **ContentView** view with the code in Listing 8-26. Run the application on your iPhone and press the Analyze button. You should see the categories detected in the file displayed on the screen. In this example, three categories are identified: dog, dog_bow_wow, and dog_bark.

Every time a sound is identified, the analyzer returns the time range in which it occurred. With this information, we can show the user not only the categories detected in a file but also the exact moment when each occurrence appears. The time range is provided as two **CMTime** values, which allows us to determine precisely when the sound happened. The following are the changes we need to introduce in our observer to store these values.

Listing 8-27: Storing the time at which each sound is found

```
import SwiftUI
import SoundAnalysis

struct Findings {
   let name: String
   let start: TimeInterval
}
class AudioObserver: NSObject, SNResultsObserving {
   var findings: [Findings] = []

   func request(_ request: any SNRequest, didProduce result: any SNResult) {
      if let results = result as? SNClassificationResult {
         let classifications = results.classifications
         let sorted = classifications.sorted { $0.confidence
            > $1.confidence }

         if let classification = sorted.first, classification.confidence
            > 0.5 {
            let name = classification.identifier
            let time = results.timeRange.start.seconds
            findings.append(Findings(name: name, start: time))
         }
      }
   }
}
```

This time we define a structure called **Findings** to store the values. The structure includes a **name** property to store the detected category and a **start** property to store the time in seconds when the sound was identified. As before, we save these values in the observer's **findings** property, but because the analyzer can detect multiple categories within a single sound and handle many sounds in the same range, we must process the results to extract only what we need. In this case, we care only about the most significant category in the range, so we sort the detected categories by confidence and select the one the model is most certain about. Once we have this category, we read its name from the **identifier** property, extract the starting time in seconds from the **timeRange** property, and create a new **Findings** instance to store these values in the array.

In the **ApplicationData** class, instead of processing only the category name, we must now create a string that includes both the category and the time when it was found. The following are the changes we need to make in our **analyzeSound()** method.

Listing 8-28: Showing the time and category of each sound

```
func analyzeSound() async {
   do {
      guard let fileURL = Bundle.main.url(forResource: "dogbark",
         withExtension: "mp3") else { return }

      let request = try SNClassifySoundRequest(
         classifierIdentifier: .version1)
      let analyzer = try SNAudioFileAnalyzer(url: fileURL)
```

```
        let observer = AudioObserver()
        try analyzer.add(request, withObserver: observer)
        await analyzer.analyze()

        result = ""
        for finding in observer.findings {
           result += "\(finding.start) - \(finding.name)\n"
        }
     } catch {
        print("Error: \(error)")
     }
  }
```

The code to set up the analyzer remains the same; we just had to add a **for in** loop at the end to read the values and append them to the **result** property so they can be displayed to the user, as shown below.

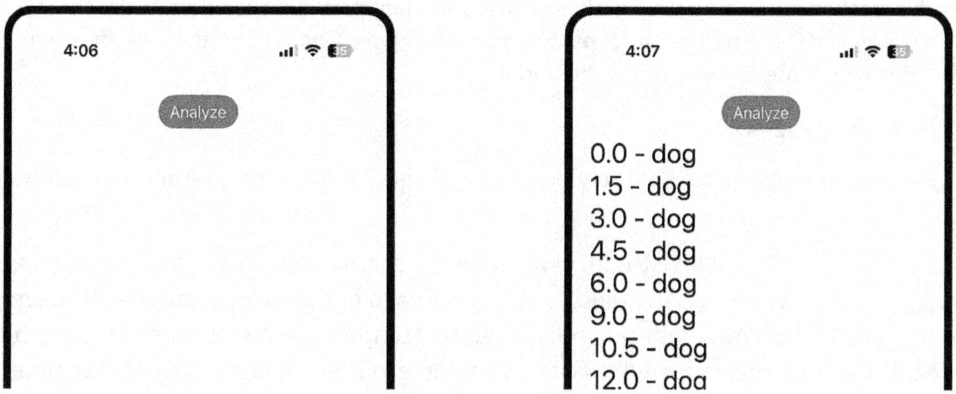

Figure 8-13: *Audio timing*

Do It Yourself

Update the AudioObserver.swift file with the code in Listing 8-27 and the **analyzeSound()** method in the **ApplicationData** class with the code in Listing 8-28. Run the application on your iPhone and press the Analyze button. You should see the list of all occurrences of sound categories in the file, as shown in Figure 8-13, right.

Live Audio Analysis

As we mentioned earlier, the **Sound Analysis** framework also allows us to analyze a live stream of audio, such as audio coming from a video feed or the microphone. To support this type of analysis, the framework provides the **SNAudioStreamAnalyzer** class. The following is the initializer for this class.

SNAudioStreamAnalyzer(format: AVAudioFormat)

This initializer creates an analyzer for live audio. The **format** argument specifies the format of the audio we want to analyze.

The **SNAudioStreamAnalyzer** class includes the following methods to perform the analysis.

add(SNRequest, **withObserver:** SNResultsObserving)

This method adds a request to the analyzer. The first argument is the request to add, and the **withObserver** argument is the observer object used to process the results.

analyze(AVAudioBuffer, **atAudioFramePosition:** AVAudioFramePosition)

This method performs the analysis. The first argument provides the audio buffer to analyze, and the **atAudioFramePosition** parameter is a 64-bit integer that specifies the frame where the analysis should be performed.

completeAnalysis()

This method tells the analyzer that there are no more audio buffers available to process.

To process a live audio stream, we need to access the audio source, such as the microphone, retrieve chunks of audio, and process each buffer independently. We have used this same workflow before when handling live transcription, but this time the procedure is simpler. The audio analysis model accepts multiple buffer formats, and the analyzer can process each chunk as it arrives, so we no longer need to convert the samples to 16-bit signed integers or create an asynchronous sequence to provide the values. However, we still must rely on the tools offered by the **AVFoundation** framework to request permission to use the microphone, configure the audio session, and use an audio engine to obtain the buffers to analyze. The following is our implementation.

Listing 8-29: Analyzing live audio

```
import SwiftUI
import Observation
import SoundAnalysis
import AVFoundation

@Observable class ApplicationData {
   var result: String = ""

   var audioEngine = AVAudioEngine()
   var audioAnalyzer: SNAudioStreamAnalyzer?
   var observer: SNResultsObserving?

   static let shared: ApplicationData = ApplicationData()
   private init() { }
```

```
    func setupAudioSession() async {
        do {
            // Check authorization to access Microphone
            if AVCaptureDevice.authorizationStatus(for: .audio)
                != .authorized {
                guard await AVCaptureDevice.requestAccess(for: .audio)
                    else { return }
            }
            // Set up audio session
            let audioSession = AVAudioSession.sharedInstance()
            try audioSession.setCategory(.playAndRecord, mode: .spokenAudio)
            try audioSession.setActive(true,
                options: .notifyOthersOnDeactivation)
        } catch {
            print("Error: \(error)")
        }
    }
    func startAnalysis() async {
        do {
            let inputFormat = audioEngine.inputNode.inputFormat(forBus: 0)
            let outputFormat = audioEngine.inputNode.outputFormat(forBus: 0)
            audioAnalyzer = SNAudioStreamAnalyzer(format: inputFormat)

            let request = try SNClassifySoundRequest(
                classifierIdentifier: .version1)
            observer = AudioObserver()
            try audioAnalyzer?.add(request, withObserver: observer!)

            audioEngine.inputNode.installTap(onBus: 0, bufferSize: 4096,
                format: outputFormat) { buffer, time in
                 Task.detached(priority: .userInitiated) { [weak self] in
                    await self?.audioAnalyzer?.analyze(buffer,
                        atAudioFramePosition: time.sampleTime)
                }
            }
            audioEngine.prepare()
            try audioEngine.start()
        } catch {
            print("Error: \(error)")
        }
    }
    func stopRecording() async {
        audioEngine.stop()
        audioEngine.inputNode.removeTap(onBus: 0)
        audioAnalyzer?.completeAnalysis()
        result = ""
    }
}
```

This class includes three methods: the **setupAudioSession()** method to request permission to use the microphone and configure the audio session, the **startAnalysis()** method to create the analyzer, begin listening to the microphone, and process the incoming audio buffers, and the **stopRecording()** method to end the process. The audio session and analyzer are configured as before, but because we are working with a continuous stream of audio, we must use the **SNAudioStreamAnalyzer** class to create the analyzer and process each buffer from the microphone with the class' own **analyze()** method.

Because we are working with a live stream of audio, we cannot wait for the process to finish before retrieving the results, we must access the values as they are produced by the observer, which means the observer must remain alive for the entire duration of the process, so along with the properties to store the audio engine and the analyzer, we also defined the **observer** property to store a reference to the observer object. The following is the implementation of this object.

Listing 8-30: Identifying the categories in real time

```
import SwiftUI
import SoundAnalysis

class AudioObserver: NSObject, SNResultsObserving {
   var appData = ApplicationData.shared

   func request(_ request: any SNRequest, didProduce result: any SNResult) {
      if let results = result as? SNClassificationResult {
         let classifications = results.classifications
         for classification in classifications {
            if classification.confidence > 0.5 {
               Task { @MainActor in
                  appData.result = classification.identifier
               }
            }
         }
      }
   }
}
```

The code for this observer is the same as the one we used earlier to retrieve every category in a file, but now the values are retrieved in real time. There are several ways to accomplish this. In this case, we decided to keep it simple by getting a reference to our **ApplicationData** object and assign the values directly to the **result** property.

From the view, we need to call the **setupAudioSession()** method to request permission to use the microphone as soon as the interface appears on the screen, and then provide a button to start and stop the process.

Listing 8-31: Controlling the analysis of live audio

```
import SwiftUI

struct ContentView: View {
   @State private var appData = ApplicationData.shared
   @State private var isRecording: Bool = false

   var body: some View {
      VStack {
         Button(action: {
            if isRecording {
               Task {
                  await appData.stopRecording()
```

```
            }
         } else {
            Task {
               await appData.startAnalysis()
            }
         }
         isRecording.toggle()
      }, label: {
         Image(systemName: isRecording ? "stop.fill" :
            "microphone.square")
      })
      .font(Font.system(size: 28))
      .buttonStyle(.glass)

      Text(appData.result)
         .padding()
      Spacer()
   }
   .padding()
   .onAppear {
      Task {
         await appData.setupAudioSession()
      }
   }
  }
}
```

Do It Yourself

Update the ApplicationData.swift file with the code in Listing 8-29, the **AudioObserver** class with the code in Listing 8-30, and the **ContentView** view with the code in Listing 8-31. Remember to add the microphone capability in the Signing & Capabilities panel, as shown in Figures 8-4 and 8-5. Run the application on your iPhone and press the button to activate the microphone. Talk, sing, or make any sound. You should see the name of the detected sound category on the screen.

IMPORTANT

In this example, we use a reference to the **ApplicationData** object to get the values from the observer in real time. Although this approach is valid, we can also use a publisher or subject from the **Combine** framework to make the values accessible from any part of the code. To learn more about the **Combine** framework, read our book *SwiftUI Framework for Masterminds*. For more information on audio recording, read our book *Advanced SwiftUI for Masterminds*.

Chapter 9
Siri

9.1 - App Intents Framework

The most powerful feature enabled by Apple Intelligence is not something we build directly into our apps, but the system's ability to perform tasks from anywhere at the user's command. With Apple Intelligence, users can ask Siri to execute an action such as playing a video, retrieving information, or storing data, and Siri automatically determines which app to use and completes the task without even opening the app.

This feature is not available automatically. Every app must expose its functionality so the system knows which actions it can perform. To provide this information, our app needs to define two things: an App Intent for every action we want to make available to the system, and shortcuts that give users access to those actions. Once this information is in place, users can tell Siri what to do, Siri receives this order and activates a shortcut, the shortcut triggers an intent, and the intent executes the action in our app, as shown below.

Figure 9-1: *Using App Intents*

> **IMPORTANT**
>
> At the time of writing, Apple is actively improving Siri and integrating Apple Intelligence into the system. Some of the features described in this chapter may not behave as expected or may not yet be fully reliable. Test these examples in your own projects to determine what works best for you and your users.

App Intents

The first step in telling the system which actions our app can perform is defining an App Intent. An app intent is a Swift structure that we define in our project like any other. The only difference is that we do not create an instance of this structure; we simply define it, and the compiler reads this definition and automatically generates the code needed to expose the action to the system. To define the structure, the framework provides the `AppIntent` protocol. The following are the properties and methods required by this protocol.

title

This property sets the title of the intent. It is a **LocalizedStringResource** structure with a string that can later be localized to the user's language and locale when the intent is created.

description

This property sets the description of the intent. It is a **IntentDescription** structure that contains a **LocalizedStringResource** structure with a string that can later be localized to the user's language and locale when the intent is created.

perform()

This method is executed when the intent is triggered. The method performs the action and then returns a structure that conforms to the **IntentResult** protocol to report the result.

The structure can also define the following property to configure the intent's behavior.

supportedModes

This property sets a value that determines how the intent behaves. It is a structure of type **IntentModes**. This structure includes the **background** property to specify whether the intent can run in the background, the **foreground** property to require the app to be open, and the **foreground(ForegroundMode)** method to return a foreground mode with a specific behavior. The method receives a **ForegroundMode** structure that defines the mode. This structure includes the properties **deferred**, **dynamic**, and **immediate**.

When the user asks Siri to perform a task, the system finds the correct intent and executes the **perform()** method. In this method, we must carry out the action in our app and then return the result of the operation. The result is returned as a structure that conforms to the **IntentResult** protocol. The following is one of the methods defined by this protocol to create an instance of this structure.

result(value: Value, **dialog:** IntentDialog, **view:** Content)

This method creates a structure used to return the result of the intent to the system. The **value** argument is the value produced by the intent, the **dialog** argument is an **IntentDialog** structure that contains a **LocalizedStringResource** with the text we want the system to display or Siri to say to the user, and the **view** argument is the view used to present the results.

There are multiple versions of this method to return different types of values and combinations of values, but every returned value must conform to a specific protocol, so unless we are returning an empty result, we must declare the return value to conform to the corresponding protocol. The following are the available protocols.

ReturnsValue<Value>

This protocol defines a result that returns a value to the system. The protocol is generic, so it must specify the data type of the value being returned.

ProvidesDialog

This protocol defines a result that returns a text to display or say to the user.

ShowsSnippetView

This protocol defines a result that returns a view to the system.

The following example illustrates how to define a simple intent that shows a string on the screen with the name of the user's favorite movie.

Listing 9-1: Defining an app intent

```
import SwiftUI
import AppIntents

struct ShowMovie: AppIntent {
   static let title: LocalizedStringResource = "Show Movie"
   static let description = IntentDescription("Shows your favorite
      movie.")

   static let supportedModes: IntentModes = .foreground(.immediate)

   @MainActor
   func perform() async throws -> some IntentResult {
      let appData = ApplicationData.shared
      appData.message = "Your favorite movie is Rambo!"
      return .result()
   }
}
```

This code defines a structure called **ShowMovie** that conforms to the **AppIntent** protocol, so it will be compiled as an app intent by Xcode when we build our app. The structure implements all the protocol requirements. We define the **title** and **description** properties to provide the intent's title and description, the **supportedModes** property to request the system to open our app as soon as the intent is triggered (**foreground(.immediate)**), and the **perform()** method to carry out the action. The purpose of this intent is to open the app and assign a string to an observable object to display a message on the screen, so we get a reference to our app's observable object (**ApplicationData**) and change the value of one of its properties to send the message to the view (**message**). Note that in this case, the intent does not need to return any value, so we declare the return type as some **IntentResult** and return an empty **result()** method.

Since the purpose of this intent is simply to open the app and display a message on the screen, our observable object needs only a single property, as shown below.

Listing 9-2: Defining our app's observable object

```
import SwiftUI
import Observation

@Observable class ApplicationData {
   var message: String = "No Message"

   static let shared: ApplicationData = ApplicationData()
   private init() { }
}
```

For the view, we only need to display the value of the **message** property on the screen.

Listing 9-3: Defining our app's interface

```
import SwiftUI

struct ContentView: View {
   @State private var appData = ApplicationData.shared

   var body: some View {
      VStack {
         Text(appData.message)
            .padding()
         Spacer()
      }
      .padding()
   }
}
```

The purpose of an app intent is to define an action that our app can perform, but to execute that intent we need to create a shortcut. For testing purposes, we can manually create a shortcut from the Shortcuts app. This is an app provided by Apple that users can use to create different types of shortcuts and automations to perform tasks on the system, including executing the intents in our app. To create a shortcut, we need to open the app, press the plus button in the top-right corner (Figure 9-2, number 1), search for the name of our app (Figure 9-2, number 2), and select the intent (Figure 9-2, number 3).

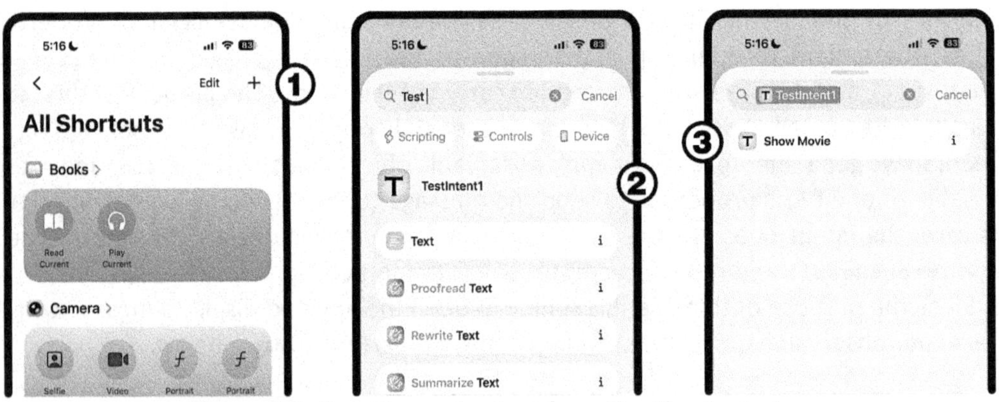

Figure 9-2: *Creating a shortcut from the Shortcuts App*

This creates an item in the Shortcuts app that we can tap at any time to execute our intent. Figure 9-3 shows what the interface looks like when we run the app for the first time and the result we see after tapping the shortcut.

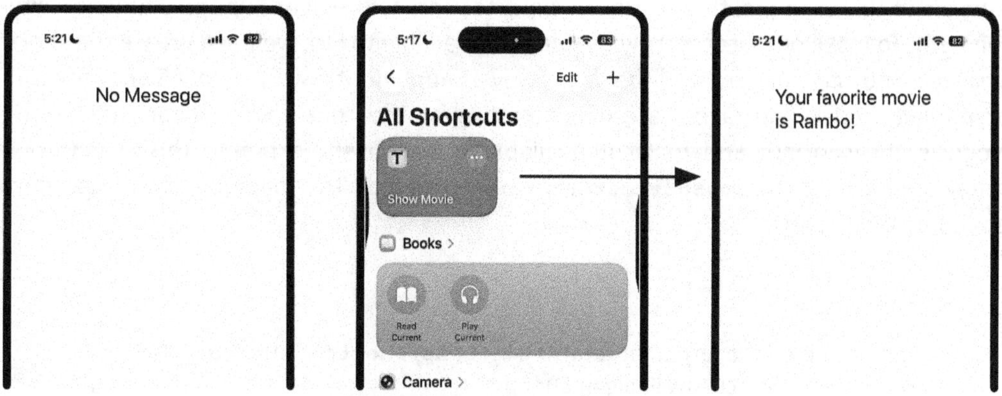

Figure 9-3: *Using a shortcut*

Do It Yourself

Create a new Multiplatform project. Create a Swift file called AppIntents.swift for the code in Listing 9-1 and another file called ApplicationData.swift for the code in Listing 9-2. Update the **`ContentView`** view with the code in Listing 9-3. Run the application on your iPhone. You should see the message "No Message" on the screen. Open the Shortcuts app (If the app was removed from your iPhone, you can reinstall it from the App Store). Tap the + button (Figure 9-2, number 1), search for the name of you app and select it (Figure 9-2, number 2). You should see the Show Movie intent. Tap on it to create a shortcut. Go back to the main screen. You should see a new view representing your shortcut (Figure 9-3, center). Tap the shortcut to run it. Your app should open, and you should see a new message on the screen, as shown in Figure 9-3, right.

IMPORTANT

Besides the **`AppIntent`** protocol, the framework includes several others designed for specific kinds of actions. Some let you create intents that play or record audio, others let you play videos or open URLs. Each protocol provides the system with the information it needs to perform the action. For more information, visit our website and follow the links for this chapter.

App Shortcuts

Although we can define an intent and let the user create a shortcut from the Shortcuts app, as we did in this example, this approach expects users to discover our app's functionality on their own. To make our intents truly usable and available to Siri, we must create the shortcut ourselves. Shortcuts are created the same way as app intents; we define a Swift structure in our project, and Xcode takes care of generating all the code required for the system to recognize the shortcut and make it available to the user. To define this structure, the framework includes the **AppShortcutsProvider** protocol. The following are the properties defined by the protocol.

appShortcuts

This is a computed property that returns a list of **AppShortcut** structures that represent every shortcut available in our app.

shortcutTileColor

This property sets an enumeration of type **ShortcutTileColor** with values that represent the color we want to assign to the shortcut's background in the Shortcuts App. The possible values are **blue**, **grape**, **grayBlue**, **grayBrown**, **grayGreen**, **lightBlue**, **lime**, **navy**, **orange**, **pink**, **purple**, **red**, **tangerine**, **teal**, and **yellow**.

negativePhrases

This property sets a structure of type **NegativeAppShortcutPhrases** that contains an array of **NegativeAppShortcutPhrase** structures with strings that represent the phrases we want Siri to ignore.

A structure that conforms to the **AppShortcutsProvider** protocol is simply a container for all the shortcuts in our app. The shortcuts themselves are defined by **AppShortcut** structures. This structure provides the following initializer to create a shortcut.

```
AppShortcut(intent: Intent, phrases: [AppShortcutPhrase],
shortTitle: LocalizedStringResource, systemImageName: String)
```

This initializer creates a shortcut from the values provided by the arguments. The **intent** argument is an instance of the intent that the shortcut runs, the **phrases** argument is an array containing the phrases Siri will respond to, the **shortTitle** argument is a localizable string with the shortcut's title, and the **systemImageName** argument is a string with the name of the SF Symbol used to represent the shortcut in the Shortcuts app and Spotlight.

When we define a shortcut, it appears in the Shortcuts app and in Spotlight when users search for our app, but it can also be run through Siri. To make Siri recognize our shortcuts, we must provide phrases for the user to say, and each phrase must include the name of our app. For example, if we want to define a phrase the user can speak to have our app return information about a movie, we can specify the string "Show me information about the movie Rambo in My App", where "My App" is the name of our app. The name of our app must be present in every phrase we want Siri to recognize. We can place it at the end, as in this example, or anywhere in the phrase, but it must always appear so Siri knows which app the user wants to interact with. To ensure that we specify the correct value (and to allow the use of alternative names, as we will see later), the framework includes the **AppShortcutPhraseToken** enumeration, which defines the following value.

applicationName

This value represents the name of the application. When the app is compiled, this value is replaced by the name of the app and alternative names if available.

The following example defines a shortcut that allows Siri to run our **ShowMovie** intent. The implementation is simple. We define a structure that conforms to the **AppShortcutsProvider** protocol, and then initialize an **AppShortcut** structure to represent the shortcut and assign it to the **appShortcuts** property, as shown below.

Listing 9-4: Defining a shortcut to run our intent

```
struct TestIntentsShortcuts: AppShortcutsProvider {
    static var appShortcuts: [AppShortcut] {
        AppShortcut(
            intent: ShowMovie(),
            phrases: [
                "Show me my favorite movie in \(.applicationName)",
                "Find my favorite movie in \(.applicationName)"
            ],
            shortTitle: LocalizedStringResource("Get Movie"),
            systemImageName: "star.circle"
        )
    }
}
```

This shortcut defines two phrases that Siri can recognize: "Show me my favorite movie in My App" and "Find my favorite movie in My App." The result is the same as before: the shortcut runs, the **ShowMovie** intent is triggered, and the app opens to display a message on the screen. The difference is that the user no longer needs to open the Shortcuts app to perform the action. Instead, they can simply say either phrase to Siri, and the action is performed immediately.

Do It Yourself

Add the **TestIntentsShortcuts** structure defined in Listing 9-4 to the AppIntents.swift file created earlier (below the **ShowMovie** structure). Run the application on your iPhone. Make sure that Siri is enabled in the Settings app (Apple Intelligence & Siri -> Talk & Type to Siri) and that the option to allow Siri to respond when the device is locked is also enabled

(Apple Intelligence & Siri -> Allow Siri When Locked). Close the app, activate Siri by saying "Hey, Siri," and then say "Show me my favorite movie in My App" (replace My App with the name of your app). The system may ask you to turn on shortcuts for the app to be able to use them. Press Turn On. The app should open and a message should be displayed on the screen, as before (see Figure 9-3, right).

Siri is not limited to recognizing only the phrases defined by the shortcut. It can also recognize similar expressions. For example, if we say something like "What is my favorite movie in My App," Siri will still run the shortcut as before. To test which phrases work and which ones we should add to guide Siri toward the correct response, Xcode provides a tool called App Shortcut Previews. This option is available in the Product menu, as shown below.

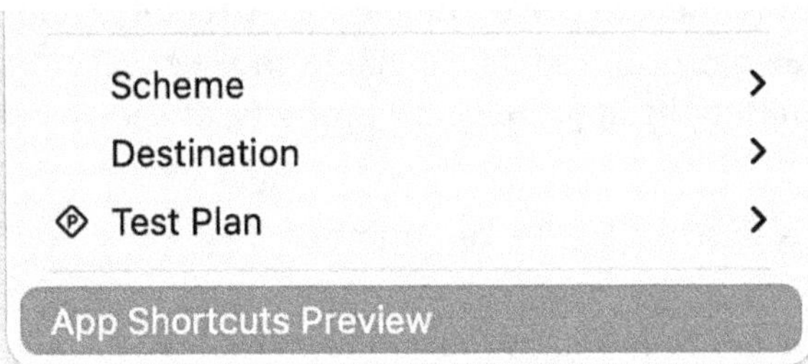

Figure 9-4: *App Shortcut Previews option*

When we select this option, a window opens where we can test Siri prompts in the languages and dialects supported by our app. If the phrase is recognized by Siri, we will see the name of the app intent that will be run when the user says that phrase, or a message indicating that no match was found. For example, a prompt that does not include the name of the app will fail, but a prompt with an expression similar to those defined by the shortcut will trigger the intent, as shown below.

Figure 9-5: *Testing prompts for Siri*

The name of our app in this example is TestIntent1. For the prompts to work, the user must mention this full name. If our app has a name that is difficult to pronounce, as in this case, or does not fit naturally into the expressions we want to suggest to Siri, we can provide alternatives. Xcode does not include any tool to define these alternative names, so we must declare them manually in the app's info.plist file. The option is available in the project's settings. We must click on the name of the project at the top of the Navigator area, open the Info panel (Figure 9-6, number 1), and then press the + button on the first item in the list to add a new key (Figure 9-6, number 2).

Figure 9-6: *Adding key to info.plist*

The key that defines alternative names is called **`INAlternativeAppNames`**. This key takes an array of dictionaries, so we first need to insert the key and declare its value type as an array, as shown below.

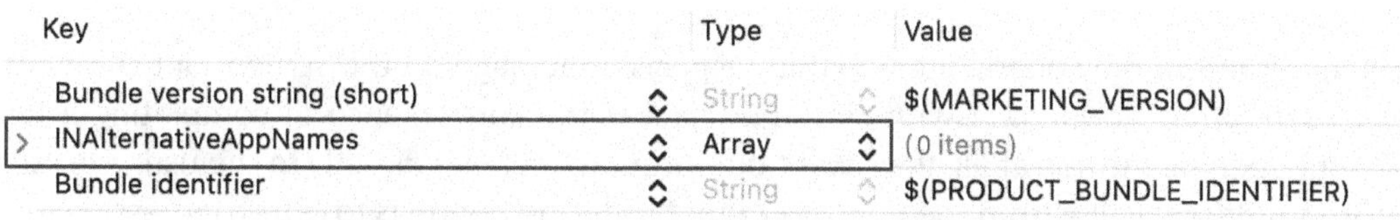

Figure 9-7: *Adding the INAlternativeAppNames key*

Now that we have the **`INAlternativeAppNames`** array, we can add items to it with the alternative names we want to use for our app. The names are defined as dictionaries, with **`INAlternativeAppName`** as the key and the alternative name as the value, as shown below.

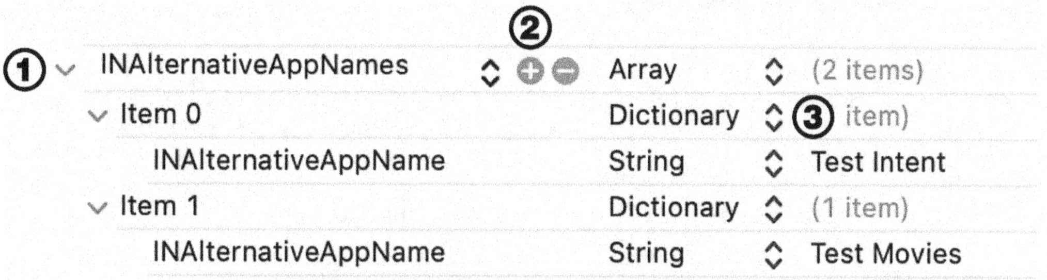

Figure 9-8: *Adding the alternative names*

To add a name, we must make sure that the arrow of the item is pointing down (Figure 9-8, number 1), and click the item's + button (Figure 9-8, number 2). The items are automatically named and numbered, but they are declared as type String, so we must change the type to Dictionary (Figure 9-8, number 3) and then press the + button on this item to add a value. Each value must contain the **`INAlternativeAppName`** key and the alternative name we want for our app. In this example, we created two names, "Test Intent" and "Test Movies," so the user can now say something like "Show me my favorite movie in Test Movies," and Siri will respond as before.

Do It Yourself

Click on the project's name at the top of the Navigator area, open the Info panel (Figure 9-6, number 1), and click the + button on the first item in the list to add a new key (Figure 9-6, number 2). Insert the key **INAlternativeAppNames** and set its type to Array (Figure 9-7). Click the arrow to open the item (Figure 9-8, number 1) and press the + button (Figure 9-8, number 2). Click the arrow to open the new item, change its type to Dictionary (Figure 9-8, number 3), and press the + button to add a new value. Declare **INAlternativeAppName** as the key and the alternative name for the app as the value, as shown in Figure 9-8. You can add as many names as you want, but they must be related to the original name. Run the application on your iPhone and ask the question again to Siri, but this time use an alternative name to represent the app. The intent should open the app and show a message on the screen, as before.

Dialog

So far, our intent only opens the app and displays a message on the screen, but this is not how users prefer to interact with Siri. They expect the convenience of completing a task without opening the app at all. If we want our intent to respond directly to the user, we must return a different value from the **perform()** method. One option is to return a message that Siri can display on the screen or speak to the user. To do this, we must declare that the value returned by this method conforms to the **ProvidesDialog** protocol and return an **IntentResult** that contains the message, as shown below.

Listing 9-5: Returning a dialog for Siri

```
struct ShowMovie: AppIntent {
   static let title: LocalizedStringResource = "Show Movie"
   static let description = IntentDescription("Shows your favorite
      movie.")

   static let supportedModes: IntentModes = .background

   @MainActor
   func perform() async throws -> some IntentResult & ProvidesDialog {
      let message = "Your favorite movie is Rambo!"
      return .result(
         dialog: IntentDialog(stringLiteral: message)
      )
   }
}
```

This intent produces the same response as before, but instead of opening the app, it runs the process in the background and returns the text to the system so Siri can display it on the screen or say it to the user. What Siri does depends on the state of the device. If the device is locked, Siri will speak the words, but if you are actively using the device, Siri will display the message on the screen, as shown below.

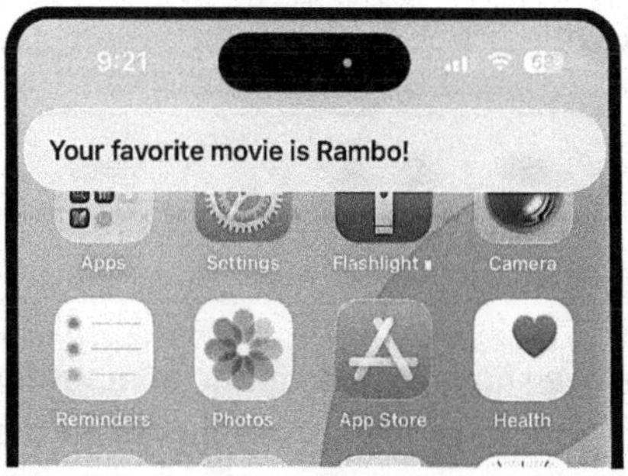

Figure 9-9: *Siri showing the response on the screen*

Do It Yourself

Update the **ShowMovie** structure with the code in Listing 9-5. For this example to work, you need the **TestIntentsShortcuts** structure introduced in Listing 9-4. Run the application on your iPhone. Go to the Home screen and ask Siri, "Show me my favorite movie in My App" (replace My App with the name of your app or an alternative name). You should see a message on the screen, as shown in Figure 9-9. Lock your phone, set it aside, wait a few seconds, and give Siri the same instruction as before. This time, Siri should speak the response out loud.

Parameters

In previous examples, we have always returned the same string as a response, but we can let the user request more specific values. For example, instead of asking only for their favorite movie, we can let users ask for a movie they love or a movie they hate. When the set of possible values is limited, we can present those options through an enumeration. The framework provides the **AppEnum** protocol to define an enumeration that works with intents. This protocol conforms to the **TypeDisplayRepresentable** and **CaseDisplay-Representable** protocols, which require the following properties.

typeDisplayRepresentation

This property sets a **TypeDisplayRepresentation** structure with a localizable string that describes the purpose of the enumeration.

caseDisplayRepresentations

This property sets a dictionary that maps the enumeration cases to **DisplayRepresentation** structures with strings that describe each case.

To provide the enumeration as input to our intent, we need to declare it as a parameter. Parameters represent the input Siri should expect the user to provide to the intent. When the user's expression triggers an intent, Siri looks for the intent's parameters and tries to identify values in the expression that match their types. To create these parameters, the framework provides the following property wrapper.

@Parameter

This is a shortcut for a property wrapper of type **IntentParameter** that turns a property into an input of an intent.

In the following example, we show how to define an enumeration to let users ask for the movie they love or hate, and how to process this value from the intent and the shortcut.

Listing 9-6: Using an enumeration to provide options

```
import SwiftUI
import AppIntents

enum MovieTypes: String, AppEnum {
   case love
   case hate

   static let typeDisplayRepresentation: TypeDisplayRepresentation =
      "Type of Movie"

   static let caseDisplayRepresentations:
      [MovieTypes: DisplayRepresentation] = [
      .love: "Love",
      .hate: "Hate"
   ]
}
struct ShowMovie: AppIntent {
   static let title: LocalizedStringResource = "Show Movie"
   static let description = IntentDescription("Shows movies you love or
      hate.")

   static let supportedModes: IntentModes = .background

   @Parameter
   var movieType: MovieTypes

   @MainActor
   func perform() async throws -> some IntentResult & ProvidesDialog {
      var movie = "Undefined"
      if movieType == .love {
         movie = "Rambo"
      } else if movieType == .hate {
         movie = "Pulp Fiction"
      }
      return .result(
         dialog: IntentDialog("The movie is \(movie)")
      )
   }
}
```

```
struct TestIntentsShortcuts: AppShortcutsProvider {
    static var appShortcuts: [AppShortcut] {
        AppShortcut(
           intent: ShowMovie(),
           phrases: [
              "Show me the movie I \(\.$movieType) in \(.applicationName)",
              "Find the movie I \(\.$movieType) in \(.applicationName)"
           ],
           shortTitle: LocalizedStringResource("Get Movie"),
           systemImageName: "star.circle"
        )
    }
}
```

The enumeration must not only conform to the **AppEnum** protocol and implement its required properties, but also return associated **String** values to give Siri an idea of the text it should recognize. In this example, we define an enumeration called **MovieTypes** that meets these requirements. We declare the cases as usual, and then implement the **caseDisplayRepresentations** property to associate each case with its corresponding string ("Love" and "Hate").

In the intent, we declare a parameter called **movieType** to store the value selected by the user, and then check this value in the **perform()** method to produce the correct response. If the value is **love**, the movie returned is "Rambo," otherwise, the movie returned is "Pulp Fiction". The value of the **movieType** parameter is also used in the shortcut to tell Siri what input to expect from the user. Note that because the value is determined at run time, we declare **movieType** as a placeholder for the property's binding value (**\.$movieType**) instead of using the property directly. As a result, we can ask Siri "Show me the movie I *love* in My App" or "Show me the movie I *hate* in My App", and Siri will produce different responses for each input.

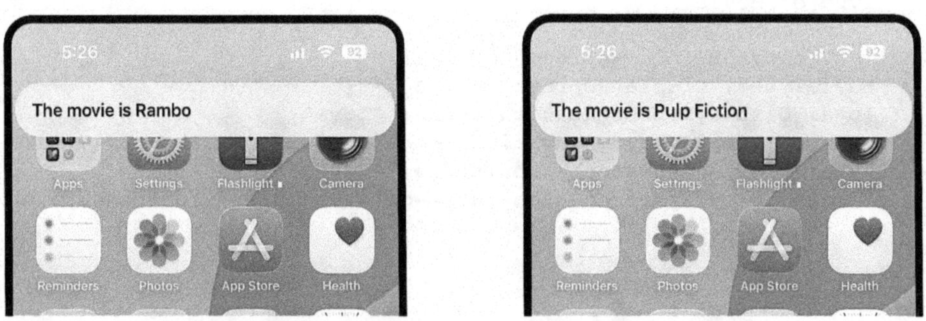

Figure 9-10: *Different responses for different inputs*

Do It Yourself

Update the AppIntents.swift file with the code in Listing 9-6. Run the application on your iPhone and ask Siri to show you the movie you hate or the movie you love. The response should change depending on what you ask, as shown in Figure 9-10.

Other than Siri, the shortcuts we define in our app also appear in the Shortcuts app and Spotlight. When we add a parameter with a fixed number of options for the user to choose from, as in the previous example, these options are automatically turned into icons in those systems, allowing the user to perform the action by simply tapping the screen. In our example, we assigned only strings to each case, so the system will use standard icons to represent them. To customize these icons, we can declare the **DisplayRepresentation** structure ourselves. For this purpose, the structure provides the following initializer.

DisplayRepresentation(title: LocalizedStringResource, **subtitle:** LocalizedStringResource?, **image:** DisplayRepresentation.Image?)

This initializer creates a **DisplayRepresentation** structure that defines how the type should appear on the screen. The **title** argument is a localized string that provides the type's title, the **subtitle** argument is a localizable string that provides the type's subtitle, and the **image** argument is a structure with the image we want to use to represent the type. This structure includes initializers to load an image from data, by name, or from a URL.

In the following example, we show how to use SF Symbols to create the icons for each option in our intent.

Listing 9-7: Customizing the options

```
enum MovieTypes: String, AppEnum {
   case love
   case hate

   static let typeDisplayRepresentation: TypeDisplayRepresentation =
      "Type of Movie"

   static let caseDisplayRepresentations:
      [MovieTypes: DisplayRepresentation] = [
      .love: DisplayRepresentation(title: "Love",
        image: DisplayRepresentation.Image(systemName: "heart")),
      .hate: DisplayRepresentation(title: "Hate",
        image: DisplayRepresentation.Image(systemName: "arrowshape.down"))
   ]
}
```

Now, when we search for our app in Spotlight, we see our app's icon, followed by an icon that represents the shortcut we have created before in the Shortcuts app, and two icons for the available options. If we tap in any of the options, we will see a window with the response, as shown below.

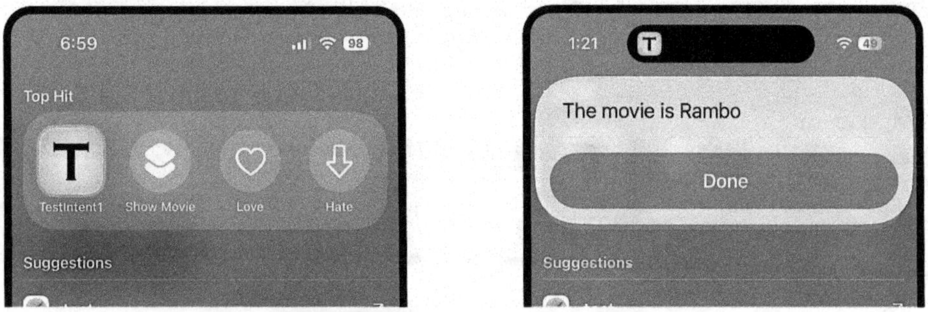

Figure 9-11: *Options in Spotlight*

Do It Yourself

Update the **MovieTypes** enumeration with the code in Listing 9-7. Run the application on your iPhone. Close the app. Drag your finger down from the center of the screen to activate Spotlight. Search for the name of your app. You should see the list of icons that represent the available options, as shown in Figure 9-11, left. Tap an icon to run the shortcut. You should see a window with the response, as shown in Figure 9-11, right.

The **@Parameter** attribute is a shortcut for creating a property wrapper from the **IntentParameter** class. This class provides several initializers that we can use with the **@Parameter** attribute to configure the parameter. The following is the most frequently used.

@Parameter(title: LocalizedStringResource, **default:** Value, **requestValueDialog:** IntentDialog)

This initializer creates a parameter with the configuration and properties determined by the arguments. The **title** argument specifies a title that identifies the parameter, the **default** argument specifies the value used by default, and the **requestValueDialog** argument specifies the dialog the intent uses to ask the user for a value.

When we declare the parameter's **requestValueDialog** argument, the intent asks the user for a value before running the **perform()** method. For example, if we want Siri to ask the user what type of movie he or she wants to see when no type is specified, we can include a dialog for the **movieType** parameter, as shown below.

Listing 9-8: Requesting a value for a parameter

```
struct ShowMovie: AppIntent {
   static let title: LocalizedStringResource = "Show Movie"
   static let description = IntentDescription("Shows movies you love or
      hate.")

   static let supportedModes: IntentModes = .background
```

```
   @Parameter(title: "Movie Type", requestValueDialog:
      IntentDialog("What type of movie?"))
   var movieType: MovieTypes

   @MainActor
   func perform() async throws -> some IntentResult & ProvidesDialog {
      var movie = "Undefined"
      if movieType == .love {
         movie = "Rambo"
      } else if movieType == .hate {
         movie = "Pulp Fiction"
      }
      return .result(
         dialog: IntentDialog("The movie is \(movie)")
      )
   }
}
```

For this to work in our example, we need to trigger the intent with an ambiguous request. For instance, we can add a prompt that does't mention the type of movie we want to retrieve.

Listing 9-9: Using an ambiguous prompt

```
struct TestIntentsShortcuts: AppShortcutsProvider {
   static var appShortcuts: [AppShortcut] {
      AppShortcut(
         intent: ShowMovie(),
         phrases: [
            "Show me a movie in \(.applicationName)",
            "Show me the movie I \(\.$movieType) in \(.applicationName)"
         ],
         shortTitle: LocalizedStringResource("Get Movie"),
         systemImageName: "star.circle"
      )
   }
}
```

Now, if the user includes the type of movie in the prompt (`love` or `hate`), the intent responds as before, but if the user asks Siri, "Show me a movie in My App," the intent first shows the dialog specified by the parameter to ask the user to choose a type, as shown below.

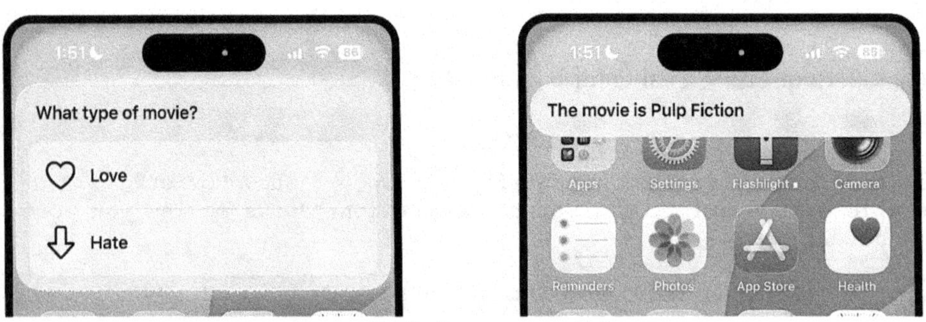

Figure 9-12: *Parameter dialog*

Do It Yourself

Update the **ShowMovie** structure with the code in Listing 9-8 and the **TestIntentsShortcuts** structure with the code in Listing 9-9. Run the application on your iPhone and ask Siri, "Show me a movie in My App." Siri should ask you to select a value, as shown in Figure 9-12, left. Say the word "Love" or "Hate" to Siri (you can also say something like "The first one" or "The second one"). After the value is selected, Siri should show you the answer with the corresponding movie, as shown in Figure 9-12, right.

In the previous example, the parameter requests a dialog when no value is provided by the user, but there may be other conditions that also require additional information. For example, besides asking users for values they forgot to specify, we may need to resolve an ambiguous result or request confirmation. For situations like these, the **IntentParameter** class defines the following methods.

requestValue(IntentDialog**)**

This method shows the dialog specified by the argument to ask the user to provide a value for the parameter and returns it.

requestConfirmation(for: Value, **dialog:** IntentDialog, **view:** ViewType**)**

This method shows a dialog asking the user to confirm the value of the parameter and returns a Boolean value with the response. The **for** argument is the value we want to confirm, the **dialog** argument is the dialog we want to show to the user, and the **view** argument is the snippet view displayed when requesting confirmation.

requestDisambiguation(among: [Value], **dialog:** IntentDialog**)**

This method shows a dialog asking the user to choose from a set of possible values, and it returns the value selected by the user. The **among** argument is an array containing the ambiguous values the user must choose from, and the **dialog** argument is the dialog we want to show to the user.

These methods are used when we need additional input from the user. For example, if the user triggers the intent but has not provided a value for the **movieType** parameter, we can call the **requestValue()** method to request one. This is similar to what we did earlier with the **requestValueDialog** argument, but because this method is called from the **perform()** method, we can check any condition we need before presenting the dialog. To determine whether the user provided a value or not, we must declare the parameter as optional, as shown below.

Listing 9-10: Requesting a value when necessary

```
struct ShowMovie: AppIntent {
   static let title: LocalizedStringResource = "Show Movie"
```

```
    static let description = IntentDescription("Shows movies you love or
      hate.")

    static let supportedModes: IntentModes = .background

    @Parameter
    var movieType: MovieTypes?

    @MainActor
    func perform() async throws -> some IntentResult & ProvidesDialog {
      if movieType == nil {
         movieType = try await $movieType.requestValue("What type of
         movie?")
      }
      var movie = "Undefined"
      if movieType == .love {
         movie = "Rambo"
      } else if movieType == .hate {
         movie = "Pulp Fiction"
      }
      return .result(
         dialog: IntentDialog("The movie is \(movie)")
      )
    }
}
```

In this case, we just make sure a value was provided. If the user says, "Show me a movie in My App," the value of **movieType** will be **nil**, so the intent executes the **requestValue()** method to ask the user to choose a value for the parameter (**love** or **hate**).

Every time a parameter method is called, the intent shows a dialog to the user. We can present as many dialogs as necessary to produce a response. For example, we can ask the user for a value if one was not provided, as we just did, and also ask the user to confirm whether the selected value is correct. In the following intent, we use the **requestConfirmation()** method to ask users if they are sure they want to see the movie they hate.

Listing 9-11: Showing multiple dialogs

```
struct ShowMovie: AppIntent {
    static let title: LocalizedStringResource = "Show Movie"
    static let description = IntentDescription("Shows movies you love or
      hate.")

    static let supportedModes: IntentModes = .background

    @Parameter
    var movieType: MovieTypes?

    @MainActor
    func perform() async throws -> some IntentResult & ProvidesDialog {
      if movieType == nil {
         movieType = try await $movieType.requestValue("What type of
            movie?")
      }
```

```
      var movie = "Undefined"
      if movieType == .love {
         movie = "Rambo"
      } else if movieType == .hate {
         let confirmation = try await $movieType.requestConfirmation(
            for: movieType!,
            dialog: IntentDialog("Are you sure you want to see the movie
               you hate?")
         )
         if confirmation {
            movie = "Pulp Fiction"
         }
      }
      return .result(
         dialog: IntentDialog("The movie is \(movie)")
      )
   }
}
```

The **requestConfirmation()** method returns a Boolean value that represents the user's response. In this case, we ask users whether they want to see the movie when they have selected the value **hate**. If the answer is Yes, the method returns **true** and we show the movie "Pulp Fiction"; otherwise, we show the value "Undefined". The result is the same as before, but now there are more steps involved. If the user does not provide a value, the intent asks for one. If the value selected by the user is **love**, Siri shows the response immediately; but if the value selected is **hate**, Siri asks for confirmation, as shown below.

Figure 9-13: *Multiple dialogs*

Do It Yourself

Update **ShowMovie** structure with the code in Listing 9-11. Run the application on your iPhone. Ask Siri, "Show me a movie in My App." Say "Hate" to select the **hate** value. Siri should then ask if you want to see the movie. Say "Yes." You should see a message with the movie Pulp Fiction on the screen, as shown in Figure 9-13.

Another method available from a parameter is **requestDisambiguation()**. This method can be used when two or more values are available and we do not know which one to return. For example, if the user asks for a favorite movie and there are multiple movies marked as favorite, we need to ask the user which one they prefer. Of course, to implement this kind of functionality, we need to work with real data so we can retrieve the values we need. In this case, we have to ask the app for the movies marked as favorite and then let the user pick one. To provide a list of movies to choose from, we can modify our **ApplicationData** class, as shown below.

Listing 9-12: Updating the data model to store a list of movies

```
import SwiftUI
import Observation

@Observable class ApplicationData {
   var message: String = "No Message"
   var listMovies: [Movies] = []

   static let shared: ApplicationData = ApplicationData()
   private init() {
      listMovies = [
         Movies(title: "Terminator", image: "movie1", favorite: false),
         Movies(title: "Avatar", image: "movie2", favorite: false),
         Movies(title: "Toy Story", image: "movie3", favorite: true),
         Movies(title: "Terminator 2", image: "movie4", favorite: false),
         Movies(title: "Frozen", image: "movie5", favorite: true)
      ]
   }
}
struct Movies: Identifiable {
   let id: UUID = UUID()
   var title: String
   var image: String
   var favorite: Bool
}
```

To store each movie, we define a structure called **Movies**. The structure includes a property called **id** to store a **UUID** value to identify the movie, and three additional properties to store the title, a string with the name of the file that contains the cover image, and a Boolean value that indicates whether the movie is the user's favorite. In the **ApplicationData** class, we define a new property called **listMovies** to store an array of **Movies** structures, and initialize it with a list of five movies so we have some data to work with.

Now we can search for the user's favorite movies from the intent, and if two or more are marked as favorites, we can call the **requestDisambiguation()** method to ask the user to pick one, as shown below.

Listing 9-13: Disambiguating a parameter

```
import SwiftUI
import AppIntents

struct ShowMovie: AppIntent {
```

```
    static let title: LocalizedStringResource = "Show Movie"
    static let description = IntentDescription("Shows your favorite
       movie.")

    static let supportedModes: IntentModes = .background

    @Parameter(default: "Undefined")
    var movie: String

    @MainActor
    func perform() async throws -> some IntentResult & ProvidesDialog {
       let appData = ApplicationData.shared
       let favorites = appData.listMovies.filter({ $0.favorite })
       if favorites.count > 1 {
          let titles = favorites.map(\.title)
          movie = try await $movie.requestDisambiguation(among: titles,
             dialog: IntentDialog("Which movie?"))
       } else if let favorite = favorites.first {
          movie = favorite.title
       }
       return .result(
          dialog: IntentDialog("Your favorite movie is \(movie)")
       )
    }
}
struct TestIntentsShortcuts: AppShortcutsProvider {
    static var appShortcuts: [AppShortcut] {
       AppShortcut(
          intent: ShowMovie(),
          phrases: [
             "Show me my favorite movie in \(.applicationName)",
             "Find my favorite movie in \(.applicationName)"
          ],
          shortTitle: LocalizedStringResource("Get Movie"),
          systemImageName: "star.circle"
       )
    }
}
```

In this example, we are not expecting the user to provide the name of the movie, but we still had to implement a parameter so we can call the **requestDisambiguation()** method on it and store the result. To get Siri to ignore this parameter and not ask for a value, we give it a value by default ("Undefined"). In the **perform()** method, we first filter the **listMovies** property to find the movies whose **favorite** property is **true**, and then get the title depending on the number of results. If more than one movie is found, we ask the user to choose one; otherwise, we check whether a movie is available and retrieve its title. Note that because we are asking only for favorite movies, we update the prompts in the shortcut to make them generic again. Now the user can say "Show me my favorite movie in My App", and if two or more are available, Siri will ask them to select one.

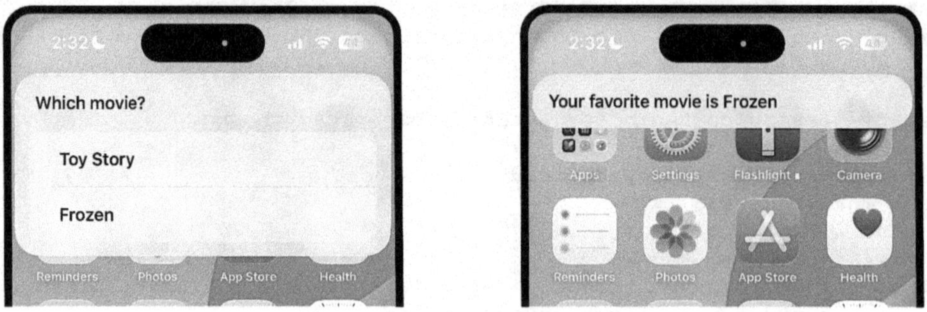

Figure 9-14: *Disambiguation*

Do It Yourself

Update the ApplicationData.swift file with the code in Listing 9-12 and the AppIntents.swift file with the code in Listing 9-13. Download the images **movie1.jpg**, **movie2.jpg**, **movie3.jpg**, **movie4.jpg**, and **movie5.jpg** from our website and add them to the Assets Catalog (We will use these images later). Run the application on your iPhone and say to Siri, "Show me my favorite movie in My App." You should see a list of all the movies whose **`favorite`** property is **`true`**. Tell Siri which movie you prefer. You should see a message with the name of that movie on the screen, as shown in Figure 9-14. Change the values of the **`favorite`** properties of the movies in the **`ApplicationData`** class to see how Siri responds when only one or no movies are marked as favorites.

Parameters represent the input of an intent, so Siri looks for those values in the user's expression. If the user does not provide a value, Siri asks a question to obtain the information it needs to perform the intent. As we did with enumeration values earlier (see Listing 9-8), we can also guide Siri to ask for specific values. For example, we can allow the user to ask for movies and then have Siri ask for the specific name of the movie they want to see, as shown below.

Listing 9-14: Asking users for specific values

```
import SwiftUI
import AppIntents

struct ShowMovie: AppIntent {
   static let title: LocalizedStringResource = "Find Movie"
   static let description = IntentDescription("Finds a movie.")

   static let supportedModes: IntentModes = .background

   @Parameter(title: "Title", requestValueDialog: "What's the movie you
      want to see?")
   var search: String

   @MainActor
   func perform() async throws -> some IntentResult & ProvidesDialog {
```

```
        let appData = ApplicationData.shared
        let movie = appData.listMovies.first(where: {
           $0.title.localizedCaseInsensitiveContains(search)
        })
        var movieTitle = "Undefined"
        if let movie = movie {
           movieTitle = movie.title
        }
        return .result(
           dialog: IntentDialog("The movie is \(movieTitle)")
        )
     }
  }
  struct TestIntentsShortcuts: AppShortcutsProvider {
     static var appShortcuts: [AppShortcut] {
        AppShortcut(
           intent: ShowMovie(),
           phrases: [
              "Show me a movie in \(.applicationName)",
              "Find a movie in \(.applicationName)"
           ],
           shortTitle: LocalizedStringResource("Get Movie"),
           systemImageName: "magnifyingglass.circle"
        )
     }
  }
```

In this example, we define a parameter with a dialog and trigger the intent with generic prompts, so when the user performs a prompt, Siri immediately asks for a value. In this case, we expect the user to provide the name of a movie, so we use the **localizedCaseInsensitiveContains()** method to search our data model for a movie whose title contains the words provided by the user and return the full title to Siri. If a movie is found, we see the title on the screen; otherwise, we see the message "Undefined".

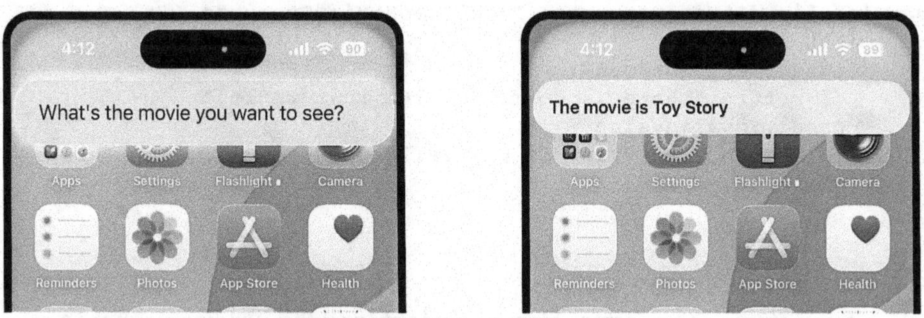

Figure 9-15: *Finding a movie*

Do It Yourself

Update the AppIntents.swift file with the code in Listing 9-14. Run the application on your iPhone. Ask Siri, "Show me a movie in My App." Siri should ask you which movie. Say something like "Toy" or "Frozen". Siri should respond with the full name of the movie, as shown in Figure 9-15.

Errors

In the previous examples, if a movie was not found, we just showed the value "Undefined" to the user. Although this may be an appropriate response in some cases, it is usually better to show an error. The challenge is that, because the intent is run by the system, we cannot simply throw an error and handle it later. Instead, we must define an error that Siri can process and use to produce a localized response. For this purpose, the Foundation framework defines the **CustomLocalizedStringResourceConvertible** protocol. This protocol requires the following property.

> **localizedStringResource**
>
> This property returns a **LocalizedStringResource** structure with a localizable string that describes the current error.

To define the errors we can throw in our intent, we must declare an enum type that conforms to the **Error** and **CustomLocalizedStringResourceConvertible** protocols, define the cases that represent each error, and implement the **localizedStringResource** property to return the messages we want Siri to show to the user when these errors occur. The following example shows how to define an **enum** with two possible errors.

Listing 9-15: Defining errors for an intent

```
import Foundation

enum ErrorIntent: Error, CustomLocalizedStringResourceConvertible {
   case movieNotFound
   case invalidValue

   var localizedStringResource: LocalizedStringResource {
      switch self {
         case .movieNotFound:
            return "There is no movie with that title."
         case .invalidValue:
            return "The value is not valid."
      }
   }
}
```

Now we can throw these errors from our intent, and Siri will know what to say to the user. For example, we can throw the **movieNotFound** error when we can't find the movie the user is looking for, as shown below.

Listing 9-16: Throwing errors from an intent

```
struct ShowMovie: AppIntent {
   static let title: LocalizedStringResource = "Find Movie"
   static let description = IntentDescription("Finds a movie.")
```

```
    static let supportedModes: IntentModes = .background

    @Parameter(title: "Title", requestValueDialog: "What's the movie you
       want to see?")
    var search: String

    @MainActor
    func perform() async throws -> some IntentResult & ProvidesDialog {
       let appData = ApplicationData.shared

       let movie = appData.listMovies.first(where: {
          $0.title.localizedCaseInsensitiveContains(search)
       })
       guard let movie = movie else {
          throw ErrorIntent.movieNotFound
       }
       return .result(
          dialog: IntentDialog("The movie is \(movie.title)")
       )
    }
}
```

The code is the same as before, but now, after searching for a movie, we use a **guard** statement to retrieve the movie's title. If we succeed, we return a message with the title as before; otherwise, we throw the **movieNotFound** error. The system receives this error and shows the corresponding message to the user, as shown below.

Figure 9-16: *Intent error*

Do It Yourself

Create a new file called ErrorIntent.swift for the code in Listing 9-15. Update the **ShowMovie** structure in the AppIntents.swift file with the code in Listing 9-16. Run the application on your iPhone and ask Siri, "Show me a movie in My App." Ask for a movie that is not on the list. You should see the error on the screen, as shown in Figure 9-16.

App Entity

Up to this point, we have used parameters of type **AppEnum** to recognize a fixed set of values and parameters of type **String** to recognize individual values, but we can also work with custom data types. For this purpose, the framework provides the **AppEntity** protocol. With this protocol, we can define structures that serve as a bridge between the intent and our app's data, exposing the information Siri needs to process the user's request. For instance, if we want Siri to interact with the **Movies** structure from our previous examples, we must define a structure that conforms to the **AppEntity** protocol and includes properties that represent the movie's title, image, and favorite value.

The properties of an App Entity are declared like any other, but if we want them to be recognized by Siri, we must expose them to the system. For this purpose, the framework provides the **@Property** property wrapper. This property wrapper is created from the **EntityProperty** class, which offers several initializers. The following is the one we use to expose the properties of an entity.

@Property(title: LocalizedStringResource)

This property wrapper exposes an entity property to the system. The **title** argument specifies the name the system uses to recognize the property. If no argument is provided, the system determines the property title from the name of the property.

In addition to these properties, the protocol also requires the implementation of the following.

typeDisplayRepresentation

This property sets a **String** value the interface uses to represent the entity.

displayRepresentation

This property sets a **DisplayRepresentation** structure that provides the values used to present the entity to the user.

defaultQuery

This property sets a structure that provides access to the values in the app's data model.

Before creating our first **AppEntity** structure, there is one more thing we need to consider. Because intents can be defined in our app as well as in extensions and external frameworks, it is unsafe to access our app's data model directly, as we have done in previous examples. To ensure that intents, entities, and queries always have access to the data, we must declare our data model as a dependency. For this purpose, the framework provides the **@Dependency** property wrapper to declare a dependency and the **AppDependencyManager** class to register dependencies. The **AppDependencyManager** class includes the **shared** property to access the instance responsible for managing the dependencies for our app, along with the following method to add a dependency.

```
add(dependency: Closure)
```

This method registers a dependency. The **dependency** argument is a closure that creates and returns the instance we want to register as a dependency.

Because intents can be triggered at any time, we must register the dependencies we need as early as possible. In this case, our intents need access to the data model, so we create an instance of the `ApplicationData` class and add it to the manager as soon as the app is launched, as shown below.

Listing 9-17: Registering a dependency

```
import SwiftUI
import AppIntents

@main
struct TestIntent1App: App {
   init() {
      let appData = ApplicationData.shared
      AppDependencyManager.shared.add { appData }
   }
   var body: some Scene {
      WindowGroup {
         ContentView()
      }
   }
}
```

Now that we have easy access to the data model, we can define the entities. The following example shows how to define a simple `AppEntity` structure to provide access to the movies in our data model. Because we are working with the same data model as before, the `AppEntity` structure must include the properties required to manage the values of the `Movies` structure. The following is our implementation.

Listing 9-18: Defining an App Entity

```
import SwiftUI
import AppIntents

struct MovieEntity: AppEntity, Identifiable {
   let id: UUID

   @Property(title: "Movie Title")
   var title: String

   let image: String
   let favorite: Bool

   static let typeDisplayRepresentation = TypeDisplayRepresentation(
      name: "Movie")
   var displayRepresentation: DisplayRepresentation {
```

```
        DisplayRepresentation(
            title: "\(title)",
            subtitle: "Favorite: \(favorite ? "Yes": "No")",
            image: DisplayRepresentation.Image(named: image)
        )
    }
    static let defaultQuery = MovieQuery()

    init(movie: Movies) {
        self.id = movie.id
        self.image = movie.image
        self.favorite = movie.favorite
        self.title = movie.title
    }
}
```

To identify each value, the **AppEntity** structure must conform to the **Identifiable** protocol and implement the **id** property with an identifier the system can use to locate the data in our app. In this case, our app is using **UUID** values to identify each movie, so we use the same value for the entity (Apple recommends using only **UUID**, **String**, or **Int** values to identify entities).

Our intent allows users to find movies by title, so we apply the **@Property** property wrapper to the **title** property to expose it to the system. To load the values, we initialize the structure with an instance of the **Movies** structure and pass the values from one property to another. Note that because the **title** property is exposed to the system, we must initialize it last.

IMPORTANT

The framework also includes a macro called **@ComputedProperty** that we can use to expose properties to Siri and automatically initialize them with the values of our custom data type. For more information, visit our website and follow the links for this chapter.

The structure assigned to the **defaultQuery** property is the one that retrieves the information from our data model. The framework provides the **EntityQuery** protocol to define this structure and additional protocols to extend its functionality. The following are the ones currently available.

EntityQuery

This protocol defines the basic functionality for an entity query. It includes methods to return a single entity and a list of suggested entities.

EntityStringQuery

This protocol defines a method that returns the entities that match a string.

EntityPropertyQuery

This protocol defines methods that return the entities whose properties match the required values.

EnumerableEntityQuery

This protocol defines a method that returns all the entities available.

UniqueAppEntityQuery

This protocol defines a method that returns a unique entity.

The system requires our structure to conform at least to the **EntityQuery** protocol. The following are the methods defined by this protocol.

entities(for: [Entity.ID])

This method receives an array of entity identifiers and must return another array with the entity structures associated with the values that match those identifiers.

suggestedEntities()

This method returns an array of entity structures representing the values we want to suggest to the user.

The **entities()** method is used by the Shortcuts App to identify the entities selected by the user when running a shortcut, so it is not needed for our application but it is required by the protocol. In the following example, we show how to define a simple query that implements this method and also the **suggestedEntities()** method to present the user with a list of favorite movies.

Listing 9-19: Defining a query for an App Entity

```
struct MovieQuery: EntityQuery {
   @Dependency var appData: ApplicationData

   func entities(for identifiers: [MovieEntity.ID]) async throws
      -> [MovieEntity] {
      let list = await appData.listMovies
      let filtered = list.filter { identifiers.contains($0.id) }
      return filtered.map { MovieEntity(movie: $0) }
   }
   func suggestedEntities() async throws -> [MovieEntity] {
      let movies = await appData.listMovies
      var favorites = movies.filter { $0.favorite }
      if favorites.isEmpty {
         let total = min(3, movies.count)
         favorites = Array(movies[0..<total])
      }
      return favorites.map { MovieEntity(movie: $0) }
   }
}
```

In this example, we first define a property with the **@Dependency** property wrapper to give the query access to our data model. Now the query methods can read the **listMovies** property in this object to retrieve the list of available movies. The **entities()** method receives an array of identifiers from the system, finds the **Movies** structures that match those identifiers, and returns an array of **MovieEntity** structures created from those values. The **suggestedEntities()** method follows a similar process, but in this case we filter the movies by the value of the **favorite** property to include only the user's favorite titles.

Once we have the entity structure that defines the entity values and the query structure that creates the entities from the values in the data model, we can define an intent. The intent for this example works the same as before, but now the parameters must be declared as type **MovieEntity**, as shown below.

Listing 9-20: Defining an intent to work with App Entities

```
struct FindMovie: AppIntent {
   static let title: LocalizedStringResource = "Find Movie"
   static let description = IntentDescription("Finds a movie by title.")

   static let supportedModes: IntentModes = .background

   @Parameter(title: "Movie")
   var movie: MovieEntity

   func perform() async throws -> some IntentResult & ProvidesDialog {
      .result(dialog: IntentDialog("The movie is \(movie.title)"))
   }
}
struct TestIntentsShortcuts: AppShortcutsProvider {
   static var appShortcuts: [AppShortcut] {
      AppShortcut(
         intent: FindMovie(),
         phrases: [
            "Show me a movie in \(.applicationName)"
         ],
         shortTitle: LocalizedStringResource("Show Movies"),
         systemImageName: "magnifyingglass.circle"
      )
   }
}
```

This intent takes a parameter of type **MovieEntity** called **movie**. When the user asks Siri a generic prompt such as "Show me a movie in My App", the system checks this parameter, and since no specific value has been provided, it calls the **suggestedEntities()** method in the **MovieQuery** structure to get a list of movies to suggest, waits for the user to pick one, and then calls the **perform()** method in the intent with the result, as shown below.

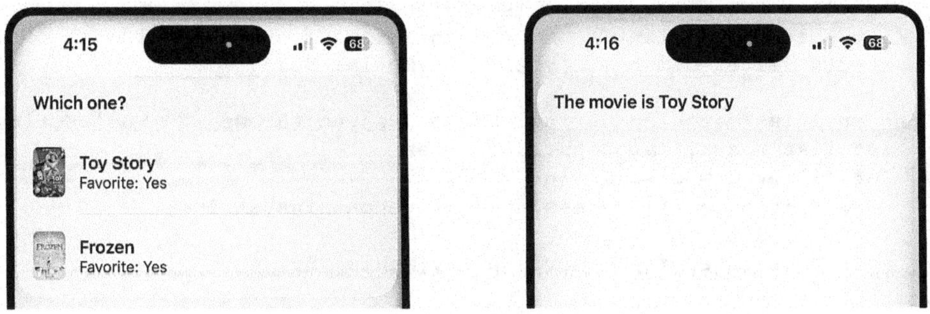

Figure 9-17: *Using an App Entity to pick a movie*

Do It Yourself

Update the **App** structure in your project with the code in Listing 9-17. Remove all the code in the AppIntents.swift file. Add to this file the code in Listing 9-18, the **MovieQuery** structure defined in Listing 9-19, and the **FindMovie** and **TestIntentsShortcuts** structures defined in Listing 9-20. Remember to download the images for the movies from our website and add them to the Assets Catalog. Run the application on your iPhone and ask Siri "Show me a movie in My App". You should see a list of favorite movies on the screen. Say the name of one of those movies. You should see a message with the name of the movie on the screen. Note that the list of movies is created from the values returned by the entity's **displayRepresentation** property.

In the previous example, we implemented the **suggestedEntities()** method. When Siri needs a value, it calls this method to prompt the user to pick one, but we can also allow users to ask Siri directly for the movie they want to see. For this purpose, we need to make the query structure conform to the **EntityStringQuery** protocol and implement the following method.

entities(matching: String)

This method receives a string with the term Siri wants us to search and returns an array of entities that match that value.

In the following example, we modify the **MovieQuery** structure to implement this method, so now, instead of showing suggestions, Siri will ask for a name.

Listing 9-21: Defining a search query

```
struct MovieQuery: EntityQuery, EntityStringQuery {
   @Dependency var appData: ApplicationData

   func entities(for identifiers: [MovieEntity.ID]) async throws
      -> [MovieEntity] {
```

```
        let list = await appData.listMovies
        let filtered = list.filter { identifiers.contains($0.id) }
        return filtered.map { MovieEntity(movie: $0) }
    }
    func entities(matching string: String) async throws -> [MovieEntity] {
        let list = await appData.listMovies
        let filtered = list.filter {
            $0.title.localizedCaseInsensitiveContains(string)
        }
        return filtered.map { MovieEntity(movie: $0) }
    }
}
```

The **entities(matching:)** method searches for the movie name in the data model and returns all the entities that match that value. If only one movie is found, the intent assigns that value to the **movie** parameter and calls the **perform()** method to return the result, but if two or more movies are found, Siri automatically presents the list to the user for disambiguation. For example, if we ask for the movie "Terminator", the method will find two matches, so Siri shows both movies on the list for the user to choose from, as shown below.

***Figure 9-18:** Asking Siri for a movie*

Do It Yourself

Update the **MovieQuery** structure with the code in Listing 9-21. Run the application on your iPhone and ask Siri "Show me a movie in My App". Siri will ask you for the name of the movie. Say "Terminator". Siri should show you a list with two movies to choose from, as shown in Figure 9-18, center. Say "Terminator Two". You should see a message with the name of that movie on the screen.

At the moment, Siri cannot extract information from the user's expression unless the value we expect the user to provide comes from a fixed set of options. For example, Siri cannot extract the title "Terminator" from the expression "Open the movie Terminator in My App". We were able to do this with **AppEnum** values before because these data types contain a predefined set of entries (see Listing 9-6), but **AppEntity** values are dynamic, which means new values can be added or removed at any time, and therefore Siri is yet not able to recognize them. As we have seen in previous examples, we can work around this limitation by having Siri request a single value, either by implementing the **entities(matching:)** method in our query or by using the dialog options introduced earlier. But if our app still needs the user to provide a value in the prompt, the framework includes the option to turn dynamic values into fixed values. For this purpose, the **AppShortcutsProvider** protocol includes the following method.

> **updateAppShortcutParameters()**
>
> This method updates the parameters of the shortcuts in an **AppShortcutsProvider** structure.

This method creates a predefined set of shortcuts based on the values available for the parameter. All we need to do is interpolate the parameter in our shortcuts and call this method as soon as the app is loaded and whenever the values change. For our example, we can call it in the app's initializer, after the dependency is registered, as shown below.

Listing 9-22: Updating the parameters in our shortcuts

```
import SwiftUI
import AppIntents

@main
struct TestIntent1App: App {
    init() {
        let appData = ApplicationData.shared
        AppDependencyManager.shared.add { appData }
        TestIntentsShortcuts.updateAppShortcutParameters()
    }
    var body: some Scene {
        WindowGroup {
            ContentView()
        }
    }
}
```

When the user includes a value in the prompt, the system calls the query methods to find an entity that matches that value. If we want the user to be able to pick any movie from our data model, the query must implement a method that returns them all. For this purpose, we can conform to the **EnumerableEntityQuery** protocol. The protocol defines the following method.

> **allEntities()**
>
> This method is called when the system needs a list of all the entities available. It must return an array of **AppEntity** structures representing all the values in the data model.

The **EnumerableEntityQuery** protocol inherits from the **EntityQuery** protocol, so we must implement the **entities()** method to return the entities that match an identifier, as always, and also the **allEntities()** method to return every movie in our data model, as shown below.

Listing 9-23: Returning an array with all the movies in our data model

```
struct MovieQuery: EnumerableEntityQuery {
   @Dependency var appData: ApplicationData

   func entities(for identifiers: [MovieEntity.ID]) async throws
      -> [MovieEntity] {
      let list = await appData.listMovies
      let filtered = list.filter { identifiers.contains($0.id) }
      return filtered.map { MovieEntity(movie: $0) }
   }
   func allEntities() async throws -> [MovieEntity] {
      let list = await appData.listMovies
      return list.map { MovieEntity(movie: $0) }
   }
}
```

Now users can ask for any movie they want, but we still need to tell Siri which shortcuts they can use to access this functionality. The following code shows some possible phrases we can use.

Listing 9-24: Shortcuts with parameters

```
struct TestIntentsShortcuts: AppShortcutsProvider {
   static var appShortcuts: [AppShortcut] {
      AppShortcut(
         intent: FindMovie(),
         phrases: [
            "Show me the movie \(\.$movie) in \(.applicationName)",
            "Show me \(\.$movie) in \(.applicationName)",
            "Open \(\.$movie) in \(.applicationName)",
            "Find the movie \(\.$movie) in \(.applicationName)"
         ],
         shortTitle: LocalizedStringResource("Show Movies"),
         systemImageName: "magnifyingglass.circle"
      )
   }
}
```

These shortcuts include the **movie** parameter, so the user can ask Siri "Show me the movie Terminator in My App", and the intent will find the movie in our data model and Siri will display it on the screen.

Do It Yourself

Update the **App** structure in your project with the code in Listing 9-22, the **MovieQuery** structure with the code in Listing 9-23, and the **TestIntentsShortcuts** structure with the code in Listing 9-24. Run the application on your iPhone and ask Siri "Show me the movie Frozen in My App". You should see a message with the name of the movie on the screen.

Try other expressions and movie titles to see how Siri responds. Remember to call the **updateAppShortcutParameters()** method every time the values in the data model are updated.

IMPORTANT

This feature is intended for a limited set of values. You shouldn't call the **updateAppShortcutParameters()** method or implement the **allEntities()** method if you expect the user to store a large number of entries. In those cases, you should instead use the dialog methods to instruct Siri to ask the user for a value, as we did in previous examples.

Snippet View

When the user is wearing AirPods or not looking at the phone, Siri speaks the response out loud, but if the user is actively interacting with the device, the system shows the response on the screen. Until now, we have returned a simple dialog, but we can also present a custom view. These views are called *Snippet Views*. To present a snippet view, we must configure the **perform()** method to return a value that conforms to the **ShowsSnippetView** protocol and include an instance of our view in the result, as shown in the following example.

Listing 9-25: Showing a snippet view

```
struct FindMovie: AppIntent {
   static let title: LocalizedStringResource = "Find Movie"
   static let description = IntentDescription("Finds a movie by title.")
   static let supportedModes: IntentModes = .background

   @Parameter(title: "Movie")
   var movie: MovieEntity

   func perform() async throws -> some IntentResult & ProvidesDialog
      & ShowsSnippetView {
      .result(
         dialog: IntentDialog("The movie is \(movie.title)"),
         view: MovieView(movie: movie)
      )
   }
}
```

This intent returns both a dialog and a snippet view. The dialog presents a message that Siri can speak, while the snippet view receives an instance of the **MovieEntity** structure to show the values on the screen. To define a snippet view, we can use structural views such as **VStack** and **HStack**, along with **Text** and **Image** views to build the content. The following is the view for our example.

Listing 9-26: Designing a snippet view

```
import SwiftUI

struct MovieView: View {
   let movie: MovieEntity

   var body: some View {
      VStack {
         Image(movie.image)
            .resizable()
            .scaledToFit()
            .frame(height: 200)
            .padding(.top)
         Text(movie.title)
            .font(.title)
      }
   }
}
```

The **MovieView** view receives an instance of the **MovieEntity** structure that represents the movie selected by the user and displays the image and title, as shown below.

Figure 9-19: *Snippet view*

Do It Yourself

Update the **FindMovie** structure in the AppIntents.swift file with the code in Listing 9-25. Create a new SwiftUI file called MovieView.swift for the view in Listing 9-26. Run the application on your iPhone and ask Siri to show you a movie, as before. You should see the snippet view with the image and title of the movie on the screen, as shown in Figure 9-19.

The snippet view in the previous example is static, with just an image and a title, but we can also present views that the user can interact with. These interactive views are not presented from a standard app intent but from an intent that conforms to the **SnippetIntent** protocol. The protocol defines the functionality needed to present these views, so all we need to do is conform to the protocol and define the structure as before. In the following example, we define a snippet intent that shows a view with a button that allows users to set the movie as their favorite.

Listing 9-27: Defining a snippet intent

```
import SwiftUI
import AppIntents

struct FavoriteIntent: SnippetIntent {
    static let title: LocalizedStringResource = "Set Favorite"

    @Parameter
    var movie: MovieEntity

    @MainActor
    func perform() async throws -> some ShowsSnippetView {
        .result(
            view: MovieView(movie: movie)
        )
    }
}
```

Although this is enough to present the view, snippet intents cannot be triggered directly from a shortcut, so we must first create a normal app intent that responds to Siri and triggers the snippet intent. To trigger the snippet intent, the **perform()** method of the app intent must return a value that conforms to the **ShowsSnippetIntent** protocol, and the **result()** method must include the **snippetIntent** argument with an instance of the snippet intent we want to trigger, as shown below.

Listing 9-28: Defining an app intent to trigger a snippet intent

```
struct FindMovie: AppIntent {
    static let title: LocalizedStringResource = "Find Movie"
    static let description = IntentDescription("Finds a movie by title.")
    static let supportedModes: IntentModes = .background

    @Parameter(title: "Movie")
    var movie: MovieEntity

    func perform() async throws -> some ProvidesDialog & ShowsSnippetIntent {
        .result(
            dialog: IntentDialog("Movie:"),
            snippetIntent: FavoriteIntent(movie: $movie)
        )
    }
}
```

Now, when the user performs a shortcut, such as asking Siri to show a movie, the **FindMovie** intent is triggered. This intent then triggers the **FavoriteIntent** intent, and this intent opens the **MovieView** view to present the interactive interface to the user.

To create the interactive view, we cannot simply add buttons and perform tasks in the app as we normally do, we must trigger additional intents that carry out the actions for us. To trigger these intents, the SwiftUI framework provides the following control views.

```
Button(intent: AppIntent, label: Closure)
```

This view creates a button that triggers an app intent. The **intent** argument is an instance of the intent we want to trigger, and the **label** argument is a closure that returns the label for the button.

```
Toggle(LocalizedStringKey, isOn: Bool, intent: AppIntent)
```

This view creates a toggle that triggers an app intent. The first argument is a localized string that specifies the label for the toggle, the **isOn** argument determines whether the toggle is on or off, and the **intent** argument is the app intent we want to trigger when the state of the toggle changes.

In the view for our example, we need a button that calls an intent that changes the value of the **favorite** property of the selected movie, so users can set the movie as their favorite from the snippet.

Listing 9-29: Defining an interactive view

```
import SwiftUI
import AppIntents

struct MovieView: View {
   let movie: MovieEntity

   var body: some View {
      VStack {
         Image(movie.image)
            .resizable()
            .scaledToFit()
            .frame(height: 200)
            .padding(.top)
         HStack {
            Text(movie.title)
               .font(.title)
            Button(intent: ChangeFavoriteIntent(movie: movie), label: {
               if movie.favorite {
                  Image(systemName: "heart.fill")
                     .foregroundStyle(.red)
               } else {
                  Image(systemName: "heart")
                     .foregroundStyle(.gray)
               }
            })
         }
      }
   }
}
```

To show the current state of the movie, we display a heart icon. If the value of the **favorite** property is **true**, we show a red heart; otherwise, the heart is gray. When the button is pressed, an intent is triggered. This is a normal **AppIntent** structure, but there are two important considerations. First, this intent is designed to be triggered only by a button in an interactive snippet, so we cannot allow the user to access it in any other way. For this purpose, the **AppIntent** protocol provides the following property.

isDiscoverable

This type property sets a Boolean value that determines whether the intent appears in the Shortcuts app or Spotlight.

The other consideration relates to how the intent is initialized. To change the value of the movie's **favorite** property, we need to pass an instance of the **MovieEntity** structure to the intent, but the system must also be able to initialize the intent without this value. For this reason, we define two initializers: one without parameters for the system and another with a **MovieEntity** parameter for the button. The following is the implementation of the **ChangeFavoriteIntent** intent used by our button.

Listing 9-30: Defining the app intent for the interactive view

```
import SwiftUI
import AppIntents

struct ChangeFavoriteIntent: AppIntent {
   static let title: LocalizedStringResource = "Change favorite"
   static let isDiscoverable: Bool = false

   @Dependency var appData: ApplicationData
   @Parameter
   var movie: MovieEntity

   init() {}
   init(movie: MovieEntity) {
      self.movie = movie
   }
   @MainActor
   func perform() async throws -> some IntentResult {
      if let index = appData.listMovies.firstIndex(where: {
         $0.id == movie.id }) {
         appData.listMovies[index].favorite.toggle()
      }
      return .result()
   }
}
```

When this intent is triggered, we access the app's data model to retrieve the **Movies** structure in the **listMovies** array that represents the selected movie, and then call the **toggle()** method on its **favorite** property to change its value. If the property was **true**, it becomes **false**, and vice versa. Each time the button in the snippet is pressed, the value of this property is toggled, the snippet is automatically recreated, and the heart icon displayed by the button updates its color, as shown below.

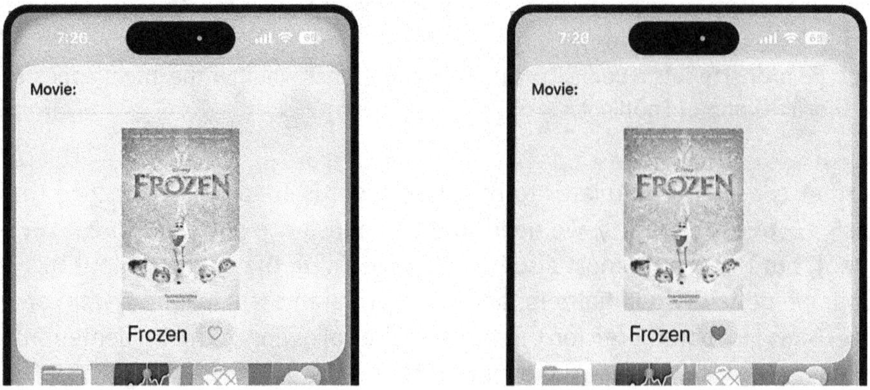

Figure 9-20: *Interactive snippet*

Do It Yourself

Create a new Swift file called FavoriteIntent.swift for the code in Listing 9-27. Update the **FindMovie** structure in the AppIntents.swift file with the code in Listing 9-28 and the **MovieView** view with the code in Listing 9-29. Create a new Swift file called ChangeFavoriteIntent.swift with the code in Listing 9-30. Run the application on your iPhone and ask Siri to show you a movie, as before. The intent should open a view with the movie and a heart next to the title, as shown in Figure 9-20. Tap the heart to change it.

In the previous example, we used a single interactive snippet to perform one action in our app (changing the favorite status of the selected movie), but there are situations in which users may need to perform multiple tasks to achieve the result they want. For these cases, the system allows us to present multiple interactive snippets in sequence. The following is the method defined by the **AppIntent** protocol for this purpose.

requestConfirmation(actionName: ConfirmationActionName, **snippetIntent:** Snippet)

This method presents an interactive snippet with buttons to confirm or cancel the task. The **snippetIntent** argument is the snippet intent we want to present, and the **actionName** argument is a structure that defines the purpose and label of the confirmation button. The structure includes the properties **add**, **addData**, **book**, **buy**, **call**, **checkIn**, **continue**, **create**, **do**, **download**, **filter**, **find**, **get**, **go**, **log**, **open**, **order**, **pay**, **play**, **playSound**, **post**, **request**, **run**, **search**, **send**, **set**, **share**, **start**, **startNavigation**, **toggle**, **turnOff**, **turnOn**, and **view**.

To demonstrate how to implement this method, we will simulate the process of ordering copies of a movie. The intent will ask the user to select a movie, then display an interactive view to choose the number of copies, and finally present a view to confirm the order, as shown below.

***Figure 9-21:** Confirmation snippet*

There are many ways to implement an application like this. To keep it simple, we will update our previous project and store the number of copies along with the movies. The following are the changes we need to make in our data model.

Listing 9-31: Storing ordered copies

```
import SwiftUI
import Observation

@Observable class ApplicationData {
   var message: String = "No Message"
   var listMovies: [Movies] = []

   static let shared: ApplicationData = ApplicationData()
   private init() {
      listMovies = [
         Movies(title: "Terminator", image: "movie1", favorite: false,
            order: 0),
         Movies(title: "Avatar", image: "movie2", favorite: false,
            order: 0),
         Movies(title: "Toy Story", image: "movie3", favorite: true,
            order: 0),
         Movies(title: "Terminator 2", image: "movie4", favorite: false,
            order: 0),
         Movies(title: "Frozen", image: "movie5", favorite: true,
            order: 0)
      ]
   }
}
struct Movies: Identifiable {
   let id: UUID = UUID()
   var title: String
   var image: String
   var favorite: Bool
   var order: Int
}
```

Now that we have a way to store the copies ordered by the user, we need to define a **`MovieEntity`** structure that includes these values so we can access the orders from the entities when necessary.

Listing 9-32: Storing the orders in the movie's entity

```
import SwiftUI
import AppIntents

struct MovieEntity: AppEntity, Identifiable {
   let id: UUID

   @Property(title: "Movie Title")
   var title: String

   let image: String
   let favorite: Bool
   let order: Int

   static let typeDisplayRepresentation = TypeDisplayRepresentation(name:
"Movie")
   var displayRepresentation: DisplayRepresentation {
      DisplayRepresentation(
         title: "\(title)",
         image: DisplayRepresentation.Image(named: image)
      )
   }
   static let defaultQuery = MovieQuery()

   init(movie: Movies) {
      self.id = movie.id
      self.image = movie.image
      self.favorite = movie.favorite
      self.order = movie.order
      self.title = movie.title
   }
}
```

The query for this entity can be similar to the previous example, but in this case it is better to let users provide the name of the movie to Siri. For this purpose, we need to make the structure conform to the **EntityStringQuery** protocol and implement the **entities(matching:)** method, as shown below.

Listing 9-33: Defining a query to search for movies by title

```
struct MovieQuery: EntityQuery, EntityStringQuery {
   @Dependency var appData: ApplicationData

   func entities(for identifiers: [MovieEntity.ID]) async throws ->
[MovieEntity] {
      let list = await appData.listMovies
      let filtered = list.filter { identifiers.contains($0.id) }
      return filtered.map { MovieEntity(movie: $0) }
   }
   func entities(matching string: String) async throws -> [MovieEntity] {
      let list = await appData.listMovies
      let filtered = list.filter {
         $0.title.localizedCaseInsensitiveContains(string)
      }
```

```
      return filtered.map { MovieEntity(movie: $0) }
   }
}
```

The app intent that starts the whole process must receive a movie from Siri, then present a snippet intent to let users select the number of copies they want, and finally return a view to display the result of the transaction. The following is our implementation of this intent and the shortcut required to get Siri to respond.

Listing 9-34: Triggering the snippet intent from the app intent

```
struct OrderMovie: AppIntent {
   static let title: LocalizedStringResource = "Order Movie"
   static let description = IntentDescription("Order a movie from the
      store.")
   static let supportedModes: IntentModes = .background

   @Dependency var appData: ApplicationData

   @Parameter(title: "Movie")
   var movie: MovieEntity

   @MainActor
   func perform() async throws -> some ProvidesDialog & ShowsSnippetView {
      try await requestConfirmation(
         actionName: .order,
         snippetIntent: OrderIntent(movie: $movie)
      )
      let movieData = appData.listMovies.first(where: {
         $0.id == movie.id })
      let title = movieData?.title ?? "Undefined"
      let order = movieData?.order ?? 0

      return .result(
         dialog: IntentDialog("Confirmation:"),
         view: ConfirmOrderView(movieTitle: title, orders: order)
      )
   }
}
struct TestIntentsShortcuts: AppShortcutsProvider {
   static var appShortcuts: [AppShortcut] {
      AppShortcut(
         intent: OrderMovie(),
         phrases: [
            "Order a movie in \(.applicationName)",
            "Buy a movie in \(.applicationName)"
         ],
         shortTitle: LocalizedStringResource("Order Movie"),
         systemImageName: "cart"
      )
   }
}
```

We can implement the **requestConfirmation()** method as many times as needed to trigger multiple snippet intents. If the user presses the Cancel button at any point in this process, no other method will be called and the entire task will be cancelled. In this case, we need only one method to trigger the snippet intent that presents the view with buttons users can press to select the number of copies they want. The following is our implementation of this intent.

Listing 9-35: Implementing the snippet intent

```
import SwiftUI
import AppIntents

struct OrderIntent: SnippetIntent {
   static let title: LocalizedStringResource = "Place Order"

   @Parameter
   var movie: MovieEntity

   @MainActor
   func perform() async throws -> some ShowsSnippetView {
      .result(
         view: OrderView(movie: movie)
      )
   }
}
```

This snippet intent simply receives a reference to the **MovieEntity** structure representing the movie selected by the user and presents the interactive view. The view must receive this value, display the movie on the screen, and provide the buttons that allow the user to select the number of copies, as shown below.

Listing 9-36: Defining the interactive view

```
import SwiftUI
import AppIntents

struct OrderView: View {
   let movie: MovieEntity

   var body: some View {
      VStack {
         Image(movie.image)
            .resizable()
            .scaledToFit()
            .frame(height: 200)
            .padding(.top)
         Text(movie.title)
            .font(.title)
         HStack {
            Button(intent: QuantityIntent(movie: movie, quantity: -1),
               label: {
               Image(systemName: "minus.circle.fill")
                  .font(.largeTitle)
```

```
                    .foregroundStyle(.red)
            })
            Text("\(movie.order)")
                .font(.title)
            Button(intent: QuantityIntent(movie: movie, quantity: 1),
                label: {
                Image(systemName: "plus.circle.fill")
                    .font(.largeTitle)
                    .foregroundStyle(.green)
            })
            Text("Copies")
                .font(.title)
        }.padding()
    }
  }
}
```

Every time a button is pressed, we trigger an additional intent to update the orders in our data model. This intent receives a copy of the **MovieEntity** structure and a value called **quantity** that indicates whether the user wants to decrease the number of copies (-1) or increase it (1). The intent must use these values to calculate the new number of copies to order, as shown below.

Listing 9-37: Defining the intent to process the orders

```
import SwiftUI
import AppIntents

struct QuantityIntent: AppIntent {
    static let title: LocalizedStringResource = "Change favorite"
    static let isDiscoverable: Bool = false

    @Dependency var appData: ApplicationData

    @Parameter
    var movie: MovieEntity
    @Parameter
    var quantity: Int

    init() {}
    init(movie: MovieEntity, quantity: Int) {
        self.movie = movie
        self.quantity = quantity
    }
    @MainActor
    func perform() async throws -> some IntentResult {
        if let index = appData.listMovies.firstIndex(where: {
            $0.id == movie.id }) {
            appData.listMovies[index].order += quantity
            if appData.listMovies[index].order < 0 {
                appData.listMovies[index].order = 0
            }
        }
        return .result()
    }
}
```

This intent takes the values received from the buttons and uses them to modify the number of orders for the movie. To do this, we first get the index of the **Movies** structure that represents the selected movie, and then change the value of the movie's **order** property based on the **quantity** parameter to permanently store the new order in the data model, so we can access this value later from anywhere in our app.

The **QuantityIntent** intent doesn't return any value, but after it is performed, the system triggers the snippet intent again and the view is updated to show the current number of orders on the screen, as shown in Figure 9-21, center.

The **requestConfirmation()** method implemented in the app intent shows a button labeled Order (see Listing 9-34). When this button is pressed, the process is confirmed and the system continues executing the instructions in the **perform()** method. In this case, we get the movie's title and current value of the **order** property from the data model and then return a view with these values. The purpose of this view is to confirm that the order has been placed. The following is our implementation.

Listing 9-38: Confirming the order

```
import SwiftUI
import AppIntents

struct ConfirmOrderView: View {
   let movieTitle: String
   let orders: Int

   var body: some View {
      VStack {
         Text(movieTitle)
            .font(.title.bold())
         if orders > 0 {
            Text("Copies ordered:")
               .font(.body)
            Text("\(orders) copies")
               .font(.title)
               .foregroundStyle(.green)
         } else {
            Text("No copies ordered")
               .font(.title)
               .foregroundStyle(.red)
         }
      }.padding()
   }
}
```

The application is ready. Now we can ask Siri "Order a movie in My App," and Siri will show a view where we can select the number of copies to order and confirm the transaction, as shown in Figure 9-21.

Do It Yourself

Start from the project you have been using so far in this section. Update the ApplicationData.swift file with the code in Listing 9-31. Remove all the code in the AppIntents.swift file. Add to this file the code in Listing 9-32, the **MovieQuery** structure in Listing 9-33, and the **OrderMovie** and **TestIntentsShortcuts** structures from Listing 9-34. Create a file called OrderIntent.swift for the code in Listing 9-35, a file called OrderView.swift for the view in Listing 9-36, a file called QuantityIntent.swift for the code in Listing 9-37, and another one called ConfirmOrderView.swift for the view in Listing 9-38. Run the application on your iPhone and ask Siri "Order a movie in My App." Siri should ask you which movie to order. Say "Frozen." You should see the movie on the screen, along with buttons to select the number of copies to order, as shown in Figure 9-21. Say "Order" to Siri or press the button. You should see a new view showing the result of the transaction.

IMPORTANT

In this example, we only display the result of the transaction on the screen. In a real application, you could store the order in a different structure, send the values to a server, or perform additional processing. For more information on how to work with interactive snippets, visit our website and follow the links for this chapter.

Siri Tips

Most users will not know the phrases they can say to Siri to unlock our app's functionality, so we must help them discover these features. Although we can design our own views or use the **TipKit** framework to provide this guidance, the **App Intents** framework already includes a built-in view that presents a familiar design and automatically generates a helpful message based on our shortcuts. The following is the view's initializer.

```
SiriTipView(intent: AppIntent, isVisible: Bool)
```

This initializer creates a view that shows a tip explaining what the user can say to unlock an app feature. The **intent** argument is an instance of the app intent the view should reference, and the **isVisible** argument is a Binding property that determines whether the view is visible or not.

To present these views, we need a Binding property of type **Bool** to determine whether the view is visible. For this purpose, we can use a simple State property, an observable property from our data model, or implement the **@AppStorage** property wrapper to store the value permanently in User Defaults. The following example shows how to implement these views with a simple State property.

Listing 9-39: Showing Siri tips

```
import SwiftUI
import AppIntents

struct ContentView: View {
   @State private var appData = ApplicationData.shared
   @State private var showingSiriTip: Bool = true

   var body: some View {
      VStack {
         SiriTipView(intent: OrderMovie(), isVisible: $showingSiriTip)

         Text(appData.message)
            .padding()
         Spacer()
      }
      .padding()
   }
}
```

The view takes the first phrase from the shortcut associated with the app intent, adds the corresponding values, and displays it on the screen. For example, if we add a Siri tip to the application created in the previous section, we will see the message "Order a movie in My App," as shown below.

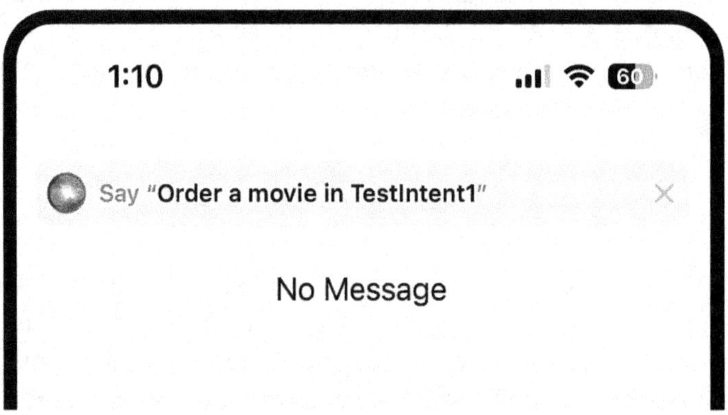

Figure 9-22: *Siri Tips*

Do It Yourself

Update the `ContentView` view with the code in Listing 9-39. Run the application on your iPhone. You should see the Siri tip on the screen, as shown in Figure 9-22.

IMPORTANT

In this chapter, we explored the technologies that currently work reliably with Siri, but there are many other features that we can already implement in the Shortcuts app and Spotlight, and Apple continues to improve the system and expand its capabilities. For more information and updates on the **App Intents** framework and Siri, visit Apple developer's website at **developer.apple.com**.

Chapter 10
Additional Models

10.1 - Custom Models

In addition to using the models provided by Apple, we can also train our own by using Create ML. This is an app provided by Apple that has been designed for training machine learning models directly on the Mac. Create ML manages every step of the training process and provides a streamlined, user-friendly workflow that generates high-performance models ready to be integrated into our applications. All we need to do is supply the appropriate data, and Create ML takes care of the rest.

Create ML

The Create ML app comes bundled with Xcode and can be launched from the Open Developer Tool option in Xcode's menu (Figure 10-1, number 1).

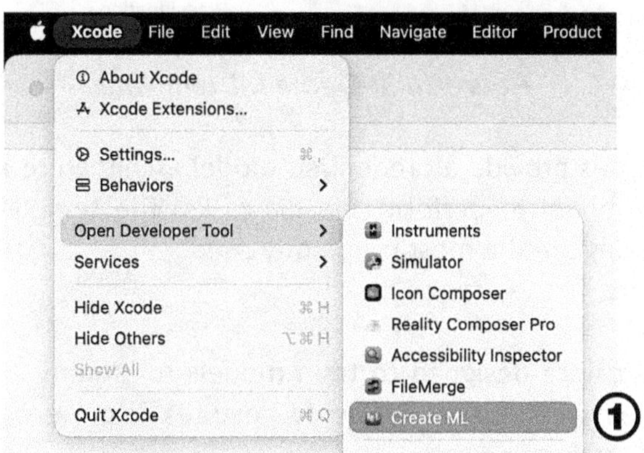

Figure 10-1: *Create ML option*

The welcome screen includes buttons on the left to create a new project or open an existing one, and a panel on the right displaying a list of recent projects.

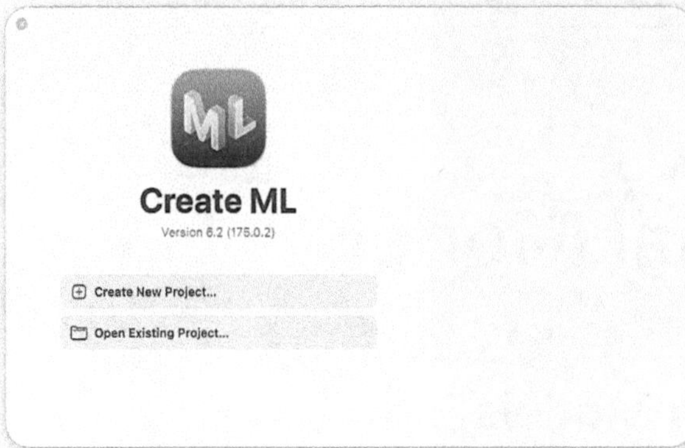

Figure 10-2: *Create ML app*

If we click on the option to create a new project, the app shows a list of templates to select from.

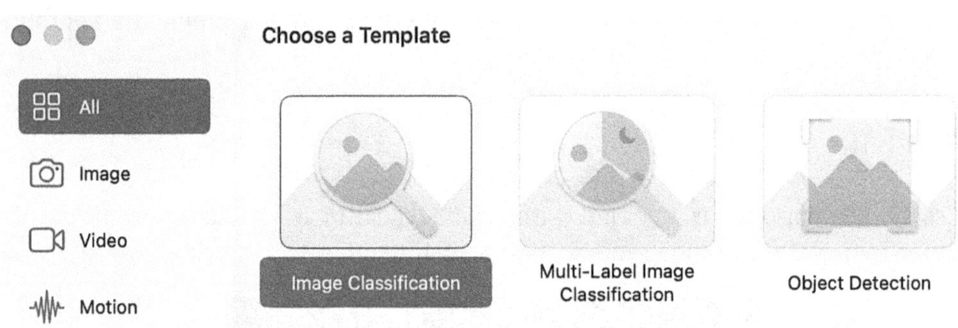

Figure 10-3: *Create ML templates*

Create ML templates provide a predefined model architecture and all the parameters necessary to train a model to perform specific tasks. The templates are organized into categories. The following are the most frequently used.

Image
: These templates are designed to train models to identify objects in an image, determine their locations, and classify gestures (e.g., recognizing whether an image contains a dog or a cat).

Video
: These templates are designed to identify actions in a video clip as well as hand gestures (e.g., determining the type of exercise a person is performing).

Text
: These templates are designed to determine the topic or sentiment of a text, or to tag text based on its function within the context (e.g., identifying the mood of an online comment).

Table
: These templates are designed to predict values based on other variables (e.g., estimating the price of a house based on the number of rooms it has or its distance from amenities).

IMPORTANT

Create ML templates not only provide predefined model architectures tailored to specific tasks, but they can also perform transfer learning, a machine learning technique that leverages pre-trained models. This means that our models can be trained on top of Apple's existing models, benefiting from their capabilities while focusing only on the tasks we define, similar to the adapters created in Chapter 5 for Foundation Models. This approach reduces model size and accelerates training without sacrificing functionality or effectiveness. For more information, visit our website and follow the links for this chapter.

After selecting a template and entering all the required information for the project, we are taken to the main interface, where we can provide the data needed to train the model.

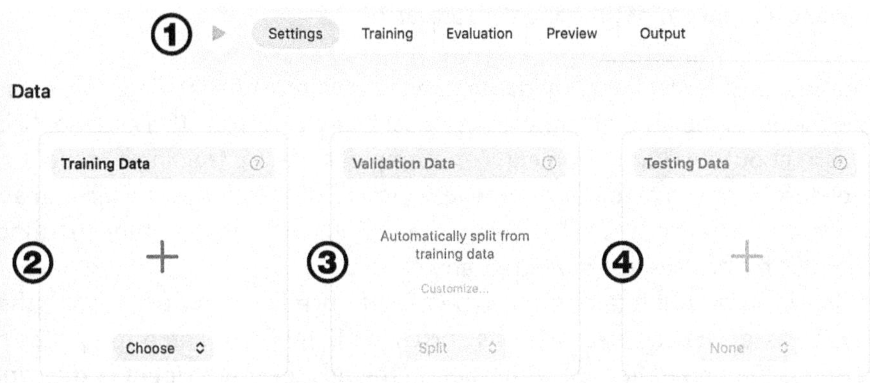

Figure 10-4: *Create ML interface*

The interface includes a toolbar at the top with a button to start training the model (Figure 10-4, number 1) and options to open additional panels. These include the **Settings** panel, where we provide the data for training; the **Training** panel, where we can visualize the training process; the **Evaluation** panel, which shows how well the model performs; the **Preview** panel, where we can test the model; and the **Output** panel, where we can download the trained model to use in our app.

Do It Yourself

Open Xcode, go to the Xcode menu at the top of the screen, select Open Developer Tool, and click Create ML (Figure 10-1, number 1). Click Create New Project, select the Image Classification template (Figure 10-3), and press Next. Enter the project's name, your name, and a description that specifies the purpose of the model. Press Next again and select a folder to store the file. (Create ML generates a single file for the project.) You should now see the interface shown in Figure 10-4.

The first step to train a model is to provide the data. The Settings panel includes options to import three sets of data: the Training data (Figure 10-4, number 2), the Validation data (Figure 10-4, number 3), and the Testing data (Figure 10-4, number 4).

Training Data
This is the dataset used to train the model. In general, the larger this set is, the more accurate the model becomes. For example, if the model's purpose is to determine whether a picture contains a dog or a cat, this set should include as many pictures of dogs and cats as possible.

Validation Data
This dataset is used to evaluate the model's performance during training, helping the system decide when the model has learned enough. We can provide our own set for validation, but Create ML can create its own from the training data.

Testing Data
This dataset is used to test the model after training. Since the data in this set is not included in the previous datasets, the model has never seen it before, making it a reliable measure of the model's accuracy.

The datasets used for training, validation, and testing must be labeled. This means that every image, sound, video, or text in these sets must be associated with a label so the system knows the correct output during training. For example, if we are training a model to detect whether a picture contains a dog or a cat, every picture of a dog must be labeled as "Dog" and every picture of a cat as "Cat," allowing the system to verify whether the model has been successfully trained to recognize dogs and cats.

Depending on the template and the type of data used to train the model, there are several ways to associate the data with its corresponding labels. Some templates require CSV files (Comma-Separated Values) with labels in the header row to identify the content of each column. Others, such as the Object Detection template, require a JSON file that includes not only the labels for each file but also the coordinates of the objects within the images. However, when working with images, sound, or text, the labels can be taken from the names of the files or the folders where they are located. For example, Figure 10-5 below shows the contents of a dataset used to train a model that can recognize different types of fruits.

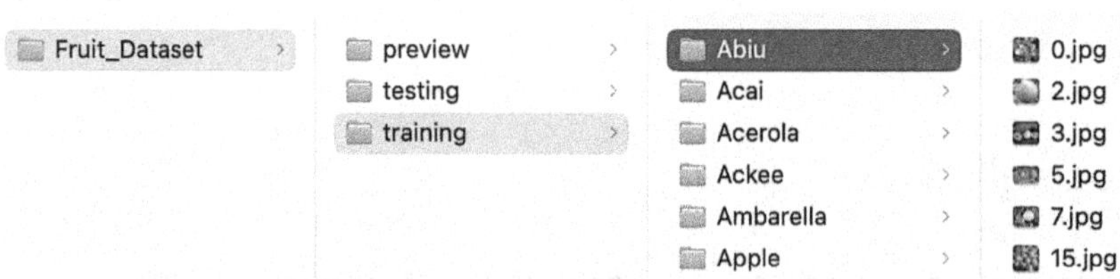

Figure 10-5: *Dataset for image classification*

This dataset contains three folders: **preview**, **testing**, and **training**. The **training** and **testing** folders include subfolders named after the fruits they contain. For example, the **Apple** folder contains pictures of apples, and the **Banana** folder contains pictures of bananas, so Create ML can use these folder names as labels for the files.

Once we have assigned the appropriate labels to our dataset, we can use it to train the model. The first step is to load the training data. The option is available in the Settings panel (Figure 10-4, number 2). For example, if we want to use the dataset shown in Figure 10-5 to train a model to identify fruits, we need to drag the **training** folder into the Training Data section (We can also press the + button in the Training Data section and open the folder). Create ML loads the files and displays the number of images loaded, along with all the classes (fruits) it has detected. In this case, our training dataset contains 98 folders (98 types of fruits) with 400 images each, so Create ML creates 98 classes to represent each type of fruit and loads a total of 39200 pictures, as shown below.

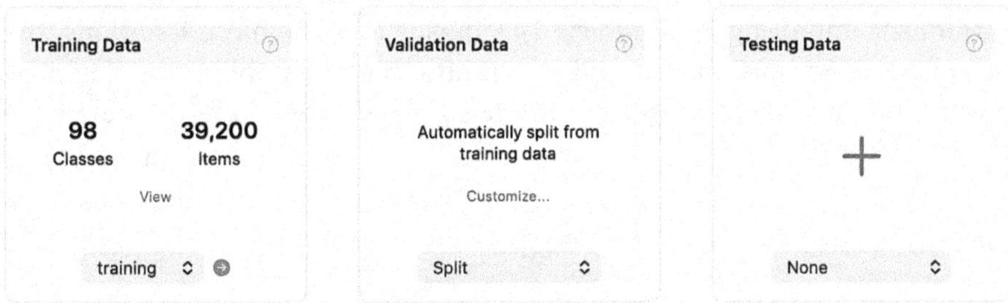

Figure 10-6: *Training data*

The next step is to provide the Validation data. This is the set of images that the system uses to check the model while training. These images are different than those in the training set, so the model is tested against new information. To create this set, we can provide our own images or let the system create the data by taking some images from the Training data. Since in this example we have enough images to work with, we let the system create this set for us, so the only thing left is to load the Testing data (Figure 10-4, number 4). In our example, this means dragging the **testing** folder into to the Testing Data box. Once the images are dragged into the box, Create ML detects the classes and loads the files, as shown below.

Figure 10-7: *Testing data*

Depending on the template, Create ML provides different options for configuration. For image classification, we have the option to change the feature extractor.

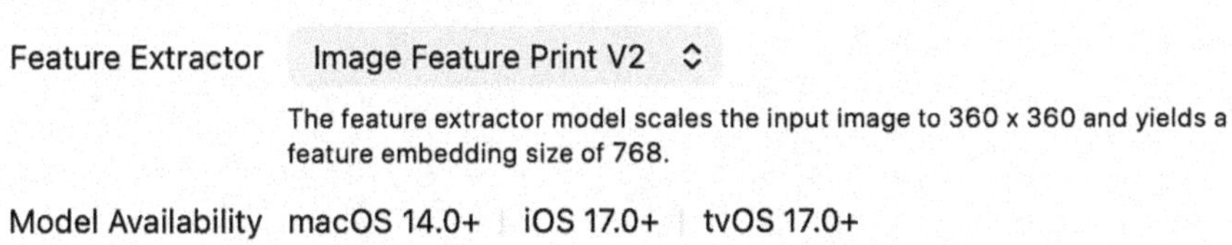

Figure 10-8: *Feature Extractor*

The feature extractor in the image classification template resizes the images to match the model's input requirements. There are two options we can choose from: Image Feature Print V1, which scales images to 299×299 pixels, and Image Feature Print V2, which scales them to 360×360 pixels. Higher resolution provides more details for the model to analyze, so the Image Feature Print V2 extractor typically delivers better results.

Another option available for image classification, which also appears in other templates, is the number of iterations we want the system to perform when training the model. Iterations, also known as *epochs*, are complete passes through the entire training dataset. Each iteration allows the model to adjust its parameters based on the whole data in the dataset, gradually improving its accuracy. This means that the more iterations, the better results we get. But we must also consider that after a certain point, the model reaches a level of accuracy that cannot longer be improved, so we have to find a balance. For our example, we set it to 25.

Figure 10-9: *Iterations*

When creating image classification models, Create ML can generate additional variations of the images in the dataset through a process called *data augmentation*. Data augmentation is a training technique used to artificially expand and diversify the dataset by applying transformations to the original images. For example, the images can be flipped, cropped, or rotated.

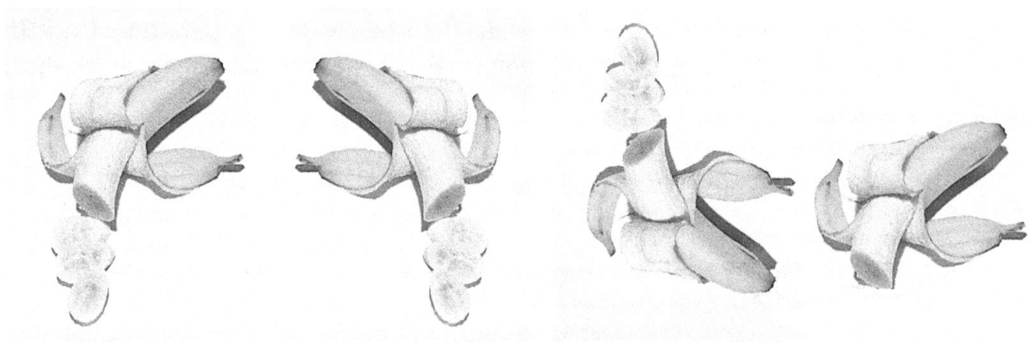

Figure 10-10: *Data augmentation*

In our example, we already have enough images to train a reliable model to identify fruits, but if we want to add more, we just have to select the options at the bottom of the Settings panel.

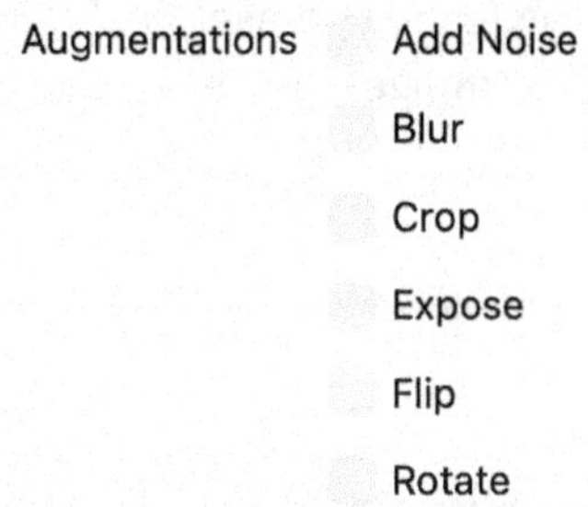

Figure 10-11: *Data Augmentation options*

After the data and settings are ready, we can start training the model. The button to initiate the process is located at the top of the window (Figure 10-4, number 1). After pressing this button, Create ML switches to the Training tab to display the progress. The system begins by preparing the data (feature extraction), which may take a few minutes depending on the size of the dataset and whether the images need to be adjusted to meet the model's requirements.

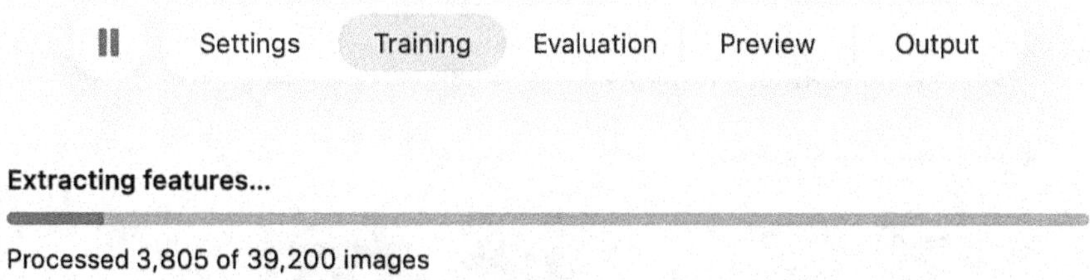

Figure 10-12: *Feature extraction*

Once this process is complete, the training begins. The system sends the images to the model one by one and checks the output. If an image does not match its label, the system determines the error and adjusts the model's parameters to reduce it (we will explore this process in detail in Chapter 11). The system processes all the images in the dataset and then repeats the cycle as many times as specified by the number of iterations set in the Settings panel. We can monitor the training progress on the screen, as shown below.

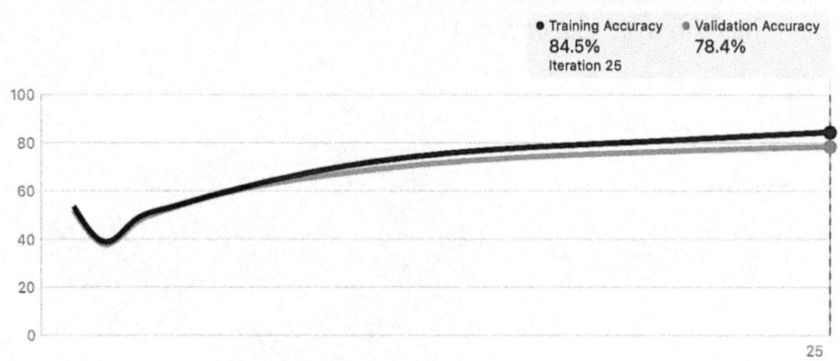

Figure 10-13: *Training progress*

This chart already shows the level of accuracy achieved by the model during training, but we can obtain more detailed information from the Evaluation panel. This panel displays the results of testing the model with the testing dataset, including overall accuracy, the number of correctly and incorrectly identified images, and even the specific classes the model found most confusing.

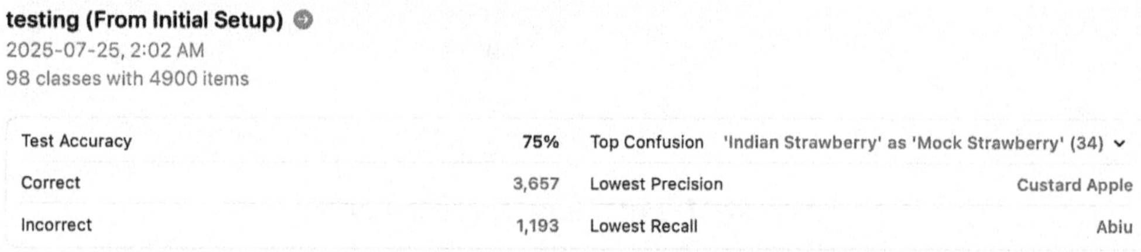

Figure 10-14: *Testing results*

Below the testing results, the panel shows a list with the results class by class. There is also a button called Explore, that replaces this list with all the images in the testing data, so we can check them one by one to identify the problem.

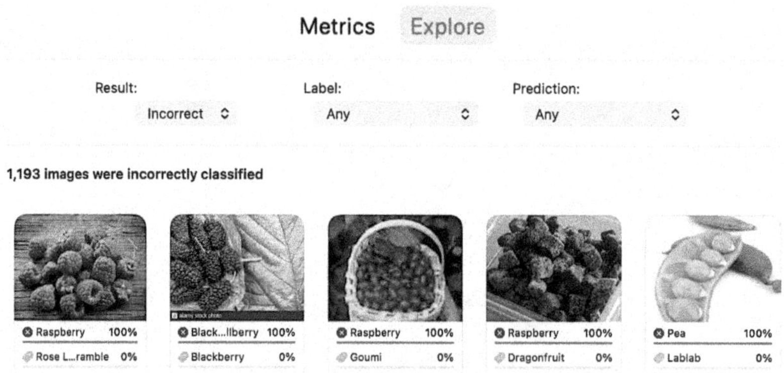

Figure 10-15: *Exploring the results*

We can also test the model with additional images using the Preview panel. To do this, we simply have to drag the files into the panel, and the model will automatically identify the fruit in the selected image. For example, Figure 10-16 shows the result after we added the images from the **preview** folder in our dataset and selected image number 4. The model successfully identifies the fruit as a coconut.

Figure 10-16: *Previews*

Do It Yourself

Download the **fruitdataset.zip** file from our website. This file contains the dataset shown in Figure 10-5. Uncompress the file, select the **training** folder, and drag it into the Training Data box (Figure 10-4, number 2). After a few seconds, the results from loading this data should appear inside the box (Figure 10-6). Next, drag the **testing** folder into the Testing Data box (Figure 10-4, number 4). Choose the Image Feature Print V2 option for the Feature Extractor (Figure 10-8), set the number of iterations to 25 (Figure 10-9), and click the toolbar button to start the training (Figure 10-4, number 1). Create ML will open the Training panel and begin the feature extraction process (Figure 10-12). After a few minutes, this will be replaced by a chart showing the training progress (Figure 10-13). Once the process is complete, open the Preview panel and drag images from the **preview** folder into this panel (Figure 10-16). Select the images to see if the model is capable of recognizing the fruits.

IMPORTANT

The Fruits dataset was extracted from a larger dataset available at **www.kaggle.com**. To find more datasets for testing and training models, visit **www.kaggle.com/datasets**. For more information on this particular dataset, visit our website and follow the links for this chapter.

After we are satisfied with the training results, we can open the Output panel to get information about the model we just created. In this panel, we can see a detailed description of the model's characteristics and two tabs: one called *General*, which provides basic information such as the model's name and description, and another called *Predictions*, which displays the types of inputs the model accepts and the outputs it produces. In our example, the inputs are color images with a resolution of 360 × 360 pixels (Figure 10-17, number 1), and the outputs are `String` values representing the fruit names (Figure 10-17, number 2).

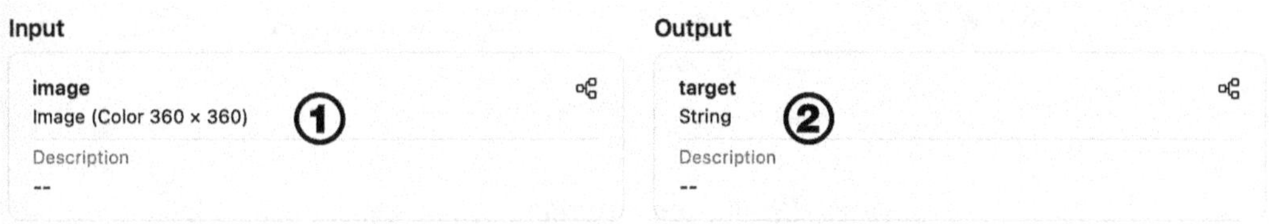

Figure 10-17: *Input and Output*

Create ML generates the model but does not produce an output file. To export the model to a file, we need to press the Get button in the top-right corner of the Output panel (Figure 10-18, number 1).

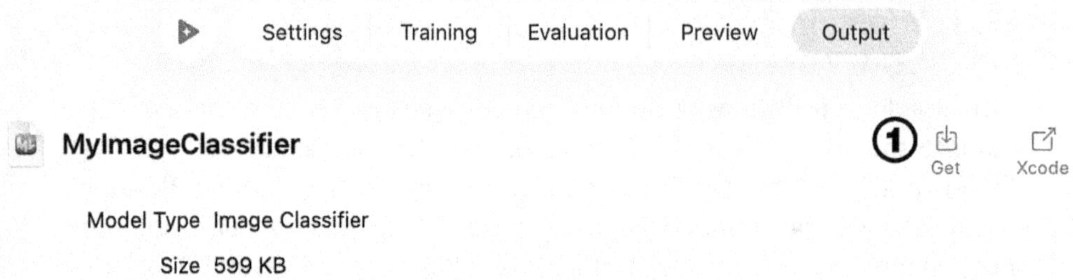

Figure 10-18: *Model file*

Clicking the Get button opens a dialog window where we can choose a folder to save the file. The file is saved in the Core ML format with the **mlmodel** extension. This format is designed by Apple to store machine learning models that can run on Apple devices, as we will see next.

> **Do It Yourself**
>
> Open the Output panel and click the Predictions tab to review the model's inputs and outputs (Figure 10-17). Press the Get button to export the model (Figure 10-18). Next, we will learn how to use this model in our Xcode project.

Core ML

Apple provides the **Core ML** framework to integrate Core ML models into our applications. This is a comprehensive framework that includes all the necessary tools to run models and handle inputs and outputs. The first step to using a Core ML model in an app is to drag the **mlmodel** file into the Xcode project, as we do with any other resource.

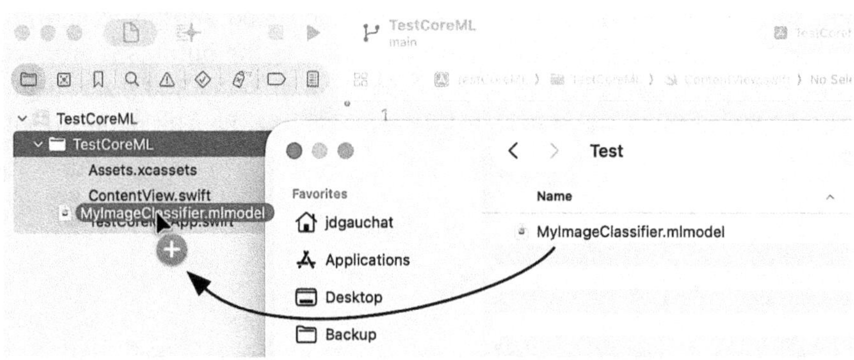

Figure 10-19: *Adding a model to the project*

After adding the file to the project, we can click it to open the model in the editor. The editor displays details about the model and provides panels where we can inspect its inputs and outputs, preview the model as we did earlier in the Create ML app, and visualize its internal structure.

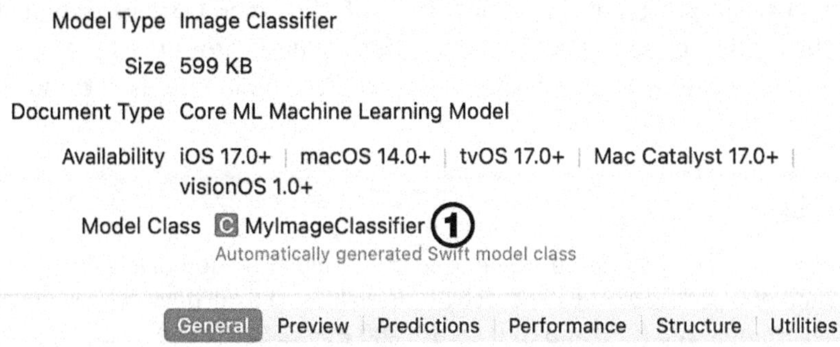

Figure 10-20: *Model in Xcode*

Do It Yourself

Create a new Multiplatform project. Drag the **mlmodel** file generated by Create ML in the previous section into the Navigation area (Figure 10-19). If you have not completed the previous steps to train the model, you can download the **MyImageClassifier.mlmodel** file from our website. Click the file to open the model in the editor. Click the Predictions tab to review the model's expected input values and the outputs it produces.

When a Core ML model is added to an Xcode project, Xcode automatically generates a Swift class for interacting with the model (Figure 10-20, number 1). This class includes the necessary properties and methods for supplying input and reading output, but the signatures of these properties and methods vary depending on the type of model we use. For example, the class generated for an image classifier model, like the one we have just created, includes a property called `target` of type `String`, which returns the name of the object identified in the image; another property called `targetProbability`, which returns a dictionary containing the model's confidence levels for the most significant objects; and the following method to provide the image to be processed.

prediction(image: `CVPixelBuffer)`

This method generates predictions based on the value provided by the argument. The **image** argument is a `CVPixelBuffer` value with the raw pixels of the image we want our model to identify.

When the model's class is initialized, it requires us to provide the model's configuration. The **Core ML** framework includes the following class for this purpose.

MLModelConfiguration

This class creates an object with options and settings that control how the model is loaded and executed.

In most cases, simply creating an instance of the **MLModelConfiguration** class is sufficient for the model to work. However, the class includes properties that can be used to customize the configuration to meet specific needs. The following is the most frequently used.

computeUnits

This property specifies the devices to be used for running the model. It is an enumeration of type **MLComputeUnits** with the values **all** (all devices), **cpuOnly** (CPU cores only), **cpuAndGPU** (CPU and GPU cores), and **cpuAndNeuralEngine** (CPU cores and Neural Engine).

With these tools, we are ready to use the model in our app. The process involves creating an instance of the class generated by Xcode to represent the model (in our case, this is the **MyImageClassifier** class), and then calling the **prediction()** method provided by this class whenever we need the model to identify the fruit in an image.

Because initializing the model may consume resources, it is better to do it once and then reuse it wherever needed. For our example, we will create a separate class to manage the model and prepare the data, as shown below.

Listing 10-1: Loading the model

```
import SwiftUI
import CoreML

class ModelProvider {
   var model: MyImageClassifier?
   let images = ["preview01", "preview02", "preview03", "preview04",
      "preview05", "preview06", "preview07", "preview08", "preview09",
      "preview10"]

   static let shared = ModelProvider()
   private init() {
      let config = MLModelConfiguration()
      self.model = try? MyImageClassifier(configuration: config)
   }
   func prediction(image: String) -> String {
      var className = "Not Sure"
      if let model = model, let input = convertImage(image: image) {
         do {
            let prediction = try model.prediction(image: input)
            className = prediction.target
         } catch {
            print(error)
         }
      }
      return className
   }
}
```

This class includes a property called **model** to store the **MyImageClassifier** object and a property called **images** to store an array of **String** values representing the names of the images we will use for testing. To load the model, we first create an **MLModelConfiguration** object to supply configuration values (although some models may not require configuration), and then use it to instantiate the model's class.

Below the initialization method, we define a custom method called **prediction()**. This method takes a **String** representing the name of the image to be identified, then loads and converts the image using a helper method that will be defined next, and finally calls the model's **prediction()** method with the processed image. The model analyzes the image and returns the name of the fruit. When the prediction is complete, the result is stored in the **target** property, which we return to the view to show it to the user.

The model's **prediction()** method does not take an image directly, but rather a buffer containing the raw data that represents each pixel in the image. This means that any image we want the model to process must first be converted to the **CVPixelBuffer** format. The following is the method we defined for this purpose.

Listing 10-2: Processing an image

```
func convertImage(image: String) -> CVPixelBuffer? {
   #if os(macOS)
   guard let image = NSImage(named: image) else {
      return nil
   }
   guard let cgImage = image.cgImage(forProposedRect: nil, context: nil,
      hints: nil) else {
      return nil
   }
   #else
   guard let uiImage = UIImage(named: image), let cgImage =
      uiImage.cgImage else {
      return nil
   }
   #endif

   let ciImage = CIImage(cgImage: cgImage)
   let width = 360
   let height = 360

   var pixelBuffer: CVPixelBuffer?
   CVPixelBufferCreate(kCFAllocatorDefault, width, height,
      kCVPixelFormatType_32BGRA, nil, &pixelBuffer)
   guard let buffer = pixelBuffer else { return nil }

   let context = CIContext()
   context.render(ciImage.transformed(by: CGAffineTransform(scaleX:
      CGFloat(width) / ciImage.extent.width, y: CGFloat(height)
      / ciImage.extent.height)), to: buffer, bounds: CGRect(x: 0, y: 0,
      width: width, height: height), colorSpace:
      CGColorSpaceCreateDeviceRGB()
   )
   return buffer
}
```

Since in this example we are working with images stored in the Asset Catalog, the method receives only the image's name, not the image itself. Therefore, we must first load the image as an **NSImage** object if the app is running on a Mac, or as a **UIImage** object if it is running on a mobile device, and then convert it into a **CVPixelBuffer**.

There are several ways to convert an image into a pixel buffer. In this case, we use a simple approach that leverages tools provided by the **Core Image** framework (see Chapter 7, Listing 7-31). We begin by defining a **pixelBuffer** variable to hold the buffer, and then call the **CVPixelBufferCreate** function to create it. Note that image classification models require the buffer to have a specific size (for our model, the required size is 360 by 360 pixels) and to be created in the 32-bit BGRA format. If the buffer is created successfully, we can then copy the image into it and return it. To do this, we create a Core Image context and call its **render** method to transfer the image into the buffer. This method requires scale values that determine how the image should be scaled (either shrunk or stretched) to fit the buffer, as well as a color space to preserve the original colors.

IMPORTANT

The **convertImage()** method in Listing 10-2 is not part of the model or involved in any machine learning process, but it is necessary to adapt the images to the requirements of the model. Converting the images to **CVPixelBuffer** values is required for models that work with images or videos, but other models expect different values that may not need any conversion at all. We will see more examples in Chapter 11.

To test our model, we are going to create an app with a simple interface that displays a list of images to choose from. When an image is selected, a second view opens showing the selected image along with a button that calls our **prediction()** method to identify the fruit.

Figure 10-21: *Interface to test our model*

The first step is to add the images to the Asset Catalog. In this example, we use the ten images located in the **preview** folder of our dataset.

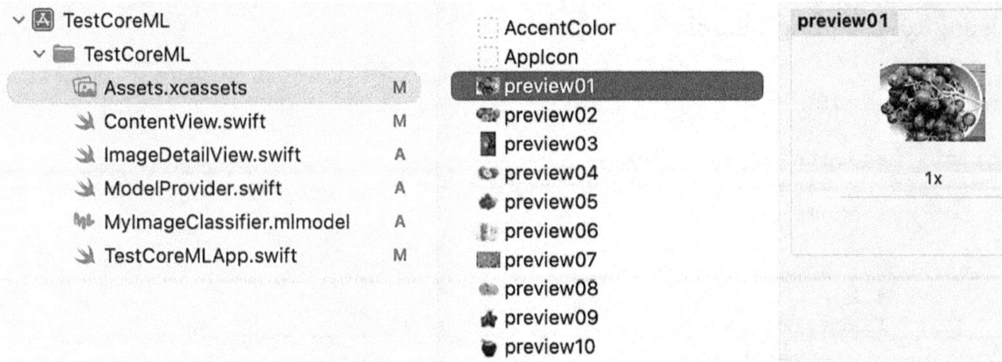

Figure 10-22: *Preview images in the Asset Catalog*

For the initial view, we need to create a grid that displays all the images and opens a secondary view when one is selected, as shown below.

Listing 10-3: Loading the images

```
import SwiftUI

struct ContentView: View {
   let guides = [
      GridItem(.adaptive(minimum: 150))
   ]
   var body: some View {
      NavigationStack {
         ScrollView {
            LazyVGrid(columns: guides) {
               ForEach(ModelProvider.shared.images, id: \.self) { image in
                  NavigationLink(destination:
                     ImageDetailView(imageName: image)) {
                     Image(image)
                        .resizable()
                        .scaledToFit()
                        .clipped()
                        .cornerRadius(8)
                        .shadow(radius: 3)
                  }
               }
            }
         }.padding()
      }
   }
}
```

This view uses a **ForEach** loop to iterate over the image names stored in the **images** property of the **ModelProvider** class and creates **Image** views to display those images on the screen. When the user taps an image, the **NavigationLink** opens a second view called **ImageDetailView** to allow the user to process the selected image with our model, as shown below.

Listing 10-4: Getting a prediction

```
import SwiftUI

struct ImageDetailView: View {
   @State private var className: String = ""
   let imageName: String

   var body: some View {
      VStack {
         Image(imageName)
            .resizable()
            .scaledToFit()
            .frame(width: 200, height: 200)
            .padding()
         Button("Identify") {
            let provider = ModelProvider.shared
            let prediction = provider.prediction(image: imageName)
            className = prediction
         }.buttonStyle(.borderedProminent)
         .padding()
         Text(className)
         Spacer()
      }
   }
}
#Preview {
   ImageDetailView(imageName: ModelProvider.shared.images.first!)
}
```

This view includes an **Image** view to display the selected image and a button to allow the user to ask the model to identify the fruit. When the button is pressed, we get a reference to the **ModelProvider** object and call the **prediction()** method. This method returns the name of the fruit identified by the model, so we assign it to a **State** property and show it on the screen.

Do It Yourself

In the project created earlier to add the model, create a new file called ModelProvider.swift for the code in Listing 10-1. Add the **convertImage()** function from Listing 10-2 to the **ModelProvider** class (below the **prediction()** function). Open the **preview** folder in the fruits dataset and drag the images into the Asset Catalog (Figure 10-22). Update the **ContentView** view with the code in Listing 10-3. Create a new SwiftUI file called ImageDetailView.swift for the view in Listing 10-4. Run the application on your computer or device. Select an image and press the Identify button. You should see the name of the fruit below the button, as shown in Figure 10-21, right.

Pre-trained Models

In addition to the Core ML models we create using the Create ML app, we can also implement models trained by other people. Apple provides several models that we can experiment with, available at **https://developer.apple.com/machine-learning/models/**. Examples include the ResNet-50 model, which recognizes the main object in an image; the BERT-SQuAD model, which finds answers to questions in a text document; and the Updatable Drawing Classifier model, which can be used and train to identify users' drawings.

Using these models is just like using our custom models; we need to download the **mlmodel** file, add it to the project, and follow the same steps as before to load it in code and perform predictions. As an example, we can use a simple model trained on the MNIST dataset. MNIST is a well-known dataset created in 1998 to train and test early machine learning models for recognizing handwritten digits. The MNIST model works with small images of 28 × 28 pixels. Although we can create our own images to test the model, there are many datasets available online for this purpose. Most of these datasets include thousands of images for training and testing, but since the model is already trained, we only need a few images to evaluate it. For this example, we will use a simple dataset that includes training images and a few preview samples. (The files are available on our website.)

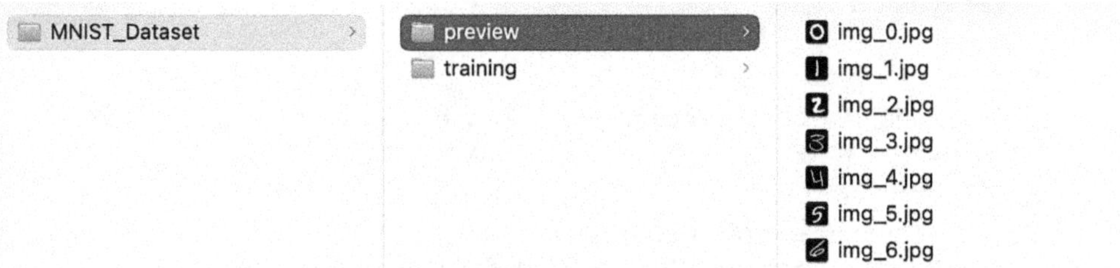

Figure 10-23: *MNIST dataset*

Once the model and images are added to the project, all that remains is to update the code to work with this model. The model takes an image and returns a number corresponding to the digit it contains, so the code will be the same we used in the previous example, with just a few minor changes to the `ModelProvider` class, as shown below.

Listing 10-5: Adapting our class to work with the MNIST model

```
import SwiftUI
import CoreML

class ModelProvider {
   static let shared = ModelProvider()
   let model: MNISTClassifier?
   let images = ["img_0", "img_1", "img_2", "img_3", "img_4", "img_5",
      "img_6", "img_7", "img_8", "img_9"]

   private init() {
      let config = MLModelConfiguration()
      self.model = try? MNISTClassifier(configuration: config)
   }
```

```
    func prediction(image: String) -> String {
        var className = "Not Sure"
        if let model = model, let input = convertImage(image: image) {
            do {
                let prediction = try model.prediction(image: input)
                className = String(prediction.classLabel)
            } catch {
                print(error)
            }
        }
        return className
    }
    func convertImage(image: String) -> CVPixelBuffer? {
        #if os(macOS)
        guard let image = NSImage(named: image) else {
            return nil
        }
        guard let cgImage = image.cgImage(forProposedRect: nil,
            context: nil, hints: nil) else {
            return nil
        }
        #else
        guard let uiImage = UIImage(named: image), let cgImage =
            uiImage.cgImage else {
            return nil
        }
        #endif

        let ciImage = CIImage(cgImage: cgImage)
        let width = 28
        let height = 28

        var pixelBuffer: CVPixelBuffer?
        CVPixelBufferCreate(kCFAllocatorDefault, width, height,
            kCVPixelFormatType_OneComponent8, nil, &pixelBuffer)
        guard let buffer = pixelBuffer else { return nil }

        let context = CIContext()
        context.render(ciImage.transformed(by: CGAffineTransform(scaleX:
            CGFloat(width) / ciImage.extent.width, y: CGFloat(height)
            / ciImage.extent.height)), to: buffer, bounds: CGRect(x: 0, y: 0,
            width: width, height: height), colorSpace:
            CGColorSpaceCreateDeviceRGB()
        )
        return buffer
    }
}
```

We only had to performed a few changes to this class to work with the MNIST model instead of our custom classifier. First, we define the **model** property to be of type **MNISTClassifier** to load the MNIST model. Since we are using a different set of images, we also update the names in the **images** property. The **prediction()** method returns the model's output in a property called **classLabel**, so we read this property to obtain the predicted number. Finally, in the **convertImage()** method, we need to change the buffer size to 28 × 28 pixels, and because the model works with buffers of type **OneComponent8**, we also modify the arguments of the **CVPixelBufferCreate()** method to meet this requirement.

The views are the same as before. The initial view displays a list of images, and when the user selects one, a second view opens showing the image along with a button to ask the model to identify the number, as shown below.

Figure 10-24: *MNIST model prediction*

Do It Yourself

Go to **https://developer.apple.com/machine-learning/models/**, scroll down until you find the MNIST model, click View Details, and press the Download button to download the **MNISTClassifier.mlmodel** file. (The file is also available on our website.) Drag this file into the Xcode project created for the previous example. Download the **MNIST_Dataset.zip** file from our website, uncompress it, open the **preview** folder, and drag the images from this folder into your project's Asset Catalog (Figure 10-23). Update the `ModelProvider` class with the code in Listing 10-5. Run the application on your computer or a device. Select an image and press the Identify button. You should see the number identified by the model displayed on the screen, as shown in Figure 10-24, right.

IMPORTANT

In addition to the models provided by Apple, many developers are constantly training and converting models to share with the community. To find more Core ML models for your applications, visit **https://huggingface.co/models?library=coreml**.

10.2 - External Models

In addition to the models provided by Apple and those we can train ourselves, we can also implement external models in our applications. External models are built on massive data centers and therefore have access to enormous computing power and training datasets.

These models can provide advanced capabilities such as natural language processing, image generation, and code completion that significantly outperform anything we can achieve with our own models running on a personal device. By connecting our apps to these external services, we can extend their functionality far beyond what local models can deliver.

OpenAI

Each company that offers these models provides its own tools, so there is no universal procedure to integrate them into our apps. In this section, we work with the models provided by OpenAI (the same ones that power ChatGPT), but the general approach applies to most commercial models available to developers today.

API Key

The first step to gain access to an external model is to create an account with the service provider. For OpenAI, this can be done through their website at **www.openai.com**. Once there, we need to sign up for an account on the API Platform. At the moment, this option appears when we hover the mouse over the Log In button.

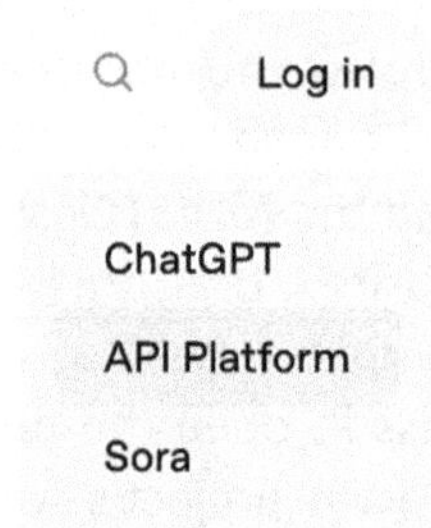

Figure 10-25: *Logging in to the API Platform*

The way we access external models is through an API. This API processes our requests and returns the model's responses, so the first thing we see when we open the platform is the API documentation.

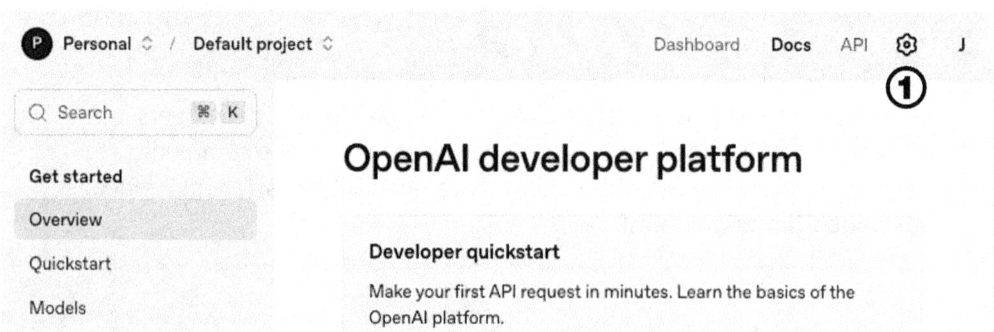

Figure 10-26: *API Documentation*

To manage our account, we need to click the Settings button in the top-right corner of the home page (Figure 10-26, number 1). The panel now displays options to keep track of our account, such as organizing projects, controlling the budget, and checking usage.

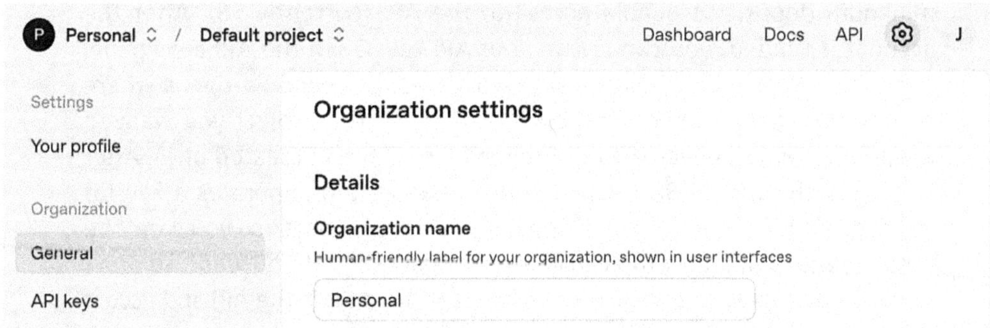

Figure 10-27: *Account settings*

The first step we need to take to set up our account is to fund it. Every company requires a minimum deposit to allow us to use their services. At the time of writing, OpenAI's minimum deposit is $5. This option is available in the Billing panel.

Figure 10-28: *OpenAI billing system*

To identify who is sending the requests and charge our account, these systems use API keys. An API key identifies our account, and therefore must be included in every request to the system, otherwise we will receive an error. The option to create these keys is available in the API Keys panel, as shown below.

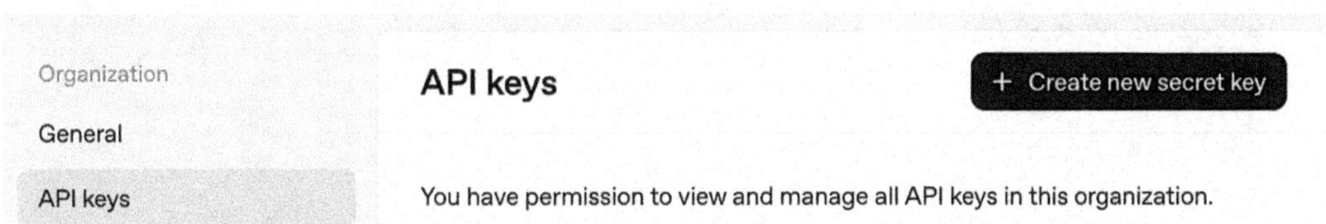

Figure 10-29: *API Keys*

Do It Yourself

Visit OpenAI's website at **www.openai.com**. Find the Log In button on the top-right side of the home page, hover over the button, and select the API Platform option (Figure 10-25). Follow the steps to sign up and set up your account. Once you have access to the platform, click on the Settings button (Figure 10-26, number 1), open the Billing panel, and click the Add to Credit Balance button to fund the account (Figure 10-28). Make the minimum deposit to enable access to the API (currently $5). After the account is funded, you can create your API key. Open the API Keys panel and press Create New Secret Key (Figure 10-29). A window opens where you can insert the name for the key and select the project you want to assign the key to (select Default Project if you haven't created one). After you press the Create Secret Key button, the system generates a key for your account. Copy and save this key in a safe place, because you won't be able to retrieve it later. (You can create as many keys as you want, so don't worry if you forget to save it.) Now you are ready to use the API and access OpenAI models, as we will see next.

API

The API takes instructions, provides the information in those instructions to the model, and then returns the model's response. We send these instructions and receive the responses using JSON files. JSON (JavaScript Object Notation) is a lightweight format used to store and exchange data. It organizes information in key–value pairs, making it both easy for humans to read and easy for machines to parse. For example, below is a JSON snippet with the minimum instructions required to send a user prompt to the OpenAI API.

Listing 10-6: JSON request for the OpenAI API

```
{
    "input": [{
        "role": "system",
        "content": "System instructions"
    }, {
        "role": "user",
        "content": "User prompt"
    }],
    "model": "gpt-5",
    "max_output_tokens": 2000,
    "store": false
}
```

The first instruction is called **input**. This tells the API which values we want the model to process. In this case, we provide two: the system instructions and the user's prompt. As with the Foundation Models studied in Chapter 5, the instructions tell the system how it should process the prompt, and the prompt provides the actual request from the user. Next, we include instructions to configure the request. In our example, we specify the model to use (gpt-5), the maximum number of tokens the model should generate in its response (2000), and whether the model should store the response in case the user asks the same question again (false).

> **IMPORTANT**
>
> In this and the following examples, we use the gpt-5 model, although other options are available. Each model has its own characteristics and cost. Currently, OpenAI recommends gpt-5 (for coding and multitasking), gpt-5-mini (for specialized tasks), and gpt-5-nano (for a cost-effective solution). The complete list is available at **https://platform.openai.com/docs/models**.

Once we have the JSON code with the instructions we want to send to the API, we must convert it into a **Data** structure and create a URL request to send it to OpenAI servers. There are many ways to implement these steps. For our example, we will define the JSON data using dictionaries, convert these dictionaries into data with the **JSONSerialization** class, and then decode the response with the **JSONDecoder** class. The following is our implementation for this example.

Listing 10-7: Sending requests to the OpenAI API

```
import SwiftUI
import Observation

@Observable class ApplicationData {
   var response: AttributedString = ""
   var prompt: String = ""

   static let shared: ApplicationData = ApplicationData()
   private init() { }

   func sendPrompt() async {
      guard !prompt.isEmpty else { return }

      // Prepare JSON instructions
      let content: [[String: String]] = [
         ["role": "system", "content": "You are a friendly AI that likes
         to chat with the user."],
         ["role": "user", "content": prompt]
      ]
      let jsonbody: [String: Any] = [
         "model": "gpt-5",
         "input": content,
         "store": false,
         "max_output_tokens": 2000
      ]
      guard let jsonData = try? JSONSerialization.data(withJSONObject:
         jsonbody) else { return }

      // Prepare URL request
      let apikey = "[YOUR-API-KEY]"
      guard let url = URL(string: "https://api.openai.com/v1/responses")
         else { return }
```

```
        var urlRequest = URLRequest(url: url)
        urlRequest.httpMethod = "POST"
        urlRequest.httpBody = jsonData
        urlRequest.addValue("Bearer \(apikey)",
           forHTTPHeaderField: "Authorization")
        urlRequest.addValue("application/json",
           forHTTPHeaderField: "Content-Type")

        // Send request and process response
        do {
           let (data, urlResponse) = try await URLSession.shared.data(
              for: urlRequest)
           if let httpResponse = urlResponse as? HTTPURLResponse {
              if httpResponse.statusCode == 200 {
                 let chatresponse = try JSONDecoder()
                    .decode(ChatResponse.self, from: data)
                 for item in chatresponse.output {
                    if item.type == "message", let content = item.content {
                       for part in content {
                          if part.type == "output_text",
                             let answer = part.text {
                             var newResponse = AttributedString(
                                "\(answer)\n\n")
                             newResponse.font = .system(size: 16,
                                weight: .regular)
                             response.append(newResponse)
                          }
                       }
                    }
                 }
              } else {
                 response = AttributedString("Error \(httpResponse
                    .statusCode): \(String(data: data, encoding: .utf8) ??
                    "No additional information.")")
              }
           }
        } catch {
           response = AttributedString("Error accessing the API: \(error)")
        }
        prompt = ""
     }
  }
```

The **sendPrompt()** method defined in Listing 10-7 is the one we call from the views with the prompt entered by the user. The method checks whether the prompt is empty, and then creates the JSON data with this value. This data is then converted into a **Data** structure using the **data()** method of the **JSONSerialization** class and sent with the request. To perform the request, we need three values: the URL that points to the API (in this case, **https://api.openai.com/v1/responses**), the JSON data we just created, and our API key. (This is just for testing purposes. As we will see later, the API key should NEVER be included in our application.) After building the request, we open a URL session and process the response.

The response from OpenAI's servers also comes back as JSON, so we can use a Swift structure and the **JSONDecoder** class to decode it and read its values. The structure we use to process the server's response must match the structure of the JSON data we receive. In this case, the response returned by the API contains key/value pairs that are nested and organized in lists, so we must nest our structures accordingly, as shown below.

Listing 10-8: Structure to process the JSON response from the API

```
import SwiftUI

struct ChatResponse: Codable {
    let output: [OutputItem]

   struct OutputItem: Codable {
      let id: String
      let type: String
      let status: String?
      let content: [ContentPart]?
      let role: String?

      struct ContentPart: Codable {
         let type: String
         let text: String?
      }
   }
}
```

The **ChatResponse** structure includes an **output** property that stores a list of **OutputItem** structures, and each **OutputItem** structure contains a **content** property that stores a **ContentPart** structure with the model's response. This means that to read the model's response, we need to navigate through these structures until we find the correct **text** property containing the value we want. For this purpose, in the **sendPrompt()** method defined in Listing 10-7, we created a **for in** loop to read every item in the output, searched for the item of type "message", then used another **for in** loop to read the **content** property of this item, searched for the item of type "output_text", and finally read the **text** property of this item to get the response.

When we perform a request, our app sends data to the server and then waits for the response. This means that the app must manage both outgoing and incoming connections. To prevent abuse, these connections are not enabled by default, but we can enable them from the project's settings. All we need to do is open the Signing & Capabilities panel, locate the App Sandbox section, and check the appropriate boxes, as shown below.

Figure 10-30: *Enabling connections*

The last step is to design the interface. For this example, we are going to use a layout similar to the one we created in Chapter 5 when working with Foundation Models. The interface includes a **TextField** for the user to type a prompt and a **Text** view to display the response from the model.

Listing 10-9: Taking the user's prompt and showing the response from the model

```
import SwiftUI

struct ContentView: View {
   @State private var appData = ApplicationData.shared
   @State private var position = ScrollPosition(idType: String.self)
   @State private var inProgress: Bool = false

   var body: some View {
      VStack {
         ScrollView {
            Text(appData.response)
               .padding()
               .textSelection(.enabled)
               .id("textID")
         }
         .frame(minWidth: 350, maxWidth: .infinity, minHeight: 300,
            alignment: .leading)
         .background(Color.gray.opacity(0.2))
         .clipShape(RoundedRectangle(cornerRadius: 12))
         .scrollPosition($position)
         HStack {
            TextField("Insert Prompt", text: $appData.prompt)
               .textFieldStyle(.roundedBorder)
               .disabled(inProgress)
            Button("Send") {
               inProgress = true
               Task {
                  if !appData.prompt.isEmpty {
                     // Insert prompt in chat box
                     var newPrompt = AttributedString(
                        "\(appData.prompt)\n\n")
                     newPrompt.font = .system(size: 16, weight: .bold)
                     appData.response.append(newPrompt)
                     // Send prompt to model
                     await appData.sendPrompt()
                     inProgress = false
                  }
               }
            }
            .buttonStyle(.borderedProminent)
            .disabled(inProgress)
         }
      }
      .padding()
      .onChange(of: appData.response) {
         position.scrollTo(edge: .bottom)
      }
   }
}
```

This view includes a button that calls the **sendPrompt()** method with the prompt entered by the user. This is similar to what we did in Chapter 5, the only difference is that now we use an additional property called **inProgress** to disable the text field and the button while the response is being processed. Figure 10-31 shows what we see after sending the prompt "Hello".

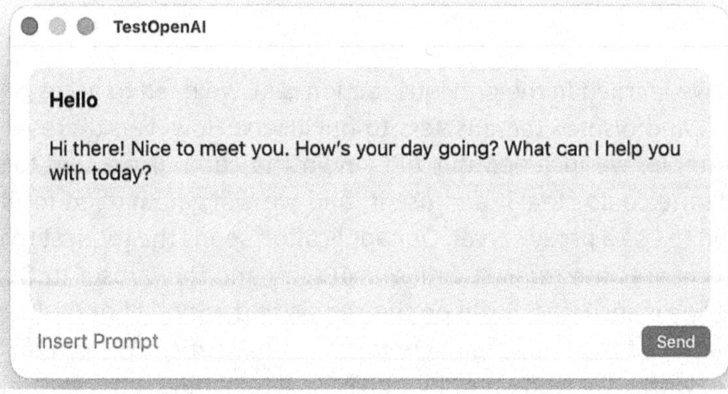

***Figure 10-31:** Interacting with OpenAI model*

Do It Yourself

Create a new Multiplatform project. Create a new Swift file called ApplicationData.swift for the code in Listing 10-7. Replace the value of the **apikey** constant in the **sendPrompt()** method with your OpenAI key. Create another Swift file called ChatResponse.swift for the structure in Listing 10-8. Update the **ContentView** view with the code in Listing 10-9. Open the project's settings, go to the Signing & Capabilities panel, scroll down to the App Sandbox section, and check the Incoming and Outgoing boxes (Figure 10-30). Run the application on your Mac, type a prompt, and press the Send button. After a few seconds, you should see the model's response on the screen, as shown in Figure 10-31. This example is for testing purposes only. You should NEVER include your API key in your application. In the next section, we will learn how to use a proxy server to protect this key.

IMPORTANT

When we receive a response from the server, we must check for errors. There are two types of errors: those returned by the URL request and those returned by the model. In the **sendPrompt()** method, we check for both. First, we examine the value of the **statusCode** property, which indicates the success of the request. There are many possible values returned by OpenAI's servers: 200 means the request was successful, 400 indicates a problem with the request, 401 indicates an authentication error, 429 indicates that the rate limits for the API have been exceeded, and 500 indicates a server-side issue on OpenAI's end. The other possibility is that the model itself returns an error. For this reason, when we receive a status code other than 200, we also print the returned JSON data along with the value so we can inspect what happened.

Cloudflare

In practice, what we learned in the previous section is all we need to access OpenAI models, perform requests, and display the answers to our users. However, there is one important issue. In that example, we included our API key in the code. If we ship this key with our application, someone could steal it and use it, and we will get charged for it. To avoid this situation, we need to use a proxy server. Our application sends the request to the server, and then the server prepares the request with our API key and forwards it to OpenAI's servers. This way, the API key is securely stored on the server, and nobody but us can access it.

There are many options available to create this proxy server. We can build a traditional server using frameworks like Node.js or Python's Flask to handle requests and forward them to OpenAI, use cloud platforms that allow us to deploy simple APIs without maintaining the infrastructure ourselves, or use serverless apps. Among these options, serverless apps have quickly become the most popular. They let us define small functions that run only when called, that automatically scale with demand, and keep our API key securely hidden from users.

Of all the companies providing serverless services, Cloudflare has become the choice for many developers because of its low cost, ease of use, and the tools it offers, some of which have been specifically designed for AI development. The service we are most interested in is Workers. Workers are lightweight applications that handle HTTP requests. They are usually written in JavaScript and run on Cloudflare's global network of servers, which allows them to deliver fast and reliable responses.

Workers

Cloudflare charges based on usage, but it also offers a free plan we can use to test the service and start deploying our apps. As always, the first step is to open an account. The website is available at **www.cloudflare.com**. After signing up, we must open the Workers & Pages panel (Figure 10-32, number 1) and click the Create Application button to set up a new Worker (Figure 10-32, number 2).

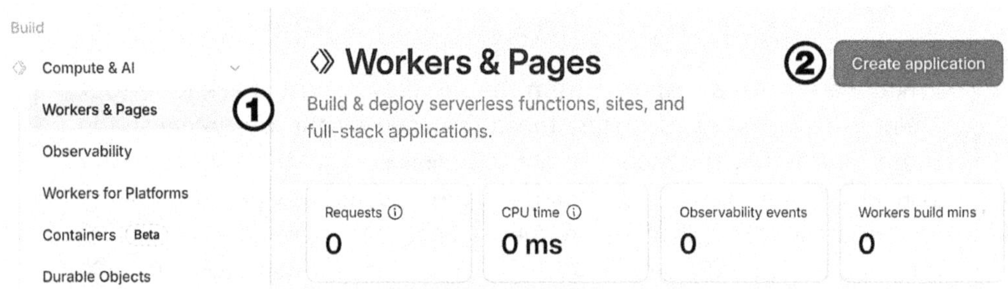

Figure 10-32: *Creating a Worker*

The platform offers many templates to choose from. For our example, the best option is to start with a simple Hello World! template (Figure 10-33, number 1).

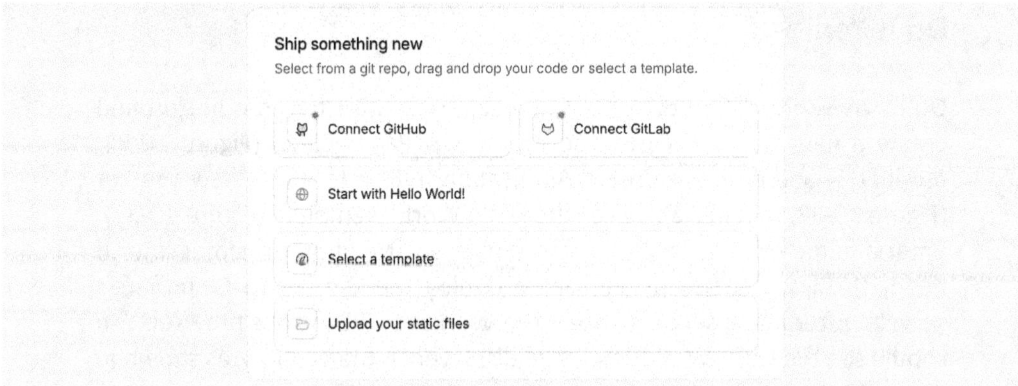

Figure 10-33: *Selecting a template*

After selecting the template, the system displays the generated code and lets us choose a name for the Worker. This name not only identifies the Worker but also becomes part of the URL we will use later to access it, as shown below.

Figure 10-34: *Defining the Worker's name and URL*

To create the Worker with the selected name, we must click the Deploy button at the bottom of the screen. The Worker is immediately deployed to Cloudflare's global network and, after a few seconds, is ready to use. If we open the Worker's URL in a browser, we will be greeted with a Hello World! message.

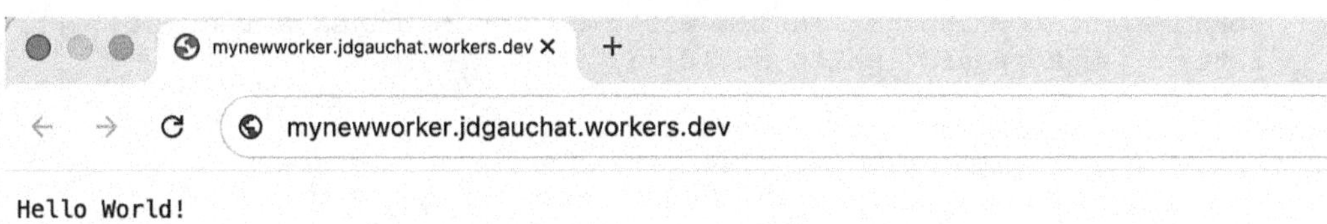

Figure 10-35: *Accessing the Worker*

Do It Yourself

Go to **www.cloudflare.com**. Click the Log In or Start for Free button and create a new account. Open the Workers & Pages panel (Figure 10-32, number 1) and click the Create Application button to add a new Worker (Figure 10-32, number 2). Select the Hello World! template (Figure 10-33). Enter a name (you can create more Workers with different names later if needed). Click the Deploy button to deploy the Worker to Cloudflare's servers. After a few seconds, open the Worker's URL in your browser. You should see the Hello World! message displayed in the window, as shown in Figure 10-35.

Cloudflare provides an online editor that we can use to modify the Worker's code. This option is available when we select a Worker from the platform's home page. To access it, we need to click Account Home in the left panel, select the Worker's name, and then click the Edit Code button (Figure 10-36, number 1).

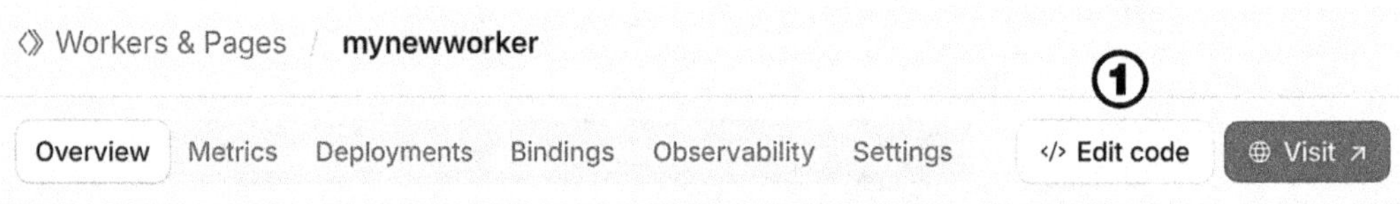

Figure 10-36: *Edit Code button*

When we click this button, the editor displays the Worker's code on the left and a testing panel on the right. The following code is what we see when we create a Worker with the Hello World! template.

Listing 10-10: Worker's code

```
export default {
  async fetch(request, env, ctx) {
    // You can view your logs in the Observability dashboard
    console.info({ message: 'Hello World Worker received a request!' });
    return new Response('Hello World!');
  }
};
```

The code generated by Cloudflare for our Worker is written in JavaScript. It includes an asynchronous function called **`fetch()`** that runs whenever a request is received by the server. This function must process the request and return a response. In this case, the code simply prints a message to Cloudflare's console and then creates and returns a new **`Response`** object with the text "Hello World!", which is why we see this message when we access the Worker from a browser.

Of course, this is just sample code to demonstrate how Workers work, but we can make any changes we want. For example, the following code stores a text in a constant and then returns a response with that text.

Listing 10-11: Editing the Worker's code

```
export default {
  async fetch(request, env, ctx) {
    const message = "This is my Worker!";
    return new Response(message);
  }
};
```

For this new Worker to become available, we must deploy it to Cloudflare's servers by pressing the Deploy button in the top-right corner of the screen. After that, when we open the Worker in a browser, instead of the previous message, we will see the message "This is my Worker!".

Do It Yourself

Open your Cloudflare account and click on the Account Home option in the left panel. You will see information about your account and a list of the Workers you have already created. Select the Worker you want to edit, then click the Edit Code button in the top-right corner (Figure 10-36, number 1). The Worker's code will appear on the screen. Replace this code with the code in Listing 10-11. Press the Deploy button in the top-right corner to deploy the Worker to Cloudflare's servers. Open the Worker's URL in your browser again. You should see the message "This is my Worker!" displayed in the browser's window.

IMPORTANT

Workers can be programmed in JavaScript, as well as in other languages such as TypeScript and Rust. JavaScript is the most common choice because it is also the language used to run applications in the browser. In this chapter, we explain some JavaScript features, but to gain a deeper understanding of how Workers operate and how JavaScript works in general, read our book *HTML5, CSS, and JavaScript for Masterminds*.

Wrangler

The code editor provided by Cloudflare works well for making changes to simple Workers that don't require additional data. However, because the service is serverless, if we need to install extra resources, we must develop the Worker on our local computer and then upload it to Cloudflare's servers. For this purpose, Cloudflare provides a tool called *Wrangler*. Wrangler is a command-line tool that we run from the Terminal app on our computer. It includes features for creating, developing, testing, and deploying serverless apps and related resources to Cloudflare's servers.

Wrangler is distributed as a Node.js package. Node.js is a program that allows us to run JavaScript code outside the browser, so to use Wrangler, we must first install Node.js and its dependencies. There are many versions of Node.js available, and not all of them are compatible with Wrangler. To make sure that we are running the correct version, we must work with a Node.js version manager called NVM. To install NVM, we must open Terminal and type the following command.

Listing 10-12: Installing Node.js Version Manager

```
curl -o- https://raw.githubusercontent.com/nvm-sh/nvm/v0.40.3/install.sh |
bash
```

Now that we have the Node.js version manager installed, we can use it to install Node.js. Currently, Wrangler requires the latest version. To see the versions available, we can run the following command.

Listing 10-13: Listing version available of Node.js

```
nvm ls-remote
```

This command displays a list of all the versions of Node.js available to download. At this moment, the latest is v24.6.0, so we can copy this string and run the following command to download the package.

Listing 10-14: Downloading the latest version of Node.js

```
nvm install v24.6.0
```

Do It Yourself

Open the Terminal app and type the command in Listing 10-12 to install NVM. To finish the installation, close Terminal and open it again. You can check that NVM is properly installed by typing **nvm -v**. You should see the NVM version on the screen. Next, type the command in Listing 10-13 to display the list of Node.js versions available for download, and the command in Listing 10-14 to install Node.js (replace the version number with the latest one shown in the list). This installs Node.js and the Node.js package manager called npm. To confirm that both applications have been installed correctly, type **node -v** and **npm -v**. You should see the versions of these applications on the screen.

After the installation is complete, we need to create a folder to store our Workers. Although we can create this folder from Terminal, it is easier to do it from Finder. For these examples, we have created a folder called **workers** inside a **Projects** folder. To navigate to this folder from Terminal, we need to copy the path, as shown below.

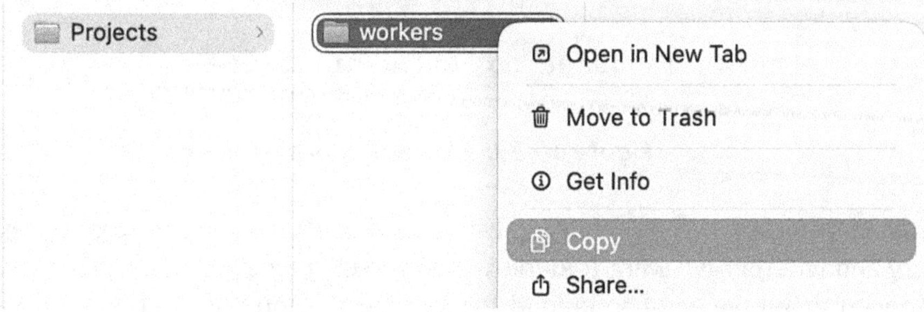

Figure 10-37: *Folder to store Workers*

As we have already seeing in Chapter 5 (see Figure 5-27), this copies the entire folder path to the clipboard, so we can go back to Terminal, type **cd** and paste the path to jump straight into the **workers** folder (e.g., **cd /Users/jdgauchat/Projects/workers**), as shown below.

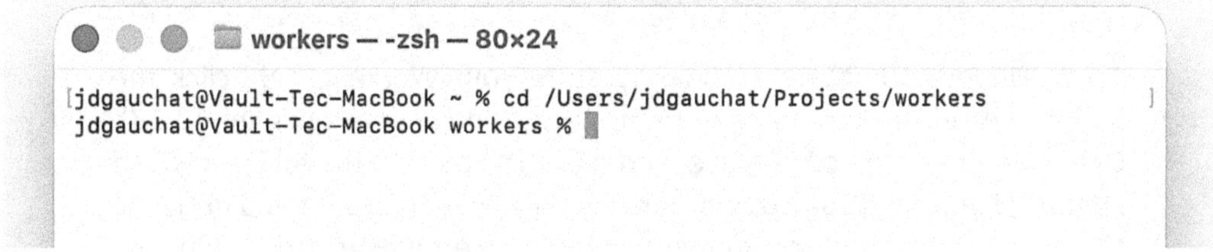

Figure 10-38: *Navigating to the **workers** folder in Terminal*

The next step is to create our Worker inside this folder. The following command creates a folder with all the files required by the Worker and deploys it to Cloudflare servers.

Listing 10-15: Creating a Worker

```
npm create cloudflare@latest -- mynewworker
```

The manager asks us to add the **create-cloudflare** package (we must select **Yes**), and then asks a series of questions to determine what we want to create. The questions may appear in a different order and include different options depending on the current version. At the time of writing, we are asked to select the category, a template, and the programming language. To work with the OpenAI API, we should select **Hello World example** for the category, **Worker only** for the template, and **JavaScript** for the programming language, as shown below.

```
│
├ What would you like to start with?
│ category Hello World example
│
├ Which template would you like to use?
│ type Worker only
│
├ Which language do you want to use?
│ lang JavaScript
│
```

Figure 10-39: Worker options

The manager usually asks two more questions: whether we want to store the project in a repository and whether we want to deploy the Worker right away. In this case, we do not need a repository, but we want to upload the Worker to Cloudflare servers, so we should select **No** for the first question and **Yes** for the second one. After this, the manager opens the browser to prompts us to log in to our Cloudflare account. Once we authorize Wrangler to access our account, the manager creates a folder containing all the files for the Worker, deploys the Worker to Cloudflare servers, and opens the browser to show it on the screen.

Do It Yourself

Go to Finder and create a folder to store your Workers, right-click the folder and select Copy to copy the path to the clipboard (Figure 10-37). Open Terminal, type **cd**, a space, and paste the path to the folder (e.g., **cd /Users/jdgauchat/Projects/workers**). Finally, type the command in Listing 10-15 to create a worker. Remember to replace **mynewworker** with the name you want to assign to your Worker. Please be aware that if you use a name that already exists, the code created for the new Worker will replace the old one.

The manager creates a folder with the Worker's name and all the files the Worker needs, including the JavaScript file with the sample code. This file may be called **index.js** or **worker.js**, depending on the version of the system we are using, and it is located inside the **src** folder, as shown below.

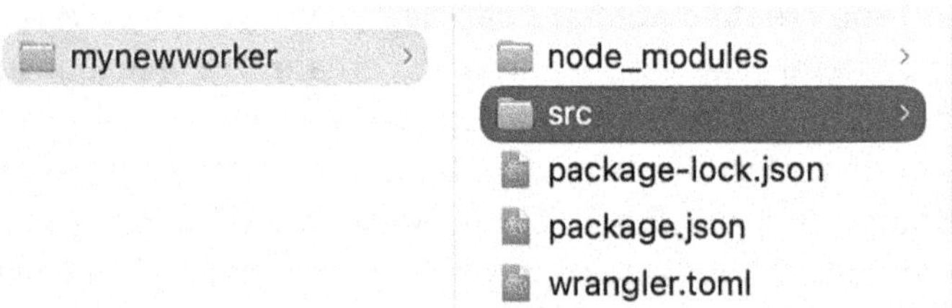

Figure 10-40: Worker's files and folders

From this point on, we can edit this code on our computer and upload it to Cloudflare servers. To edit the **worker.js** file, we can use Xcode or any other editor such as Visual Studio

Code (**code.visualstudio.com**). After we modify the file, we must upload it again to Cloudflare servers to make the changes available to our users. To deploy the Worker, we must type the following command from the Worker's folder.

Listing 10-16: Deploying a Worker

```
npx wrangler deploy
```

The **npx** command comes with **npm** and allows us to run commands from a package without installing it globally on the computer. In this case, we use it to execute the **deploy** command from the Wrangler package. After we type this command, the Worker is uploaded again to Cloudflare servers and all the changes we made become available to everyone.

Do It Yourself

Open the **worker.js** file from the **src** folder in Xcode and change the text in the response, as we did in Listing 10-11 (e.g., "This is my local Worker"). Open Terminal, type **cd mynewworker** to open the Worker's folder (Replace **mynewworker** with the name of your Worker), and type the command **npx wrangler deploy** from this folder to deploy the Worker to Cloudflare servers. Enter your Worker's URL in a browser. You should see the updated text on the screen. For a list of the commands you can use in Terminal to navigate to folders and work with files, visit our website and follow the links for this chapter.

IMPORTANT

If you want to run the Worker locally, you can type the command **npx wrangler dev**. This command starts a local server that allows us to test the Worker on our computer. The server runs on port 8787, so after starting it, we can open the URL **http://localhost:8787/** in a browser to run the Worker.

OpenAI Library

Our Worker is now set up and ready to send requests to the OpenAI API. The first step we need to take is to store our API key securely on the server. The option is available on our Cloudflare's account in the Worker's Settings panel (Figure 10-41, number 1).

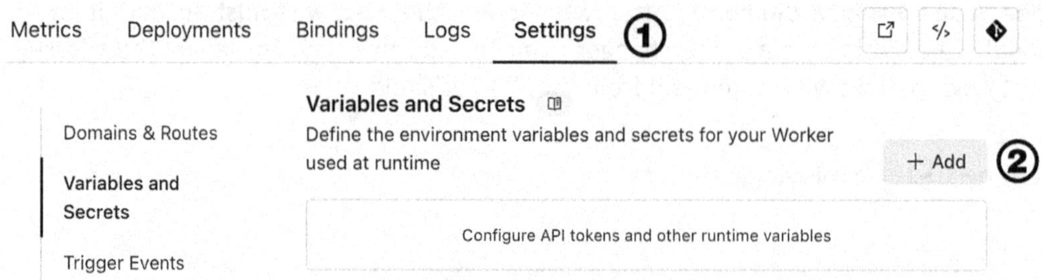

Figure 10-41: *Variables and Secrets*

The panel includes a section called *Variables and Secrets*, and in this section, we will find a button on the right to add a variable (Figure 10-41, number 2). When we click this button, a window opens where we can choose the type of value to store (Secret), specify the name to identify it, and enter the value (our API key).

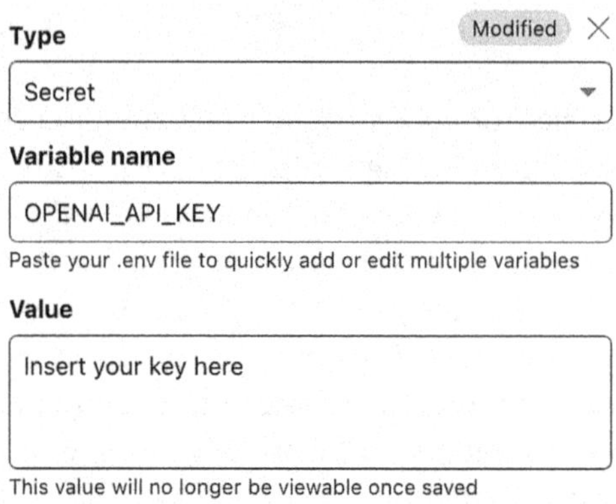

Figure 10-42: *Creating a secret key*

Do It Yourself

Go to your Cloudflare account, click on Account Home, click on the name of the Worker, and open the Settings tab (Figure 10-41, number 1). In the Variables and Secrets section, click Add (Figure 10-41, number 2), select the type Secret, enter a name to identify the variable (e.g., OPENAI_API_KEY), paste your OpenAI key in the Value field, and press the Deploy button to save it.

Once our key is securely stored on Cloudflare's servers, we can start sending requests to the OpenAI models from our Worker. To do this, the Worker needs access to the OpenAI library. The following is the command we need to run from the Worker's folder to install this library in our computer.

Listing 10-17: Installing OpenAI API

```
npm install openai
```

This command creates a folder inside our Worker with all the code required to perform requests to OpenAI models and process their response. Now we can import this library from our Worker and perform requests to OpenAI servers. The following code shows a simple implementation.

Listing 10-18: Accessing OpenAI models from the Worker

```
import OpenAI from "openai";

export default {
  async fetch(request, env, ctx) {
    const openai = new OpenAI({
      apiKey: env.OPENAI_API_KEY
    })
    try {
      const response = await openai.responses.create({
        model: "gpt-5",
        input: "[{ role: 'user', content: 'Hello' }]",
        store: false,
        max_output_tokens: 2000
      });
      return new Response(JSON.stringify(response))
    } catch(e) {
      return new Response(JSON.stringify({ error: e.message }), {
        status: 500 });
    }
  }
};
```

As illustrated by this example, we first must import the OpenAI library and then create the request in the **`fetch()`** method. The request is built using the **`OpenAI`** object, which accepts an object for configuration. In this case, we specify the **`apiKey`** option with our API key (the same value we securely stored in the previous step).

The OpenAI API includes the **`create()`** method to perform a request. This method takes an object with the request's parameters, sends the request to OpenAI's servers, and waits for the response. Once the data from OpenAI servers arrives, we convert it into JSON with the **`stringify()`** method and send it back as a response.

In this example, we send the message "Hello" to the gpt-5 model, so after deploying this new Worker to Cloudflare's servers, if we open the Worker from our browser, we will see JSON code as a response, as shown below.

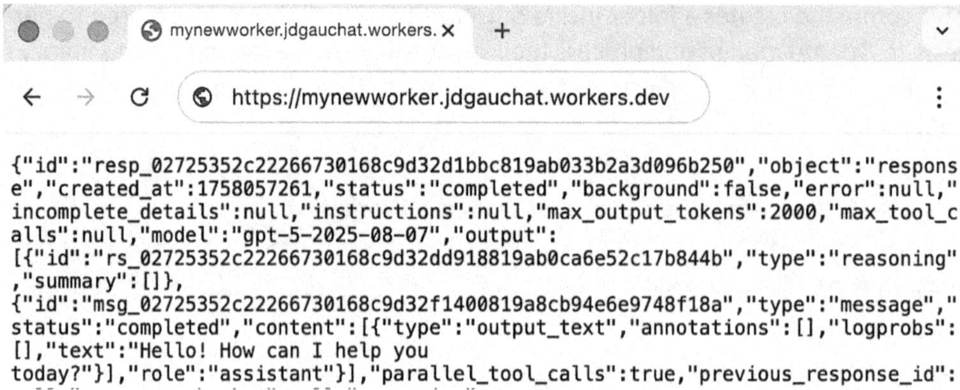

Figure 10-43: *OpenAI response*

> **Do It Yourself**
>
> Open the Worker's folder in Terminal. Type the command **npm install openai** to install the OpenAI library. You should see a new folder called **openai** inside the **node_modules** folder. Update the **worker.js** file with the code in Listing 10-18. Type the command **npx wrangler deploy** to deploy the Worker to Cloudflare servers again. Enter your Worker's URL in a browser. After a few seconds, you should see the JSON response on the screen, as shown in Figure 10-43.

> **IMPORTANT**
>
> The code for the OpenAI API is loaded and added to the Worker in the background. If you go to your Cloudflare account and try to edit the code in the browser, you will see many additional lines above your own code.

Implementation

In the last example, we always performed the same request and sent the same prompt to the model. Of course, this is not what we want. Instead, we want to take the user's prompt, send it to the Worker, and display the response back to the user. This means that the application must be programmed to send the user's prompt to the Worker, and the Worker must be programmed to integrate this prompt into the request, forward it to the OpenAI model, and send back the response to the application. For this, we can start from the previous application (see Listing 10-7). All we need to do is modify our `ApplicationData` class, as shown next.

Listing 10-19: Using a Worker from our app

```
import SwiftUI
import Observation

class ApplicationData {
   var response: AttributedString = ""
   var prompt: String = ""

   static let shared: ApplicationData = ApplicationData()
   private init() { }

   func sendPrompt() async {
      guard !prompt.isEmpty else { return }

      // Prepare JSON instructions
      let jsonbody: [[String: String]] = [["role": "user",
         "content": prompt]]
      guard let jsonData = try? JSONSerialization.data(withJSONObject:
         jsonbody) else { return }

      guard let url = URL(string: "https://mynewworker.jdgauchat.workers
         .dev") else { return }

      // Prepare URL request
      var urlRequest = URLRequest(url: url)
      urlRequest.httpMethod = "POST"
      urlRequest.httpBody = jsonData
      urlRequest.addValue("application/json",
         forHTTPHeaderField: "Content-Type")

      do {
         let (data, urlResponse) = try await URLSession.shared.data(
            for: urlRequest)
         if let httpResponse = urlResponse as? HTTPURLResponse {
            if httpResponse.statusCode == 200 {
               let chatresponse = try JSONDecoder().decode(ChatResponse
                  .self, from: data)
               for item in chatresponse.output {
                  if item.type == "message", let content = item.content {
                     for part in content {
                        if part.type == "output_text",
                           let answer = part.text {
                           var newResponse = AttributedString(
                              "\(answer)\n\n")
                           newResponse.font = .system(size: 16,
                              weight: .regular)
                           response.append(newResponse)
                        }
                     }
                  }
               }
            } else {
               response = AttributedString("Error \(httpResponse
                  .statusCode): \(String(data: data, encoding: .utf8) ??
                  "No additional information.")")
            }
      }
```

```
        } catch {
           response = AttributedString("Error accessing the API: \(error)")
        }
        prompt = ""
     }
}
```

Since the Worker now handles preparing and sending the request, this code only needs to create the JSON object with the user's prompt and send it to the Worker. Note that now the request is not send to the OpenAI URL, but to the Worker's URL.

With this code, we are sending the user's prompt to the Worker. Now we need to modify the Worker to receive this value and prepare the request.

Listing 10-20: Sending the user's prompt from the Worker

```
import OpenAI from "openai";

export default {
  async fetch(request, env, ctx) {
    const openai = new OpenAI({
      apiKey: env.OPENAI_API_KEY
    })
    try {
      const userPrompt = await request.json()

      const messages = [
        {
          role: "system",
          content: "You are a friendly AI that likes to chat with the
             user."
        },
        ...userPrompt
      ];

      const response = await openai.responses.create({
        model: "gpt-5",
        input: messages,
        store: false,
        max_output_tokens: 2000
      });
      return new Response(JSON.stringify(response))
    } catch(e) {
      return new Response(JSON.stringify({ error: e.message }), {
        status: 500 });
    }
  }
};
```

The **fetch()** method receives the request from our application. This request contains data in its body, which we parse into JSON with the **json()** method and then combine with the rest of the instructions for the API. In this case, we add a system prompt (instructions for the model on how to behave) but keep the rest of the request unchanged.

After deploying this Worker to Cloudflare's servers, we can run our app and send messages to the OpenAI model. The result is the same as before, but this time the request is routed through the Worker.

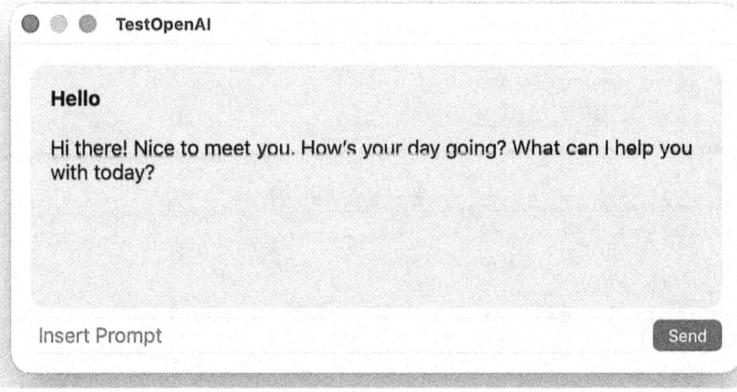

Figure 10-44: *Chatting with the model through the Worker*

Do It Yourself

In this example, we assume we are working with the project started in the previous section (see Listing 10-7). You will need the `ApplicationData` class from Listing 10-7, the `ChatResponse` structure from Listing 10-8, and the `ContentView` view from Listing 10-9. Update the `ApplicationData` class with the code in Listing 10-19 and replace the URL in the code with your Worker's URL. Update the **worker.js** file with the code in Listing 10-20. Open the Worker's folder in Terminal and type the command **npx wrangler deploy** to deploy the Worker to Cloudflare's servers. Run the application on your Mac. You should be able to chat with the model, as shown in Figure 10-44.

The OpenAI API provides several ways to configure requests and customize responses. For example, we can use Function Calling to connect models with external tools (similar to Tool Calling in Foundation Models), or generate structured outputs to ensure the response follows a JSON schema we define (similar to Guided Generation in Foundation Models). The list of options is extensive, and it is not the purpose of this book to cover them all. Fortunately, they share similar characteristics and are implemented in much the same way as with other AI systems and models. For instance, if we want to receive a structured response from the OpenAI model, we follow a process similar to the one used previously with Foundation Models: we define the JSON schema, send it with the request, and then convert the response into a Swift structure. The next example demonstrates how to implement this procedure.

The Worker we need for this example is similar to the one we used before, but now we must specify the format of the JSON object we want the model to return. In the following example, we define a format that requires the model to include the name of the city the user is talking about, the country where that city is located, the language spoken in that country, the currency used, and a list of tourist attractions.

Listing 10-21: Creating a JSON schema for the model

```
import OpenAI from "openai";

export default {
  async fetch(request, env, ctx) {
    const openai = new OpenAI({
      apiKey: env.OPENAI_API_KEY
    })
    try {
      const userPrompt = await request.json()
      const messages = [
        {
          role: "system",
          content: "Determine the city referenced by the user and return
              information about it."
        },
        ...userPrompt
      ];
      const format = {
        "format": {
            "type": "json_schema",
            "name": "Info-Cities",
            "schema": {
              "type": "object",
              "properties": {
                "city": {
                  "type": "string",
                  "description": "The name of the city."
                },
                "country": {
                  "type": "string",
                  "description": "The country where the city is located."
                },
                "language": {
                  "type": "string",
                  "description": "The main spoken language in the city."
                },
                "currency": {
                  "type": "string",
                  "description": "The official currency used in the city."
                },
                "attractions": {
                  "type": "array",
                  "description": "Five tourists attractions in this
                      city.",
                  "items": { "type": "string" },
                }
              },
              "required": ["city", "country", "language", "currency",
                  "attractions"],
              "additionalProperties": false
            },
            "strict": true
        }
      };
```

```
      const response = await openai.responses.create({
        model: "gpt-5",
        input: messages,
        text: format,
        store: false,
        max_output_tokens: 2000
      });
      return new Response(JSON.stringify(response))
    } catch(e) {
      return new Response(JSON.stringify({ error: e.message }), {
        status: 500 });
    }
  }
};
```

The format includes a property called **required**, which provides a list of all the parameters the response must include, and another called **strict**, which specifies whether the model should strictly follow the instructions. After defining the format, we add it to the request as the value of the **text** instruction. The rest of the parameters remain the same.

The **ApplicationData** class doesn't change much either. We need to create a JSON object with the user's prompt and send the request to the Worker, but this time the response is returned as JSON rather than plain text, so we must convert it into a Swift structure to read its values, as shown below.

Listing 10-22: Parsing a JSON response

```
import SwiftUI
import Observation

class ApplicationData {
   var response: AttributedString = ""
   var prompt: String = ""

   static let shared: ApplicationData = ApplicationData()
   private init() { }

   func sendPrompt() async {
      guard !prompt.isEmpty else { return }

      // Prepare JSON instructions
      let jsonbody: [[String: String]] = [["role": "user",
         "content": prompt]]
      guard let jsonData = try? JSONSerialization.data(withJSONObject:
         jsonbody) else { return }
      guard let url = URL(string: "https://mynewworker.jdgauchat.workers.
         dev") else { return }

      // Prepare URL request
      var urlRequest = URLRequest(url: url)
      urlRequest.httpMethod = "POST"
      urlRequest.httpBody = jsonData
      urlRequest.addValue("application/json",
         forHTTPHeaderField: "Content-Type")
```

```
        do {
            let (data, urlResponse) = try await URLSession.shared.data(
                for: urlRequest)

            if let httpResponse = urlResponse as? HTTPURLResponse {
                if httpResponse.statusCode == 200 {
                    let chatresponse = try JSONDecoder().decode(ChatResponse
                        .self, from: data)
                    for item in chatresponse.output {
                        if item.type == "message", let content = item.content {
                            for part in content {
                                if part.type == "output_text",
                                    let answer = part.text {
                                    let message = try parseCity(text: answer)
                                    var newResponse = AttributedString(
                                        "\(message)\n\n")
                                    newResponse.font = .system(size: 16,
                                        weight: .regular)
                                    response.append(newResponse)
                                }
                            }
                        }
                    }
                } else {
                    response = AttributedString("Error \(httpResponse
                        .statusCode): \(String(data: data, encoding: .utf8) ??
                        "No additional information.")")
                }
            }
        } catch {
            response = AttributedString("Error accessing the API: \(error)")
        }
        prompt = ""
    }
    func parseCity(text: String) throws -> String {
        let citydata = Data(text.utf8)
        let cityresponse = try JSONDecoder().decode(CityResponse.self,
            from: citydata)

        var message = "\(cityresponse.city ?? "Undefined")\n"
        message += "\(cityresponse.country ?? "Undefined")\n"
        message += "\(cityresponse.language ?? "Undefined")\n"
        message += "\(cityresponse.currency ?? "Undefined")\n"
        message += "\(cityresponse.attractions?.joined(separator: ",") ??
            "Undefined")\n\n"
        return message
    }
}
```

In this example, we create a new method called **parseCity()** to turn the JSON object into a Swift structure. The following is the definition of this structure.

Listing 10-23: Structure to parse the JSON response

```
import SwiftUI
```

```
struct CityResponse: Codable {
   let city: String?
   let country: String?
   let language: String?
   let currency: String?
   let attractions: [String]?
}
```

Now we can send a prompt with the name of a city and receive a response that includes all these values.

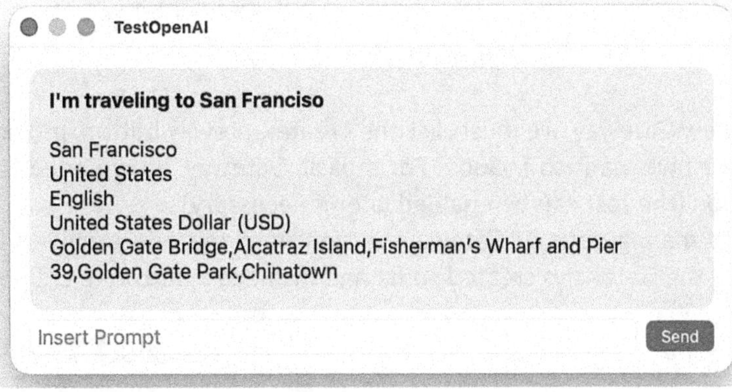

Figure 10-45: *JSON response*

Do It Yourself

Update the **worker.js** file with the code in Listing 10-21. Open the Worker's folder in Terminal and type the command **npx wrangler deploy** to deploy the Worker to Cloudflare's servers. Update the **ApplicationData** class with the code in Listing 10-22. Create a new Swift file called CityResponse.swift with the structure in Listing 10-23. Run the application and enter the name of a city. You should see something similar to Figure 10-45.

AI Gateway

Every time we send a prompt to OpenAI, our account is charged. The cost depends on the model we are using. In our examples, we have always used the gpt-5 model, but as mentioned earlier, other models are also available. The rates are quite affordable, but extensive use can lead to high charges. Hiding our API key with a Worker is extremely important to prevent abuse, but it is not the perfect solution. To avoid unexpected charges, we can periodically replace our API key, but sometimes that is not enough. To better control usage and prevent abuse, Cloudflare offers a service called AI Gateway.

AI Gateway allows us to funnel all our AI requests through a single system, which makes it easier to track cost, enforce limits, and add guardrails for safety. The system is available on the AI menu, as shown below.

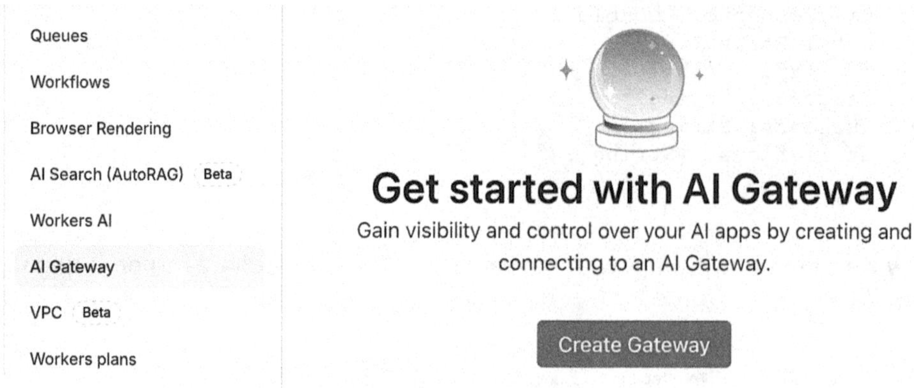

Figure 10-46: *AI Gateway*

To create a new Gateway, we must click the Create Gateway button, provide a name, and select the features we want to include. For a basic Gateway, all we need is to enable the Collect logs option (the rest can be enabled later if necessary).

The panel to manage our AI Gateways is similar to the one provided for Workers. It shows a list of all the Gateways created so far and includes a button to create more.

Figure 10-47: *Gateway list*

For the Gateway to control API usage, we must assign the Gateway URL to the OpenAI API in our Worker, so all requests pass through it. We can find the information we need in the Overview panel. Below Metrics, there is a section called Usage Examples with sample code that show how to use the Gateway with each service provider. Figure 10-48, below, shows what we see when we select the OpenAI option.

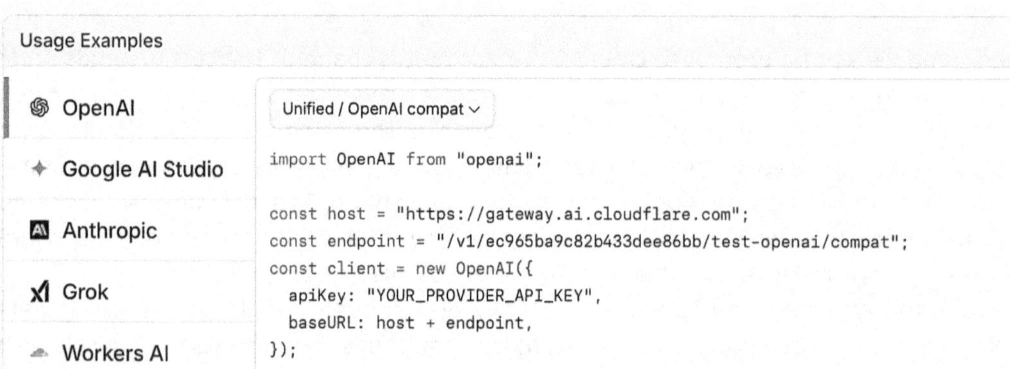

Figure 10-48: *Usage examples*

We can copy and paste this code into our Worker as it is, or add the **baseURL** argument with the Gateway URL ourselves, as shown below.

Listing 10-24: Using a Gateway

```
const openai = new OpenAI({
    apiKey: env.OPENAI_API_KEY,
    baseURL: 'https://gateway.ai.cloudflare.com/v1/beds5633nbsndb2bjb334dd/
        test-openai/compat'
})
```

Do It Yourself

Go to your Cloudflare account, open the AI Gateway panel, and click the Create Gateway button (Figure 10-46). Enter a name for the Gateway and press the Create button. From the Gateway panel, select the Gateway you just created (Figure 10-47), go down to the Usage Examples section, select OpenAI (Figure 10-48), and update the Worker with the Gateway URL, as we did in the code of Listing 10-24. Now all your requests will go through the Gateway, allowing you to control and manage your app's traffic and consumption.

Chapter 11

Neural Networks

11.1 - How Neural Networks Work

Apple has not only integrated artificial intelligence models across its platforms, but has also designed hardware capable of running and training these models. Apple computers use unified memory, a shared memory architecture that allows the CPU (central processing unit) and GPU (graphics processing unit) to access the same pool of memory. This means that all system memory is available for machine learning tasks, making these computers ideal not only for running artificial intelligence models, but also for training them and conducting our own experiments. With Apple computers, we can learn how neural networks work, explore different architectures, and train custom models from scratch.

Network Architecture

As explained in Chapter 2, a neural network is composed of a mesh of interconnected neurons, each represented by a mathematical unit known as a perceptron. Each perceptron connects to other perceptrons, and its activation value directly influences the activation values of the perceptrons that follow in the network. The magnitude of this influence is determined by the strengths of the connections, known as *weights*, along with an additional parameter called the *bias*. Using these values, we compute the activation of each perceptron sequentially until the network produces a final result, as shown below.

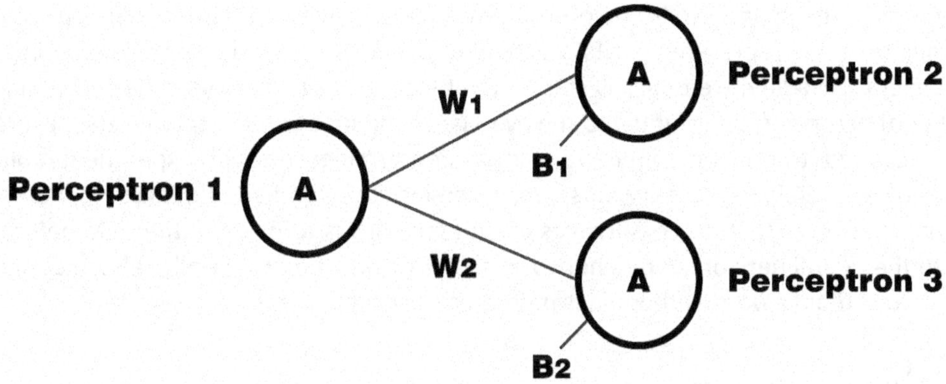

Figure 11-1: *Perceptrons connectivity*

This diagram illustrates how information flows through the network and how individual perceptrons contribute to the final output. In this example, perceptron 2 and perceptron 3 receive input from perceptron 1, so their activation values depend on the activation value of perceptron 1 and the values of the weights and biases they are associated with (**W1** and **B1** for perceptron 2, and **W2** and **B2** for perceptron 3).

The output of the network depends on the number of perceptrons it contains, their initial activation values, and the values of the weights and biases associated with each perceptron in the network. There are many ways to organize and connect these perceptrons to achieve the desired results, but in the most commonly used architecture, perceptrons are arranged in layers, with each perceptron connected to every perceptron in the subsequent layer.

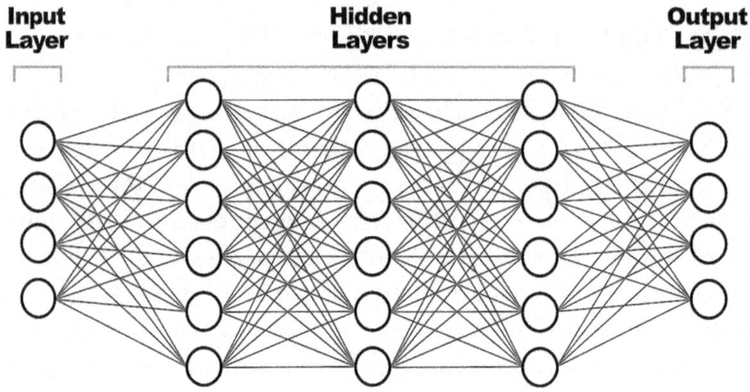

Figure 11-2: *Neural Network Layers*

In this common architecture, perceptrons are usually referred to as *neurons* or *nodes*. The first layer of neurons is called the *input layer*, and it is responsible for receiving all the values the network needs to process. The subsequent layers, known as *hidden layers*, identify associations between the inputs and the outputs, while the final layer, called the *output layer*, is responsible for delivering the results.

The first step in building a neural network is deciding how many neurons each layer should contain, which largely depends on the type of input and output the network is expected to process. For example, if we want to design a network that determines whether an image contains a dog or a cat, the input layer must include enough neurons to represent every pixel in the image, while the output layer needs only two neurons, one representing dogs and the other representing cats. The hidden layers, by contrast, are more experimental. As a general guideline, we typically start with at least two hidden layers, each containing a number of neurons roughly equal to the average of the input and output layers. Regardless of the scenario, the final architecture is always determined through experimentation and may involve multiple neural networks, preprocessing steps, and additional components. For instance, networks that process images often apply filters to prepare the data before it is sent to the neural network, while networks that work with text typically rely on additional models to compute word embeddings before processing or generating text.

Training Cycle

Once the network architecture is defined, we must initialize the weights and biases for each neuron and then train the network (gradually modify the weights and biases) until it produces the desired results. The complete process is described below.

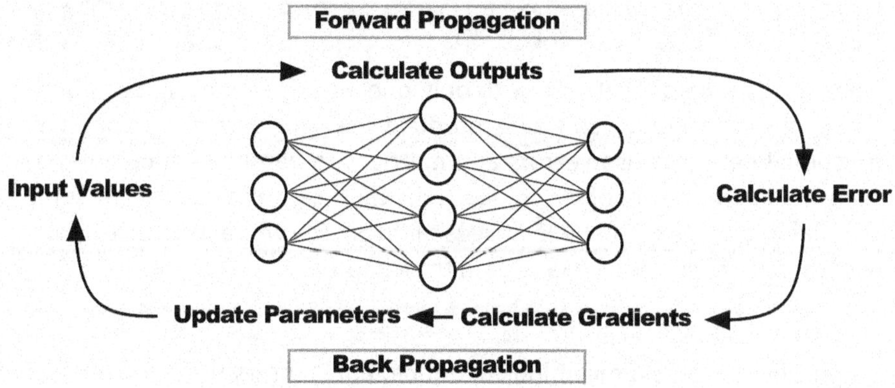

Figure 11-3: *Network Training Process*

The training process begins by initializing the network's parameters (weights and biases) with small random values, usually close to zero. Using these initial parameters along with the input values, the network calculates the activation of each neuron, one layer at a time, until it reaches the output layer in a process known as **forward propagation**. The values produced by the output layer are then compared with the expected results to compute the error (also called *loss* or *cost*). Once the error is known, we determine how much each parameter should be adjusted to reduce it, and we use these values (called *gradients*) to update the parameters in a process called **backpropagation**. With the updated parameters, the network processes the next input values and repeats the cycle until the error becomes small enough for the network to be useful or we decide that the training is complete.

Forward Propagation

The first concept we need to understand is forward propagation. Forward propagation is the process in which we compute the output of a neural network based on the input values and the network's parameters (weights and biases). We begin by assigning the input values as the activation values of the neurons in the input layer, and then compute the activation values of the neurons in the subsequent layers using the corresponding weights and biases, until we reach the output layer. To illustrate how this process works, we will use a very simple network composed of an input layer, a hidden layer, and an output layer, with only one neuron per layer, as shown below.

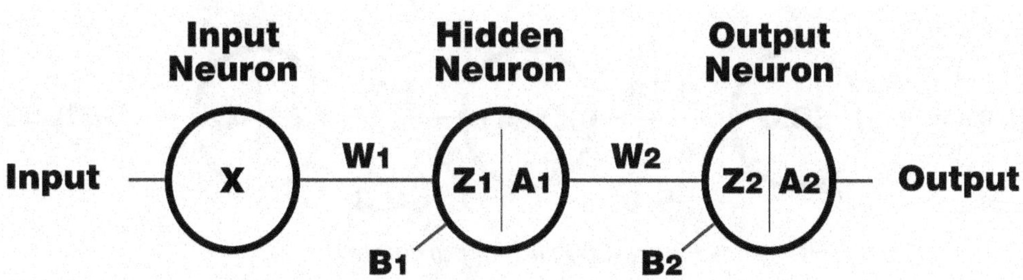

Figure 11-4: *Simple network*

IMPORTANT

Since this is a simple network with only one neuron per layer, it can only accept a single input value and produce a single output. In contrast, functional networks use vectors and matrices to handle multiple inputs, such as all the pixels of an image, and they can also process several samples at once (e.g., multiple images of dogs). We will learn how to work with more complex networks later in this chapter.

The graphic in Figure 11-4 might look daunting, but it shows the same process we have already studied in Chapter 2, except this time instead of a single neuron we have three neurons arranged in sequential layers. We begin by assigning the input value (**X**) to the input neuron. This value becomes the activation of this neuron, so no further calculation is needed at this step. The next step is to calculate the activation of the hidden neuron (**A1**). As before, this is done by multiplying the input (**X**) by the weight (**W1**) and then adding the bias (**B1**). This gives us the weighted sum for the hidden neuron (**Z1**). Once we have this value, we apply an activation function to obtain the activation value of this neuron (**A1**), as shown below.

$$Z1 = X * W1 + B1$$
$$A1 = f(Z1)$$

Figure 11-5: *Calculating the activation value of the hidden neuron*

After obtaining the activation value of the hidden neuron, we can use it as the input for the output neuron and calculate its activation value in the same way.

$$Z2 = A1 * W2 + B2$$
$$A2 = f(Z2)$$

Figure 11-6: *Calculating the activation value of output neuron*

As always, the process is easier to understand if we use real numbers. Figure 11-7 below shows the values we are going to use for our example. The weights were randomly set to 0.10 and 1.2, and the biases to -5.0 and 3.0.

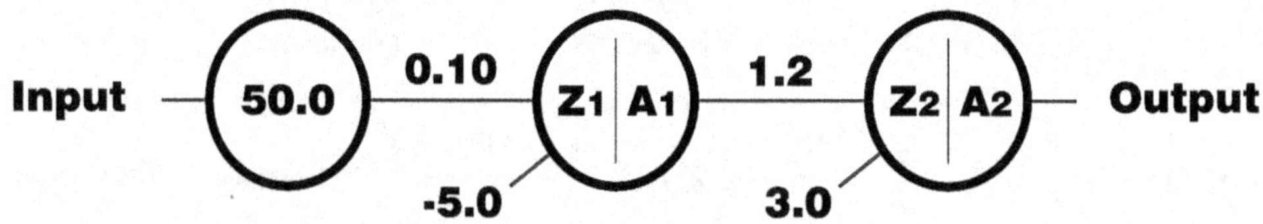

Figure 11-7: *Initial parameters*

The idea is to calculate the output when the input is equal to 50.0, so we first get the weighted sum of the hidden neuron (**Z1**).

$$Z1 = X * W1 + B1 = 50.0 * 0.10 + (-5.0) = 5 - 5 = 0.0$$

Figure 11-8: *Calculating the weighted sum for the hidden neuron*

Now that we have the weighted sum for the hidden neuron (**0.0**), we need to calculate its activation value (**A1**) using an activation function. Activation functions are required to introduce flexibility into the network. Without them, the network would only perform simple straight-line calculations and would not be able to learn more complex patterns. In Chapter 2, we used a simple step function that returns 0 if the result is negative and 1 if it is equal to or greater than zero, but there are others available, each with its own advantages and disadvantages. Figure 11-9 below shows the mathematical formulas of the activation functions most frequently used in modern neural networks.

Linear	ReLU	Sigmoid	tanh
$f(x) = x$	$\begin{cases} x \text{ if } x > 0 \\ 0 \text{ if } x <= 0 \end{cases}$	$\dfrac{1}{1 + e^{-x}}$	$\dfrac{e^{x} - e^{-x}}{e^{x} + e^{-x}}$

Figure 11-9: *Activation functions*

Again, this might look complicated, but these are actually very simple formulas. The **Linear** activation function simply returns the **Z** value without any change, the **ReLU** function returns the same value if it is greater than 0, or 0 otherwise, the **Sigmoid** function raises Euler's number (**e**) to the power of negative **Z** and then normalizes the result to return a value between 0 and 1, and the **tanh** function works in a similar way, but it subtracts and adds the results to return a value between –1 and 1. So for example, if we use the **Sigmoid** function to determine the activation value of a neuron that has a weighted sum of 5, the calculation is performed as follows.

$$A = \frac{1}{1 + e^{-5}} \approx \frac{1}{1 + 0.006738} \approx \frac{1}{1.006738} \approx 0.9933$$

Figure 11-10: *Sigmoid activation function*

As we have already mentioned, every activation function has its advantages and disadvantages, and which one we use depends on the network architecture and the task we want to accomplish. The **Linear** activation function is often used in the output layer of small networks when we want to perform a regression task, that is, when the network must produce a numerical value that can be directly applied or interpreted (for example, when we want to predict the price of a house based on its attributes and location). The **ReLU** activation function is widely used in modern neural networks because it is simple to compute and very effective for training deeper networks. The **Sigmoid** function was widely used in the past because it produces values between 0 and 1, which made it suitable for representing probabilities, but because it is less efficient, it is now only used in small networks or in the output layer for binary classification tasks. And finally, the **tanh** function is similar to the sigmoid, but it produces values between –1 and 1, which can sometimes make training more stable by centering the outputs around zero.

For our small neural network, we are going to use the **Sigmoid** function to calculate the activation value of the hidden neuron (**A1**), as shown below.

$$A1 = \frac{1}{1 + e^{-Z1}} = \frac{1}{1 + e^{-0}} = \frac{1}{1 + 1} = \frac{1}{2} = 0.50$$

Figure 11-11: *Applying the Sigmoid function to our network*

To get the value of **A1**, we use the value of **Z1** calculated earlier. In this case, **Z1** is **0.0**, and any number raised to the power of **0** is equal to **1**. This gives us the formula **1 / (1 + 1)**, which is equal to **1 / 2**, which gives us the result **0.50**.

Once we have the value of **A1**, we can use it as the input for the neuron in the output layer and calculate its activation value. The process is the same as before: we multiply the input by the weight and add the bias to get the weighted sum (**Z2**).

$$Z2 = A1 * W2 + B2 = 0.50 * 1.2 + 3.0 = 3.60$$

Figure 11-12: *Calculating the weighted sum for the output neuron*

Because we want the network to produce a value we can use directly, we will not apply an activation function to this neuron. In this case, the weighted sum itself becomes the neuron's activation value (**A2**). Since this neuron belongs to the output layer, its value represents the final output of the network. With the current configuration, this means that every time we input the value **50** into the network, the output will be **3.60**, as shown below.

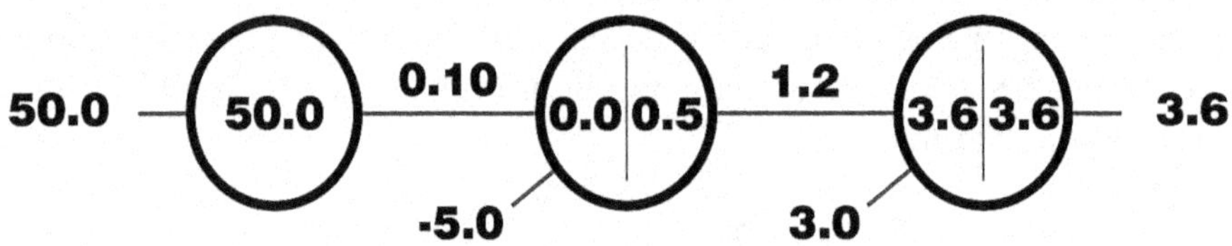

Figure 11-13: *Full forward pass*

Manually calculating the outputs of a neural network, as we did so far, is only practical when dealing with a very small number of neurons. Once we move on to more complex and practical networks, the number of calculations becomes so large that only computers can handle them. This means that if we want to turn our simple network into something useful, we must translate everything we have done so far into code. There are many ways to organize the code for building and training a neural network. In our case, we will begin by creating a class to store all the values the network needs to function, as shown below.

Listing 11-1: Storing the values of a neural network

```
import SwiftUI

class NetworkData {
   let input: Double = 50.0
   let target: Double = 15.0
```

```
    var weight1: Double = 0.10
    var bias1: Double = -5.0
    var weight2: Double = 1.2
    var bias2: Double = 3.0

    var z1: Double = 0.0
    var a1: Double = 0.0

    var gradW2: Double = 0.0
    var gradB2: Double = 0.0
    var gradW1: Double = 0.0
    var gradB1: Double = 0.0
}
```

The first two properties of our **NetworkData** class provide the input value (**50.0**) and the value we want the network to produce for that specific input (**15.0**). Next are the values for the weights and biases of each layer, as defined earlier in Figure 11-7. The remaining properties are used to store the values produced by the network and to support training, as we will see later.

As always, it is best to separate the functionality of our application from the user interface and views, so we decided to perform the training process of our network in an observable object. First, we will use this class to perform the forward pass.

Listing 11-2: Performing the forward pass

```
import SwiftUI
import Observation

@Observable class ApplicationData {
    var logs: String = ""
    var training: Bool = false

    @ObservationIgnored var data: NetworkData!

    static let shared: ApplicationData = ApplicationData()
    private init() { }

    func trainNetwork() {
        logs = ""
        training = true
        data = NetworkData()

        // Forward propagation
        let output = forwardPass()

        // Show output
        let last = String(format: "%.6f", output)
        logs += "Last Output: \(last)\n"
    }
    func forwardPass() -> Double {
        // Calculate hidden layer
        data.z1 = data.input * data.weight1 + data.bias1
        data.a1 = 1 / (1 + exp(-data.z1))
```

```
        // Calculate output layer
        let output = data.a1 * data.weight2 + data.bias2
        return output
    }
}
```

This class defines two observable properties for the views: one called **logs**, which displays the values produced by the network on the screen, and another called **training**, which notifies the views when the training starts and ends. It also defines a property called **data** to store an instance of the previously introduced **NetworkData** class, and a method called **trainNetwork()** to carry out the training process.

The **trainNetwork()** method is called from the views whenever we want to start the training process. Inside this method, we first initialize the properties to ensure we always start from scratch and then call another method called **forwardPass()** to perform forward propagation. In **forwardPass()**, we begin by calculating the weighted sum for the neuron in the hidden layer (**data.z1**), then compute its activation value using the sigmoid function (**data.a1**), and finally use this value to calculate the activation value of the output neuron (**output**). The output value is returned by the function and assigned to the **logs** property to display it on the screen. Note that to calculate the sigmoid function we use the **exp()** function provided by the **Foundation** framework. Using this functions, we calculate Euler's constant raised to the power of the negative weighted sum (**-data.z1**).

Now we just need a simple interface to let the user manage the training process. The following view includes a **Text** view to display the logs and a button to call the **trainNetwork()** method.

Listing 11-3: Controlling the training process

```
import SwiftUI

struct ContentView: View {
    @State private var appData = ApplicationData.shared

    var body: some View {
        VStack {
            Text("Neural Network")
            ScrollView {
                Text(appData.logs)
                    .font(Font.system(size: 18))
            }
            Button("Train Network") {
                appData.trainNetwork()
            }.disabled(appData.training)
        }
        .frame(minWidth: 300, maxWidth: 600, minHeight: 300, maxHeight: 600)
        .padding()
    }
}
```

When the user presses the button, the **trainNetwork()** method creates an instance of the **NetworkData** class with all the values for the network and calls the **forwardPass()**

method to process the input through the network and return the output. In this case, the input is **50.0** and the output produced by the network from the current weights and biases is **3.60**, exactly the same output we had manually calculated before.

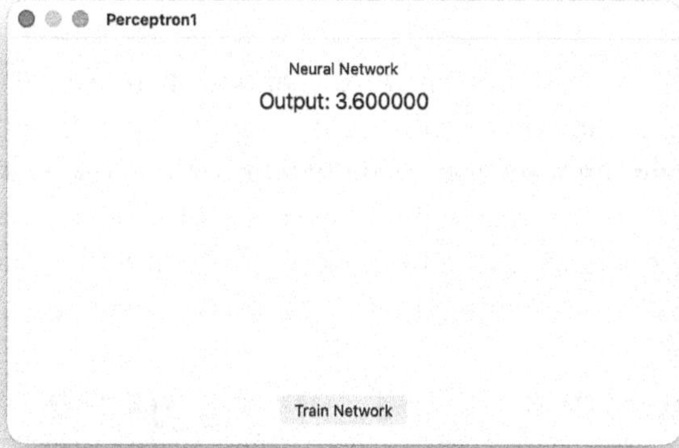

Figure 11-14: *Network output*

Do It Yourself

Create a new Multiplatform project. Create a Swift file called NetworkData.swift for the class in Listing 11-1. Create another Swift file called ApplicationData.swift for the class in Listing 11-2. Update the `ContentView` view with the code in Listing 11-3. Run the application on your Mac and press the Train Network button. You should see the message "Output: 3.600000" on the screen, as shown in Figure 11-14.

Error Functions

So far, our simple network receives the input value **50.0** and produces the output **3.60**. If this were the output we were expecting, the network would be working correctly and no adjustments would be necessary, but that is almost never the case. Since networks are initialized with random values, the output is rarely what we expect. In our example, we want the network to output **15.0** whenever it receives **50.0** as input, which means we need to train it.

The first step in training a network is to calculate the error. In our example, the value produced by the network is **3.60** and our target value is **15.0**, so we can say that the network currently produces an error of **11.40** (**15.0 – 3.60**). Although this gives us an idea of how far the network is from the expected result, this method is not reliable. More complex networks can take multiple inputs and return multiple outputs, so we need to calculate the error for every output and then get an average to know how wrong the network is. For example, if one output is off by **5** and another is off by **7**, we need to add these two values and divide by two to get the average error. In this case, **5 + 7** is **12** and **12/ 2** is equal to **6**, so the average error of the network is **6**, as shown below.

$$\begin{array}{ll} \text{output} = 9 \quad \text{target} = 4 \\ \text{output} = 8 \quad \text{target} = 1 \end{array} \rightarrow \begin{array}{l} 9 - 4 = 5 \\ 8 - 1 = 7 \end{array} \rightarrow \frac{5 + 7}{2} = \frac{12}{2} = 6$$

Figure 11-15: *Mean Error*

This is called the **Mean Error** (average error), and while it provides a general idea of the network's performance, it can still be misleading. For example, if one output is off by **−3.0** and another by **+3.0**, their differences cancel out when averaged, giving the impression that the network is performing well when, in fact, both outputs are incorrect. To avoid this issue, a common solution is to square the differences before summing them. By doing this, all errors become positive values, ensuring that none are canceled out, as shown below.

$$\begin{array}{ll} \text{output} = 6 \quad \text{target} = 9 \\ \text{output} = 4 \quad \text{target} = 1 \end{array} \rightarrow \begin{array}{l} (6 - 9)^2 = (-3)^2 = 9 \\ (4 - 1)^2 = (3)^2 = 9 \end{array} \rightarrow \frac{9 + 9}{2} = 9$$

Figure 11-16: *Mean Squared Error*

In this example, we assume that when the network outputs **6**, the expected value is **9**, and when it outputs **4**, the expected value is **1**. This yields an error of **−3** for the first sample and **+3** for the second sample. If we simply average these errors, the result is **0**, which incorrectly suggests that the network is accurate. By squaring the errors, however, both become positive, providing a more meaningful measure of the network's inaccuracy. This approach to calculating the network's error is called **Mean Squared Error** (MSE) and is defined by the following formula:

$$E = \frac{1}{n} \sum_{i=1}^{n} (\text{output}_i - \text{target}_i)^2$$

Figure 11-17: *Mean Squared Error formula*

This formula is simply a mathematical way of expressing what we just did in Figure 11-16. The sigma symbol (∑) means "sum of," the **n** at the top indicates the total number of samples, while the expression at the bottom (**i** = **1**) shows that we start the calculation with the first sample. For each sample, we subtract the target value from the network's output, square the result, and add all those squared values together. Finally, we multiply the total by **1/n**, which is the same as dividing by the number of samples. This gives us the mean squared error, or the average squared difference between the predicted values (outputs) and the expected values (targets).

MSE is useful when we want the network to predict numerical values, but when the goal is to classify data into categories (for example, determining whether an image contains a dog or a cat), a better error function is the **Cross-Entropy Loss**. Instead of looking at numerical distance, Cross-Entropy compares two sets of probabilities: the correct ones (the target values) and the ones predicted by the network. The bigger the difference between these two, the larger the error will be. For classification problems with multiple categories (classes), Cross-Entropy is defined as follows.

$$E = -\sum_{i=1}^{n} \textbf{target}_i * \log(\textbf{output}_i)$$

Figure 11-18: *Cross-Entropy Loss formula*

This formula is also easy to understand. For each sample, it multiplies the target value by the natural logarithm of the predicted value, adds all the results together, and then returns the negative of that sum. The main difference with the MSE function is that the targets are written as **one-hot encoded** vectors. These are simple arrays made up of ones and zeros that show which category is correct. For example, in a network that classifies images as either dogs or cats, the array **[1, 0]** would represent "dog," while **[0, 1]** would represent "cat." The network's predicted probabilities for the two output neurons are then compared to these vectors to calculate the error, as shown below.

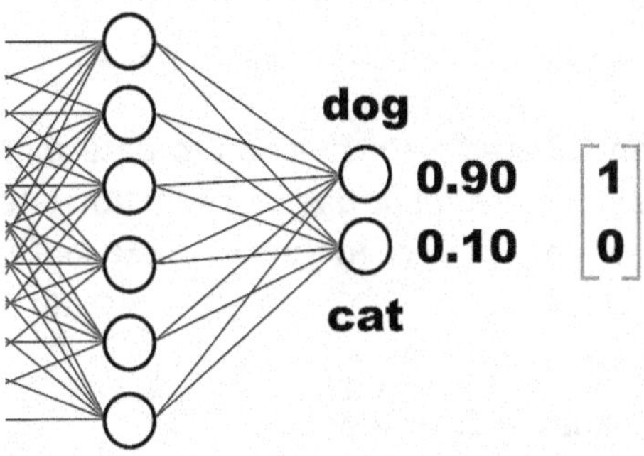

- (1 * log(0.90) + 0 * log(0.10))
- (1 * -0.10536051565783 + 0)
- (-0.10536051565783)
≈ 0.10536051565783

Figure 11-19: *Cross-Entropy errors*

In this example, the first neuron in the output layer produces a value of **0.90** and the second neuron produces a value of **0.10**. Since we are processing the image of a dog, the target is represented by the one-hot encoded vector **[1, 0]**. To calculate the error, we multiply the first target value (**1**) by the natural logarithm of the corresponding output (**0.90**), and then add the second target value (**0**) multiplied by the natural logarithm of its corresponding output (**0.10**). Because anything multiplied by **0** is **0**, the second term disappears, and we only need to calculate the logarithm of **0.90**. The final error is approximately **0.105**, which makes sense because the output neuron for "dog" is already very close to 1, so the error is small. However, one of the key strengths of the Cross-Entropy Loss function is that it heavily penalizes predictions that are confidently wrong. For example, in Figure 11-20 below, we can see the types of errors produced when the same network outputs a different set of values.

output = [0.90, 0.10]   - (1 * log(0.90) + 0 * log(0.10)) ≈ 0.105
output = [0.40, 0.60]   - (1 * log(0.40) + 0 * log(0.60)) ≈ 0.916
output = [0.01, 0.99]   - (1 * log(0.01) + 0 * log(0.99)) ≈ 4.605

Figure 11-20: *Cross-Entropy errors*

In this example, we see that when the network is almost correct, as in the first case, the error is very small (the target is **1** and the neuron's output is **0.90**, yielding an error of **0.105**). When the prediction is less accurate, as in the second case, the error increases (the target remains **1**, but the output is **0.40**, giving an error of **0.916**). Finally, when the network is completely wrong, as in the last case, the error becomes much larger (**4.605**), strongly indicating that the network requires a significant adjustment.

IMPORTANT

Mean Squared Error and Cross-Entropy Loss are the most widely used error functions, but there are many others. Some are variations of these functions, while others are experimental or specialized functions that researchers use to improve performance and develop new network architectures. For more information, visit our website and follow the links for this chapter.

For our example, we are going to use the Mean Squared Error function to determine how far off the network's prediction is. (We will apply the Cross-Entropy Loss function later in this chapter.) The following are the changes we need to introduce to the **`trainNetwork()`** function to calculate the error and show it to the user.

Listing 11-4: Calculating the error with the Mean Squared Error function

```
func trainNetwork() {
    logs = ""
    training = true
    data = NetworkData()

    // Forward propagation
    let output = forwardPass()

    // Calculate error
    let error = pow((output - data.target), 2)
    logs += "Error: \(String(format: "%.6f", error))\n"

    // Show output
    let last = String(format: "%.6f", output)
    logs += "Output: \(last)\n"
    training = false
}
```

This method works the same as before, but after performing forward propagation, we calculate the error using the output returned by the **`forwardPass()`** function, our target value (**15**), and the **`pow()`** method from the **Foundation** framework to raise the result to the power of **2**. In this case, we don't need to calculate the average error, since our simple network only handles one input and one output. When we run the application and call the **`trainNetwork()`** method again, the interface shows an error of **129.96**.

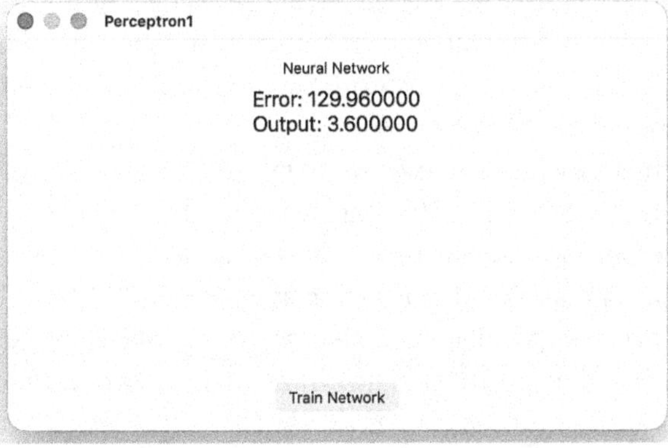

Figure 11-21: *Network's error*

Do It Yourself

Update the **`trainNetwork()`** function in the **`ApplicationData`** class with the code in Listing 11-4. Run the application and press the Train Network button. You should see the error displayed on the screen, as shown in Figure 11-21.

Back Propagation

Now that we can calculate the error, the next step is to train the network to reduce it. This means adjusting the weights and biases so that the output moves closer to the desired value. While there are different ways to approach this task, the most effective method is to calculate exactly how much each parameter should change to minimize the error using derivatives. Derivatives are mathematical tools that allow us to measure the rate of change in a system. For example, Figure 11-22 below shows a water pipe with a valve. The valve has four different positions to regulate the flow of water (**X**), and depending on its position, the amount of water flowing through the pipe will change (**Y**).

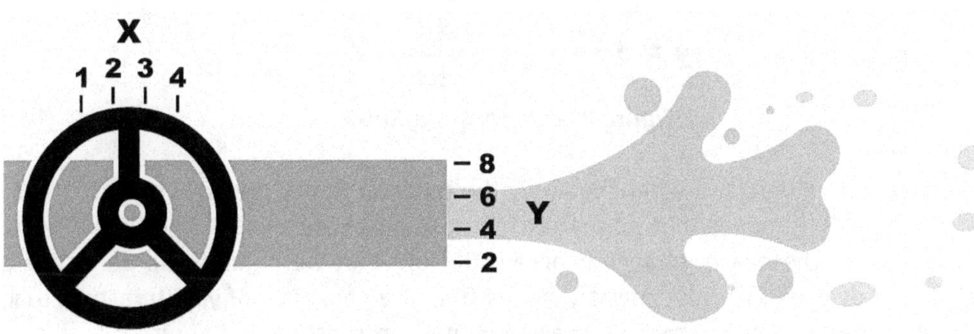

Figure 11-22: *Rate of change*

In this example, we assume that when the valve is set to **1**, the water flow is **2**; when set to **2**, the flow is **4**; at **3**, the flow is **6**; and at **4**, the flow is **8**. This shows that the rate of change in the system is **2**, meaning every time the valve increases by **1** unit, the water flow increases by **2**. Mathematically, this relationship can be expressed as **y = 2x**, where **y** represents the water flow and **x** represents the valve position. Since the rate of change is constant at **2**, the derivative of this function (the rate of change) is simply **2**.

Because this system shows a simple linear relationship between the valve and the flow of water, we were able to determine the derivative of the function numerically. However, this is not always the case. In many situations, the functions that describe the relationship between two variables, such as **X** and **Y**, can become very complex. In those cases, we need to calculate the derivative analytically. This means that instead of working with numbers, we use algebraic expressions and apply specific rules to find the derivative of a function in symbolic form.

IMPORTANT

The process of finding the derivative of a function is called *differentiation*. When we differentiate a function, we apply a set of rules that describe how the function changes with respect to its variable. Differentiation is especially important in neural networks because it tells us how much to adjust the weights and biases in order to reduce the error and improve performance. In this section, we will focus only on the aspects of differentiation needed for our examples. If you want to explore the topic in greater depth, there are many free tutorials and courses available online. For more information, visit our website and follow the links for this chapter.

There are many derivative rules that help us find the rate of change for any variable in a system, and the one we apply depends on the characteristics of the function. The simplest of these is the **Constant Rule**, which states that whenever a function contains a constant not associated with a variable, the derivative of that constant is **0**. Figure 11-23 below shows the application of this rule in a simple function.

Function	Derivative
$y = 18$	$\frac{dy}{dx} = 0$

Figure 11-23: *Constant Rule*

This is easy to understand when we apply the function to our previous example. If **Y** is always equal to 18, it means that no matter the position of the valve **X**, the flow of water never changes, so the rate of change is always **0**. Note that we defined the derivative as **dy/dx** (read as **dy** over **dx**). This notation means "the rate of change of **y** with respect to **x**," or in simpler words, "how much **y** changes every time **x** increases by one unit."

Another derivative rule is the **Power Rule**. The Power Rule states that when a variable is raised to a power, the derivative can be found by multiplying the expression by that power and then reducing the power by one. In simple terms, we bring the exponent down as a multiplier and decrease it by one to obtain the new expression, as shown below.

Function	Derivative
$y = x^3$	$\frac{dy}{dx} = 3x^{3-1} = 3x^2$

Figure 11-24: Power Rule

In this case, **x** is raised to the power of **3**, so to find the derivative we bring down the exponent as a multiplier of **x**, and then reduce the exponent by one, which gives us the derivative $3x^2$.

Another simple rule is the **Constant Multiple Rule**. This rule states that whenever a function includes a constant multiplied by a variable or expression, the constant can be carried through unchanged, and we only need to calculate the derivative of the variable or expression. For example, in the following function the constant **5** is multiplied by x^3. To apply the rule, we temporarily set aside the **5**, calculate the derivative of x^3, and then bring the **5** back into the result.

Function	Derivative
$y = 5x^3$	$5\frac{dy}{dx} = 3x^{3-1} = 5 * 3x^2 = 15x^2$

Figure 11-25: Constant Multiple Rule

These two rules, the Power Rule and the Constant Multiple Rule, are the same ones we applied earlier to determine the derivative of the function used to calculate the flow of water (**y = 2x**). Figure 11-26 below illustrates the steps we follow to obtain the derivative of this function.

Function	Derivative
$y = 2x$	$2\frac{dy}{dx} = 1x^{1-1} = 1x^0 = 2 * 1 = 2$

Figure 11-26: Applying derivative rules

In this example, we first apply the Constant Multiple Rule to set aside the **2**, then use the Power Rule to calculate the derivative of **x**, and finally bring the **2** back and calculate the result. Note that **x** is naturally raised to the power of **1**. When we subtract **1** from the exponent, we get **0**, and any value raised to the power of **0** equals **1**. This means that the derivative of **x** is **1**, and multiplying it by **2** gives us **2** (the same rate of change we found earlier).

There are a few additional rules that are useful when working with complex functions, like the ones we find in neural networks. One of these is the **Sum Rule**. This rule states that the derivative of a sum is equal to the sum of the derivatives. In other words, if two or more functions are added together, we can differentiate each function separately and then add the results. For example, if we consider the function $y = x^2 + x^4$, we can apply the Sum Rule to calculate its derivative, as shown below.

$$\frac{d\,(x^2 + x^4)}{dx} = \frac{d}{dx}(x^2) + \frac{d}{dx}(x^4) = 2x + 4x^3$$

Figure 11-27: *Sum Rule*

In this example, we differentiate each term of the function separately. The derivative of x^2 is **2x**, and the derivative of x^4 is $4x^3$. We then add these results together, giving the final derivative of the function as $2x + 4x^3$.

A similar rule is the **Difference Rule**. This rule states that the derivative of a difference is equal to the difference of the derivatives. In other words, if two functions are subtracted, we can differentiate each one separately and then subtract the results. For example, if we consider the function $y = x^2 - x^4$, we can apply the Difference Rule to calculate its derivative, as shown below.

$$\frac{d\,(x^2 - x^4)}{dx} = \frac{d}{dx}(x^2) - \frac{d}{dx}(x^4) = 2x - 4x^3$$

Figure 11-28: *Difference Rule*

There is also the **Product Rule**, which is used to differentiate a function expressed as the multiplication of two or more expressions. To apply it, we multiply the first expression by the derivative of the second, then we multiply the second expression by the derivative of the first, and finally we add those two results together. For example, if we consider the function $y = x^2 * x^4$, we can apply this rule to calculate its derivative, as shown below.

$$\begin{aligned}\frac{d\,(x^2 * x^4)}{dx} &= (x^2)\frac{d}{dx}(x^4) + (x^4)\frac{d}{dx}(x^2) \\ &= (x^2) * (4x^3) + (x^4) * (2x) \\ &= 4x^5 + 2x^5 \\ &= 6x^5\end{aligned}$$

Figure 11-29: *Product Rule*

In this example, we multiply the first expression (x^2) times the derivative of the second (x^4), plus the second expression (x^4) times the derivative of the first (x^2). This gives us $x^2 * 4x^3 + x^4 * 2x$. When multiplying terms with the same base, we can simplify the equation by adding the exponents ($x^2 * x^3 = x^5$ and $x^4 * x = x^5$), so we get the expression $4x^5 + 2x^5$. Finally, since the variables in this function have the same exponent (x^5), we can add the coefficients to get the final derivative of the function ($6x^5$).

Another similar rule is the **Quotient Rule**, which is used to differentiate a function defined as the division of two expressions. To apply it, we multiply the denominator by the derivative of the numerator, subtract the numerator multiplied by the derivative of the denominator, and then divide the entire result by the denominator squared. For example, if we consider the function $y = x^2 / x^4$, we can apply this rule to calculate its derivative, as shown below.

$$\frac{d\left(\frac{x^2}{x^4}\right)}{dx} = \frac{(x^4)\frac{d}{dx}(x^2) - (x^2)\frac{d}{dx}(x^4)}{(x^4)^2}$$

$$= \frac{(x^4) * (2x) - (x^2) * (4x^3)}{(x^4)^2}$$

$$= \frac{(2x^5) - (4x^5)}{x^8} = \frac{-2x^5}{x^8} = \frac{-2}{x^3}$$

Figure 11-30: *Quotient Rule*

> **IMPORTANT**
>
> In these examples, we could have simplified the expressions first and then differentiate the result. For instance, the function $y = x^2 * x^4$ can be simplified to $y = x^6$ (when a variable is multiplied by itself, the exponents are added). Differentiating this gives the same result as before ($6x^5$), but the Product and Quotient Rules become essential when we need to differentiate more complex functions, such as the Sigmoid or the Cross-Entropy Loss functions.

Lastly, the most interesting differentiation rule, and the most relevant for neural networks, is the **Chain Rule**. This rule is based on the concept of nested functions. It states that when we have one function inside another, we can differentiate the outer function first while keeping the inner function unchanged, and then multiply this derivative by the derivative of the inner function. For example, if we consider the function $y = (x^2 + 10)^3$, we can apply this rule to calculate its derivative. The first step is to split the nested functions into two and calculate their derivatives, as shown below.

Function	Inner Function	Outer Function
$y = (x^2 + 10)^3$	$u = x^2 + 10$	$y = (u)^3$
	$\frac{du}{dx} = 2x + 0$	$\frac{dy}{du} = 3u^2$
	$\frac{du}{dx} = 2x$	$\frac{dy}{du} = 3(x^2 + 10)^2$

Figure 11-31: *Differentiating nested functions*

The inner function in this case is $x^2 + 10$. The derivative of a constant is always **0**, so the derivative of this function is just **2x**. Next, we use this function to define the outer function ($(u)^3$) and differentiate it to get $3u^2$. Finally, we replace the inner function (**u**) with the original expression to get the final derivative of the outer function ($3(x^2 + 10)^2$).

Now that we have the derivative of **u** with respect to **x** (inner function) and the derivative of **y** with respect to **u** (outer function), we can calculate the derivative of **y** with respect to **x** by multiplying both derivatives, as shown below.

$$\frac{dy}{dx} = \frac{dy}{du} * \frac{du}{dx} \qquad \frac{dy}{dx} = 3(x^2 + 10)^2 * 2x = 6x(x^2 + 10)^2$$

Figure 11-32: *Chain Rule*

The Chain Rule is required when we need to determine how one variable changes with respect to another in a system involving multiple nested functions. To make this idea clearer, we can expand our water pipe analogy.

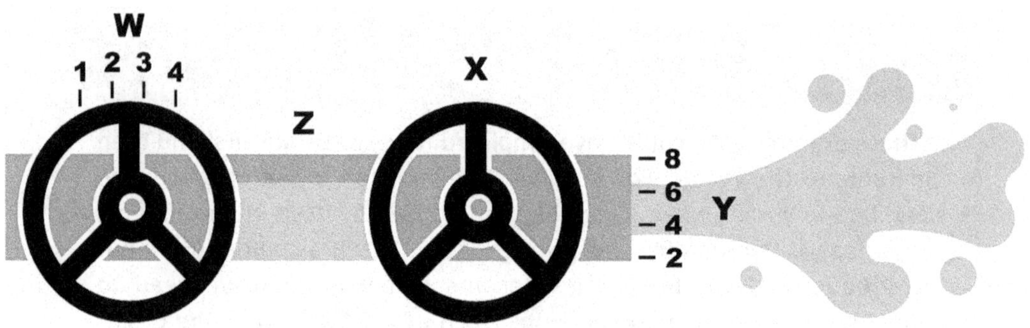

Figure 11-33: *Chain of variables*

In the previous system, we calculated the rate of change of **Y** with respect to **X**; in other words, how much **Y** changes every time the position of valve **X** is adjusted (see Figure 11-22). In algebraic terms, this is written as **dy/dx** (the derivative of **y** with respect to **x**). In this new system, however, we want to determine the rate of change of **Y** with respect to **W**, that is, how much **Y** changes when valve **W** is adjusted. But now there is an additional variable in between. **Y** does not depend directly on **W**; instead, **Y** depends on **Z** (the pressure after valve **W**), and **Z** depends on **W**. To calculate the rate of change of **Y** with respect to **W**, we must apply the Chain Rule. First, we must calculate the rate of change of **Y** with respect to **Z** (**dy/dz**), then the rate of change of **Z** with respect to **W** (**dz/dw**), and multiply them together, as shown below. (Note that when measuring the rate of change between Y and W, we treat X as constant.)

$$\frac{dy}{dw} = \frac{dy}{dz} * \frac{dz}{dw}$$

Figure 11-34: *Chain Rule to measure water flow*

The calculations are the same as before. For example, if we assume that the function **z = 2w** defines how the valve **W** affects the water pressure **Z** and the function **y = 1/4z** determines how the water pressure **Z** affects **Y**, we can apply the Chain Rule to determine how much **Y** changes when the valve **W** is adjusted, as shown below.

$$\frac{d\left(\frac{1}{4}z\right)}{dz} = \frac{1}{4}z^0 = \frac{1}{4} \qquad \frac{d\,(2w)}{dw} = 2w^0 = 2$$

$$\frac{dy}{dw} = \frac{dy}{dz} * \frac{dz}{dw} = \frac{1}{4} * 2 = \frac{2}{4} = \frac{1}{2}$$

***Figure 11-35:** Rate of change of Y with respect to W*

In this example, we first calculate **dy/dz**. The function is **y = 1/4z**. Using the Power Rule, the exponent of **z** drops from **1** to **0**, so z^0 = **1**, and the derivative is therefore **1/4** (meaning that for every unit increase in **z**, **y** increases by one-quarter). Next, we calculate **dz/dw**. The function is **z = 2w**. Again, using the Power Rule, the exponent of **w** drops from **1** to **0**, so w^0 = **1**, and the derivative is therefore **2** (meaning that for every unit increase in **w**, **z** increases by **2**). Now that we have the partial derivatives, we can determine how changes in **w** influence **y** by applying the Chain Rule. Multiplying **dy/dz** (**1/4**) by **dz/dw** (**2**) gives us **1/2**, which means that for every unit increase in **w**, **y** increases by a half.

How the Chain Rule works in this system is easy to understand if we think about the parameters of our analogy. For every unit we increase **W**, the pressure **Z** increases by **2** units. For every unit increase in **Z**, the flow **Y** increases by one-quarter. So when we increase **W** by **1**, **Z** increases by **2**, and **Y** increases by **2 * 1/4 = 1/2**. This matches exactly the rate of change we obtained by applying the Chain Rule. And this principle holds true no matter how many steps there are in the chain. By multiplying the derivatives of the intermediate steps, we obtain the rate of change between the first and last variables.

The Chain Rule is fundamental in neural networks because activation functions are applied to weighted sums, and therefore they create this kind of nested structure with a long chain of variables that we need to follow to determine how each parameter affects the error. We can see this clearly in our simple neural network (see the `forwardPass()` function in Listing 11-2). To calculate the weighted sum for the hidden neuron ($\mathbf{Z_1}$), we multiplied the input by the weight ($\mathbf{W_1}$) and added the bias ($\mathbf{B_1}$). This value was then passed through the sigmoid function to calculate the neuron's activation value ($\mathbf{A_1}$). That activation value was used next to calculate the weighted sum of the output neuron, and finally we used that output value to calculate the error. These steps form a series of nested functions, with the outermost function being the error function. Figure 11-36 below shows all the variables involved.

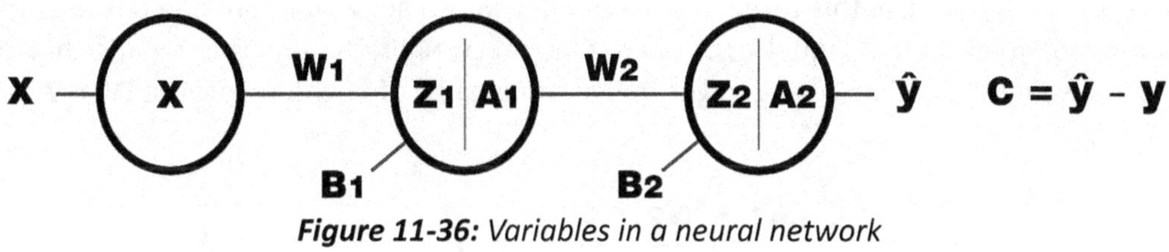

***Figure 11-36:** Variables in a neural network*

IMPORTANT

This diagram uses a slightly different notation from the previous one. We represent the input as **X**, the output as **ŷ** (read as "Y hat"), the target as **Y**, and the error as **C** (for Cost). This is the standard notation found in most books and online courses, so it is the one we will use for the rest of this chapter.

The purpose of using the Chain Rule in a neural network is to determine how much each parameter (weights and biases) influences the error so we can adjust them to make the network more accurate. In other words, we need to calculate the rate of change of **C** (the error) with respect to each parameter, working backwards from the error function in a process called *backpropagation*. For example, to calculate how **C** changes with respect to $\mathbf{W_2}$, we apply the following chain.

$$\frac{dC}{dW_2} = \frac{dC}{d\hat{y}} * \frac{d\hat{y}}{dW_2}$$

Figure 11-37: *Rate of change of C with respect to* W_2

Since we want to determine the rate of change of the error with respect to every single parameter, we must always begin by determining how the output (**ŷ**) affects the error (**dC/dŷ**), and then go backwards until we reach each parameter. In our example, we are using the square error function (**(ŷ - y)²**). This is already a nested function, so to calculate this derivative, we need to follow the same procedure as before (see Figure 11-31 and 11-32).

$$\frac{dC}{d\hat{y}} = \frac{d\,(\hat{y} - y)^2}{d\hat{y}} = 2(\hat{y} - y) * (1 - 0) = 2(\hat{y} - y)$$

Figure 11-38: *Rate of change of C with respect to ŷ*

We first calculate the derivative of the outer function **(ŷ - y)²**. By the Power Rule, this becomes **2(ŷ - y)**. Next, we differentiate the inner function **(ŷ - y)**. Since **y** is constant its derivative is **0**, and the derivative of **ŷ** is 1. Multiplying the two results, we obtain **dC/dŷ = 2(ŷ - y)**.

Now that we have determined how **ŷ** influences **C**, we need to determine how $\mathbf{W_2}$ influences **ŷ** ($\mathbf{d\hat{y}/dW_2}$). In this case, we are not applying an activation function to the output neuron, so the output is equal to $\mathbf{Z_2}$, and $\mathbf{Z_2}$ is the weighted sum. This means that the function we need to differentiate to get the rate of change of **ŷ** with respect to $\mathbf{W_2}$ is $\mathbf{Z_2 = A_1 * W_2 + B_2}$.

$$\frac{d\hat{y}}{dW_2} = \frac{d\,(A_1 * W_2 + B_2)}{dW_2} = A_1 * 1 + 0 = A_1$$

Figure 11-39: *Rate of change of ŷ with respect to* W_2

Because we are differentiating with respect to $\mathbf{W_2}$, both $\mathbf{A_1}$ and $\mathbf{B_2}$ are treated as constants. Using the Constant Rule, the derivative of $\mathbf{B_2}$ is **0**, and using the Constant Multiple Rule, we factor out $\mathbf{A_1}$ from the multiplication, differentiate $\mathbf{W_2}$ (which gives **1**), and then multiply back by **A1**. This gives the final result: $\mathbf{d\hat{y}/dW_2 = A_1}$.

Now that we have both derivatives, $\mathbf{dC/d\hat{y}}$ and $\mathbf{d\hat{y}/dW_2}$, we can apply the Chain Rule to combine them and obtain $\mathbf{dC/dW_2}$.

$$\frac{dC}{dW_2} = \frac{dC}{d\hat{y}} * \frac{d\hat{y}}{dW_2} = 2(\hat{y} - y) * A_1$$

Figure 11-40: *Rate of change of C with respect to* W_2

At this point, we know how the weight ($\mathbf{W_2}$) affects the error (**C**). Now we need to do the same for the bias ($\mathbf{B_2}$). The process is very similar. We start from the error function ($\mathbf{dC/d\hat{y}}$), then differentiate $\hat{y}$ with respect to $\mathbf{B_2}$, and finally apply the Chain Rule again to get $\mathbf{dC/dB_2}$. We already have $\mathbf{dC/d\hat{y}}$ ($\mathbf{2(\hat{y} - y)}$), so all we need is to calculate $\mathbf{d\hat{y}/dB_2}$, and multiply both derivatives, as shown below.

$$\frac{d\hat{y}}{dB_2} = \frac{d\,(A_1 * W_2 + B_2)}{dB_2} = 0 + B_2^0 = 0 + 1 = 1$$

$$\frac{dC}{dB_2} = \frac{dC}{d\hat{y}} * \frac{d\hat{y}}{dB_2} = 2(\hat{y} - y) * 1 = 2(\hat{y} - y)$$

Figure 11-41: *Rate of change of C with respect to* B_2

Because this time we are differentiating with respect to $\mathbf{B_2}$, both $\mathbf{A_1}$ and $\mathbf{W_2}$ are treated as constants (the derivative is **0**). That means we only need to differentiate $\mathbf{B_2}$, whose derivative with respect to itself is **1**. Applying the Chain Rule, we multiply this result by $\mathbf{dC/d\hat{y}}$, so the rate of change of **C** with respect to $\mathbf{B_2}$ is $\mathbf{2(\hat{y} - y)}$.

At this point, we have calculated the rate of change of the weight and bias that affects the output neuron ($\mathbf{W_2}$ and $\mathbf{B_2}$). The derivative of the weight is $\mathbf{2(\hat{y} - y) * A_1}$ and the derivative of the bias is $\mathbf{2(\hat{y} - y)}$. Now we must do the same for the remaining parameters in our network: $\mathbf{W_1}$ and $\mathbf{B_1}$. The process is as always, but this time we must pass through more intermediate functions and variables, since we not only have two weighted sums but also the sigmoid function used to compute the activation value of the hidden neuron. Figure 11-42 below shows the chain of derivatives we must compute to get the rate of change of **C** with respect to $\mathbf{W_1}$.

$$\frac{dC}{dW_1} = \frac{dC}{d\hat{y}} * \frac{d\hat{y}}{A_1} * \frac{dA_1}{dZ_1} * \frac{dZ_1}{dW_1}$$

Figure 11-42: *Rate of change of C with respect to* W_1

The chain of derivatives in a neural network can extend to hundreds of terms. A quick way to check that the chain has been written correctly is to cancel out the terms that appear in both the numerator and the denominator, until we are left with the derivative we want to calculate, as shown below.

$$\frac{dC}{dW_1} = \frac{dC}{\cancel{d\hat{y}}} * \frac{\cancel{d\hat{y}}}{\cancel{A_1}} * \frac{\cancel{dA_1}}{\cancel{dZ_1}} * \frac{\cancel{dZ_1}}{dW_1}$$

Figure 11-43: *Validating the chain*

This time, after differentiating the error function, instead of differentiating **ŷ** with respect to W_2, as we did before, we must differentiate it with respect to A_1, because A_1 is the variable through which the output connects to W_1. Since we already calculated **dC/dŷ = 2(ŷ - y)**, the next derivative we need is $d\hat{y}/dA_1$, taken from the definition of $Z_2 = A_1 * W_2 + B_2$.

$$\frac{d\hat{y}}{dA_1} = \frac{d\,(A_1 * W_2 + B_2)}{dA_1} = A_1^0 * W_2 + 0 = 1 * W_2 = W_2$$

Figure 11-44: *Rate of change of ŷ with respect to* A_1

Because we differentiate with respect to A_1, W_2 remains the same, the derivative of A_1 is A_1 raised to the power of **0**, which is equal to **1**, B_2 is treated as a constant so its derivative is equal to **0**, and therefore we get $d\hat{y}/dA_1 = W_2$.

The next derivative is dA_1/dZ_1. This is the most complex derivative in our network because it requires differentiating the sigmoid function. Figure 11-45 below shows how we perform this calculation.

$$\frac{dA_1}{dZ_1} = \frac{d\,(1 + e^{-Z})^{-1}}{dZ_1} = -(1 + e^{-Z})^{-2} * (-e^{-Z}) = \frac{e^{-Z}}{(1 + e^{-Z})^2}$$

$$= \frac{1}{1 + e^{-Z}} * \frac{e^{-Z}}{1 + e^{-Z}} = \frac{1}{1 + e^{-Z}} * \frac{(1 + e^{-Z}) - 1}{1 + e^{-Z}}$$

$$= \frac{1}{1 + e^{-Z}} * \left(\frac{1 + e^{-Z}}{1 + e^{-Z}} - \frac{1}{1 + e^{-Z}}\right) = \frac{1}{1 + e^{-Z}} * \left(1 - \frac{1}{1 + e^{-Z}}\right)$$

Figure 11-45: *Differentiating the Sigmoid function*

Although it may look intimidating at first, the derivative of the sigmoid function is actually straightforward. The only differentiation rule we need is the Power Rule, the rest is just algebraic simplification. We begin by rewriting the fraction as a power function, $(1 + e^{-z})^{-1}$, which makes it easier to differentiate. Applying the Power Rule to differentiate the nested functions gives us the expression $-(1 + e^{-z})^{-2} * (-e^{-z})$. After differentiating, we convert the expression back into fraction form, multiply the terms, and simplify step by step until we obtain a much simpler function. The key insight is that this derivative can be expressed entirely in terms of the sigmoid function itself: it is the sigmoid multiplied by one minus the sigmoid. If we denote the sigmoid by **S**, then the derivative is $dA_1/dZ_1 = S * (1 - S)$.

Lastly, we need to calculate the derivative dZ_1/dW_1, which means differentiating W_1 in the function $Z_1 = X * W_1 + B_1$ (the weighted sum of the hidden neuron).

$$\frac{dZ_1}{dW_1} = \frac{d\,(X * W_1 + B_1)}{dW_1} = X * W_1^0 + 0 = X * 1 = X$$

Figure 11-46: *Rate of change of Z_1 with respect to W_1*

At last, we have all the partial derivatives required to compute **dC/dW$_1$**. All we need to do is to apply the Chain Rule (see Figure 11-42).

$$\frac{dC}{dW_1} = 2(\hat{y} - y) * W_2 * (S * (1 - S)) * X$$

Figure 11-47: *Derivative of the error function with respect to W_1*

Of course, our work is not over, we still need to calculate the rate of change of **C** with respect to the bias (**B1**). Fortunately, most of the derivatives we need have been calculated already, as shown in the expression below.

$$\frac{dC}{dB_1} = \frac{dC}{d\hat{y}} * \frac{d\hat{y}}{A_1} * \frac{dA_1}{dZ_1} * \frac{dZ_1}{dB_1}$$

Figure 11-48: *Rate of change of C with respect to B_1*

The only partial derivative we don't have yet is **dZ1/dB1**, which means differentiating **B$_1$** in the function **Z$_1$ = X * W$_1$ + B$_1$** (the weighted sum of the hidden neuron).

$$\frac{dZ_1}{dB_1} = \frac{d\,(X * W_1 + B_1)}{dB_1} = 0 + B_1^0 = 1$$

Figure 11-49: *Rate of change of Z_1 with respect to B_1*

Since we are differentiating with respect to **B$_1$**, all other variables are treated as constants, so after differentiating **B$_1$**, we get **1**. Now we can apply the Chain Rule again to get the derivative **dC/dB$_1$**.

$$\frac{dC}{dB_1} = 2(\hat{y} - y) * W_2 * (S * (1 - S)) * 1$$

Figure 11-50: *Derivative of the error function with respect to B_1*

After completing these steps, we now have all the derivatives required to calculate the rate of change of the error with respect to every parameter in the network. This means that we are ready to translate the process into code and begin training our network. Since we already computed all the necessary values during forward propagation, and our `NetworkData` class includes properties to store them (see Listing 11-1), all we need is to define a method to perform the calculations.

Listing 11-5: Performing backpropagation

```
func backPropagation(output: Double) {
    // Calculate Output layer
    data.gradW2 = 2 * (output - data.target) * data.a1
    data.gradB2 = 2 * (output - data.target) * 1

    // Calculate Hidden layer
    let sigmoidDerivative = data.a1 * (1 - data.a1)
    data.gradW1 = 2 * (output - data.target) * data.weight2
        * sigmoidDerivative * data.input
    data.gradB1 = 2 * (output - data.target) * data.weight2
        * sigmoidDerivative * 1
}
```

The **backPropagation()** method in Listing 11-5 receives the output produced by the **forwardPass()** method and then calculates the derivatives. We begin with the parameters in the output layer (**W_2** and **B_2**). First, we use the function derived earlier to compute the rate of change of **C** with respect to **W_2** (see Figure 11-40), and then we do the same for the bias (see Figure 11-41).

After computing the derivatives for the output layer, we continue with the hidden layer. Here, we apply the functions for **dC/dW_1** and **dC/dB_1** (see Figures 11-47 and 11-48). Note that since the derivative of the sigmoid function appears twice in these calculations, we evaluate it first to save time, and because we have already stored the result of the sigmoid in the **a1** property during forward propagation, we reuse that value instead of calculating the sigmoid function again.

Do It Yourself

Add the method in Listing 11-5 to the **ApplicationData** class (below the **forwardPass()** method). We will use the values produced by this method in the next section to optimize the network.

IMPORTANT

Backpropagation is a straightforward process, but because it involves many steps, it can be difficult to grasp at first. In this section, we use the water pipe analogy proposed by Brandon Rohrer on his website (**www.brandonrohrer.com**). However, there are many other tutorials and examples online that present the idea in different ways and can make the concept easier to understand. For more information, visit our website and follow the links for this chapter.

Optimization

Now that we know how much each parameter influences the error, we can start adjusting them to reduce it. This process is called *Optimization*, and it is carried out using a method known as gradient descent. Gradient descent has long been used to find the values that minimize the output of a function. The concept is straightforward: if we picture the function as a curve on a graph, then finding the minimum is like moving downhill along the curve until reaching the lowest point. By repeatedly adjusting the parameters in this downhill direction, we gradually approach the minimum, as illustrated below.

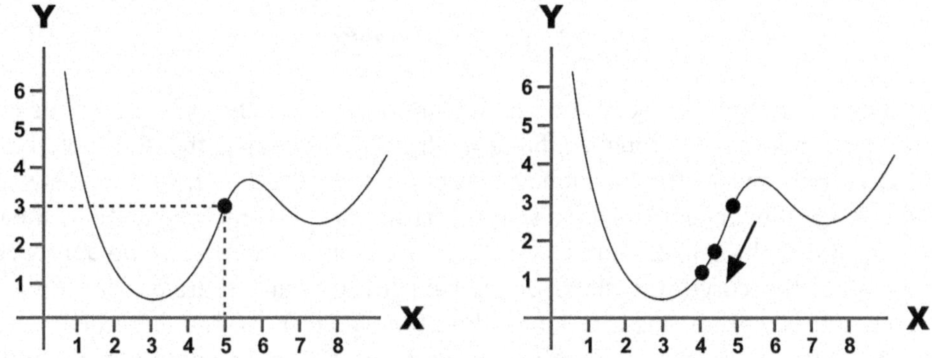

Figure 11-51: *Gradient descent*

Figure 11-51 shows the graphical representation of a function. The curve is obtained by taking different values of **X**, calculating the corresponding output of the function, and plotting the points where each **X** value intersects with its result on the **Y** axis. In the graph on the left, we see that when **X = 5**, the function returns **Y = 3**. If our goal is to find values of **X** that make the function return a smaller output (a smaller **Y**), we need to move downhill along the curve. The graph on the right illustrates this idea. Starting from our initial point on the curve, we adjust **X** step by step in the downhill direction until we approach the lowest value of **Y** possible.

The process is easy to follow in a two-dimensional graph like this one, but neural networks work with hundreds or even thousands of values at once, creating a multidimensional surface that we cannot visualize. To handle this complexity, we use the derivatives we calculate during backpropagation. A derivative tells us not only the rate of change of one variable with respect to another, but also the slope of the tangent line at a given point on the curve, as shown below.

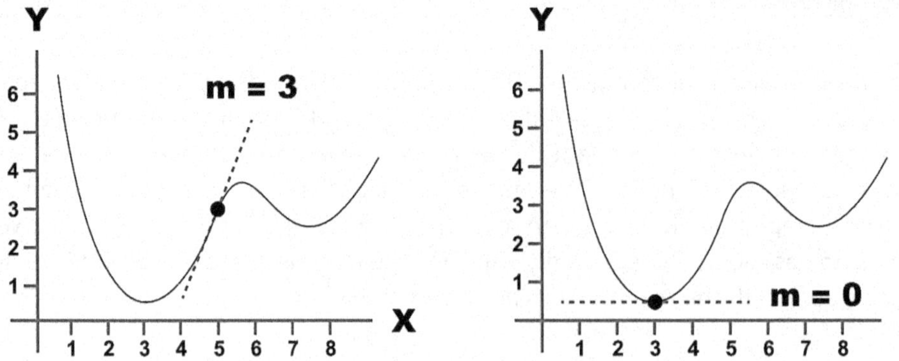

Figure 11-52: *Gradient descent*

The tangent line can be thought of as the line that passes through two points on the curve. If those points are brought infinitesimally close together, the slope of that line becomes the derivative of the function at that point. In Figure 11-52, we can see why this matters: at **X** = **5**, the tangent line has a slope of **3** (the slope is usually denoted by the letter **m**), while at **X** = **3**, the tangent line has a slope of **0**. This shows that as we approach the lowest point of the curve, the slope of the tangent line, and therefore the derivative, approaches zero. By examining the slope values (derivatives), we can determine both the direction in which we need to adjust the parameters to reduce the output of the function and the rate at which we should make those adjustments in order to reach the lowest point of the function.

This is how we optimize a network: we calculate the derivatives during backpropagation and then use these values to adjust the parameters in order to reduce the error. However, finding the lowest point of a function using derivatives introduces two challenges. First, if we rely only on the rate of change given by the derivatives, the parameter values may jump around the curve, making it hard to settle at the lowest point (Figure 11-53, left). Second, because neural networks process many values at once, the error function can have multiple low points. In such cases, we might end up in a local minimum instead of the absolute lowest point, known as the global minimum (Figure 11-53, right).

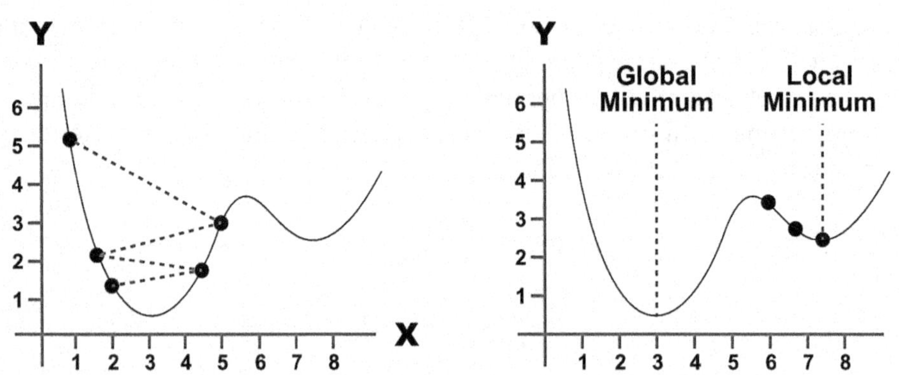

Figure 11-53: *Issues with gradient descent*

There are many strategies we can follow to avoid these issues. The most common is to use a learning rate, a small value that, when applied to the rate of change of each parameter, gradually leads us to the optimal result. As shown in the right graph of Figure 11-51, applying a learning rate reduces the error one small step at a time, increasing the chances of reaching a minimum. To reduce the risk of getting trapped in a local minimum, some systems use random batches of samples when training (for example, feeding the network images in random order instead of sequentially). Others adjust the learning rate over time, or even experiment with random variations of it, and researchers are constantly developing new strategies to achieve the best results. In our case, we are working with a simple network that processes just one input and produces one output, so using a learning rate alone is enough to optimize the parameters. The following is the method we will use to perform this optimization.

Listing 11-6: Optimizing the neural network

```
func optimization(rate: Double) {
   data.weight1 = data.weight1 - rate * data.gradW1
   data.bias1 = data.bias1 - rate * data.gradB1
   data.weight2 = data.weight2 - rate * data.gradW2
   data.bias2 = data.bias2 - rate * data.gradB2
}
```

The **optimization()** method takes the learning rate we want to use (**rate**), multiplies that value by the derivative of each parameter, and subtracts the result from the parameter's current value. We subtract because the derivative (or gradient) indicates the direction in which the error increases, and our goal is to update the parameters in the opposite direction to reduce the error.

Now that we have the **backPropagation()** method to calculate the derivatives for each parameter and the **optimization()** method to update the network, we can combine them to perform a round of training. The following are the changes we need to introduce in the **trainNetwork()** method to test this process.

Listing 11-7: Testing optimization

```
func trainNetwork() {
   logs = ""
   training = true
   data = NetworkData()

   // Forward propagation
   let output = forwardPass()

   // Calculate error
   let error = pow((output - data.target), 2)
   logs += "Error: \(String(format: "%.6f", error))\n"

   // Back propagation
   backPropagation(output: output)

   // Optimization
   optimization(rate: 0.01)
```

```
    // Show output
    let last = String(format: "%.6f", forwardPass())
    logs += "Output: \(last)\n"
    training = false
}
```

This method follows the same steps as before: we initialize the values to start training from scratch and then perform a forward pass to calculate the output. After computing the error, however, we now call the **backPropagation()** and **optimization()** methods to update the parameters of the network. In this example, we use a learning rate of **0.01**, but the ideal value depends on factors such as the type of input data, the network's configuration, and the optimization strategy being applied.

When we run the application and press the Train Network button, the **trainNetwork()** method performs one round of optimization, giving us a better result than before (a value closer to our target of **15.0**), as illustrated in Figure 11-54.

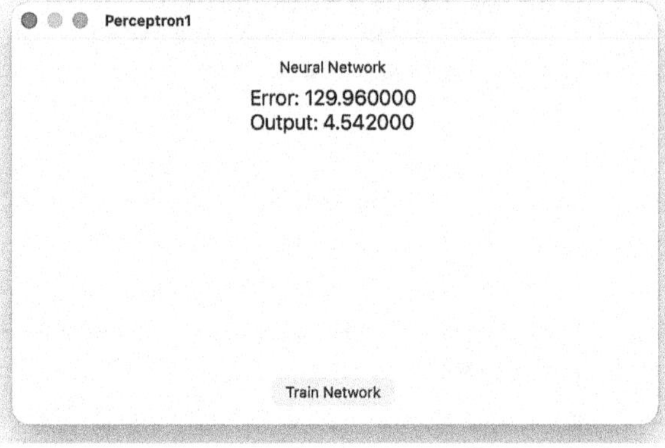

Figure 11-54: *Output after one round of optimization*

Do It Yourself

Add the **optimization()** method from Listing 11-6 to the **ApplicationData** class (below the **backPropagation()** method). Update the **trainNetwork()** method with the code in Listing 11-7. Run the application and press the Train Network button. You should see an output similar to Figure 11-54. After these changes, the network's output should be **4.542**, which is an improvement over the previous result of **3.60**, but still far from our target value of **15.0**. In the next section, we will learn how to continue training the network to move closer to this target.

IMPORTANT

The optimization method we are using in this example is the foundation of most training processes and is commonly known as Stochastic Gradient Descent (SGD). Over time, many other algorithms have been developed to improve speed, stability, and accuracy, including Momentum, RMSProp, Adam, and AdaGrad, among others. For more information, visit our website and follow the links for this chapter.

Training

In the previous example, we completed one round of the training process. This is usually called an *iteration*, which refers to a single update of the network's parameters. An iteration can occur after processing just one input value, as in our case, or after processing a batch of data. For instance, if we have 1,000 images and we process them in batches of 100, it will take 10 iterations to go through all the images once.

Because the parameters are updated gradually, the network typically needs to process the entire dataset many times before producing acceptable results. One full pass through the dataset is called an *epoch*. Training a network often requires hundreds or even thousands of epochs. In practice, this means running through the data repeatedly until the error is minimized or reduced to a satisfactory level.

In our example, we determined that about 200 epochs with a learning rate of 0.01 are needed to train the network to output the expected value (**15.0**). To accomplish this, we use a **for in** loop and call the **backPropagation()** and **optimization()** methods during each iteration to calculate the gradients and update the parameters.

Listing 11-8: Training the neural network

```
func trainNetwork() {
    let epochs = 200
    let learningRate = 0.01

    // Restart networks values
    logs = ""
    data = NetworkData()
    training = true

    for pass in 0..<epochs {
        // Forward propagation
        let output = forwardPass()

        // Calculate Error
        let error = pow((output - data.target), 2)
        if pass % 10 == 0 {
            logs += "Error: \(String(format: "%.6f", error))\n"
        }
        // Back propagation
        backPropagation(output: output)

        // Optimization
        optimization(rate: learningRate)
    }
    // Show output after training
    let last = String(format: "%.6f", forwardPass())
    logs += "Output: \(last)\n"
```

```
    training = false
}
```

At each cycle of the **for in** loop, the **backPropagation()** method recalculates the derivatives based on the most recent error, and the **optimization()** method applies gradient descent to update the parameters to reduce the error. Note that we use the modulo operator (**%**) to print the current error every 10 cycles.

Figure 11-55 below shows the results of training. After 200 epochs, the error is reduced to almost zero and the output is very close to **15.0**. In other words, we have successfully trained our simple network to always produce the value **15.0** whenever the input is **50.0**.

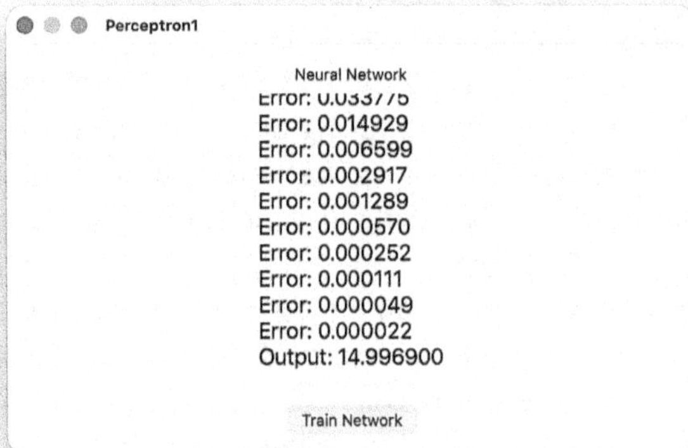

Figure 11-55: *Network training*

Do It Yourself

Update the **trainNetwork()** method in the **ApplicationData** class with the code in Listing 11-8 and run the application on your Mac again. Press the Train Network button. You should see the error gradually decrease and a final output that is close to our expected value (**15.0**).

IMPORTANT

In practice, the error almost never reaches exactly zero, and the network's output rarely matches the expected value perfectly. This is due to many factors, including the approximations made during optimization, the limited amount of data available, and the inherent complexity of the problem being solved. Despite these limitations, networks remain useful because the error can be reduced enough for the model to make accurate predictions.

11.2 - MLX Framework

Our simple neural network, with just one neuron per layer, already requires handling many values and performing complex computations, so it's easy to imagine how much harder the task becomes once we add more neurons to try to build something useful. As the number of neurons and parameters grows, the work quickly increases in complexity. To tackle this problem, companies have developed libraries that automate essential tasks such as storing values, calculating derivatives, and optimizing the network. Some of the most popular are TensorFlow, PyTorch, Keras, MXNet, and JAX. For a time, Apple lagged behind in this area, but it recently introduced a new framework called *MLX*, designed to compete with the leaders in the field. MLX was specifically built to take advantage of Apple Silicon, allowing anyone with a Mac to design and test neural networks from scratch. Originally created for Python, the most widely used language in machine learning, MLX now has a Swift version, making the framework not only fast but also easy to use for Apple developers.

The **MLX** framework comes as a package that we need to add to our project. This option is available in the project settings, as shown in Figure 11-56, below. First, we must click on the project's name in the Navigator area (number 1), then click on the project itself (number 2), select the Package Dependencies tab (number 3), and finally click the + button at the bottom of the panel to add a new package (number 4).

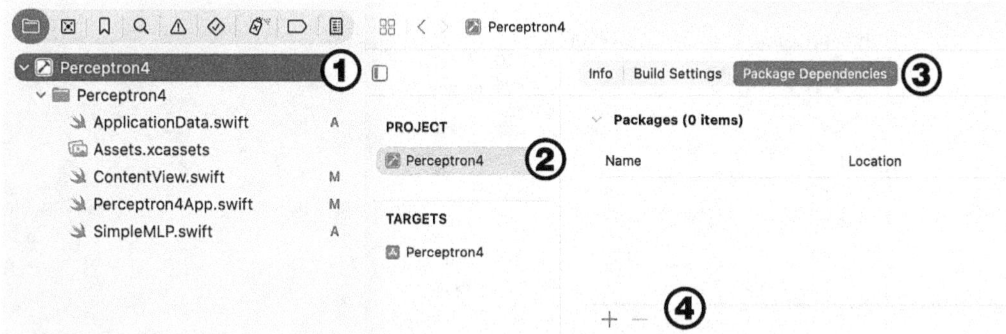

Figure 11-56: *Package Dependencies*

Packages are added from the web, which means we must provide the URL that Xcode uses to download it. The **MLX** framework is hosted on GitHub at **https://github.com/ml-explore/mlx-swift**. After entering this URL, Xcode displays information about the package, and includes the Add Package button at the bottom of the panel to add it.

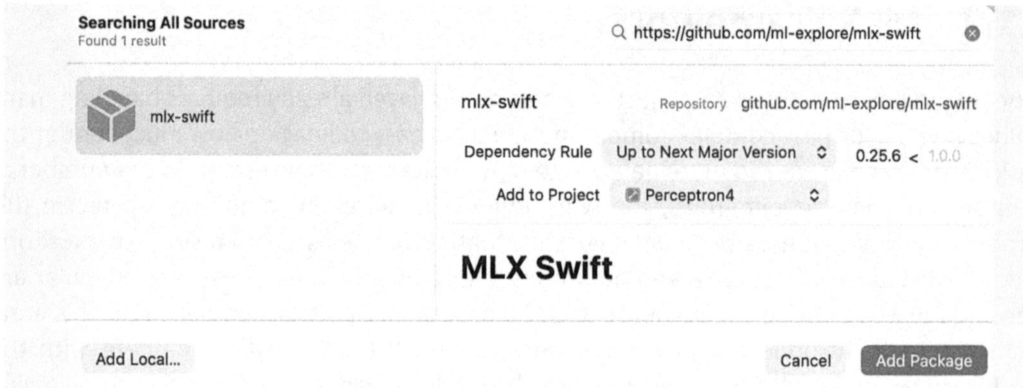

Figure 11-57: *Adding a package*

The mlx-swift package includes not only the **MLX** framework but also additional frameworks that can simplify our work. The ones we typically need are **MLX**, **MLXNN**, and **MLXOptimizers**. MLX provides the core functionality, MLXNN offers tools to design and initialize neural networks, and MLXOptimizers contains the utilities required to optimize them, including access to widely used optimizers such as SGD, Adam, RMSProp, and others. To add these frameworks to our project, in the following window, we need to assign them to the target using the option on the right, and then press the Add Package button again.

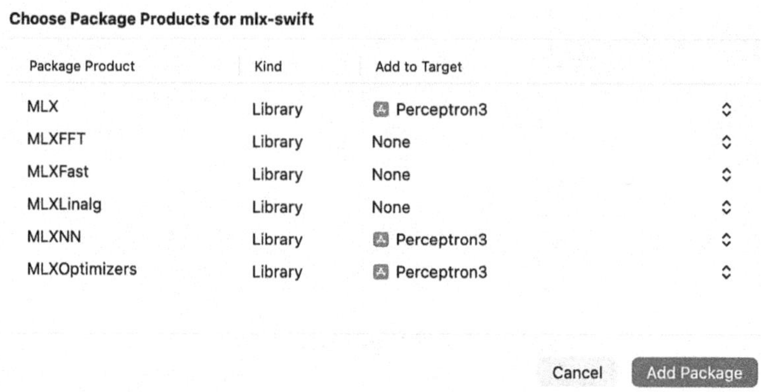

Figure 11-58: *Adding frameworks to the target*

MLX is more efficient when it offloads most operations to the GPU, so it requires the tools provided by the **Metal** framework to function properly. To install these tools, we must select the Settings option from the Xcode's menu at the top of the screen, go to the Components panel (Figure 11-59, number 1), and download the latest version of the Metal Toolchain (Figure 11-59, number 2).

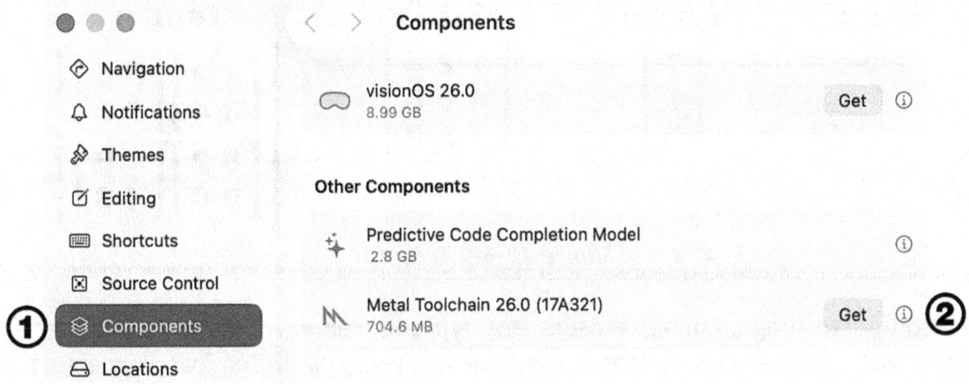

Figure 11-59: *Installing Metal Toolchain*

Do It Yourself

Create a new Multiplatform project. Open the project's settings, open the Package Dependencies tab, and press the + button to add a package, as shown in Figure 11-56. Copy and paste the URL **https://github.com/ml-explore/mlx-swift** into the field at the top of the window and press Return (Figure 11-57). With the MLX package selected, click the Add Package button. A list of available frameworks will appear, as shown in Figure 11-58. Select the target for the **MLX**, **MLXNN**, and **MLXOptimizers** frameworks (you may need to scroll through the list), and press the Add Package button again. You should now see the mlx-swift package added to your project. Open the Xcode menu at the top of the screen, select Settings, open the Components panel, and click on the Get button to download the Metal Toolchain, as shown in Figure 11-59.

Network Data

The process of designing and training a neural network with MLX is very similar to what we've done so far, except now we can take advantage of the framework to handle much of the heavy lifting for us. One important task that MLX simplifies is data management. In practical neural networks, we often need to process a large number of inputs, such as all the pixels in an image, and produce specific outputs, such as the category or class the image belongs to. In between, the network must also process large amounts of data in the hidden layers. To store and manage all these values, neural networks use structures called *Tensors*. Tensors are multidimensional numerical arrays that can have zero or more dimensions. A tensor with a single number is called a *Scalar* (0 dimensions), a tensor with a linear array of numbers is a *Vector* (1 dimension), a tensor with a table of rows and columns is a *Matrix* (2 dimensions), and any structure with three or more dimensions is simply called a *Tensor*, as illustrated in Figure 11-60.

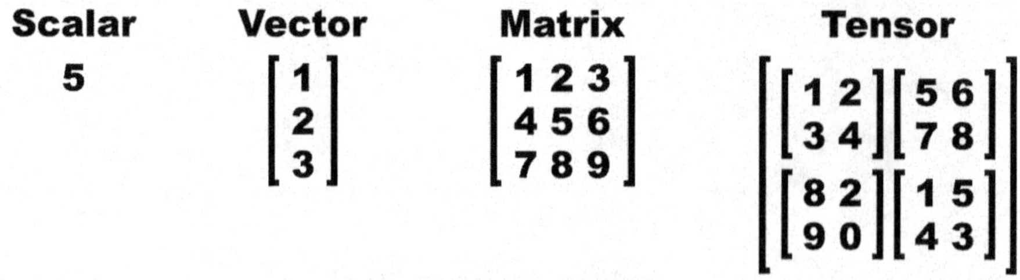

Figure 11-60: *Tensors*

In computer programming, tensors are typically represented as multidimensional arrays. In MLX, these values are stored using the **`MLXArray`** class. The following are some of the most frequently used initializers.

`MLXArray``(Data, Shape?)`

This initializer creates an **`MLXArray`** object using the data and configuration provided by its arguments. The first argument is a scalar or vector containing the values to store, and the second argument is an array of integers that defines the dimensions of the tensor (optional if the dimensions can be inferred from the values).

`MLXArray(converting:`` Array, Shape?)`

This initializer converts a Swift array of **`Double`** values into an **`MLXArray`** with values of type **`Float32`**. The **converting** argument is the array of **`Double`** values to convert, and the second argument is an array of integers that defines the dimensions of the tensor (optional if the dimensions can be inferred from the array).

MLX arrays work with specific precision data types. For integers, they support **`Int16`**, **`Int32`**, and **`Int64`**, and for floating-point values, they support **`Float16`** and **`Float32`** (note that **`Float64`** is supported, but not on the GPU). When values are provided directly, MLX converts them into **`Float32`** by default. For example, if we provide a single number, **`MLXArray`** stores it as a scalar of type **`Float32`** (a zero-dimensional tensor), and if we provide an array of numbers, **`MLXArray`** creates a vector of **`Float32`** values (a one-dimensional tensor), as shown below.

Listing 11-9: Creating scalars and vectors with the `MLXArray` class

```
import Playgrounds
import MLX

#Playground("Testing MLXArray") {
   let scalar = MLXArray(6)
   // array(6, dtype=int32)

   let vector = MLXArray([1, 2, 3])
   // array([1, 2, 3], dtype=int32)
}
```

In this example, we use the **#Playground** macro to test some **MLXArray** structures in our project. This macro simply simulates Playground behavior on an Xcode project, so we can incorporate code into our files without affecting the application and see the results of executing that code on the canvas. The first property in this example creates a scalar with the value 6, and the second creates a vector with the values 1, 2, and 3, so we will see the values **array(6, dtype=int32)** and **array([1, 2, 3], dtype=int32)** on the canvas. Note that to be able to use the **#Playground** macro, we must import the **Playground** framework, and to access the **MLXArray** class, we must import the **MLX** framework that we previously added to the project.

Do It Yourself

Create a new file called Tensors.swift for the code in Listing 11-9. Open the canvas in the editor and press the refresh button if necessary. You should see each property displayed with their corresponding values. Use this file to test the rest of the examples in this section.

In the previous example, MLX inferred the data types from the values. Since the values were integers, the **MLXArray** was created with values of type **Int32**, but neural networks typically require 32-bit floating-point values. To create **MLXArray** objects of this type, we can define the array first and then pass it to the initializer, as shown below.

Listing 11-10: Creating vectors of type `Float32`

```
import Playgrounds
import MLX

#Playground("Testing MLXArray") {
   let swiftArray: [Float32] = [1, 2, 3]
   let vector = MLXArray(swiftArray)
   //array([1, 2, 3], dtype=float32)
}
```

If we are working with standard arrays created in Swift, they are usually of type **Double**. To convert these arrays into **Float32**, the **MLXArray** class provides the **MLXArray(converting:)** initializer.

Listing 11-11: Converting arrays of type `Double`

```
import Playgrounds
import MLX

#Playground("Testing MLXArray") {
   let swiftArray = [1.0, 2.0, 3.0]
   let vector = MLXArray(converting: (swiftArray))
   // array([1, 2, 3], dtype=float32)
}
```

The tensors we have created so far are 0-dimensional (scalars) and 1-dimensional (vectors). To create tensors with more dimensions, we can specify their shape. For example, we can create a matrix with three rows and three columns, like the one shown in Figure 11-60.

Listing 11-12: Creating a matrix

```
import Playgrounds
import MLX

#Playground("Testing MLXArray") {
    let matrix = MLXArray([1, 2, 3, 4, 5, 6, 7, 8, 9], [3, 3])
    // array([[1, 2, 3],
    //        [4, 5, 6],
    //        [7, 8, 9]], dtype=int32)
}
```

When creating a multidimensional tensor, we provide the values as a vector and then declare the shape as an array of integers, where each number specifies the size of one dimension. In the example of Listing 11-12, the array [3, 3] defines a matrix with three rows and three columns. MLX then arranges the values in the array according to this specification.

The **MLXArray** class also includes type methods to create pre-populated matrices that are often required when processing values in neural networks. The following are the most frequently used.

zeros(Shape, **type:** Type)

This type method creates a matrix with the dimensions specified by the first argument, and with all values set to 0. The **type** argument defines the data type of the values (e.g., **Int16.self**).

ones(Shape, **type:** Type)

This type method creates a matrix with the dimensions specified by the first argument, and with all values set to 1. The **type** argument defines the data type of the values (e.g., **Int16.self**).

eye(Int, **m:** Int?, **k:** Int, **type:** Type)

This type method creates an identity matrix, which is a matrix with all values set to 0 except along the diagonal. The first argument specifies the number of rows, the **m** argument specifies the number of columns, the **k** argument determines which diagonal is set to 1, and the **type** argument defines the data type of the values (e.g., **Int16.self**).

linspace(Start, Stop, **count:** Int)

This type method generates a vector with evenly spaced numbers over a specified interval. The first argument specifies the starting value of the vector, the second argument specifies the ending value, and the **count** argument is an integer that defines how many values the vector will contain.

The following example shows a practical application of these methods and the types of values they produce. Note that if no type is specified, these methods create matrices with values of type **Float32**, but we can change this by declaring the **type** argument, as we did with the **zeros()** method.

Listing 11-13: Creating pre-populated matrices and vectors

```
import Playgrounds
import MLX

#Playground("Testing MLXArray") {
    let zeros = MLXArray.zeros([2, 3], type: Int16.self)
    // array([[0, 0, 0],
    //        [0, 0, 0]], dtype=int16)

    let ones = MLXArray.ones([2, 3])
    // array([[1, 1, 1],
    //        [1, 1, 1]], dtype=float32)

    let identity = MLXArray.eye(3, m: 3)
    // array([[1, 0, 0],
    //        [0, 1, 0],
    //        [0, 0, 1]], dtype=float32)

    let vector = MLXArray.linspace(Float32(0), Float32(1), count: 5)
    // array([0, 0.25, 0.5, 0.75, 1], dtype=float32)
}
```

The **MLXArray** class also includes properties and methods to get information about the tensor and access the values. The following are the most frequently used.

size

This property returns an integer with the total amount of items in the array.

ndim

This property returns an integer with the numbers of dimensions of the array.

dtype

This property returns an enumeration with a value that represents the data type of the items in the array. The enumeration is of type **DType** and includes the cases **float16**, **float32**, **float64**, **int8**, **int16**, **int32**, **int64**, and more.

item()

This method returns the scalar value of an item in the array.

The following example implements these properties and method on a vector created with the **linspace()** method.

Listing 11-14: Reading the configuration and accessing the items of an array

```
import Playgrounds
import MLX

#Playground("Testing MLXArray") {
    let vector = MLXArray.linspace(Float32(0), Float32(1), count: 5)
    // array([0, 0.25, 0.5, 0.75, 1], dtype=float32)

    let size = vector.size
    // 5

    let dimensions = vector.ndim
    // 1

    let type = vector.dtype
    // .float32

    let item: Double = vector[1].item()
    // 0.25
}
```

The **linspace()** method creates a vector with five values. Therefore, the **size** property returns 5 (five items), the **ndim** property returns 1 (a vector has only one dimension), and the **dtype** property returns **.float32** (the vector was created from **Float32** values). To access each value, we specify its index and call the **item()** method. This method returns the value as a number of the type declared for the property. In this case, we declared the property **item** as type **Double**, so the method returns the value at index 1 (0.25) converted to **Double**.

The **MLX** framework also provides methods to perform operations on the values within the tensor, such as finding the largest or smallest value in a matrix. The following are the most frequently used.

all(Array, axis: Int, keepDims: Bool)

This method returns a Boolean value indicating whether the elements in the tensor are all true. The first argument is the **MLXArray** we want to process, the **axis** argument specifies whether the check is performed across columns (0) or rows (1), and the **keepDims** argument determines whether the reduced dimensions are preserved.

max(Array, axis: Int, keepDims: Bool)

This method returns an **MLXArray** containing the maximum values from the original array. The first argument is the **MLXArray** we want to process, the **axis** argument specifies whether the search is performed across columns (0) or rows (1), and the **keepDims** argument determines whether the reduced dimensions are preserved.

min(Array, axis: Int, keepDims: Bool)

This method returns an **MLXArray** containing the minimum values from the original array. The first argument is the **MLXArray** we want to process, the **axis** argument specifies whether the search is performed across columns (0) or rows (1), and the **keepDims** argument determines whether the reduced dimensions are preserved.

```
argMax(Array, axis: Int, keepDims: Bool)
```

This method returns an **MLXArray** containing the index of the maximum value from the original array. The first argument is the **MLXArray** we want to process, the **axis** argument specifies whether the search is performed across columns (0) or rows (1), and the **keepDims** argument determines whether the reduced dimensions are preserved.

```
mean(Array, axis: Int, keepDims: Bool)
```

This method returns an **MLXArray** containing the mean (average) values from the original array. The first argument is the **MLXArray** we want to process, the **axis** argument specifies whether the mean is calculated across columns (0) or rows (1), and the **keepDims** argument determines whether the reduced dimensions are preserved.

```
sum(Array, axis: Int, keepDims: Bool)
```

This method returns an **MLXArray** containing the sum of the values from the original array. The first argument is the **MLXArray** we want to process, the **axis** argument specifies whether the sum should be performed across columns (0) or rows (1), and the **keepDims** argument determines whether the reduced dimensions are preserved.

```
std(Array, axis: Int, keepDims: Bool, ddof: Int)
```

This method returns an **MLXArray** containing the standard deviation of the original array. The first argument is the **MLXArray** we want to process, the **axis** argument specifies whether the calculation is performed across columns (0) or rows (1), the **keepDims** argument determines whether the reduced dimensions are preserved, and the **ddof** argument (delta degrees of freedom) is an integer that adjusts the divisor used in the calculation (0 computes the population standard deviation and 1 computes the sample standard deviation).

```
variance(Array, axis: Array, keepDims: Bool, ddof: Int)
```

This method returns an **MLXArray** containing the variance of the original array (a measure of how far the values in a set are spread around their mean). The first argument is the **MLXArray** we want to process, the **axis** argument specifies whether the calculation is performed across columns (0) or rows (1), the **keepDims** argument determines whether the reduced dimensions are preserved, and the **ddof** argument (delta degrees of freedom) is an integer that adjusts the divisor used in the calculation (0 computes the population standard deviation and 1 computes the sample standard deviation).

Some of these methods are used to prepare the input values before feeding them into the network, while others are used to process the network's output. For example, the `std()` and `variance()` methods are often applied to input data such as images to help normalize pixel values, making them easier to work with (for example, by scaling values so they fall within a consistent range, such as 0 to 1). Methods like `all()` can be used to evaluate conditions on the output, such as checking whether all predictions meet a certain criterion. The following example demonstrates how some of these methods are used. We will revisit several of them later in more practical situations.

Listing 11-15: Processing the items of a tensor

```
import Playgrounds
import MLX

#Playground("Testing MLXArray") {
    let matrix = MLXArray([9, 2, 3, 0, 5, 6], [2, 3])
    // array([[9, 2, 3],
    //        [0, 5, 6]], dtype=int32)

    let all = all(matrix)
    // array(false, dtype=bool)

    let max = max(matrix, axis: 0)
    // array([9, 5, 6], dtype=int32)
}
```

There are two ways to use these methods: we can process the entire array or specify an axis. In this example, we first call the **all()** method on the entire array. This method checks whether all the values in the array evaluate to true and returns a single Boolean result: **true** if all items are true, or **false** otherwise. When working with numbers, the method determines truth by comparing values to zero (0 is treated as false, and any nonzero value is treated as true). Since our sample array contains a zero, the method concludes that not all values are true and returns **false**. On the other hand, the call to the **max()** method specifies the axis 0, which means the operation is performed across the columns, so the method returns the maximum value in each column. Because the matrix has three columns, the result is a vector with three values [9, 5, 6].

> **IMPORTANT**
>
> Most of these methods, as well as those we will introduce next, are available both as instance methods of the **MLXArray** class and as part of the **MLX** framework. Therefore, they can be called directly on an **MLXArray** instance, as we did in Listing 11-14, or as standalone methods with the array specified as an argument (as we did in Listing 11-15).

Forward Propagation

Once the network values are stored, we need to process them to obtain the results we want. The **MLXArray** class provides a variety of methods for performing these operations. In this section, we will introduce those that are mostly used during forward propagation. The following are the ones that are applied to process individual values.

abs()

This method returns a new array containing the absolute values of the items in the original array.

```
round()
```

This method returns a new array with the values rounded to the nearest integer.

```
pow(Exponents)
```

This method returns a new array with the values raised to the power of the exponents specified by the argument. The argument can be either a single number or an **MLXArray** containing multiple exponents.

```
exp()
```

This method returns a new array with **e** raised to the power of each value in the original array.

In the following example, we test these methods on a vector with values from -1 to 1. Note that since the original vector is of type **Float32**, all the values produced by these methods are also of type **Float32**.

Listing 11-16: Performing operations on the values of a vector

```
import Playgrounds
import MLX

#Playground("Testing MLXArray") {
   let vector = MLXArray.linspace(Float32(-1), Float32(1), count: 6)
   // array([-1, -0.6, -0.2, 0.2, 0.6, 1], dtype=float32)

   let absolute = vector.abs()
   // array([1, 0.6, 0.2, 0.2, 0.6, 1], dtype=float32)

   let round = vector.round()
   // array([-1, -1, -0, 0, 1, 1], dtype=float32)

   let power = vector.pow(2)
   // array([1, 0.36, 0.04, 0.04, 0.36, 1], dtype=float32)

   let exp = vector.exp()
   // array([0.367879, 0.548812, 0.818731, 1.2214, 1.82212, 2.71828],
dtype=float32)
}
```

In addition to performing operations on the items in a single array, we can also perform operations between arrays. Among others, the **MLX** framework provides the following methods for this purpose.

```
add(Array, Array)
```

This method returns a new **MLXArray** object containing the result of the element-wise addition of the two arrays provided as arguments.

```
multiply(Array, Array)
```

This method returns a new **MLXArray** object containing the result of the element-wise multiplication of the two arrays provided as arguments.

matmul(Array, Array)

This method returns a new **MLXArray** containing the result of the dot product of the two arrays provided as arguments.

transposed(Array)

This method returns a new **MLXArray** with the elements of the provided array transposed.

These methods serve different purposes. The **add()** and **multiply()** methods are used when we need to compute values element by element. This is required when applying activation functions, scaling values, or combining gradients. The following example demonstrates how to add and multiply two vectors.

Listing 11-17: Performing operations between two tensors

```
import Playgrounds
import MLX

#Playground("Testing MLXArray") {
    let vector1 = MLXArray(converting: [1, 2, 3])
    let vector2 = MLXArray(converting: [4, 5, 6])

    let add = add(vector1, vector2)
    // array([5, 7, 9], dtype=int32)

    let multiply = multiply(vector1, vector2)
    // array([4, 10, 18], dtype=int32)
}
```

The operations performed by these methods are straightforward. They process the elements one by one in order, add or multiply them, and then return a new **MLXArray** with the results. For example, when we add the two vectors, 1 is added to 4, 2 to 5, and 3 to 6, producing the array [5, 7, 9].

On the other hand, the **matmul()** method performs a dot product. A dot product takes two lists of numbers of the same length, multiplies the numbers at matching positions, and then adds the results together. This is exactly the operation needed to calculate the weighted sum for each neuron. The following example applies the dot product to two vectors to illustrate how it works.

Listing 11-18: Performing the dot operation

```
import Playgrounds
import MLX

#Playground("Testing MLXArray") {
    let vector1 = MLXArray(converting: [1, 2, 3])
    let vector2 = MLXArray(converting: [4, 5, 6])
```

```
    let dotProduct = matmul(vector1, vector2)
    // array(32, dtype=float32)
}
```

In this case, the result is 32. The **matmul()** method takes the values of the first vector, multiplies them in order with the corresponding values of the second vector, and then adds the results. The complete operation is: (1* 4) + (2 * 5) + (3 * 6) = 32.

In this example, we applied the dot product to two vectors. However, neural networks usually work with matrices or higher-dimensional tensors. In those cases, matrix multiplication generalizes the dot product: each element of the resulting matrix is obtained by taking the dot product of a row from the first matrix and a column from the second. To perform this operation, the number of columns in the first matrix must match the number of rows in the second. For example, if we have a matrix with dimensions 2×3 (2 rows and 3 columns), we cannot multiply it by another 2×3 matrix, because the first has 3 columns while the second has only 2 rows. However, we can use the **transposed()** method to adjust one of the matrices so the operation is valid, as shown below.

Listing 11-19: Transposing a matrix

```
import Playgrounds
import MLX

#Playground("Testing MLXArray") {
    let matrix = MLXArray([1, 2, 3, 4, 5, 6], [2, 3])
    // array([[1, 2, 3],
    //        [4, 5, 6]], dtype=int32)

    let transposed = transposed(matrix)
    // array([[1, 4],
    //        [2, 5],
    //        [3, 6]], dtype=int32)
}
```

In this example, we create a matrix with two rows and three columns, and then transpose it into a matrix with three rows and two columns. Note that the method simply flips the matrix, converting rows into columns and columns into rows.

Although the **MLX**, **MLXNN**, and **MLXOptimizers** frameworks provide all the tools needed to design and train a network, they also include methods for performing these operations manually when necessary. The following are the most frequently used.

relu(Array)

This method applies the Rectified Linear Unit (ReLU) to the values of the **MLXArray** passed as the argument. This is equivalent to using the **max()** method to compare each value with 0.

sigmoid(Array)

This method applies the sigmoid function to the values of the **MLXArray** passed as the argument.

```
softmax(Array, axes: [Int], precise: Bool)
```

This method performs the softmax function on the values of the **MLXArray** passed as the argument. The **axes** argument determines the axes we want the method to consider, and the **precise** argument specifies whether the function will be numerically precise when performing the calculations.

The **relu()** and **sigmoid()** methods calculate the activation values of neurons as before, but we haven't implemented the **softmax()** method yet. This method is typically used in the output layer to convert raw output values into probabilities. The method normalizes the outputs so that they sum to 1, allowing us to interpret each value as the probability that the input belongs to a particular class, as shown in the following example.

Listing 11-20: Calculating the softmax on the values of an output layer

```
import Playgrounds
import MLX

#Playground("Testing MLXArray") {
   let vector = MLXArray(converting: [9, 2, 3, 0, -2, 4])
   // array([9, 2, 3, 0, -2, 4], dtype=float32)

   let softmax = softmax(vector)
   // array([0.989836, 0.000902613, 0.00245356, 0.000122155, 1.65319e-05,
0.00666946], dtype=float32)

   let percentage = round(multiply(softmax, 100))
   // array([99, 0, 0, 0, 0, 1], dtype=float32)
}
```

In this example, we define a vector with six numbers to simulate the output of a network with six neurons in its output layer. The **softmax()** method takes these values and normalizes them, ensuring that all outputs are between 0 and 1 and that they add up to 1, so they can be interpreted as probabilities. This becomes clear when we call the **multiply()** method next to scale the values by 100 and then use the **round()** method to round the results. The resulting array shows the probability that each neuron represents the correct class expressed as a percentage. In this case, the first neuron has a probability of 99%, meaning that the class it represents is the one the network has identified as correct.

There is one more thing to know about MLX arrays. The **MLX** framework is lazy, meaning that calculations on **MLXArray** values are deferred until the results are actually needed. In most cases, we don't have to do anything, once the values are used, the system automatically performs the necessary calculations. However, there are situations where we need to trigger the process manually. In such cases, we can use the following method.

```
eval(Array...)
```

This method evaluates **MLXArray** values. The argument is a list of one or more **MLXArray** objects, separated by commas.

As we will see later, this method is often required to force the system to initialize the network's parameters and carry out the optimization process.

IMPORTANT

Working with vectors, matrices, and higher-dimensional tensors is a constant in machine learning. Understanding how to use and apply these tools is essential for anyone who wants to design and train their own networks. In this section, we introduced the most frequently used methods for performing the core operations required in neural networks, but how these methods are implemented and combined depends on the network's architecture and the goals we want to achieve. To expand your knowledge, many free courses and books are available online. For more information, visit our website and follow the links for this chapter.

Loss Functions

The **MLXNN** framework includes functions to calculate a network's loss (the error). The following are the ones we use to calculate the Mean Squared Error and the Cross-Entropy Loss we introduced earlier, but others are also available.

```
mseLoss(predictions: Array, targets: Array, reduction: LossReduction)
```

This method calculates the Mean Squared Error. The **predictions** argument is the **MLXArray** containing the network's outputs, the **targets** argument is the **MLXArray** containing the expected values, and the **reduction** argument is an enumeration that determines how the errors are reduced. The possible values are **mean** (returns the average error), **sum** (adds up all the errors), and **none** (returns the array of error values as-is).

```
crossEntropy(logits: Array, targets: Array, weights: Array?, axis: Int, labelSmoothing: Float, reduction: LossReduction)
```

This method calculates the Cross-Entropy Loss. The **logits** argument is the **MLXArray** containing the network's raw outputs before normalization, the **targets** argument is the **MLXArray** containing the expected values, the **weights** argument is an optional **MLXArray** that we can use to assign greater importance to specific samples or classes, the **axis** argument specifies the dimension that represents the classes, with -1 (the last dimension) used by default, the **labelSmoothing** argument controls how much probability is spread across classes to prevent the model from becoming overly confident in a single class, and finally, the **reduction** argument is an enumeration that determines how the errors are reduced. The possible values are **mean** (returns the average error), **sum** (adds up all the errors), and **none** (returns the array of error values as-is).

Back Propagation

The **MLXNN** framework can also handle the calculation of derivatives (gradients) for backpropagation. For this purpose, the framework includes the following method.

```
valueAndGrad(model: Model, Closure)
```

This method creates a function that computes both the model's loss and its gradients. The **model** argument is a reference to the model object (an object that inherits from the `Module` class), and the second argument is a closure or a function that defines how the error is computed.

This method returns a function that can be used to calculate the loss and gradients during each cycle of the training process. (We will see how to apply this later.)

Optimization

The tools for optimization are provided by the **MLXOptimizers** framework, which defines several classes for creating network optimizers such as SGD, Adam, and others. The following are the initializers of the most frequently used.

```
SGD(learningRate: Float, momentum: Float, weightDecay: Float,
dampening: Float, nesterov: Bool)
```

This initializer creates an SGD optimizer. The **learningRate** argument sets the learning rate, the **momentum** argument adds a fraction of the previous update to the current one to accelerate convergence, the **weightDecay** argument applies a penalty to large weights to reduce overfitting, the **dampening** argument controls how much the momentum contribution is reduced on each update, and the **nesterov** argument enables Nesterov momentum, which adjusts when gradients are calculated to improve training accuracy and speed.

```
RMSprop(learningRate: Float, alpha: Float, eps: Float)
```

This initializer creates an RMSprop optimizer. The **learningRate** argument sets the learning rate, the **alpha** argument controls how much of the past squared gradients are retained in the moving average, and the **eps** argument is a small constant added to the denominator to improve numerical stability and prevent division by zero.

```
Adam(learningRate: Float, betas: (Float, Float), eps: Float)
```

This initializer creates an Adam optimizer. The **learningRate** argument sets the learning rate, the **betas** argument is a pair of coefficients that control the exponential decay rates of the moving averages of the gradients (first value) and the squared gradients (second value), and the **eps** argument is a small constant added to the denominator to improve numerical stability and prevent division by zero.

All these classes conform to the `Optimizer` protocol, which defines the following method for performing optimization.

```
update(model: Module, gradients: ModuleParameters)
```

This method updates the model's parameters using the provided gradients. The **model** argument is a reference to the model object (an object that inherits from the **`Module`** class), and the **gradients** argument is a dictionary of **`MLXArray`** objects containing the gradients calculated by the **`valueAndGrad()`** method.

After initializing the optimizer, we must call this method at every cycle of the training process to update the network's parameters. (We will see how to use it in a practical example later.)

Network Architecture

The last step before building our network is to define its architecture. For this purpose, the **MLXNN** framework provides the **`Module`** class, which includes all the functionality needed to manage the network's parameters. To design a network, we create a subclass of **`Module`**, define properties to store the layers, and implement the code that manages the network.

There are many types of networks and architectures we can design, and many ways to organize a **`Module`** subclass. For our examples, we will build a simple network with three layers: an input layer, a hidden layer, and an output layer. To define these layers, the framework provides a base class called **`Layers`** and several subclasses we can use. For feedforward networks with fully connected layers, like the ones we have studied in this book, the framework includes the **`Linear`** subclass.

```
Linear(Input, Output, bias: Bool)
```

This initializer creates a fully connected layer that computes the weighted sum of each neuron (it calculates the dot product of the inputs and the weights plus an optional bias term). The first argument is an integer specifying the dimension of the layer's input, the second argument is an integer specifying the dimension of the layer's output, and the **bias** argument is a Boolean that determines whether bias values are included.

In addition to defining these properties, our class must also conform to the **`UnaryLayer`** protocol and implement the **`callAsFunction()`** method. Conforming to the protocol makes the class behave like any other layer, allowing the system to understand the network's input and output behavior and enabling us to compose it with other networks when needed. The **`callAsFunction()`** method, in turn, makes the class "callable": once implemented, we can invoke the object as if it were a function, which simplifies the processing of the module in more complex systems.

The **`callAsFunction()`** method must take a value as input and return a value as output. In this case, it receives an **`MLXArray`** with the inputs, processes the values through the network, and returns another **`MLXArray`** with the outputs. However, this processing is not performed automatically, we must implement the behavior ourselves, as shown in the following example.

Listing 11-21: Defining the network

```
import MLX
import MLXNN

nonisolated class SimpleNetwork: Module, UnaryLayer {
   let hiddenLayer: Linear
   let outputLayer: Linear

   init(inputDim: Int, hiddenDim: Int, outputDim: Int) {
      self.hiddenLayer = Linear(inputDim, hiddenDim)
      self.outputLayer = Linear(hiddenDim, outputDim)
   }
   func callAsFunction(_ x: MLXArray) -> MLXArray {
      var x = hiddenLayer(x)
      x = sigmoid(x)
      return outputLayer(x)
   }
}
```

In this module, we define two properties to store and process the hidden layer and the output layer (the input layer only receives the input values, so it does not require computation). These properties are then initialized with the values passed to the class. Since these values represent the number of neurons in each layer, the hidden layer is initialized with the number of neurons in the input layer and its own number of neurons, while the output layer is initialized with the number of neurons in the hidden layer and its own number of neurons.

The **callAsFunction()** method is invoked whenever the system performs the forward pass. In this case, we first process the inputs through the hidden layer, then apply the sigmoid function to the result, pass these new values through the output layer, and finally return the output. Note that objects created from the **Linear** class also implement the **callAsFunction()** method, so we can invoke them with the values we want to process as if they were functions.

Do It Yourself

Continuing from the previous project, create a new file called SimpleNetwork.swift for the class in Listing 11-21. We will use this class in the next steps to train our network.

Training

Now that we have a class to manage our network, we can initialize it and begin training. In this example, we will reuse the same structure and views implemented before to demonstrate how to train a simple network using the **MLX** framework. We will implement the **ContentView** view defined in Listing 11-3 and our usual **ApplicationData** class to manage the process and post updates. The following code initializes this class and defines the properties needed to provide the input, specify the target, and control the training process.

Listing 11-22: Initializing the network

```
import SwiftUI
import Observation

import MLX
import MLXNN
import MLXOptimizers

@Observable class ApplicationData {
   var logs: String = ""
   var training: Bool = false

   @ObservationIgnored var model: SimpleNetwork!
   @ObservationIgnored var inputs: MLXArray!
   @ObservationIgnored var targets: MLXArray!

   static let shared: ApplicationData = ApplicationData()
   private init() {
      model = SimpleNetwork(inputDim: 1, hiddenDim: 1, outputDim: 1)
      inputs = MLXArray([50])
      targets = MLXArray([15])
   }
}
```

To illustrate how the process works, we are replicating the same simple network we created earlier with only one input neuron, one hidden neuron, and one output neuron. The input and target are also set to the same values as before: **50.0** for the input and **15.0** for the target. Note that because we are going to use the tools provided by MLX to train the network, we need to import the **MLX**, **MLXNN**, and **MLXOptimizers** frameworks.

The next step is to define the loss function. This predefined function is required by the **valueAndGrad()** method to compute the error. The method must take three arguments: the **model** argument to receive a reference to the **Module** object, the **x** argument to receive the inputs, and the **y** argument to receive the targets. The method must also return an **MLXArray** object representing the error, as shown below.

Listing 11-23: Defining the loss function

```
func lossFunction(model: SimpleNetwork, x: MLXArray, y: MLXArray) ->
MLXArray {
   mseLoss(predictions: model(x), targets: y, reduction: .mean)
}
```

In this case, we use the **mseLoss()** function to calculate the error. This function sends the inputs to the network (the model), compares the output with the targets, computes the Mean Squared Error, and returns it.

The next step is to train the network. The process is the same as before: we define the number of epochs and the learning rate, and then create a loop that calculates the gradients and optimizes the network at each cycle.

Listing 11-24: Training the network

```
func trainNetwork() {
    // Restart network values
    logs = ""
    training = true

    // Setting training values
    let epochs = 200
    let learningRate: Float = 0.01

    eval(model!)
    let gradients = valueAndGrad(model: model, lossFunction)
    let optimizer = SGD(learningRate: learningRate)

    // Training
    for pass in 0..<epochs {
        // Gradients
        let (loss, grads) = gradients(model, inputs, targets)

        // Calculate Error
        let error: Double = loss.item()
        if pass % 10 == 0 {
            logs += "Error: \(String(format: "%.6f", error))\n"
        }
        optimizer.update(model: model, gradients: grads)
        eval(model!, optimizer)
    }
    let last = model(inputs)
    logs += "Last Output: \(last.item(Float.self))\n"
    training = false
}
```

As mentioned earlier, the **MLX** framework is lazy. This means that values are not computed until they are required, so before starting the training loop we call the `eval()` method to initialize the parameters. We then create the function for calculating the gradients by calling the `valueAndGrad()` method, and create an instance of the `SGD` class to set up the Stochastic Gradient Descent optimizer that will be used to train the network.

Inside the loop, we calculate the gradients, display the current error on the screen, and call the `update()` method on the optimizer to perform the optimization. Immediately afterward, we call the `eval()` method again. This is necessary to force the system to evaluate the model's parameters so that we can work with fresh values in the next cycle. Figure 11-61 shows what appears on the screen when we press the Train Network button.

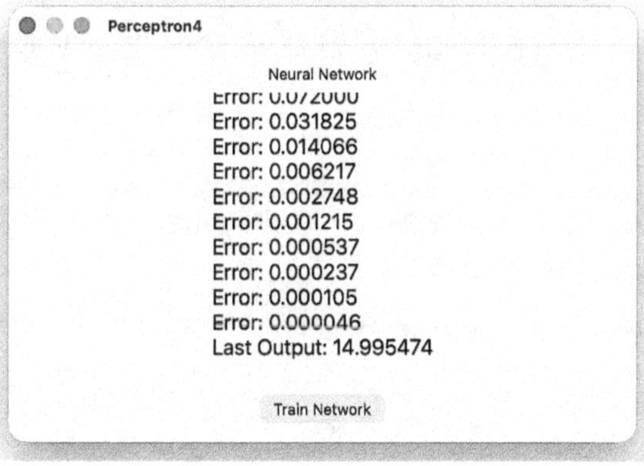

Figure 11-61: *Network training with MLX*

Do It Yourself

Create a new file called ApplicationData.swift for the code in Listing 11-22. Add the **`lossFunction()`** method from Listing 11-23 and the **`trainNetwork()`** method from Listing 11-24 to the **`ApplicationData`** class (below the initializer). For this example, you also need to update the **`ContentView`** view with the code in Listing 11-3. Run the application on your Mac and press the Train Network button. You should see something similar to Figure 11-61.

This neural network, like the one we designed from scratch before, is only useful for didactic purposes. All it does is output the value **15.0** when it receives the value **50.0** as input. While this is helpful for understanding how to design and train a network, developing models for practical use requires adding more neurons, creating deeper architectures, adjusting parameters, validating results with test data, and more. To illustrate how useful networks are designed, we will now create one that processes the Iris dataset.

The Iris dataset is a classic dataset in machine learning and statistics, often used for testing classification algorithms. It contains 150 samples of iris flowers, divided evenly into three species: Iris setosa, Iris versicolor, and Iris virginica. For each flower, the dataset provides four numerical features: sepal length, sepal width, petal length, and petal width, all measured in centimeters, as shown below.

SepalLengthCm	SepalWidthCm	PetalLengthCm	PetalWidthCm	Species
5.1	3.5	1.4	0.2	0
4.9	3.0	1.4	0.2	0
4.7	3.2	1.3	0.2	0
4.6	3.1	1.5	0.2	0
5.0	3.6	1.4	0.2	0
5.4	3.9	1.7	0.4	0
4.6	3.4	1.4	0.3	0

Figure 11-62: *Iris dataset*

The goal of the dataset is to use these features to predict the species of each flower. For this purpose, the species of flowers in the dataset are labeled with values from 0 to 2 (0 for setosa, 1 for versicolor, and 2 for virginica). For a network to be able to identify these categories (classes) from the parameters, we need several neurons per layer. The input and output layers are straightforward. In our case, there are four input values (sepal length, sepal width, petal length, and petal width), so we need four input neurons. For the output, we need to use a one-hot encoded vector to identify the classes (see Figure 11-19), which means we need three neurons to represent the three flower species. The configuration of the hidden layers is more difficult to determine and is usually chosen by trial and error. In this case, since the Iris dataset is well studied, we know that the network requires at least one hidden layer with 16 neurons. The following are the changes we need to introduce in our **`ApplicationData`** class to create this network.

Listing 11-25: Designing a network for the Iris dataset

```
import SwiftUI
import Observation

import MLX
import MLXNN
import MLXOptimizers

@Observable class ApplicationData {
   var logs: String = ""
   var training: Bool = false

   @ObservationIgnored var model: SimpleNetwork!
   @ObservationIgnored var inputTraining: MLXArray!
   @ObservationIgnored var inputTesting: MLXArray!
   @ObservationIgnored var targetTraining: MLXArray!
   @ObservationIgnored var targetTesting: MLXArray!

   static let shared: ApplicationData = ApplicationData()
   private init() {
      model = SimpleNetwork(inputDim: 4, hiddenDim: 16, outputDim: 3)

      if let (inputTraining, inputTesting, targetTraining, targetTesting)
         = loadIrisDataset() {
```

```
            self.inputTraining = inputTraining
            self.inputTesting = inputTesting
            self.targetTraining = targetTraining
            self.targetTesting = targetTesting
         }
      }
   }
```

The process is the same as before, but now we create the network with 4 input neurons, 16 hidden neurons, and 3 output neurons, and then execute a method called **`loadIrisDataset()`** to load the Iris dataset.

Loading the data used to train a network is highly dependent on the type of information being processed and the design of the network. For example, when working with text, words must be converted into numbers; when working with images, they often need to be compressed or resized; and in most cases, the data must be normalized, that is, adjusted to fall within a consistent range, usually between 0 and 1. In this case, we need to transform the values representing the flower species into one-hot encoded vectors, split the dataset into training and testing subsets, and normalize all the values to make it easier for the network to produce the correct outputs. The following is our implementation of these procedures.

Listing 11-26: Loading the Iris dataset

```
func loadIrisDataset() -> (MLXArray, MLXArray, MLXArray, MLXArray)? {
   // Loading the file from the bundle
   guard let url = Bundle.main.url(forResource: "IrisDataset",
      withExtension: "csv") else {
      return nil
   }
   guard let content = try? String(contentsOf: url, encoding: .utf8)
      else {
      return nil
   }
   let lines = content.components(separatedBy: .newlines).filter {
      !$0.isEmpty }
   let dataRows = lines.dropFirst()

   var inputValues: [[Float32]] = []
   var targetValues: [Float32] = []
   for row in dataRows {
      let columns = row.split(separator: ",")
      var listValues: [Float32] = []

      for (index, value) in columns.enumerated() {
         if let x = Float32(value), index < 4 {
            listValues.append(x)
         } else if let target = Float32(value) {
            targetValues.append(target)
         }
      }
      inputValues.append(listValues)
   }
```

```swift
    // One-Hot Encoding the species
    let hotEncoding = [[1, 0, 0], [0, 1, 0], [0, 0, 1]]
    let targetHot = targetValues.map { hotEncoding[Int($0)] }

    // Getting random indexes for splitting data
    let indices = inputValues.indices.shuffled()
    let splitIndex = Int(Double(indices.count) * 0.75)

    // Split the data into training and testing
    let inputTraining = indices[..<splitIndex].map { inputValues[$0] }
    let inputTesting = indices[splitIndex...].map { inputValues[$0] }
    let targetTraining = indices[..<splitIndex].map { targetHot[$0] }
    let targetTesting = indices[splitIndex...].map { targetHot[$0] }

    // Convert to vectors we can use for MLXArray
    let inputTrainingFlat = inputTraining.flatMap { $0 }
    let inputTestingFlat = inputTesting.flatMap { $0 }
    let targetTrainingFlat = targetTraining.flatMap { $0 }
    let targetTestingFlat = targetTesting.flatMap { $0 }

    // Convert to MLXArray
    let inputTrainingArray = MLXArray(inputTrainingFlat,
       [inputTraining.count, 4])
    let inputTestingArray = MLXArray(inputTestingFlat,
       [inputTesting.count, 4])
    let targetTrainingArray = MLXArray(targetTrainingFlat,
       [targetTraining.count, 3])
    let targetTestingArray = MLXArray(targetTestingFlat,
       [targetTesting.count, 3])

    // Calculating values for normalization
    let mean = inputTrainingArray.mean(axes: [0], keepDims: false)
    let std = inputTrainingArray.variance(axes: [0], keepDims: false)
       .sqrt()

    // Apply normalization to both training and testing data
    let eps: Float = 1e-6
    let stdSafe = std + eps
    let normalizedInputTraining = (inputTrainingArray - mean) / stdSafe
    let normalizedInputTesting = (inputTestingArray - mean) / stdSafe

    return (normalizedInputTraining, normalizedInputTesting,
       targetTrainingArray, targetTestingArray)
}
```

It is important to understand that this is not a standard procedure. How we load and preprocess the input depends on the data we are working with and the goal we want to achieve. In this case, we first load the file from the bundle. Since it is a CSV file, all values are separated by commas, so we extract each value from every sample, and then store the first four values in an array called **`inputValues`** and the last value (the species index) in another array called **`targetValues`**.

In the next step, we take the values in the **`targetValues`** array and convert them into one-hot encoded vectors. To do this, we create an array of arrays to represent each species: [1, 0, 0] represents the species at index 0, [0, 1, 0] represents the species at index 1, and [0, 0, 1] represents the species at index 2. This allows us to later compare the outputs of the three neurons in the output layer against these arrays and determine how accurate the network is (see Figure 11-19).

Now that we have all the input and target values ready, we need to split the dataset into two parts: one with the inputs and targets for training and another with the inputs and targets for testing. This way, we can use one set of samples to train the network and a different set to test how well the network performs. For this purpose, we work with the indices. We take the indices from the **inputValues** array, create a subset containing only 75% of them, and then use it to split the dataset.

Once the datasets are ready, we must convert them into **MLXArray** objects so they can be used in our MLX network. To do this, we first flatten the arrays with the **flatMap()** method. (This step is necessary because the **MLXArray** initializer does not accept multidimensional arrays and requires vectors instead.) Using these vectors, we then initialize the **MLXArray** objects with the appropriate dimensions for each set (4 for the inputs and 3 for the targets).

After this process, we have the values organized as required, but they are still unchanged from the original dataset. The next step is to normalize them. In our code, we use a process called *standardization*, which transforms the data so that each feature has a mean of 0 and a standard deviation of 1 (a measure of how much the values deviate from 0). This makes training more stable and prevents features with larger ranges (like petal length) from overpowering those with smaller ranges (like sepal width). For this purpose, we calculate the mean with the **mean()** method, the standard deviation with the **variance()** method, and then apply the normalization formula (**X' = (X - Mean(X)) \ Std(X)**) to produce the final values.

The final values are returned and assigned to properties, so we can now begin training the network. As always, the first step is to define the error function. For classification tasks like this one, it is best to use the Cross-Entropy Loss function. The following are the changes required in our **lossFunction()** method.

Listing 11-27: Defining the loss function for classification tasks

```
func lossFunction(model: SimpleNetwork, x: MLXArray, y: MLXArray)
    -> MLXArray {
    crossEntropy(logits: model(x), targets: y, reduction: .mean)
}
```

The training process is very similar to what we did before, except that this time we must adjust more parameters to achieve the desired result, which requires running more epochs (3000). The following is our updated **trainNetwork()** method.

Listing 11-28: Defining the loss function for classification tasks

```
func trainNetwork() {
    // Restart network values
    logs = ""
    training = true
```

```
    // Setting training values
    let epochs = 3000
    let learningRate: Float = 0.01

    eval(model!)
    let gradients = valueAndGrad(model: model, lossFunction)
    let optimizer = SGD(learningRate: learningRate)

    // Training
    for epoch in 0..<epochs {
        // Gradients
        let (lossValue, grads) = gradients(model, inputTraining,
            targetTraining)

        // Calculate Error
        let error: Float = lossValue.item()
        if epoch % 100 == 0 {  // Log every 100 epochs instead of 10
            logs += "Loss: \(String(format: "%.6f", error))\n"
        }
        optimizer.update(model: model, gradients: grads)
        eval(model!, optimizer)
    }
    // Testing
    var correct = 0
    let logits = model(inputTesting)
    let predictions = softmax(logits)
    let predictedLabels = argMax(predictions, axis: 1)
    let targetLabels = argMax(targetTesting, axis: 1)
    correct = (predictedLabels .== targetLabels).sum().item()
    let accuracy = Double(correct) / Double(targetTesting.shape[0]) * 100
    logs += "Final Accuracy: \(String(format: "%.2f", accuracy))%\n"
    training = false
}
```

Because we are classifying data, in addition to the network's error, we can also calculate its accuracy. Accuracy is determined by counting how many classes the network predicts correctly and dividing that number by the total number of samples. This produces a percentage that reflects how well the network performs on the dataset. In our example, we calculate this by first applying the **softmax()** function to the outputs to obtain a clear probability distribution. We then retrieve the indices of the highest values from both the arrays produced by the **softmax()** function and those stored in the **targetTesting** property, and compare them to determine how many of them match. This gives us the number of correct predictions, which we divide by the total number of samples and multiply by 100 to obtain the accuracy in percentage.

We now have everything we need to run and train our network, but there is one more change required for this example to work. In modern networks, especially classification networks like this one, it is better to use the ReLU activation function instead of the Sigmoid function for calculating the activation values of the neurons in the hidden layers. ReLU makes the network easier to train and generally more effective. In our example, all we need to do is replace the **sigmoid()** method with the **relu()** method in the **callAsFunction()** method of our **SimpleNetwork** class, as shown below.

Listing 11-29: Applying the ReLU activation function

```
func callAsFunction(_ x: MLXArray) -> MLXArray {
    var x = hiddenLayer(x)
    x = relu(x)
    x = outputLayer(x)
    return x
}
```

After we press the Train Network button, the **trainNetwork()** method takes a few seconds to finish training and then displays the result on the screen, as illustrated in Figure 11-63.

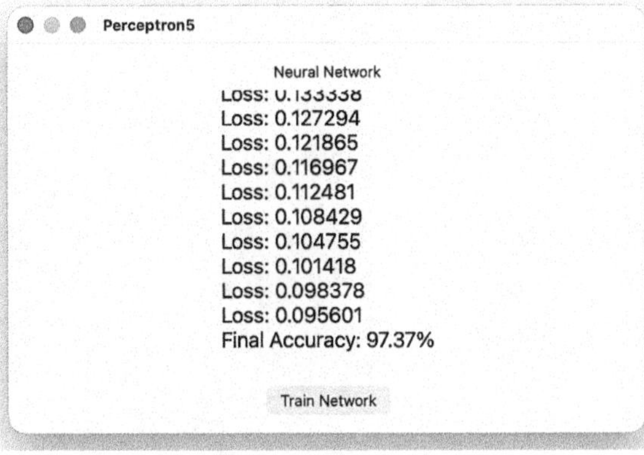

Figure 11-63: *Network's accuracy*

Do It Yourself

For this example, you can update the previous project or create a new one. If you create a new project, remember to add the MLX package again. Download the **IrisDataset.csv** file from our website and add it to your project. Update the **ApplicationData** class with the code in Listing 11-25. Add the **loadIrisDataset()** method from Listing 11-26 to the **ApplicationData** class. Update the **lossFunction()** method with the code in Listing 11-27. Update the **trainNetwork()** method with the code in Listing 11-28. Update the **callAsFunction()** method in the **SimpleNetwork** class with the code in Listing 11-29. Run the application and press the Train Network button. You should see the list of errors and the network's accuracy at the bottom of the list, as shown in Figure 11-63.

IMPORTANT

The purpose of these examples is to demonstrate how the main tools of the **MLX** framework are used to design and train neural networks, but there are many additional techniques, processes, and architectures to explore. The documentation for this framework is available online, along with numerous Swift examples showing how to build neural networks, work with LLMs, and train on larger datasets. For more information, visit our website and follow the links for this chapter.

Where To Go From Here

Every framework and model introduced in this book can be combined with others to create powerful experiences for your users. Many of the models provided by Apple can be fine-tuned with your own data using Create ML, and you can train your own models to meet your specific requirements. New public and free Core ML models are published every month, and Apple continues to introduce changes and improvements with each update. Remember to check Apple's developer website (**https://developer.apple.com/**) and specialized platforms like Hugging Face (**https://huggingface.co**) for the latest information.

The field of artificial intelligence is still experimental and continues to evolve. If you are interested in expanding your understanding of neural networks and learning how to design and train artificial intelligence models, there are courses, video tutorials, and eBooks available for free. For more information, visit our website and follow the links provided for each of the chapters in this book.

If you need help developing applications for Apple devices, take a look at the other books in our series.

Swift Programming Language for Masterminds

How to take advantage of Swift to create applications for iPhones, iPads and Macs

Learn everything you need to master the Swift programming language and build applications for iPhones, iPads, and Macs. After reading this book, you will know how to program with Swift, process information, access advanced frameworks, and organize your code to develop any application you want.

SwiftUI Framework for Masterminds

How to create professional applications for iPhones, iPads and Macs

Learn how to work with the SwiftUI framework to create amazing applications for iPhones, iPads, and Macs. After reading this book, you will know how to define interactive views, create custom layouts, build graphics and animations, store information permanently on device, and gain all the skills you need to design and develop modern applications.

Index

#

#Playground 433

@

@Environment 44
@Generable 86
@Guide 87, 89
@InstructionsBuilder 78
@Parameter 312, 315
@PromptBuilder 77
@Property 326

A

abs 438
Activation 12
activation 402
Adam 430, 444
Adapter 139
Adapters 129
adaptiveImageGlyph 47
add 291, 296, 327, 439
AlexNet 16
all 436
allEntities 333
allJoints 235
alternatives 263
analyze 291, 296
AnalyzerInput 266
analyzeSequence 262
Anthropic 30
AppEntity 327
AppIntent 301, 305, 340
Apple Intelligence 2
applicationName 307
AppShortcut 306
AppShortcutPhraseToken 307
appShortcuts 306
AppShortcutsProvider 306, 333
argMax 437
Artificial intelligence 9
assetInstallationRequest 259
AssetInventory 259
assetsUnavailable 114
AttributedString 47, 50, 53, 54, 75
availability 109
AVAudioEngine 267
AVAudioFormat 267
AVSpeechSynthesisVoice 276, 279
AVSpeechSynthesizer 276
AVSpeechSynthesizerDelegate 286
AVSpeechUtterance 276, 278
axon 10

B

backgroundColor 47
backpropagation 401, 418, 422
barcodeDetectionOptions 212
barcodeGenerator 248
BarcodeObservation 204
bestAvailableAudioFormat 265
bias 399
blendWithMask 247
boundingBox 204, 224
Button 338

C

CalculateImageAestheticsScoresRequest 201
calendarEvent 217
call 100
callAsFunction 446
cancelAnalysis 291
cancelAndFinishNow 262
captureQuality 228
caseDisplayRepresentations 311
cgImage 252, 42
Chain Rule 415
ChatGPT 21, 22, 29
CIContext 246
CIFilter 246
CIImage 245
classifications 289
ClassifyImageRequest 188

Claude 21, 22, 29
clientIdentifier 168
Cloudflare 378
CMTime 289
CMTimeRange 289
Codestral 33
Coding Assistant 21, 4, 7
colorControls 247
colorMonochrome 247
completeAnalysis 296
computeUnits 362
concurrentRequests 114
Conda 132
confidence 189, 235, 290
Configuration 168, 169
Console 7
Constant Multiple Rule 413
Constant Rule 412
Container 221
contains 158
content 219, 221, 72
Context 114
continueSpeaking 285
Core ML 18, 360
Create ML 18, 351
createCGImage 246
cropped 246
Cross-Entropy Loss 408, 410
crossEntropy 443, 453
currentLanguageCode 279
CustomLocalizedStringResourceConvertible 324

D

data 56
DataDetectorMatch 217
debugDescription 114
decodingFailure 114
Deep Belief Network 16
Deep Learning 16
default 72
defaultQuery 326
dendrites 10
Derivatives 411
description 100, 302
DetectBarcodesRequest 203
detectedData 213
DetectFaceCaptureQualityRequest 228
DetectFaceLandmarksRequest 230
DetectFaceRectanglesRequest 224
DetectHumanBodyPoseRequest 234
DetectHumanHandPoseRequest 240
DetectHumanRectanglesRequest 232
detectsHands 235
DictationTranscriber 258
Difference Rule 414
differentiation 412
DisplayRepresentation 314
displayRepresentation 326
distance 158, 236
document 213
DocumentObservation 213
dominantLanguage 144
downloadAndInstall 260
dtype 435
DynamicGenerationSchema 94, 95, 97

E

emailAddress 217
Embeddings 157
end 290
entities 329, 331
EntityProperty 326
EntityPropertyQuery 329
EntityQuery 328
EntityStringQuery 328, 331
EnumerableEntityQuery 329, 333
epoch 427
errorDescription 114
eval 442
exceededContextWindowSize 118, 120
exp 439
exposureAdjust 247
extent 245
extracted 40
eye 434

F

FaceObservation 224, 226, 228

falseColor 247
finalizeAndFinish 262
finalizeAndFinishThroughEndOfInput 265
Flask 378
flightNumber 217
focused 64
FocusState 64
foregroundColor 47
forward propagation 401
Foundation Models 18, 71

G

gaussianBlur 246
gender 280
GenerateAttentionBasedSaliencyImageRequest 196
GenerateObjectnessBasedSaliencyImageRequest 200
GeneratePersonSegmentationRequest 252
GenerationError 118
GenerationOptions 82
GenerationSchema 95
Generative Adversarial Networks 17
Genmoji 17, 46
Gradient descent 423
guardrailViolation 116

H

hasMinimumPrecision 189
hasMinimumRecall 189
heatMap 196
HumanBodyPoseObservation 235
HumanObservation 232

I

identifier 189, 280, 290
Image Playground 17, 37
ImageAestheticsScoresObservation 201
ImageCreator 42, 46
imagePlaygroundGenerationStyle 41
imagePlaygroundPersonalizationPolicy 41
imagePlaygroundSheet 38, 41
ImageRequestHandler 188
images 42
INAlternativeAppNames 309
installedLocales 259
Instructions 78, 80
IntentParameter 312, 315, 317
IntentResult 302
invalidate 169
isAvailable 112, 259
isColorInverted 204
isDiscoverable 339
isFinal 263
isPaused 285
isResponding 72
isSpeaking 285
isUtility 201
isWritingToolsActive 68
Item 219
item 435
itemString 219

J

JavaScript 383
JAX 429
joint 235
Joint 235
jointName 235
JSON 135, 372

K

Keras 429

L

landmarks 230
language 280
LanguageAvailability 177
languageConstraints 143, 147
languageHypotheses 144, 146
LanguageModelSession 101, 121, 71, 72, 79
Large Language Models 17
learning rate 427
leftHand 235

Linear 403, 445
lines 213
link 217
linspace 434
Llama 33
LM Studio 32
Locale 113, 177
LocalizedStringResource 302
localizedStringResource 324
location 235

M

makeCoordinator 54
makeUIView 54
MapKit 105
markerString 219
markerType 219
matches 67
matmul 440
Matrix 431
max 436
maximumHandCount 240
mean 437
Mean Error 408
Mean Squared Error 408, 410
measurement 217
Metal 430
min 436
Miniconda 132
Mistral 30
MLModelConfiguration 361
MLX 18, 429
MLXArray 432
MLXNN 430, 443, 445
MLXOptimizers 430, 444
modelContainer 51
Models 15
Module 445
moneyAmount 217
motionBlur 246
mseLoss 443, 447
multiply 439
multiplyBlendMode 248
MXNet 429

N

name 100, 280
Natural Language 143, 18
ndim 435
neighbors 159
neuron 10
NLEmbedding 158
NLLanguage 144, 145
NLLanguageRecognizer 143
NLTag 152
NLTagger 150
NLTagScheme 151
NLTokenizer 148
Node 378, 382
noiseReduction 247
NormalizedRect 196, 224
npm 385
npx 385
NSAttributedString 53, 54, 56, 57
NSRange 67
NVM 382

O

Ollama 32
one-hot encoded 409
ones 434
OpenAI 30, 370, 373, 386
Optimization 423, 426
outputImage 248
outputPixelFormatType 252
overallScore 201

P

parameters 402
PartiallyGenerated 107, 93
pauseSpeaking 285
payloadString 204
paymentIdentifier 217
Perceptron 12, 14
perceptron 399
perform 188, 302
performAll 188

permissiveContentTransformations 117
phoneNumber 217
pitch 226
pitchMultiplier 278
PixelBufferObservation 252
Playground 3
pointsInImageCoordinates 230
postalAddress 217
pow 439
Power Rule 412
prediction 361
prewarm 122
processString 143
Product Rule 414
Prompt 77
Property 94
ProvidesDialog 303
PyTorch 429

Q

qrCodeGenerator 248
quality 280
qualityLevel 252
Quotient Rule 414
Qwen 33

R

range 47
rate 278
rateLimited 114
recognitionLanguages 208, 209
recognitionLevel 208
RecognizeDocumentsRequest 212
RecognizedTextObservation 208
RecognizeTextRequest 208
Recurrent Neural Networks 17
refusal 116
Region 230
ReLU 403
relu 441, 455
request 289
requestConfirmation 317, 340
requestDidComplete 289
requestDisambiguation 317
requestValue 317
reset 143
respond 72, 95
Response 168, 72
Restricted Boltzmann Machine 16
Result 263
result 302
ReturnsValue 303
rightHand 235
RMSProp 430
RMSprop 444
roll 226
round 439

S

SaliencyImageObservation 196
salientObjects 196
Scalar 431
SemanticDetails 217
sendAction 63
sentenceEmbedding 158
sentimentScore 156
sepiaTone 247
SGD 430, 444
sharpenLuminance 247
shipmentTrackingNumber 218
shortcutTileColor 306
ShowsSnippetView 303
showWritingTools 63
Sigmoid 403
sigmoid 441
Siri 2, 301
SiriTipView 347
size 252, 435
SNAudioFileAnalyzer 290
SNAudioStreamAnalyzer 296
SNClassification 290
SNClassificationResult 289
SNClassifySoundRequest 289
SNResultsObserving 289
softmax 442
Sound Analysis 18
source 168
sourceLanguage 168
sourceText 168

speak 277
Speech 257
SpeechAnalyzer 259, 262, 265
SpeechTranscriber 257, 259
speechVoices 279
start 265, 290
status 177, 178
std 437
stopSpeaking 285
streamResponse 80
string 150
suggestedEntities 329
sum 437
Sum Rule 413
supplementalPayloadString 204
supportedBarcodeSymbologies 213
supportedLanguages 113, 177
supportedLocales 259
supportedModes 302
supportedRecognitionLanguages 213
supportsAdaptiveImageGlyph 54
supportsImagePlayground 44
supportsLocale 113
SwiftUIAttributes 47
symbologies 204
symbology 204
SystemLanguageModel 109, 112, 117, 139, 71

T

tag 150
tagHypotheses 151
tags 150
tanh 403
target 168
targetLanguage 168
targetText 168
temperature 84
Tensor 431
TensorFlow 429
Terminal 132
text 263, 40
Text 213
textRecognitionOptions 213
textView 65
textViewDidChange 69
textViewWritingToolsDidEnd 65
textViewWritingToolsWillBegin 65
timeRange 289
title 302
Toggle 338
toImageCoordinates 196
tokenRange 148
tokens 148
Tool 100
tool 114
ToolCallError 114
topCandidates 209
transcript 118, 208, 213
Transcript 120, 126
transcriptEntries 72
transformed 246
Transformers 17
translate 167, 180
Translation 164, 18, 210
translationPresentation 164
translations 179
TranslationSession 167
translationTask 167
transposed 440
typeDisplayRepresentation 311, 326

U

UIApplication 63
UIResponder 63, 64
UITextField 53
UITextViewDelegate 65
UIViewRepresentable 54
underlyingError 114
UniqueAppEntityQuery 329
unsharpMask 247
unsupportedGuide 114
unsupportedLanguageOrLocale 114
update 445
updateAppShortcutParameters 333
updateUIView 54
upperBodyOnly 232
url 245
usesLanguageCorrection 208

valueAndGrad 444, 447
variance 437
vector 158
Vector 431
version 168
Vision 18, 187
VisionObservation 189
voice 276
volume 278

W

weighted sum 403
weights 399
wordEmbedding 158
words 213
Workers 378
Wrangler 381
Writing Tools 17, 61
writingToolsBehavior 61, 62
writingToolsResultOptions 68

X

Xcode 19, 2, 6

Y

yaw 226

Z

zeros 434

www.ingramcontent.com/pod-product-compliance
Lightning Source LLC
LaVergne TN
LVHW080004210926
848481LV00011B/2946